A LIFE OF SIR JOHN ELDON GORST

CASS SERIES: BRITISH POLITICS AND SOCIETY
Series Editor: Peter Catterall
ISSN: 1467-1441

Social change impacts not just upon voting behaviour and party identity but also the formulation of policy. But how do social changes and political developments interact? Which shapes which? Reflecting a belief that social and political structures cannot be understood either in isolation from each other or from the historical processes which form them, this series will examine the forces that have shaped British society. Cross-disciplinary approaches will be encouraged. In the process, the series will aim to make a contribution to existing fields, such as politics, sociology and media studies, as well as opening out new and hitherto neglected fields such as management history.

Peter Catterall (ed.), *The Making of Channel 4*

Brock Millman, *Managing Domestic Dissent in First World War Britain*

Peter Catterall, Wolfram Kaiser and Ulrike Walton-Jordan (eds), *Reforming the Constitution: Debates in Twenty-Century Britain*

Brock Millman, *Pessimism and British War Policy, 1916–1918*

Adrian Smith and Dilwyn Porter (eds), *Amateurs and Professionals in Post-war British Sport*

Archie Hunter, *A Life of Sir John Eldon Gorst: Disraeli's Awkward Disciple*

Harry Defries, *Conservative Party Attitudes to Jews, 1900–1950*

A LIFE OF
SIR JOHN ELDON GORST

Disraeli's Awkward Disciple

Archie Hunter

FRANK CASS
LONDON • PORTLAND, OR

First published in 2001 in Great Britain by
FRANK CASS PUBLISHERS
Crown House, 47 Chase Side,
Southgate, London N14 5BP

and in the United States of America by
FRANK CASS PUBLISHERS
c/o ISBS, 5824 N.E. Hassalo Street
Portland, Oregon, 97213-3644

Website: www.frankcass.com

British Library Cataloguing in Publication Data

Hunter, Archie, 1929–
  A life of Sir John Eldon Gorst: Disraeli's awkward
disciple / Archie Hunter.
    p. cm. – (CASS series–British politics and society, ISSN
1467–1441)
    Includes bibliographical references (p.   ) and index.
    ISBN 0-7146-5180-X (cloth)
    1. Gorst, John Eldon, Sir 1835–1916. 2. Disraeli, Benjamin, Earl
of Beaconsfield, 1804–1881–Friends and associates. 3. Great
Britain–Politics and government–1837–1901. 4. Politicians–Great
Britain–Biography. 5. British–New Zealand– Biography.   I. Title
II. Series.
  DA565.G47 H86 2001
  941.081'092aB–dc21   2001028288

ISBN 0-7146-5180-X (cloth)
ISSN 1467-1441

Library of Congress Cataloging-in-Publication Data

Hunter, Archie, 1929–
  A life of Sir John Eldon Gorst: Disraeli's
awkward disciple. – (Cass series. British politics and
society)
  1. Gorst, Sir John Eldon, 1835–1916 2. Politicians – Great
Britain – biography 3. Great Britain – Politics and
government – 19th century
  I. Title
  941'.081'092

Printed in Great Britain by Bookcraft, Midsomer Norton, Somerset

Dedicated to the descendants of John and Mary Gorst

Contents

Illustrations

Foreword

Everybody who takes a serious interest in nineteenth-century British politics has heard of Sir John Eldon Gorst. He established Conservative Central Office in 1870 and became the Conservative Party's principal agent. Disraeli approved Gorst's appointment for which the latter was, in modern parlance, 'head-hunted'. It was a crucial moment in the history of the Party, because Gorst did a superb job and it is not too much to claim that many aspects of the modern Conservative Party stem directly from his reforms and initiatives. Though the broad country acres could be left to the reliable Tory squirearchy, urban Toryism gained its successes as a result of Gorst's foresight.

So much is known and so much is universally conceded. Yet, strangely enough, little else is now remembered about this remarkable man. Reading this striking biography of Gorst, by his descendant Archie Hunter, I repeatedly broke off in order to rebuke myself for having forgotten an illuminating fact about politics that Gorst's life illustrates. Eventually, I faced the fact that my memory was not unusually fallible on the subject. I had never known in the first place what Archie Hunter so carefully explains. Like others who pride themselves on their grasp of mid- and late-Victorian history there were alarming gaps in my knowledge. There can surely be no better recommendation of any biography than that it is packed with new information that encourages fresh thinking.

It may be objected that since Gorst was not a Prime Minister, or party leader, learning a lot more about his life can hardly have all that much impact on either our judgement or imagination. This is a gross error, perhaps derived from the modern cult of celebrity. The idea that the intellectual contribution of former generations is best assessed by discovering which of them occupied important offices is a view so wide of the mark as to be obviously wrong directly it is openly stated. Gorst was a much wiser and more far-sighted man than many who held high office.

His career demonstrates how different was the Conservative Party then to what it has subsequently become. The first difference is often mentioned, but the second, of even greater importance, is rarely stressed. These days the Conservative Party depends little upon the Duke and the Marquis. In Gorst's time the aristocratic domination of the Party was very apparent. Disraeli himself, though his own origins owed nothing to, and his outlook but a mere acquaintance with, the nobility's attitudes, found it prudent to surround himself, in and out of office, with a disproportionate number of peers. Such a climate did not help Gorst's political advancement. He was a classic example of the gifts of the educated middle classes. That such gifts were often undervalued was an inevitable by-product of arrangements that bestowed favours so easily and casually upon aristocratic background.

What is very infrequently commented upon is that the Victorian Conservative Party had a much less close commitment to capitalism, or what is now usually called the free-enterprise system, than was the case in the twentieth century. Naturally that does not mean that Victorian Tories were, in any sense, socialistic, or sought any dramatic change in the social or economic order. It is more that their assumptions did not run so strongly in the belief that they were involved in a struggle of ideologies between capitalism and socialism. Such an intense ideological battle was the essence of the twentieth century rather than of the nineteenth. Men like Gorst had no particular qualms about a measure of state intervention, because it did not occur to them that using the power of the state to rectify wrongs implied any danger to capitalism.

So, imaginative Tories like Gorst were very interested in what was called 'the condition of the people'. Throughout his adult life Gorst showed a touching concern for the poor. He was ever willing to sacrifice time and money to help society's unfortunates. Nor was his help bounded only by the bounds of charity. An intensely practical man, he sponsored, or suggested, a whole range of ideas for improving the lot of the majority. His quite unselfconscious belief that the resources of a powerful country ought to be tapped for the benefit of the many may strike the modern ear as almost simplistic. Did Gorst have no fear of the over-weening power of the state, nor dread of the endless intrusion of the bureaucracy into everyday life? The answer is that he belonged to a more confident age and judged that good could be done without ever exceeding the limits of common sense and moderation.

Though Gorst was something of a British pioneer in matters of social welfare, for he had been impressed by what Germany did for workers in terms of health, accident, persistent illness and old age pensions, I feel that perhaps his greatest social contribution was in the sphere of education. Archie Hunter sets out Gorst's record here with great lucidity and I confess that this is a part of Gorst's achievements I had largely overlooked. The reader should pay close attention to the efforts he made when he was, in effect, Minister of Education in the Salisbury Government. Gorst sought to resolve the muddle over schools and to whole education saga is a microcosm of Gorst's public life. Most of his more sweeping measures failed at first, partly because of the malign influence of Arthur Balfour, who comes badly out of this biography at nearly every point in the story, a thoroughly just view in my opinion. Finally though, Gorst is shown to have been right and it is Balfour himself, who incorporates Gorst's ideas into his own 1902 Education Bill. Gorst was a radical reformer whose ideas were in advance of lesser men, who were willing to exploit his talent and copy his suggestions. Never was the evidence clearer than in education.

Finally, can I point out the great attraction of this biography, but first dispose of what it would be wrong to regard as a defect? There is an absence of private, personal details, so beloved of some modern minds, who think themselves cheated unless they receive an exact account of the sexual mores and peccadillos of the subject, however irrelevant that may be to his primary concerns. Gorst was a man of his times. He did not leave behind a chapter and verse explanation of his emotional life. Nor does the reader need one. He can read in this story something much more startling than a tedious recitation of loves and lusts in every way similar to the thousand and one banal accounts daily on offer. In this biography one can read of a man, not merely of another world, but almost of a different galaxy. Gorst was a radical, Victorian gentleman and this is, intellectually, virtually an extinct species. There is excitement and enlightenment in learning what guided such a man, how and why he lived and what legacy he left to us.

Brian Walden

Series Editor's Preface

Sir John Eldon Gorst never attained the high offices his early talent perhaps promised. Had he stayed in New Zealand, the young colony might have given more outlet for his skills. Back in Britain, however, he never rose above junior ministerial rank. Nor was his career at the Bar crowned with the highest successes, although he did participate in some promient Victorian cases. Not least in politics, he met frustration at every turn.

Nevertheless, the puzzle is not why then publish this, the first full-length biography of Gorst, but why has it taken so long for such a work to appear? Gorst may never have occupied centre-stage. The limelight did not suit his personality: even in the Fourth Party he allowed the scene to be stolen by Lord Randolph. But he was ubiquitous behind the scenes, a kind of Victorian gadfly pricking both pomposity and consciences.

But this biography does much more than rescue Gorst from Lord Randolph's shadow. Gorst was not a maverick parliamentarian, or at least not simply that. After all, his most familiar role to history students is from Robert Blake's depiction of his role in reviving the electoral fortunes of the Conservative Party. Less familiar to those students, however, will be the way in which he was treated thereafter.

Archie Hunter's excellent biography does much to resolve the conundrum of Gorst's political career, from indefatigable Conservative Party worker to the Liberal candidate of the Edwardian era. In the modern era a defector of Gorst's eminence would be rewarded with a safe seat. Gorst instead had to fight and lose. In any case, he probably did not really see himself as a defector. The party by then led by his former colleague in the Fourth Party, A. J. Balfour, was not that for which he had played such a part in the 1874 election, any more than their Liberal opponents remained unchanged since Gladstonian days. Balfour, who comes across in these pages as at best a cautious opportunist, was not the same stamp of Conservative as Gorst. The book's sub-title is as telling as it is appropriate. Gorst indeed was 'Disraeli's awkward disciple'.

There are some parallels between the two men. Disraeli had more flair, but, more than that, his social concern was always more rhetorical than programmatic, and something to be trimmed to fit the world views of the landed grandees who still dominated the party in his day.

Gorst, by contrast, was a disciple who proved more royal than the king, posing along the way problems in his enthusiasms that Balfour, a far less skilful party manager than his predecessors, was incapable of resolving.

In these enthusiasms, however, Gorst played a part in discourses which went, as Hunter shows, far beyond the confines of the Tory Party. Gorst's important role in the debates, for instance, behind the 1902 Education Act, is here fully brought out for the first time.

This biography, however, is more than just an account of Gorst's political career. It also makes a significant contribution to our appreciation of the nature of the nineteenth-century empire, in India and particularly in New Zealand. In contrast to some recent literature suggesting a hardening of imperial attitudes in the mid-nineteenth century, Gorst's experiences in New Zealand suggest that the difficulties that fuelled the Maori King movement and the Taranaki wars were both more contingent and more complex than a simple emphasis on race might imply. That he seems eventually to have become disillusioned should not obscure the nature of Gorst's efforts to promote reconciliation between European settlers and Maori.

A life spanning from the imperial frontier living amongst the Waikato to the fringes of the Cabinet in Westminster presents a very broad canvas. I am pleased to say that Archie Hunter proves more than equal to the challenge in this fascinating biography.

Peter Catterall
Series Editor

Preface and Acknowledgements

This is the first full-length life of Sir John Eldon Gorst to be written. Gorst has, however, been of considerable interest over the years to a number of historians, who have written articles about different aspects of his career, or have included in historical studies of the age, or biographies, many details about him and his work.

For example, in the former category J. R. Vincent has written on Gorst's earliest years in Parliament, E. J. Feuchtwanger on his association with the central organisation of the Conservative Party (during which time he founded Conservative Central Office), B. B. Gilbert on him as a Conservative rebel and also on his work about children's welfare, while N. Daglish has written a number of articles about his contribution to educational reform and one piece covering his early years in New Zealand. With regard to books, Gorst plays a major part in *The Fourth Party* written by his son Harold Gorst, as he does in the chapters on the same subject in Winston Churchill's biography of his father *Lord Randolph Churchill*. Two much more recent biographies of Lord Randolph, by R. F. Foster and R. V. Rhodes James, pay marked attention to Gorst in his Fourth Party days. Also Gorst figures frequently in the pages of R. Shannon's *The Age of Disraeli* and *The Age of Salisbury*. Finally, Gorst's personality and his work as Vice-President of the Committee for the Council on Education (effectively Minister of Education) is thoroughly considered by Neil Daglish in his *Educational Policy-Making in England and Wales: The Crucible Years 1895–1911*.

Curiously, as far as I can discover, there has been virtually no attempt made by historians (Gilbert is the exception) to write about Gorst's work in the field of labour and social welfare. This is surprising in view of some of the advanced ideas and proposals Gorst brought to these subjects which were engaging the attention of reformers – these did not usually include Conservative politicans – in the late Victorian age.

My aim in this book has been to break new ground by telling the complete story of Gorst's life, bringing together what is known about his time in New Zealand, his long years in politics covering twelve elections, the first when he was aged 30 and the last when he was 74, and, to a much lesser extent, his career as a lawyer. In my last chapter I assess the contribution he made as a politician and social reformer.

There has been one particular difficulty for the biographer. Unhappily none of Gorst's own private and family papers has survived.

This has meant, inevitably, that Gorst's family life receives less attention than it deserves. To balance this, Gorst as an author and propagandist was often busy with his pen. Apart from articles he wrote on topical political and social issues, he published three books, two of which throw important light on his years in New Zealand. In addition his elder son Jack's diaries and autobiographical notes, and his younger son Harold's autobiography are a fruitful source of information. Fortunately, there is an ample supply of primary source material on Gorst's public life in the national archives and great collections. For instance the letters he wrote to three major political figures, Disraeli, Lord Randolph Churchill and Lord Salisbury, are especially revealing of the man and his views. Another bonus, albeit a less significant one, is the attraction Gorst had for the cartoonist. He has not for nothing been described as '. . . a picturesque and incalculable anomaly who always raised delightful expectations of the unexpected and the indecorous'.

I have been given permission to use Crown copyright papers in the custody of the Public Record Office. I am also grateful for permission to quote from unpublished copyright and other material in the care of the following:

- Auckland University Library, New Zealand (Fowlds papers).
- Bodleian Library, University of Oxford (Bosanquet, Bryce, Kimberley, Marvin, Middleton, Paget and Hughenden (Disraeli) papers).
- British Library (Iddesleigh and Ritchie papers).
- Brynmoor Jones Library, University of Hull (Sykes Collection).
- Cambridge University Library (correspondence of Lord Randolph Churchill).
- Conservative Central Office (minutes of National Union of Conservative and Constitutional Associations).
- Duke of Devonshire and the Chatsworth Settlement Trustees (correspondence of the 8th Duke).
- Duke University, Durham, North Carolina, USA (Kekewich papers).
- London Metropolitan Archives (Barnett papers and Charity Organisation Society records).
- Paul Lysley Esq. (diaries and autobiographical notes of Sir Eldon (Jack) Gorst: copies of these are lodged at St Antony's College, Oxford).
- The Marquess of Salisbury (papers of the 3rd Marquess).
- W. K. Stead, Esq. (Stead papers: these are lodged with Churchill Archives Centre, Churchill College, Cambridge).

- Master, Fellows and Scholars of St John's College, Cambridge (College archival material).

I should like to thank for their help the staff of the following libraries, museums, institutions and other organisations: Alexander Turnbull Library, Wellington, New Zealand; Auckland Institute and Museum, New Zealand; Bodleian Library, University of Oxford; BBC Archives (on the Bravo case); British Library; British Library of Political and Economic Science, London School of Economics; Cambridge City Library; Cambridge Union Society; Cambridge University Library; Centre for Kentish Studies, Maidstone; Crewkerne Library; Exeter Central Library; Family Welfare Association; Harris Library, Preston; Hatfield House Library; Hertfordshire County Archives; Lancashire Record Office; Lincoln's Inn Library; London Metropolitan Archives; Medway Council Archives and Local Studies Centre; Norfolk Studies Library; the Royal Commission on Historical Manuscripts; Salvation Army; Te Awamutu Museum, New Zealand; and the Uckfield Library.

I am particularly fortunate that Brian Walden has written the Foreword to this book. I am also grateful that he has confirmed Gorst's importance as a political figure, and has set my subject's contribution into a modern-day context.

Many people helped in the preparation of this book. I wish particularly to thank: my cousin Sir John Gorst, formerly MP for Hendon North, for his great encouragement and thoughtful help, which included giving me access to his own papers, reading the text and providing illustrations; Dr Neil Daglish of Victoria University of Wellington for all his advice and other assistance – invaluable in the light of his knowledge of Gorst – and for commenting so constructively on the text; my brother David Hunter and neighbour Roger Montague for reading the text and for offering valuable suggestions for improving my draft and for their infectious enthusiasm for my project.

Boyhood recollections of my subject and comments on his character were provided by my uncle Lieutenant-Colonel Anthony Hunter; his was the only direct evidence of Gorst available to me. My cousin Paul Lysley was another who gave me unstinting support, as did John Moore who provided me with much useful material from his historical archive on the Gorst family. Both were also helpful over illustrations for the book. Dr Guy Holborn, Librarian at Lincoln's Inn, found for me information on Gorst the lawyer, which I would not have discovered myself. Valuable material on Gorst's early life came from R. D. W. Rhodes, Headmaster of Rossall School; Malcolm Underwood, Archivist at St John's College, Cambridge; and from Henry Pipe of the

Cambridge Union Society. At the Bodleian Library I received unfailing help and courtesy from Colin Harris. I should also like to express my sincere thanks to Dr Peter Catterall, the Series Editor, for his many suggestions and advice on historical matters, and to Andrew Humphrys, my editor at Frank Cass Publishers, for his help during the production of this book.

Others who kindly gave me help – and I am sorry if I have not named them all – included: Professor J. H. Baker, M. J. Bosson, Tim Boyden, Bill Chadwick, Peter Corsen, Captain Guy Crowden, John Dudley, Diana Frome, Toni Fortune, Marna Fyson, John G. Gorst, Nina Gorst, Christina Gorst-Ellis, Robin Harcourt Williams, my son Archie Hunter, Bernard Lawley, the Revd Dr Warren Limbrick, John McBain, Dr Martin Maws, Dr Peter Mellini, Derek Mountain and his family, Dr Mark Nicholls, Charles Noble, Charles Ponting, Michael Ponting, the late Sir Robert Rhodes James, Sir Tatton Sykes, Gordon Taylor, and Richard Wollocombe.

My manuscript was most professionally typed by my daughter-in-law Antonia Hunter and by Joan Hawkins. Both were adept at interpreting my vile handwriting, and I am most grateful to them both for their pains and for the excellence of all their work.

My final thanks must go to my wife Mirabel who has been ever present to help with forbearance and wise judgment on the major and minor matters which inevitably assail the author.

Abbreviations

AJHR	Appendices to the Journals of the House of Representatives, Wellington, New Zealand
BL	British Library
BOD	Bodleian Library, University of Oxford
COS	Charity Organisation Society
CPD	Common Pleas Division
DNB	*Dictionary of National Biography*
EXD	Exchequer Division
FP	*The Fourth Party* (by H. E. Gorst)
HP	Hughenden Papers (correspondence of Benjamin Disraeli)
JG AN	Sir Eldon (Jack) Gorst Autobiographical Notes
JG d	Sir Eldon (Jack) Gorst diaries
Ld RC	correspondence of Lord Randolph Churchill
MK	*The Maori King* (by J. E. Gorst)
MLL	*Much of Life is Laughter* (by H. E. Gorst)
NZR	*New Zealand Revisited* (by Sir J. E. Gorst)
PD	Hansard's Parliamentary Debates
PRO	Public Record Office, Kew
QBD	Queen's Bench Division
TLR	Times Law Reports

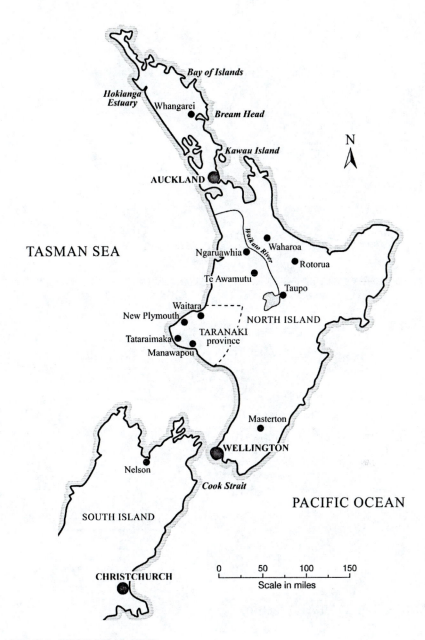

Bay of Islands

Hokianga
Estuary

Whangarei

Bream Head

Kawau Island

AUCKLAND

TASMAN SEA

Waharoa

Ngaruawahia

Rotorua

Te Awamutu

Taupo

Waitara

New Plymouth

NORTH ISLAND

Tataraimaka

TARANAKI
province

Manawapou

Masterton

WELLINGTON

Nelson

Cook Strait

PACIFIC OCEAN

SOUTH ISLAND

0   50   100   150
Scale in miles

CHRISTCHURCH

N

Waikato River

MAP 1: NEW ZEALAND

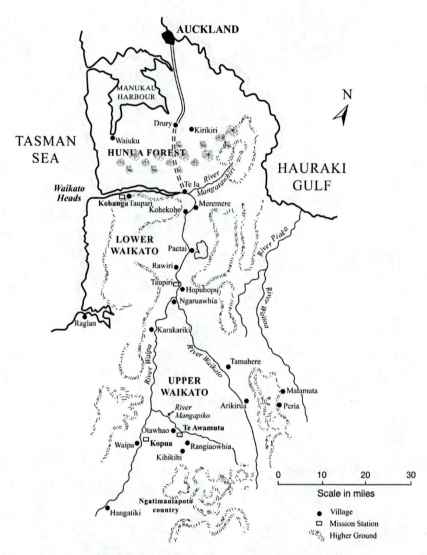

AUCKLAND

MANUKAU HARBOUR

TASMAN SEA

Drury

Waiuku

Kirikiri

HUNUA FOREST

HAURAKI GULF

Waikato Heads

Te Ia

River Mangatawhiri

Kohanga Taupari

Meremere

Kohekohe

River Piako

LOWER WAIKATO

Pactai

Rawiri

River Waioa

Taupiri

Hopuhopu

Ngaruawahia

Raglan

Karakariki

River Waipa

River Waikato

Tamahere

UPPER WAIKATO

Matamata

River Mangapiko

Arikirua

Peria

Otawhao

Te Awamutu

Waipa

Kopua

Rangiaowhia

Kihikihi

Ngatimaniapoto country

Hangatiki

| 0 | 10 | 20 | 30 |

Scale in miles

● Village

□ Mission Station

Higher Ground

MAP 2: THE WAIKATO 1860–63

— 1 —

Youth

On a cold January morning in 1860 two young men dressed for
travel might have been observed on the quayside of the great
seaport city of Liverpool. They were surrounded by a throng of
people who could only be emigrants. Alongside the quay lay a tall
four-masted ship of the clipper class, its sails furled. Activity was
immense on board and on the quay, for the ship was being loaded
with people, animals, crates, stores and luggage. It was foggy and
windless, and the opposite side of the river was invisible.

On closer inspection one of the two young men, slight and
bearded, looked desperately ill. While he was mainly silent, his
companion seemed cheerful as if he were trying to keep up the
other's spirits. Soon they were joined by two other men who had
come to see them off: relatives or friends, no doubt, of the travellers.
It was time to board. The young men made their farewells and then
walked along the short gangplank onto the ship. The one went slowly
as if walking was an effort; the other was watchful, ready to support
his friend.

The ship – the 2,305-ton *Red Jacket* owned by the White Star
Company – was due to catch the tide that afternoon. But on the
advice of the pilot its sailing was delayed on account of the fog. Then
early next morning, on 27 January, the ship with its 500 passengers
slipped from its moorings and, towed by two steamers, slowly moved
– still in mist – down the river towards the estuary. The 15,000-mile
journey to the antipodes had begun.

Two days later as the ship entered the Atlantic the bearded young
man had for the first time on the voyage dragged himself on deck. He
was leaning over the rail, which he gripped as strongly as his strength
would allow. He still looked very ill. For a moment he was watched by
the captain and a young woman passenger, to whom the captain
spoke: 'I fear we shall have to put that poor fellow in the sea before
we get to the line.'[1]

The young man was the 25-year-old John Eldon Gorst. He and his
friend Mainwaring were both destined for New Zealand. Gorst had
recently been the victim of scarlet fever, a deadly disease in those

days. However, the captain was wrong: Gorst had a tough constitution and a strong will, and would live another 56 years.

*   *   *   *

John Eldon Gorst was born in Preston on 24 May 1835, the third child and second son of Edward Chaddock Gorst, a solicitor, and his wife Elizabeth. Six more children would subsequently be born to the Gorsts, three boys and three girls. The Gorsts were a well-established family living comfortably in a three-storied Georgian house in fashionable Winckley Square in the middle of Preston, and respected in their part of Lancashire. Robert Chaddock Gorst, John's great-grandfather, was born of yeoman stock in Middlewich, Cheshire. He had made a good marriage to Mary Lowndes and moved to Preston in about 1760. His three sons did well. One went to Cambridge and was ordained. The other two became attorneys. One of them, Edward, John's grandfather, practised first at Leigh and then in Preston with the firm of Blakelock before being appointed deputy Clerk of the Peace for the County Palatine of Lancaster. His son, Edward Chaddock, born in 1803 and John's father, also went into the law, becoming a solicitor and then in turn deputy Clerk of the Peace. For many years, therefore, the Gorsts were at the centre of legal and administrative affairs in the county. John's uncle, Thomas Mee Gorst, chose the other branch of the legal profession. After graduating from St John's College, Cambridge, he was called to the Bar at the Middle Temple.

The Gorsts have been remembered in Preston as strong supporters of the Anglican church. There are memorial windows to John's grandfather Edward and his grandmother, and to various other members of the family in St John's parish church. Further, in 1856 Edward's three surviving daughters gave in their father's memory a font which still stands in the baptistry of that church. Another Gorst forebear presented communion plate to Christ Church consisting of a flagon, two chalices and two patens of silver. There are also memorials to the Gorsts in St George's church, Preston.[2] There is one other memorial to be mentioned. In Winckley Square, close to his parents' house, John's birth in 1835 was celebrated by the planting of a chestnut tree. Huge and shady, it still stands today.

About John's mother, Elizabeth, not a lot is known. She came from a prosperous family who lived in County Durham, her father being John Douthwaite Nesham of Houghton-le-Spring. She was married in 1830, had nine children and died aged 46 in December 1848 when John was 13.

When John was 5 years old an event occurred which would affect the fortunes of the Gorst family to their advantage, including, towards the end of his life, John's own. His uncle Thomas Mee inherited property under the will of Robert Lowndes of Palterton Hall in Derbyshire. This inheritance was conditional on the beneficiary taking the name Lowndes which Thomas did in 1841. Robert Lowndes had died in 1797, but his sons had no heirs. Accordingly, under his will his property passed to the family of his daughter Mary, who, as has already been mentioned, married Robert Chaddock Gorst.

In 1847 when John was 12 his elder brother Edward was sent off to Rugby, a school whose reputation had revived under its great headmaster Dr Thomas Arnold. However, for some reason – possibly it was due to his mother's death – John did not follow in his brother's scholastic footsteps; instead he went to Preston Grammar School, situated just round the corner from where he lived. He was a clever boy but no school records of the time survive, so we do not know his precise achievements, except that he was head boy. Also while there he founded and edited a school magazine, which he called *The Scholar*. This publication was printed and issued at regular intervals for a year until it ran foul of the school authorities and had to be suppressed. As Gorst was to put it himself:

> Obnoxious articles, ... written in a mocking spirit were the pretext, and they proceeded from the pen of my father. But neither as editor nor as son could I take shelter under his name, and the paper was condemned and stopped.[3]

This episode did not stop the Master of the Grammar School, G. N. Smith, himself a Cambridge graduate, from writing to the tutor at St John's College, Cambridge in April 1853 requesting Gorst's admission to the College the following October. In his letter he bore testimony to his pupil's 'excellent character and conduct' and stated that Gorst had 'a very good knowledge of Latin and Greek languages – in mathematics I have much confidence in speaking of his superior abilities and attainments ...'[4] There is an entry for Gorst in J. A. Venn's *Alumni Cantabrigiensis* which shows that he matriculated in 1853 and was a scholar.

In those days Cambridge held an honours examination in mathematics only, and until 1858 it was necessary for students to have four years' residence to obtain a degree. Gorst therefore read mathematics. His progress during his four years was smooth, and in the six examinations he took he was always placed in the first class.[5] The syllabus for the tripos in those days was an interesting mixture which included the classics, moral philosophy, logic, the study of the gospels and Acts, as well as algebra, Euclid, trigonometry, hydrostatics, mechanics, calculus and geometry. In his third year other subjects made their appearance such as astronomy, dynamics and lunar theory, optics, as well as church history covering the first three centuries of the Christian era and the Reformation. Gorst always set his sights high and in his final examinations he confidently expected to become First Wrangler, his college apparently sharing these hopes.[6] But he was to be disappointed and had to content himself with being Third Wrangler. On the day the exam results were published, friends were posted between the Senate House and Gorst's rooms in St. John's in order that the tidings should be carried to him with the least possible delay. Why he could not have gone himself to the Senate House to learn the results first-hand is unclear. At any rate the news was slow in coming and the disconsolate Gorst guessed his fate. Afterwards his coach consoled him by saying, 'I never knew a man take so high a mathematical degree who knew so little mathematics as you.'[7]

Gorst had not worked exclusively for the mathematical tripos, for he spent a good deal of time studying under Professor Living at the chemical laboratory that had just been established at Cambridge by St John's College.

It might be tempting, but almost certainly wrong, to attribute Gorst's interest in chemistry to the success in that field already being achieved by his brilliant half-brother, Edward Frankland, who had become in 1851, at the age of 26, professor of chemistry at Owen's College, Manchester. But chemistry midway through the nineteenth century was commanding the attention of many devoted to scientific research. Gorst's interest will have been another manifestation of his lively intellectual curiosity. In any case Gorst, we can be fairly sure, was unaware of his half-brother's existence, at least at this time. A word of explanation is necessary. As a very young man John's father, Edward Chaddock Gorst, had an affair with Margaret Frankland, a domestic servant employed in the Gorst household in Preston, and by her had an illegitimate son. News of Edward's indiscretion had for obvious reasons to be suppressed, and the Gorsts paid Margaret a handsome annuity which assured the boy's education and start in life as a chemist in Lancaster. Edward Frankland's career in chemistry was a distinguished one; he became President of the Chemical Society and, in 1895, was knighted.[8]

Gorst took his degree and on 31 March 1857 he was elected to a Fellowship of his College. The office of Gregson Fellow to which he had been admitted was a distinguished one for it had been founded in 1527. In addition, the Fellowship had just been vacated by Dr Bateson on his appointment as Master of the College. Gorst retained his Fellowship for a mere three years, having to relinquish it on his marriage. He was made an Honorary Fellow in 1890.

There were two other activities which caught Gorst's attention while at Cambridge. One was rowing. In the May races of 1854 he rowed No. 4 in the second boat of the Lady Margaret Boat Club, the name by which the St John's boat club was and still is known. It may well have been as a result of boat club festivities that Gorst was admonished by the Dean for bad behaviour in his second year. A very noisy party was held in his rooms in D4 New Court one winter evening. The entry in the College archives reads:

> Some [of those in his rooms] were shouting and imitating the voices of strange animals from the window to the court to the great annoyance and disgust of the neighbourhood … a Fellow was obliged to call on the Senior Dean to ask him to interfere.

The offenders, it seems, were friends of Gorst's such as the captain of boats with a reputation for rowdiness. But this was not all. Perhaps the Dean was unpopular or he may have overreacted to the high spirits displayed. Whatever it was the next night the door to the Dean's rooms was screwed up so as to make entry or exit impossible.[9] History does not relate whether the unfortunate Dean was immured or not. Accounts of what happened appeared in the local and even London papers. If he had not been one before, Gorst must have become something of a celebrity.

Gorst's other great interest while an undergraduate was the Cambridge Union Society in which he played an active part, always as a strong Conservative. The Union had not in the mid-nineteenth century quite emerged as the forcing-house for aspiring young politicians that it was to become. Nonetheless, it attracted those drawn to politics who wished, often earnestly, to debate the issues of the time. Gorst was certainly one of these.

The first time Gorst spoke at the Union was in opposition to a motion condemning trade unions. To oppose such a motion was not untypical of the man he was to become. Trade unions in the 1850s were anything but popular with run of the mill Conservatives. But then Gorst was always inclined to be highly independent in his political views. While Gorst was brought up against a conventional family background of law and administration, discussion and argument on the issues of the day may well have been encouraged by his father, who, after all, had written contentious articles for his son's school magazine. It is very likely that Gorst's independence of mind and spirit, which we shall come across throughout the pages of this history, will have had its origin at home in Preston.

Gorst soon made his mark in the Union and became Treasurer at the beginning of the Michaelmas term of 1855. This was quite an onerous position. Apart from all the work to do with accounting and the paying of bills, the Treasurer, if he was absent without good reason from any business meeting, was fined one guinea. The Union finances in Gorst's time were in a pretty parlous state but, as he recalled years later, they managed by 'exercising self-denial' largely to recover the situation.[10]

Eventually, the ultimate accolade, Gorst was elected President of the Union for the Easter term of 1857. The President had the task, or some might say the fun, of deciding on the subject for debates. The subjects Gorst chose were both serious and contentious ones, and throw some light on his character. On Tuesday 28 April the motion was: 'that this House would desire to see a measure of Parliamentary Reform passed by the new Parliament, either in the ensuing or in the subsequent session'.[11] The motion was carried by one. The country, however, would have to wait for ten years for legislation to be successfully enacted on this subject.

A week later the motion 'that the present relations of church and state are anomalous and unsatisfactory' was defeated by 34 to 27. An amendment to the motion was moved, but rejected, to the effect that the only desirable alteration in these relations concerned the collection of church rates. The subject of these rates has been long forgotten, but in those days it engendered much heat, particularly among nonconformists.[12] It was to be the unpromising subject on which Gorst was one day to make his maiden speech in the House of Commons and is one we shall discuss further in due course.

Again Union members defeated a motion in the next debate that 'the government of Louis Napoleon is founded on injustice and offers no security for the permanent welfare of France'. In the last debate of term a Mr C. A. Jones of St John's College – who was the mover of no fewer than three of the four motions that term and must surely have been a crony of Gorst's – moved: 'that this House would regret to see the admission of Jews to Parliament again rejected by the House of Lords'. Fifty-three of those members present voted and the majority was 11 against. Happily, Parliament removed the bar against Jewish members the following year. Gorst in his career as a politician was to show that he did not like to see people debarred from exercising their civic rights on grounds of religion, race or gender. Clearly, he held these views early in life and stuck to them.

After his time at Cambridge was over, Gorst decided to have what we would call today a gap year, and enjoy himself. First he borrowed his elder brother's horses and went hunting during the winter at his uncle's in County Durham. He then set off for Europe, wandering through Switzerland and the Tyrol before visiting Vienna and Prague. Next he travelled to Dresden where he settled down to learn German.[13] He was for much of his life to admire Germany and the modern and efficient way that country was governed. For these travels and the time in Germany, Gorst must have been given a decent allowance by his father who had on his brother Thomas' death a few years before succeeded to the Lowndes' property.

When Gorst returned to England in 1858, following the family legal tradition he entered the chambers of Mr Christie, an eminent conveyancer, to read law. He also began to eat his dinners at the Inner Temple, to which he had been admitted the previous year. But fate quickly intervened when his father had a stroke. Gorst must have been fond of him or else was a conscientious son, or perhaps both. He may of course have disliked London and his studies. In any event he left Mr Christie's chambers and went back to Lancashire to be near his stricken father. For work he took a teaching job at Rossall School in Fleetwood.

According to a history of Rossall, Gorst came 'as an Examiner in the summer of 1858 and remained teaching unpaid until Christmas 1859'. This, as will be seen in a later chapter, was not the last time he took no pay for his work. Gorst appeared to the boys as a somewhat flamboyant character. One of them writing over 60 years later said:

> He was a lively and energetic young man with a golden brown beard and a monocle *à la* Chamberlain. He was somewhat impatient as a teacher but keen on games. He was the virtual founder of Rossall football. [14]

The writer was absolutely correct about Gorst's energy and impatience. These were characteristics he was to display all his life. Apart from rowing at Cambridge, Gorst did not show particular interest in sport or in playing games himself. But he did always encourage the young to play, as is occasionally glimpsed in these pages.

At this time Gorst must have been undecided on what he was to do with his life and how he was to use the talents he undoubtedly possessed. As yet the law had not properly caught his attention. It must have been about now that his thoughts turned to Bishop Selwyn, the dynamic Bishop of New Zealand and Melanesia, who had preached at Cambridge in 1854.[15] Selwyn, who had rowed in the first university boat race in 1829, was also a St John's man. The likelihood is that Gorst heard Selwyn's sermons, and that the Bishop met and talked to the younger man about his work; the two men might even have remained in touch. At any rate at some stage Gorst contacted the Bishop and, as a result of what he heard, considered there was a job for him to do in the antipodes as a lay missionary.

So he discussed his future with his ailing father. He told him that he wanted a more active and adventurous life, and was considering going to the colonies. There was no family precedent for this but his father approved the plan. His elder brother, Edward, was against the idea,[16] but John did not take his advice.

After his father died in May 1859 Gorst therefore determined to cut his links with England. He wound up his teaching post at Rossall the following Christmas, and prepared for his voyage to New Zealand.

NOTES

1. FP, 26.
2. Information supplied by John Moore.
3. NZR, 257–8.
4. Records of St John's College, Cambridge.
5. Ibid.
6. A Wrangler was a person placed in the first class in the mathematical tripos at Cambridge University. Examinees were placed in order of merit.
7. FP, 24.
8. C. A. Russell, *Edward Frankland: Chemistry, Controversy and Conspiracy in Victorian England,* Cambridge, Cambridge University Press, 1996, 15–16.
9. Records of St John's College, Cambridge.
10. Paget papers, MS Autogr. e. 12, Gorst–Paget, 2 Feb. 1894.
11. Records of Cambridge Union Society.
12. The term nonconformist (or dissenter) was originally applied to someone in the Puritan section of the Church of England who refused to conform to certain practices of the church.
13. FP, 25.
14. Records of Rossall School.
15. G. Kitson Clark, *The Making of Victorian England*, London, Methuen, 1960, 153.
16. *Review of Reviews*, 4 Aug. 1891, 576.

2

Mutiny on the *Red Jacket*

A few weeks before he was due to travel out to New Zealand, Gorst contracted scarlet fever. He was very ill and nearly died. But he pulled through and managed somehow to reach Liverpool where, as we have seen, he boarded the *Red Jacket*, a clipper bound for Auckland via Melbourne.

Gorst was still ill for the first ten days or so of the voyage and must have looked grim. Soon, however, his health began to improve, and he was taking a growing interest in the voyage and in his fellow passengers. Happily descriptions of that voyage, often graphic, were recorded by Gorst in letters he wrote to a sister at the time.[1] The passage to Melbourne, round the Cape and across the Indian Ocean would take 84 days, then considered quick. During it the passengers would experience extremes of climate, including hurricane force winds, mountainous seas, ice and fog as well as the listless doldrums. Sometimes the clipper would travel 300 miles a day; at others in stifling heat the ship would be at a virtual standstill. Gorst wrote of the furious rolling of the ship:

> It was a continued struggle with toilet apparatus, books, chairs, plates, food; everything kept coming at you in the most aggressive manner, and you never enjoyed a minute's rest; even in bed it was a struggle to keep from falling out.

Gorst described the experienced captain, Samuel Reid, as being a very jolly yet cautious man. Luckily for the passengers he was also a man of resolution. Gorst liked equally the first mate, a cheerful indomitable character, who enjoyed chaff and reminded Gorst of Mark Tapley, the hero's servant in *Martin Chuzzlewit*. Officers apart, the crew were a mixed bunch and sometimes volatile. The *Red Jacket*, built in Maine, USA, had been on the Australian run for over five years and was considered by many as the most beautiful of all the clippers. She made the fastest-ever eastbound crossing of the Atlantic in 1854, taking just over 13 days.

There were two classes of passenger: saloon and steerage. Often there was friction between them. It was, for instance, a source of irritation to the steerage that they were restricted in their access to the poop, one of the more sought-after parts of the ship. Besides the British there were Germans and Italians on board as well as children of all ages. Many of them had free passages provided by colonising associations. The bait of cheap land was often as not luring them to the antipodes.

To begin with the passengers were quiet and disinclined to quarrel. But as the hot weather approached tensions mounted and rows erupted. Two of the problems were overcrowding and boredom. Nothing could be done about the former, but the endless meals which broke up the day may perhaps have alleviated the latter. Early on Gorst described the food as being 'very good'.

There was much excitement when one day the ship hit a whale, and there was a rush to see what had happened. Rarely did passengers glimpse land. The Canaries were briefly seen on the horizon. Later they passed Tristan da Cunha and the adjacent desolate island named Inaccessible. Then well south of Mauritius there were the Prince Edward Islands and a few others, alarmingly not always on the chart. No stops were made and just occasionally they saw other ships. Once they exchanged friendly signals with the *Challenger*, China-bound. On another occasion they passed an American ship sailing homewards. So close were the ships that the *Red Jacket* shook the American's sails, prompting angry language from its helmsman.

Recreational activities for the passengers were limited. Gorst carried his own supply of books, but he would have been exceptional. The scope for exercise, bar pacing the deck – the ship's dimensions in feet were 251 (length) x 44 (width)[2] – was fairly limited and there were, for instance, no deck games. Card playing in steerage was put down by those in the saloon as 'immoral and wicked' although, as Gorst observed, it went on every night in the saloon. Sometimes there was dancing, apparently to a cracked fiddle, when the two classes mixed. In due course, twice a week, concerts – purely vocal affairs – were arranged; perhaps these would more accurately be described as sing-songs. They were distinctly popular and also brought people together. Occasionally, if the ship was becalmed, boats would be lowered and rowed around. When the heat was intense the fire hoses would be brought out and turned on the male passengers on deck. Females, more modestly, would be doused in the deck-house. 'Their screams', wrote Gorst, 'are most heart-rending and disturb the whole ship.'

Bear-fighting, a kind of playful wrestling between children or even adults of the same sex, took place but accidents occurred as when a little girl fell down a hold and was nearly killed. A boy also fell down the companionway from the poop injuring himself badly. Once 'two ladies in the next berth to ours, while engaged in hot strife, came crashing through into ours, so the ardour for this pursuit [bear-fighting] has been a little cooled', Gorst commented.

For the children there was some schooling. It is difficult to imagine that Gorst did not offer his services to those in charge, for he was always wanting to instruct and improve both young and old.

There were also animals on board. These included sheep and pigs, and even a cow – housed in a horse-box lashed to the deck – to provide milk for breakfast when she was not sea-sick. The poop was a glorified 'poultry yard'. Fowls and duck apparently died in their dozens and were supposed to be thrown overboard. You ate poultry, in Gorst's view, at your own risk.

Although he found his fellow-passengers for the most part 'dull' and towards the end of the voyage sometimes 'childish', Gorst entered fully into the spirit of ship-board life. Once he tried to mediate in a quarrel in the steerage, and made a speech appealing for toleration and the freedom to give opinions. He had the honesty to record that what he said had little effect. This was not the only time he addressed groups of passengers. The desire to rise on his hind legs and speak must, with him, have been a strong one. Never afraid of taking a lead he also, when the ship reached Melbourne, wrote a petition on behalf of the passengers to the Australian authorities. More of this anon.

In a different vein he did duty as 'amateur doctor's mate' when the ship's doctor went down badly with seasickness, and did the rounds. He wrote cheerfully: 'I have not killed anybody yet and trust to reach Auckland without a case of manslaughter.' The only serious illness he mentions were two cases of smallpox early in the voyage. Both patients recovered and thankfully there were no more cases. Gorst believed most of those he attended were ill as a result of 'over-eating', which tends to confirm that the food must have been good.

Towards the end of the voyage the ship got tangled up among the rocky Poor Knights islands, 100 miles north of Auckland. This must have been an extremely hazardous time and Gorst was up nearly all night with the captain helping him to take bearings to fix their position.

There was one great drama on the voyage, which Gorst seemed to relish. This was when an ugly situation suddenly developed one evening in the South Atlantic. It all began with a great fight between the crew and some foreigners who had been teased. The chief mate intervened, and knocked down a sailor 'in the most refreshing manner', as Gorst put it, and then for good measure put him in irons to cool off. A German passenger had his nose broken and another sailor his head cut open with an iron hook.

The quarrel was patched up temporarily, but it soon broke out afresh with far more serious consequences. The sailor who had been in irons was again involved in a fracas; this time he was drunk and violent. Gorst had been taking a turn on deck at about eleven at night before turning in, when he came upon the captain, second mate and boatswain dragging this man aft, away from a crowd of sailors who were trying to rescue him. Gorst at once went to help the captain by holding the gangway against the angry crew. Another sailor was collared and he too was put in irons on the orders of the captain. There must have been considerable noise, and other passengers hurried forward to offer their assistance to the hard-pressed ship's officers. Those helping were quickly armed with 'cutlasses, bayonets and revolvers'.

By now the crew were in a mutinous state. The critical moment came at midnight when the next watch was called. At this juncture the captain resolved to arrest two more members of the crew identified as ringleaders. Therefore he, with two mates and five armed passengers one of whom was Gorst, went down to make the arrests. One of the two men elected to go quietly, but the other resisted and screamed for help from his comrades. Other sailors, thereupon, came rushing up the gangway only to be met with an array of bayonets. The first mate, by now on the scene, thrust at the leading seaman and would probably have killed him, had not the captain parried the blow, deflecting the blade of the weapon deep into the woodwork. The mutineers were beaten back. The gangways and the front of the poop were now held by armed men, many of them passengers. Gorst wrote:

> There was an awful pause while the captain went down to load his revolver. You can have no idea how ludicrous the whole affair appeared to us, though the officers thought it serious. I saw the doctor, who is a very meek man, armed with a cutlass. When the pistols were loaded the captain ... ordered the watch to haul taut the mainbrace to test their obedience, and it was done.[3]

An armed watch, fixed bayonets at the ready, was kept for the rest of the night. The four men arrested, handcuffed and with their legs chained and in stocks, were placed in a luggage storeroom.

In the morning the captain held a meeting in the saloon. He was taking no chances and obtained the agreement of the passengers to form three special watches consisting of 12 armed men. Sentries were posted in the gangway armed with 'pistols and cutlasses', while two armed men were constantly on the poop. The rest of the watch were close by in readiness for emergencies. The captain took the precaution of drawing up a document setting out these arrangements and explaining the need for passenger participation in them. The document was signed by the co-operating passengers.

In due course the mutineers were released on good behaviour, and only the original instigator of the trouble was detained. No one wanted him freed. Finally the crew, now obedient to all the captain's commands, addressed a letter to him promising to behave.

After the excitement of the mutiny the weather turned foul. Off the Cape of Good Hope fearsome winds from east-north-east drove the ship far to the south, down indeed to latitude 48⁰ 30′, which lies 1,000 miles south of the continent of Africa. One morning Gorst was roused at 7 am to see an iceberg. In fact the *Red Jacket* was surrounded by ice. No sooner were they in these treacherous ice-fields than the winds dropped and they were blanketed in fog, with visibility often down to a ghostly 300 yards. For a time four crew were posted as look-outs.

It was a relief to all passengers to make landfall at last off Cape Otway on the coast of Victoria especially as, not long before, the mizzen top-sail had been carried away for the third time on the voyage. Gorst was up betimes – it was 19 April – to witness the pilot boat come alongside at Port Philip Heads. No ship, apparently, had arrived at the Port of Melbourne for two weeks, which meant that the *Red Jacket* had beaten every vessel sailing from England at the same time. One piece of disturbing news awaited those emigrants going on to Auckland. The previous month a war between the settlers and the Maoris had broken out in North Island, New Zealand, but at least it was confined to the New Plymouth area. This was the start of the Taranaki war, and was to lead eventually to the long and bitter Maori war some three years later.

The passengers who were longing to disembark were to be frustrated, for the Victoria authorities immediately put the whole ship, and the unfortunate pilot to boot, into quarantine for smallpox. No one was allowed to leave the ship. This was when Gorst helped prepare the petition, already mentioned, which explained that everyone on board had been vaccinated and that there had been no recurrence of the disease since the initial two cases, and they were praying for release. The medical officers, though, were stony-hearted and ordered the revaccination of the ship's company and passengers. Worse, they insisted that all bedding and clothing should be fumigated and sterilised in boiling water on shore. The wretched passengers had to return to the ship in drenched clothes and with wet bedding too. Their discomfort must have been acute.

The impression may have been given that, during the long voyage, Gorst, when he was not reading or writing, was either playing the mediator, or orator, or the doctor's mate, or the navigator or just helping to quell a mutiny. This, even if partly true, is not an entirely accurate picture. For Gorst was not immune from the charms of the fair sex, and as the journey progressed he was becoming more and more romantically involved with a young lady. We have already met her talking to the captain; she was Mary Elizabeth Moore who was travelling with her parents. By the time the *Red Jacket* had reached Melbourne, John had fallen in love, proposed – probably in the Roaring Forties of all places – and been accepted.[4]

Mary and her parents were originally bound for New Zealand. But when her father heard about the Taranaki war he decided to remain for a time in Melbourne. So the engaged couple had to separate for a while until they could be married in August.

Mary came from an Anglo-Irish family. She was the daughter of Lorenzo Moore, whose father had been MP for Dublin University in the 1820s. Moore was a bit of a firebrand, and had had a rather colourful career. He had joined the East India Company at the age of 18 and had then taken to soldiering, reaching the rank of major in the 5th Madras Light Cavalry. Rashly he produced some literature critical of the Company's anti-Christian policy which his Commanding Officer ordered to be burned, thinking it likely to undermine good order and discipline. So leaving the Company's service Moore went home with his wife and three children, took a degree at Cambridge, and became a parson, a profession favoured by others in his family. He worked in several parishes before deciding in 1859 to emigrate to New Zealand, a country he eventually arrived in three years later.[5]

The journey on to Auckland, reached on 16 May, 111 days after leaving Liverpool, may have been for Gorst something of an anti-climax. If it was, the extracts from his letters do not show it. As ever he was observant and described the passing scene with his usual verve and wit.

Once, in the middle of the night, he was awakened by a loud crash as the ship took a huge plunge. There was a rain of 'boxes, books and boots' onto the floor and 'Mainwaring's tobacco boxes' were smashed to smithereens spilling tobacco all over the floor 'like a brown door mat'. Except that his brother Roland was a schoolmaster in Preston, we know little about Mainwaring with whom Gorst shared a cabin, or why he should have been travelling with so much tobacco. He makes the odd further appearance in our story, but remains nonetheless a shadowy figure.

Gorst was delighted with the beauty of the passage through the islands north of Auckland and enchanted with the setting of that town. But once on shore Auckland, then New Zealand's capital, disappointed him. The place was lighted by a 'few dim oil-lamps' and he could not see his way, stumbling into holes in the road and finally into the ruins of what turned out to be a burnt-out flour mill. This happened while he was on his way to the post-office, no doubt to post a letter to Mary. Eventually he located the building – 'a shabby wooden thing'– and, to his disgust, found it shut. His expectations were perhaps too high.

Gorst was soon greeted by Bishop Selwyn, whom he had come to assist as a lay missionary. Selwyn had already been in the country for nearly 20 years. He would stay on until 1868 when he would return home and become the Bishop of Lichfield. Later a Cambridge college would be founded in his memory. Gorst was fortunate to have this remarkable pioneer as his mentor for a time.

The plan had been that Gorst should help John Patteson in his missionary work among the cannibal tribes of Polynesia,[6] which lay at the time within Bishop Selwyn's diocese. This plan was revised when Gorst turned up at Auckland, and no doubt to Selwyn's surprise, engaged to be married. The good bishop must have decided that remote Pacific islands were not the place – at least immediately – for a young bride to begin her married life: better that the Gorsts should start off in Auckland. Patteson, whom Gorst came to know and like, became Bishop of Melanesia in 1861. Ten years later he died a martyr when he was killed by the islanders of the Santa Cruz group (now part of the Solomon Islands). Perhaps Gorst had a fortunate escape.

According to Gorst, Selwyn was the most unpopular person in the colony. His offence was that at the outbreak of the Taranaki War he had declared the sale of the disputed Maori land to the colonial government – the cause of the war – to be invalid. The occupation of the land by British troops, the Bishop made clear, was therefore unjust. These outspoken views did not apparently interfere with his relations with the Governor, Colonel Thomas Gore Browne, as Gorst was shortly to observe. Gore Browne was a decent and straightforward man who had been in the Indian army and then Governor of St. Helena before coming to New Zealand in 1855.

The Governor had invited some Maori chiefs to a conference to discuss their grievances. The meeting was to be held in the buildings of a college owned by the Melanesian mission a few miles north of Auckland opposite Rangitoto Island. Gorst and his friend Mainwaring went off to help the Bishop and his wife to prepare the buildings for the conference. Gorst found the work 'immense fun' and liked what he described as the 'freedom of colonial manners'. No one stood on his or her dignity. The Bishop 'took off his coat and waistcoat and worked like a day labourer, loading wheelbarrows with all sorts of odds and ends . . . [then he] took a broom and began to sweep, and sent us off to take a load of pumpkins to a Maori college . . .' Shortly, the Governor arrived with his ADC. As soon as the Bishop spotted them they too were put to work and helped 'on the sweeping of the building'.[7] All this greatly appealed to Gorst.

Before the preparations for the conference were complete the news came in that the missionary schooner *Southern Cross* had run aground some 80 miles north of Auckland. Happily everyone aboard was safe. At once the Bishop set out in a 20-ton schooner, the *Petrel*, to see what he could do to help, taking Gorst with him. Roads were poor or non-existent and this was the best way to reach the scene swiftly.

The little relief expedition developed into something of an adventure for Gorst. Due to strong winds the *Petrel* failed to make its first objective, the sheltered waters of the Whangerei estuary. Glad to be free of the cramped quarters of the *Petrel*'s six-foot-square cabin, the Bishop and Gorst took to a rowing boat to spend the night ashore. The boat leaked and they only just made the cove for which they were aiming. On shore a Maori village provided shelter and food. The Maoris by tradition show great hospitality to strangers. At once Selwyn was at home talking to his hosts round a fire kindled in the middle of the floor and filling the room with choking smoke.

The next day the relief party were back on the *Petrel*, and the little schooner reached the estuary safely. On shore everyone was entertained to breakfast by the local postmaster who doubled as custom-house officer, harbour-master, magistrate, policeman and other civil offices. Gorst was himself destined in two years' time similarly to fill all these posts in Upper Waikato. Next they borrowed a whaleboat and the rest of the day was spent rowing round Bream Head against adverse winds towards the scene of the wreck, which was finally reached in heavy seas in pitch dark. The spars and main sails of the *Southern Cross,* they found, had been rigged up by the crew as a tent on the beach. Under this the Bishop's party, which now included an elderly ship's carpenter, pitched their small tents, and lit a fire to make tea. Gorst's bed consisted of a strip of waterproof spread on the sand with blankets on top. They were lucky to have arrived in one piece.

The schooner, Gorst saw next day, was in quite sound condition but very deeply buried in sand so that a large part of the deck was hidden from view. They tried pumping out the water and shovelling away the sand, but their good work was undone when the tide came in. The Bishop, ever hopeful, went off to seek further help. Food supplies were by now low, so Gorst and the carpenter set out to forage. They trudged through dense forest before coming at length to a sizeable village where they finally succeeded with help from a European trader in buying a pig, at the rate of 3d a pound, for £2 12s 6d, a sum which had first to be agreed to the satisfaction of the Maori magistrate. They now set off back to the site of the shipwreck, with the pig being driven by a man and a boy. That evening there must have been a welcome feast with roast pork as the main course.

Further attempts were made to salvage the *Southern Cross* but these proved abortive. On a more positive note the party encamped on the beach received instruction in the Maori language in the evenings from the Bishop. Gorst was now concerned about the date. He was due to catch the mail boat from Auckland to Sydney, and did not want to miss it for fear of upsetting the plans for his marriage to Mary in August.

This time he set off into the interior to reach Whangarei, first by rowing boat heading upstream before progress was impeded by creeks and swamps. He then continued on foot by forest tracks through a succession of Maori villages. Often he was on his own and several times became lost. But everyone he met, including a Frenchman who gave him lodgings for the night, helped him on his way, and he finally reached his first destination just in time to catch a local sailing boat going to Auckland.

John and Mary were duly married at Geelong near Melbourne on 18 August with Mary's father performing the ceremony. Once again for the third time in a mere four months Gorst crossed the Tasman Sea, but this time with his bride. He and Mary were to live in Auckland for a little less than a year and a half before they moved to the Waikato to live among the Maoris.

NOTES

1. NZR, 5–23: Sir John E Gorst's book *New Zealand Revisited* is the main source of information about his voyage to New Zealand.
2. Information on the *Red Jacket* supplied by Bernard Lawley, and also taken from Jane Lyon, *Clipper Ships and Captains*, Mahwah, NJ, n.d.
3. NZR, 13.
4. FP, 26.
5. *Dictionary of New Zealand Biography*, vol. II, 1870–1900, M54.
6. James Cowan, *New Zealand Wars*, Wellington, Government Printer, 1922–23, 229.
7. NZR, 29.

The Maori King Movement

John Gorst set foot in New Zealand at a particularly unsettled time in North Island when relations between the Maoris and the colonists were deteriorating. At the heart of the discord was the land problem. The settlers were greedy to buy it and the Maoris were often reluctant to sell it.

The Maoris had lived in New Zealand for many centuries before the Europeans came. Some decades after Captain James Cook had circumnavigated the islands, British and Australian traders in the whaling business and in timber were having contact with the Maoris. Then in the early part of the nineteenth century the missionaries arrived on the islands. The Maoris, a race of agriculturists, resisted for some time the proselytising efforts of the missionaries but in course of time Christianity gained a firm hold. They were above all a warlike people and fighting among themselves was endemic. Land, their most important form of property, belonged to the tribe.

The process of European colonisation was slow and did not gather any real momentum before the formation in 1838 of the New Zealand Company. The British government was reluctant in these early days to impose its authority on the colonisers. Then, worried about French interest in the Islands, it sent out Captain William Hobson of the Royal Navy to treat with the Maoris.

The Treaty of Waitangi which Hobson signed with 50 chiefs at the Bay of Islands in February 1840 was something of a landmark in New Zealand's history. Later some 500 Maori leaders, mainly chiefs, added their mark to the treaty and received a blanket each for doing so. But, significantly in view of later developments over the vexed question of land, no Waikato chief signed.

By this treaty, which ran to three short articles, the chiefs ceded their sovereignty to the Queen. In return the Queen guaranteed to the chiefs the full and undisturbed possession of their lands while the chiefs yielded to the Queen the sole right of buying their land. Finally the chiefs were given the rights and privileges of British subjects. Soon after the treaty Hobson proclaimed British sovereignty over both North and South Island. At first the islands were technically part of New South Wales, but became a separate colony in 1841.

The historian, Keith Sinclair, writing in 1959, stated that the treaty 'was intended to lay a basis for a just society in which two races far apart in civilisation would live together in amity'. At the same time he observed that while almost everyone concerned received some satisfaction from the treaty it pleased no one entirely.[1] Gorst, writing in 1864 after spending three and a half years in New Zealand, was critical of the treaty's wording. He considered it one-sided, and pointed out that the Maoris were ignorant of words like 'sovereignty' and that they were without any government which 'could secure the observance of conditions on their side' to which they had agreed.[2] In Gorst's view the treaty was not much observed by either side, the Maoris regarding their own right arms to be the best protectors of their land and property.

As more and more settlers arrived in the colony so the land question began to cause increasing friction. This led to fighting between the Maoris and the land-hungry colonists. In 1845 George Grey, only 29, arrived as Governor. He was a man of strong character with marked ability, although inclined to be autocratic. He stopped the intermittent fighting, and a period of peace and relative stability followed. He encouraged missionary schools and Maori agriculture, and restored the interrupted government monopoly of buying land. Under the system the government bought land from the Maoris at 6d or 1s an acre, and sold it on to the colonists for 10s or £1 an acre, the large profit forming the basis of government revenue. Grey did little for the government of Maori districts, leaving the Maoris on the whole to fend for themselves. If it existed at all, government policy was for Maoris to be Europeanised.

By 1854 the colonists now numbering about 32,500, of whom 12,000 were in Auckland, had been clamouring for self-government. The home government had yielded to this agitation and Grey, before his departure to become Governor of the Cape, had introduced a new constitution for the colonists which set up various elected legislatures. But the interests of the Maoris were neglected and they were given only a very limited franchise. Some years later the British government accepted that responsible government was in the hands of the colonists, although the Governor, now Colonel Thomas Gore Browne, still retained control of troops and native affairs. But in principle, apart from the reserved matters, the Governor acted on the advice of his ministers. These ministers were local politicians drawn from the settler community who sat in the legislature at Auckland.

One of them, commanding the confidence of the chamber, became Premier.

The settlers were preoccupied with profits from business and farming, and ignored the welfare of the Maoris, assuming at the same time an inherent and prejudiced superiority over them. For their part the Maoris were torn between resentment against the invader and respect for his God and goods.[3] Gorst put it well when he wrote: 'Men habitually told that they emit a disagreeable smell are not likely to feel a strong affection towards the race that smells them.'[4]

Nonetheless some of the commercial achievements of the Maoris, especially those in the Waikato, were formidable. Thousands of acres were planted with wheat and other crops, and scores of flour mills were owned and operated by them.

By the early 1850s the Maoris began to be deeply dissatisfied with the amount of land being lost to the settlers. A thousand Maoris including many chiefs assembled in 1854 at Manawapou in Taranaki province in order to agree that land should no longer be sold to the *pakeha* (Europeans). This meeting was important as it marked the rise of the nationalist Maori King movement, and led four years later in 1858 to the installation at Ngaruawahia in the Waikato of an elderly and respected Maori chief, Potatau, as the Maori King. It was in this year too that the census revealed that the Europeans now outnumbered the Maoris.

The King was to an extent a symbolic figure for although he reigned with his flag, his councillors, some troops and constables, his kingdom was only a loose federation of tribes and he did not in practice rule his subjects. But the King movement was united in its common purpose of ensuring no more land was sold to settlers. Certainly Wiremu Tamihana, a leading Waikato chief and one of those responsible for setting up the Maori King, had wanted to introduce through the King movement an effective system of government among the Maoris. But the movement went well beyond this. Historians are generally agreed that the King movement was an expression of a growing sense of Maori nationalism.[5] The Maoris wished to rule themselves, and in so doing to maintain their separate identity. By claiming in the late 1850s a comprehensive jurisdiction over their own people the Kingites, unhappily, were on a collision course with both the imperial and colonial governments.

In March 1859 an event occurred in Taranaki province, where there was a history of feuding over land between Maoris and settlers, which was to develop into a major crisis. At a meeting in New Plymouth the Governor, Gore Browne, giving way to pressure from the settlers, counselled the Maoris to sell unoccupied land, promising at the same time that the government would not buy it unless the owners had agreed to sell. Whereupon Teira, a Maori sub-chief, jumped up and offered for sale a block of land at Waitara amounting to 60,000 acres. Gore Browne accepted, provided the title was good. Immediately Wiremu Kingi, a powerful chief, objected and with that abruptly left the meeting. The Governor felt he could not back down. Unfortunately, he was badly advised and, strangely ignorant of Maori land law, was unaware that land belonged to a tribe as a whole. In fact Wiremu Kingi and others had claims to part of the land. An inadequate and protracted inquiry into the title did not reveal this.

When government surveyors went in February 1860 to the site to put in pegs, they were confronted by a crowd who promptly removed the pegs. Perhaps precipitately, the government proclaimed martial law and then sent in troops to occupy the disputed land. Most of the settlers supported the Governor, but, as we have seen, some like Bishop Selwyn disagreed with the government action. Another to do so was the former Chief Justice, Sir William Martin, who wrote a pamphlet about the dispute. Strife was now inevitable and the Taranaki war began in March 1860 just before Gorst's arrival in New Zealand. For about a year there would be intermittent and inconclusive fighting, essentially confined to Taranaki, between on the one hand an uneasy combination of British troops and local militias numbering some 3,000 and on the other hand about half that number of Maori warriors.

The setttlers were forced to congregate at New Plymouth and leave their farms at the mercy of marauding bands of Maoris who had almost complete freedom of movement. In return government forces burned Maori villages and occasionally fought pitched battles, though on a small scale. The Maoris had no overall strategy, did not adopt guerrilla tactics and tended to keep to their traditional mode of war, whereby they invited attack on a fortified hill-top village (known as a *pa*) to the rear of which was bush affording the opportunity of escape. Auckland, where the Gorsts made their home, had the atmosphere of a rough frontier-cum-garrison town. Australian and Irish immigrants formed a large proportion of the population. The pioneers, who had both enterprise and ambition, were usually from the working or lower middle class. Sinclair light-heartedly comments on the frequency with which men from the English middle classes went to New Zealand because of 'bigamy or bankruptcy, disappointment or disgrace'.[6]

If the price of land in Auckland was high, so too was the average wage. Speculation was rife and men tended to use their leisure time in gambling and drinking. Gorst found some of the settlers to be 'slovenly in their habits'. Women had a civilising effect, and had consequently an especially important contribution to make to the community. Organised entertainment and cultural activities took time to develop. This did not stop a Methodist minister writing, just after the time the Gorsts were in Auckland, about the subject of gaiety in the town. In particular, he deplored the giving of balls by both 'gentry and the working class' fearing the 'dissipation of the mind' and the injury to health that they caused.[7]

The Gorsts were an adaptable couple and settled down to their new life. At the same time John, showing a lively interest in the political problems besetting the country, was raring to explore further afield. In particular he wanted to go to the Waikato and learn about the King movement at first hand. It was not long before the opportunity to go there presented itself. In October 1860 the Rev. B. Y. Ashwell invited the Gorsts to visit him at his mission station at Taupiri. There Ashwell wanted John to meet Tamihana, whom we have already mentioned. He was the chief of the Ngatihaua tribe, an intelligent and learned man and the patron of a successful Maori school at Matamata where he lived.

It proved to be a rather gruelling journey south into the hinterland, starting with a 20-mile jolt in 'a van' pulled by a horse along a rough track to the settlement of Drury. The effect of this ride, wrote Gorst, was 'very similar to that of a flogging'. There followed the next day a stage made in drenching rain of 12 miles through the Hunua forest ranges to the banks of the Waikato river. The party at the time consisted of the Gorsts, Ashwell and his daughter and two Maoris with tents and baggage. After Drury they had between them three horses, two of which were ridden by the women while Gorst and Ashwell took it in turns to ride the third animal. The following morning after a night spent in the isolated house of a settler, they met Mrs Ashwell, who had obligingly come out from Taupiri to meet them. The journey now continued by canoe through thickly wooded country, giving Gorst, an observant traveller, the chance to comment on the overhanging 'Kohai trees covered with their yellow blossoms like laburnum', on which settled black 'parson birds' sucking the nectar from their flowers. Another favourite bird was the small owl, named after its famous cry 'morepork, morepork'.

That night they were revived at a hospitable village by a delicious dish of river fish 'like whitebait' boiled by their Maori hosts. During their short stay Mary somehow lost her diamond ring. A great search was made for it but it could not be found. Some days later the local chief sent a message to the Gorsts that the ring had been found and was being returned, but the chief could not be persuaded to take any kind of reward.

At Paetai further upstream Gorst was impressed with the Maori school where he found a dozen little girls under 10, who could read Maori perfectly, knew some arithmetic and spoke a little English, although their pronunciation was 'eccentric'. At the next school, probably at Rawiri, the pupils were all boys. Gorst wrote that there were 'many such schools in the Waikato district, all self-supporting or nearly so; the natives allotted a few acres of land on which the labour of the teacher and scholars sufficed to raise enough grain and potatoes for their food'.[8] Unhappily, these promising Maori village schools would be swept away as the tide of war engulfed the country.

Before the party reached Taupiri they were hailed by an approaching Maori canoe, and learnt from two chiefs travelling in it that a Maori had been murdered away to the north-west at Waiuku on Manikau harbour. It was suspected, the chiefs said, that the murderer was a European, and if this turned out to be true then it would be war unless the culprit was given up to the Maoris for justice. Apparently, two years before both chiefs had been the assessors for the British resident magistrate. On his withdrawal they had become adherents of the King movement.

The Gorsts' visit to the Ashwells at Taupiri was a disappointment, being marred by rumours of war. As soon as his party had arrived at the mission settlement Ashwell had written to Tamihana to try to arrange a meeting between him and John Gorst. Almost at once there was news that Tamihana was coming downstream towards Taupiri at the head of a war party of 300 men. On the day of the chief's arrival at Taupiri, Gorst met him at the early hour of 6.30 a.m. Tamihana, accompanied by 'wild-looking and tattooed' followers, could not have been more friendly. He and Gorst established from the start a rapport which was to endure. Tamihana, who was mission-educated and so spoke English, said he was determined to keep the peace although the majority of his followers wanted the surrender of the suspected murderer. He also said that Ashwell's house was *tapu* (sacred) and that Gorst should continue on south to Matamata.

But John was concerned about Mary's safety and there seemed, in the circumstances in which they found themselves, no sensible alternative but to retrace their footsteps. They stopped off again at Paetai and were astonished at the transformation the peaceful village of a few days ago had undergone. The shore was now lined with large canoes and crowds of Maoris were hurrying to and fro with guns and tomahawks. The women, as was the custom, were preparing food in great ovens sunk in the ground. Everywhere there were children getting in the way. Threading his way among young men preparing for the war dance, Gorst at last found Tamihana. All the men round the chief asked who Gorst was, and whether he had anything to do with the Governor. On being told he was the friend of Ashwell the missionary, they shook his hand and made a place for him. Gorst had another talk with Tamihana who, when he learnt that the young Englishman had his wife with him, advised with obvious regret that the Gorsts should indeed both return to Auckland. But when the disturbance was over he, Tamihana, would send a deacon to collect Gorst so that he could return to the Waikato and visit Matamata.

Before moving on, Gorst was determined to see the war dance, which was disapproved of by the missionaries. It proved to be the only one danced in anger that he ever witnessed. The Maoris, armed to the teeth and wearing headbands of white feathers, divided into two groups, attackers and defenders. They began by charging around, shaking and beating themselves, chanting all the while. Gradually the noise and movement performed in unison reached a crescendo of leaping, screaming and brandishing of weapons. Gorst was enthralled by the scene. After the dance there were speeches short and to the point. There was no doubt in Gorst's mind that the warriors meant business. The new Maori King, Matutaera (he was later known as Tawhiao), who had succeeded to the throne after Potatau's death, was present and in a state of indecision as to whether or not he should advance on Auckland. But the real leader, Gorst noted, was the cautious Tamihana.[9]

The journey back to Auckland was as uncomfortable as the outward one had been. After various misadventures the Gorsts reached the town at about 8 pm in a violent storm. Gorst at once went to Bishop Selwyn's house to tell him about the advancing warriors. The Bishop thought the position was a dangerous one and decided, even at that late hour, to go off and meet the Maoris himself to try to prevent mischief. He was successful, for he was able to draw Tamihana's attention to a party of militants setting off on their own to pillage and possibly murder settlers. Tamihana with great difficulty was able to recall these hotheads. Gorst commented years later that 'the colony had really a much narrower escape than was at the time suspected'.[10]

On his first visit to the Waikato Gorst had been struck by the contrast between the material poverty of the Maori people, as reflected in their houses, clothing and food, and what he called 'their mental attainments' such as their reasoning on political subjects, and the good sense they showed in making provisions for governing themselves and for educating their children.[11] As far as their ability to govern themselves was concerned, Gorst changed his mind on this in the course of the next two years. From an administrative point of view it would not have escaped Gorst's notice how minimally the writ of the colonial government ran in the Waikato.

Gorst did not meet Tamihana again until the following year when it was learnt the chief was collecting a large party at Tamahere for the purpose of intervening in some way in the Taranaki war, still a local affair. So once again Gorst found himself travelling to Taupiri. From Ashwell's mission station Gorst rode up to Tamahere with Hota, Tamihana's eldest son. Mary was pregnant and did not accompany her husband on this trip.

Tamihana and the leading men gave Gorst a warm welcome, as they were about to start their dinner of baked mutton, potatoes and white bread. Plates were not used, each man cutting meat from the joint with his knife. After dinner a Bible containing maps was produced and Gorst was subjected by the assembled company to an examination of his knowledge of history, both ancient and modern, and geography. Gorst, a studious man, had been learning Maori and by now he would have been able to hold a conversation with his hosts in their own tongue. Later that evening Tamihana went down to the school-house where Gorst was lodged and the two men had a long *tête-à-tête*, a manifestation of the friendship developing between them.

The next day, a Sunday, Tamihana preached at the morning service. Evening prayers, held in the open, was 'almost too much for my gravity' wrote Gorst. 'The congregation was squatted down [*sic*] clothed in blankets and infested with naked babies which toddled about making a most irreverent row.' The deacon, as it was getting late, exhorted the congregation to read the responses faster and finally 'closed the service abruptly, intimating they must come earlier another evening'. Gorst's contribution to this visit took place the following morning when he gave a talk at the school on the Queen, her ministers and the House of Commons, emphasising that the affairs of New Zealand were carefully considered by these august personages and by Parliament. With an eye to the main chance he lost no opportunity in urging his audience to accept any decision made by the Commons over the war in Taranaki.[12]

A little later Gorst made another visit to Tamahere from Taupiri, this time with Ashwell, reaching the place at the very moment a number of Waikato men wounded in the Taranaki war arrived. The Maori chief explained to his visitors during the course of several long interviews what he intended to do in Taranaki. He was going as a man of peace and wanted to halt the war. He would try to persuade the leading chief, Wiremu Kingi, to write to the Governor saying – and thus presumably echoing Gorst – that the Maoris would abide by what the House of Commons decided and also requesting a cessation of hostilities. For their part both Gorst and Ashwell tried, unsuccessfully, to persuade Tamihana to go to Auckland to see the Governor.

There is no evidence that, in having discussions with Tamihana, Gorst and Ashwell were doing anything but acting on their own initiative. We can discount the possibility of their having been given an official brief. Gorst could not resist becoming involved in government affairs; he was also a man who all through his life wished to instruct people. We have already seen him as a debater at Cambridge, a schoolmaster and a giver of pep talks on board ship. He sought, usually with engaging zeal, to enlighten those with whom he came into contact, although ever industrious, he liked to have a detailed knowledge of any subject he was working up before holding forth on it.

Tamihana carried out his resolve to visit Waitara, a journey he made in March 1861 against the wishes of the Maori King, who was opposed to other Maori tribes meddling in the Taranaki quarrel. The chief met with conspicuous success in his endeavours to halt the war, after a rather reluctant Wiremu Kingi agreed to let him handle negotiations with the Europeans. He had a series of discussions with various government officials including Donald McLean, the influential Native Secretary. These resulted in a temporary truce; as events turned out, the break in the war was to last two years and so gave the parties a chance – not one taken – to resolve their differences over the disputed Waitara land. Tamihana had proposed sensibly enough that all parties should withdraw from this land. But this did not happen. Asked to meet the Governor, Tamihana once again refused to go to Auckland. He also declined to widen his discussions in Taranaki to cover such matters as property plundered in the war and the Maori King movement.[13]

Tamihana returned to Tamahere discontented with the way, as he perceived it, his friendly overtures to the British had been greeted. He sent for John Gorst, for he wished to give him an account of what had happened at Waitara. Gorst hurried south to Tamahere and met Tamihana at the school-house, giving him a cigar 'to keep him as mild as possible'. A white flag fluttered from the 'rebel' flagstaff in honour of the peace. Their talk lasted two hours. Tamihana said the Waikatos were not at all depressed by the results of their fighting with British soldiers, and there was a general readiness to fight for their King and for their national independence despite the casualties they had suffered. The Maori chief was especially sorry that his proposal for letting the House of Commons decide the merits of the land dispute – perhaps not a very practical one – had been apparently rejected. Moreover, he and his people were despondent about 'civilisation' and had taken their children away from their own Maori schools. They had also abandoned the wearing of European clothes.

At the centre of the dialogue between the two men was the question of the King movement and the land issue. Tamihana told Gorst that the Waikatos had never signed the Treaty of Waitangi and were not bound by it. He explained that the Maoris were determined to uphold the Maori King, but there was, he said, no enmity to the Queen. Their King was a figure about whom they could rally and under whom they would make laws to replace obsolete Maori customs. The King should be to the Maoris what the Governor was to Europeans, and round them both was the Queen as a protective 'hedge'.[14] Peace, Tamihana said, had not been made. Vehemently he insisted he would never give up his King.

Gorst for his part gave the chief the reasons why he thought the King movement was 'unwise', arguing that it promoted dissension among the Maoris themselves and in case of a dispute with the government it would deprive them of the Queen's protection. More tellingly perhaps, it would prevent them obtaining European money for schools, hospitals and so on. Tamihana did not dissent, but insisted nevertheless that the Maoris wanted to remain a distinct nation. When Gorst said that the British objected to the name 'King', Tamihana replied, 'Why? What is in a name?' Many years after Tamihana's death Gorst, then aged 70, paid a tribute to the Maori chief, with whom he had enjoyed many an argument. Always Tamihana had remained patient, calm and ever anxious to find out the exact meaning of an interlocutor's words. Gorst wrote:

> I have met many statesmen in the course of my long life, but none superior in intellect and character to this Maori chief …[15]

This was praise indeed. During the visits he made to Tamihana, Gorst would often be accompanied by Heta, a deacon; he described Heta as a sincere Christian, whose friendship and advice he valued.

After seeing Tamihana, Gorst thought he should report fully to the Governor what the Maori chief had said to him. Gorst was given a good hearing by Gore Browne for this was the first intelligence the Governor had received of Tamihana's state of mind since the negotiations at Waitara. The Governor confirmed that Tamihana's terms had not been accepted, nor had peace been made.

Gorst was made to repeat what he had told the Governor to the Attorney-General, and then to produce a written report which was despatched to the Colonial Office where it was in due course incorporated in a Blue Book on the situation in New Zealand. One other apparent result of Gorst's talk with Tamihana was that the Chief Justice wrote at length to the Maori chief recapitulating the government's objections to the title 'King' and urging him to see that the title was given up, or alternatively to let the Queen decide the matter.

Inexorably, Gorst was being drawn into the political arena. But not against his will. The good relations he had established with Tamihana had not been lost on the Governor, who would shortly seek to exploit this situation. A year after he had first arrived in the country, Gorst had managed to obtain a foot in both the government camp and that of a leading Maori chief. While New Zealand was only a small country in terms of population, it was none the less an achievement for a young man not quite 26 to have made this mark.

After thinking about his experiences in the Waikato and believing rightly that the government, having come to a crossroads in its relations with the Maoris, was contemplating the use of force again, Gorst reached for his pen. In May 1861 he wrote three letters under the appropriately chosen pseudonym 'Fabius' (after the Roman general who was a believer in delaying tactics) to the *New Zealander*, an Auckland newspaper. In his first letter he began with the premise broadly following the government's line that the Maori King 'should be put down'. He did not give his reasons but, if he had done, there can be little doubt that he would have said there could be no room in New Zealand for two separate governments. He then went on to suggest there were two options open to the government to overcome the King movement. One was to use military force and the other to use conciliatory means. He pointed out at some length – in no less than 108 column lines of text – the difficulties and costs of military operations.[16] Further, he saw no merit at all in a nation of 28,000,000 crushing one of 50,000. He was therefore firmly opposed to the military option.

In his second letter written on 22 May he advised that time should be allowed for reflection by both sides. He considered, not mincing his words, that the British in their actions towards the Maoris had failed woefully in their duties both as governors and as educators. In the expectations raised by the British 20 years earlier the Maoris had been cruelly disappointed. He went on to say that the Maori King movement was a revolt against the system of government introduced, and had been established partly to replace that system which the British had been unable or unwilling to afford, and partly to prevent the further alienation of Maori land.

Gorst also urged that magistrates administering English law should be appointed to go out and reside among the Maoris, who would never be 'civilised' by men 'sitting at mahogany desks in Auckland'. At the same time a comprehensive scheme for the Maoris' efficient education – in the broadest meaning of the term – should be introduced by the colonial government, who should not leave this task solely to the missionaries.[17] There was certainly some sense in what Gorst was suggesting. As a result of what he had seen with his own eyes, he wanted firm civil as opposed to military intervention by the government to remedy a situation arising not so much from maladministration as from non-administration.

Some readers today of Gorst's letters to the *New Zealander* might be shocked that Gorst could refer to the Maoris as 'savages' or as 'an inferior race'. But he would also describe the Maoris as an 'intelligent' and 'noble' people. Like all Victorians and men of his time he believed, however arrogant this may sound today, that people ruled by the British needed 'civilising' and that the British could govern the Maoris better than they could govern themselves.

While readers of the *New Zealander* were digesting what Gorst had written, the Governor was issuing a 'declaration' – it was more like an ultimatum – to the Waikato Maoris, who were assembling on 3 June for a big meeting at their capital Ngaruawahia. In it Gore Browne listed all the wrongs committed by the King movement, especially those matters concerned with waging or threatening war against the government. Adherents of the movement, the Governor stated, were trying to obtain arms and ammunition to achieve their aims by violent means.[18] There could be no mistaking the fact that the Governor was throwing out a direct challenge to the Maoris to disown the Maori King and obey the law.

Tamihana seems at this gathering to have been given *carte blanche* to defend the position adopted by the Waikato Maoris, which he did stoutly. He then wrote a letter to the Governor in which he quoted readily from the Old Testament. The Governor might not have been too pleased to read that he was regarded by Tamihana as 'headstrong', but then the Maoris were a plain-speaking race and not a people to be intimidated. The Governor took Tamihana's letter to be defiant. The die now seemed to be cast and both sides began to prepare for war.

It was at this moment that the home government intervened. The Duke of Newcastle, the Colonial Secretary, uneasy at the course of events, decided that a change of Governor was needed. So he brought back Sir George Grey, the former incumbent of the post, who had conveniently offered his services as a mediator in the Taranaki war. Grey had gained something of a reputation as being a friend of the Maoris. If anyone could rescue the situation, or so it must have been argued by the Duke, it was Grey. As for Gorst he did not, interestingly, attach much blame for the prevailing state of affairs on the departing Governor, believing its cause to be mistakes by his predecessors (this had to include Grey) and to the system of 'dual' government much disliked by Gorst, to which we will return.[19]

For a while John Gorst was distracted by a happy family event. Mary gave birth at 2.15 p.m. on 25 June 1861 to a son in the Auckland suburb of Parnell. He was christened, as was his father, John Eldon, but would always be known in the family as Jack. He was to be the first of eight children. One died as a child but the other seven would all reach adulthood. Six would marry and all would dote on their mother Mary.

Besides his work as a lay helper in the missionary field, about which little is known, Gorst had been doing some teaching. In Parnell, John had met and come to know John Kinder who was headmaster of the new grammar school there. Gorst was invited to teach at this school, and for a time he took the Greek class every morning.[20] In addition he taught Maori children on his visits to his friends the Ashwells at Hopuhopu school where one of his pupils was Hota, Tamihana's son. We can only guess how much satisfaction Gorst was obtaining from his work. Almost certainly, though, his mind was not being adequately stretched. On the other hand Gorst's interest had been caught by the problems facing the government, especially those connected with the administration of Maori affairs. Not entirely surprisingly, therefore, we find Gorst offering his services to the government.[21] He had already brought himself to the Governor's attention by his contact with Tamihana and, no doubt, by his letters to the press. There was a shortage in New Zealand of intelligent and energetic young men willing to enter government service, and his offer was accepted. The outgoing Governor and the colonial government, now headed by William Fox, had agreed that, as a start,

Gorst should be sent on a mission to the Waikato to inspect schools there.

Gorst's mission had to be delayed until the arrival in late September of the new Governor. Grey read the latest papers about the problems in the Waikato and elsewhere, commenting that Tamihana was likely to turn out 'a troublesome fellow'. Then without more ado the terms of Gorst's task were agreed in a letter dated 8 October. Besides inspecting and reporting back on all the schools, he was told to keep his ears open and learn all he could 'as to the state of things in general and the sentiments at present prevailing among the Waikato chiefs as to peace or war'.[22] Very likely Gorst's intelligence role – for this is what it undoubtedly was – was seen by the government as more important than his role as school inspector which did, however, if this were needed, provide him with useful cover.

Taking leave, then, of Mary and his baby son, Gorst set out on another journey into the Waikato. He travelled widely over the area and visited eleven schools, six of which were mission-run (later he would also visit the newly opened Bay of Islands school). On his travels he met many chiefs including, of course, his friend Tamihana whom he found ploughing land for the support of the school 'like a primitive Roman' in the Thames valley plain below the beautifully situated village of Matamata. Thirty acres were sown with wheat for the school, whose numbers had dwindled from 63 to 16. Gorst thought that Tamihana would like to have accompanied him back to Auckland, but the chief, still a man of peace, did not apparently wish to offend the increasingly influential Waikato war party.

In Kihikihi Gorst met the leader of this party, Rewi Maniapoto, describing him as 'sharp and lawyer-like'. Also there was the elderly and genial Wiremu Kingi of Waitara fame whom Rewi had taken to the Waikato in case he indulged in any backsliding with regard to the still unresolved Taranaki land dispute. After church Gorst squatted on the ground with these men and their followers. They discussed the Governors. Gore Browne was 'an eagle that came swooping down upon them from the clear sky' while Grey was 'a rat that burrowed underground out of sight and would come up in their midst when and where they least expected it'.[23] These colourful vignettes were indeed quite apt.

While touring the Waikato, Gorst, mindful of his intelligence role, warned the authorities in Auckland in a letter dated 23 October that he now felt less confident about the restoration of peace. There was, he reported, a strong feeling of distrust of anything that came from the Europeans, and whatever the Governor might propose 'some sinister motive will be suspected'.[24] The Maoris were not in the least afraid of troops being sent into the Waikato, but Rewi appeared to gauge that the army would do nothing until they had built a good road through the Hunua forest ranges. In general Gorst felt – and he was probably right – that Grey's personal influence over the Maoris had been over-rated.

From a reading of Gorst's comprehensive inspection report on his tour[25] it looks as if the state of the schools, in particular the Maori ones, had been in decline since his first visit to the Waikato a year before. But he may then of course have been a shade over-optimistic. Clothing, food, buildings and books were often in a poor way. Attendance was down and several schools had closed altogether. Some schools he praised, such as those at Kopua and Karakariki, both run by Wesleyans; at the latter school he singled out for a pat on the back the Maori teacher Martha, paid a salary of £24 per annum, who spoke English remarkably well.

Quite apart from the effects of the war clouds hanging over the Waikato, Gorst, in his report, tried to analyse why certain schools were failing educationally. Inadequate teaching and funding were two significant problems he noted. There was a shortage of good Maori teachers, many of whom were unpaid and, perhaps unmotivated, became tired of their work. The colonial government funded the mission schools indirectly insofar as they made large annual grants to the three religious bodies which had supervisory responsibilities for schools in their care. The *per capita* grant per child was £6 a year and school managers, Gorst found, all said that such an amount was inadequate; £8 a year seemed nearer the mark. In general he did not care for the funding system and thought government grants should be made direct to the schools. Grants should also be made for teachers' salaries, and suitable books should be supplied by government. He was concerned too about disease among the children. Furthermore, schools must be regularly inspected. Gorst made other proposals too to improve the efficiency of the schools, such as to furnish a model to be imitated by the Maori schools.

We do not know what became of Gorst's report, but there was much food for thought in it. Unhappily, it was a bad moment to propose reforms in districts whose chiefs were in recalcitrant mood. Gorst may not have known very much about educational administration in New Zealand when he made his inspection and wrote his report. Nonetheless he demonstrated that he had quickly grasped the main problems facing schools in the Waikato, and that he had the best interests of the children at heart. He could little have dreamed, when he was writing his report, that 34 years later he would be charged as a minister at Westminster with the responsibility for the education of the children of the British nation.

The Governor was probably more interested to hear from Gorst about the Waikato political situation than about the schools. Grey now had a plan as to how the Maori districts were to be administered. A form of semi-indirect rule, along the lines of a scheme advocated in 1858 but never put into effect, was to be set up with the country divided into 20 districts presided over by a European civil commissioner. Sub-districts would be staffed with Maori magistrates, assessors and constables, all salaried. Maori runangas (assemblies) would recommend to the Governor bye-laws that needed passing. Europeans, including doctors, would come to live among the Maoris.[26] The scheme sounded fine on paper, but was it too late?

Grey decided to announce and introduce this ambitious plan at the Bay of Islands, where he expected and received a warm welcome. William Fox, the Colonial Premier, went too and took along Gorst as his secretary. Grey's party must have been a large one for General Cameron and his staff were also part of it. This is the only time we hear of Gorst going as far north as the beautiful Hokianga estuary. The irrepressible Grey seemed to take a real pleasure, Gorst observed, in dragging the General off the road to see some huge kauri tree or visit a burial place in the swamps. Once he nearly drowned Cameron in the mud. Mischievously, Gorst commented: 'I thought he did it on purpose.'[27]

A number of meetings were held on the reforms and addressed by the Governor. One of these proceedings was enlivened by a crazy old chief with a spear who, after making a hostile oration, jumped onto the verandah where Grey was sitting and placed the spear at the Governor's throat. Gorst wrote that Grey 'did not turn a hair; he laughed at the man in a cool genial way ...' The assailant then shook the Governor warmly by the hand, and said it was all a joke.

NOTES

1.   Keith Sinclair, *A History of New Zealand*, London, Penguin, 1980, 71.
2.   MK, 38.
3.   Keith Sinclair, *The Origins of the Maori Wars*, Auckland, New Zealand University Press, 1957, 11–17; for more on relations between the races see B. J. Dalton, *War and Politics in New Zealand 1855–1870*, Sydney, Sydney University Press, 1967, 1–2, 4–8.
4.   MK, 75–6.

5. Sinclair, *History,* 114–15; W. Limbrick, *Bishop Selwyn in New Zealand, 1841–68,* Palmerston North, Dunmore Press, 1987, 97.
6. Sinclair, *History,* 101.
7. R. Ward, *Life among the Maoris of New Zealand,* London, G. Lamb, 1872, 273.
8. NZR, 122.
9. Ibid., 127.
10. Ibid., 128.
11. MK, 5.
12. NZR, 130.
13. MK, 166–7; NZR, 132, 140–1.
14. MK, 166–7; NZR, 132–3, 140–1.
15. NZR, 141.
16. *New Zealander,* 18 May 1861.
17. Ibid., 1 June 1861.
18. MK, 167–78; NZR, 147–58.
19. MK, 202.
20. M. Dunn, *John Kinder: Paintings and Photographs,* Auckland, SeTo Publishing, 1985, 27.
21. N. Daglish, 'How half-civilised people ought to be managed: John Gorst, Education and the Waikato Maoris 1860–63', *Durham and Newcastle Research Review,* vol. IX, no. 45, 1980, 138.
22. NZR, 160.
23. NZR, 163.
24. J. Rutherford, *Sir George Grey,* London, Cassell, 1961, 462.
25. Report of J. E. Gorst, Inspector of Schools, 5 Dec. 1861; AJHR, 1862, E-4, 3–11.
26. MK, 206; NZR, 167; Sinclair, *History,* 132.
27. NZR, 169.

4

On Government Service

One minute Gorst seemed to be employed by the Governor on some task and the next it was the turn of the colonial government, in the shape of William Fox, the Premier, to use him. This must have been confusing to say the least, and Gorst himself observed: 'I became an official of the British Government, whether of the imperial or colonial government was never exactly settled, and was employed in attempting to carry out their schemes for restoring confidence and peace'.[1]

This is a good moment to say something about the duality which existed over the control of the native department. The previous Governor, Gore Browne, as has been noted, retained his control of this department with the Native Secretary, Donald McLean, being responsible to him instead of to the Premier. Neither the General Assembly nor the colonial ministers, however, much liked the arrangement. Grey, on arrival, proceeded to reverse the situation and, while he still wanted to make decisions on Maori affairs himself, he transferred the responsibility for managing them to the colonial government under Fox. As Sinclair puts it: 'Both the imperial authorities and the colonial ministers wished to call the tune of Maori policy'. This was a recipe for discord and disaster. There were too many cooks. The result was that Grey and his ministers were often in a chronic state of disagreement. Gorst believed that this duality in government was one of the causes of the renewal of the war in 1863.[2]

There was, however, no doubt who was responsible for internal security, for the Governor was still in charge of the 6,000 British troops in the colony. He also possessed legislative as well as executive powers. Add to all this his prestige and experience and he was still the most powerful man in the colony.

On return from the Bay of Islands Gorst was immediately packed off by the Governor on a mission to Matamata and Peria in Upper Waikato. There, given the commission of a magistrate, he was to investigate a complaint made by Tamihana about the traffic in spirits being carried on by European traders in the Thames valley.[3] Grey was anxious to demonstrate to the Maori chiefs that the government wished to help them in putting down this illicit trade. Gorst was also given a further remit. He was to inform the chiefs about the government's new proposals, already mentioned, on governing the Maori districts; these included proposals to give force to the decisions made by runangas and to validate the bye-laws passed by them.

For some days Tamihana ruminated over the tidings he had received. It was not a good time, Gorst noted, to arrive in Upper Waikato. There were no pigs and no potatoes left to eat, and the people were relying on fern-root as their staple diet. Biscuits were unobtainable from the local traders and the small piece of meat brought by Gorst was carried off by a famished cat.

Suddenly Tamihana made up his mind to lay the proposals before three separate runangas. A runanga was a traditional Maori village assembly or court, which exercised both legislative and judicial functions. The gathering consisted of men and women as well as young and old, and any participant was entitled to put forward his or her views. Its proceedings were informal whatever the nature of the discussions.

Finding himself short of clothes Tamihana now borrowed one of Gorst's shirts and, 'wearing a belt and long pistol but no hat', jumped on a horse and quickly led the way west towards Arikirua. Here and at Tamahere, the Maoris, despite Tamihana's admirable explanation to them, were suspicious of Grey's proposals, many thinking that the Governor's real object was to do away with the Maori King.

At Ngaruawahia, the capital of the Maori King, Gorst ran into trouble. A law had been passed by the local runanga forbidding Europeans to enter the town without permission. Gorst was unaware of this. Two zealous Maori King officials, after a whispered consultation, came to turn him away. In the meantime Gorst, thirsty and not knowing what was afoot, went down to the nearby river to get a drink. To make this easier for himself he boarded a light canoe, which at once capsized throwing him into the river. Gorst was soaked. But, as he remarked, even the Maori King's men would not send away a half-drowned man till his clothes were dried and some food cooked.[4] Happily, Tamihana arrived on the scene and all was well.

The runanga at Ngaruawahia, conducted in its usual temperate manner, concluded that if the Governor would allow their King and flag to stand, then they would fall in with his plans and work with him for the common good. They were anxious, however, not to have European officials living in their midst while Tamihana spoke in favour of the idea.

During this last meeting the chiefs had shown themselves to be so keen on the passing of an effective spirits law and complained so bitterly of government neglect that Gorst took it upon himself to pledge that the Governor would act forthwith. Looking back at this rush of blood to his head, Gorst thought he had been 'criminally rash' since he knew nothing of the inside of a government office or how it worked or indeed how long it took to get anything done.

He was lucky though. He rode straight off to Kohanga as much as 50 miles down the Waikato river where he happened to catch the Governor on his way to attend a big meeting with the Maoris at Taupari (not Taupiri). Grey at once consented to an Order-in-Council being passed prohibiting the importation of spirits into the Waikato. Gorst was then despatched to Auckland to see to the paperwork. Surprisingly, in some dusty office pigeon-hole there was found a regulation drafted some years ago on this very subject. It had never been put into effect. So the necessary order was prepared and published, almost unbelievably within ten days of Gorst making his pledge to the chiefs.[5] This rapid piece of work was received with approval by the chiefs.

The Governor's meeting at Taupari was important. The preliminary business was to install there a Maori magistrate with a salary of £50 p.a.; the Maoris in Taupari were more amenable to Grey's plans than those in the Upper Waikato districts. While there the Governor inevitably became involved in discussions about the Maori King. While he made it clear he was opposed to the King, he did not give his intentions away, except that he let it be known that the army would be constructing a metalled road through the Hunua forest to the Waikato river. This was a significant announcement for the Waikato Maoris, because they saw that they could now be no longer immune to military invasion.[6] Grey, the Waikato chiefs decided, was going to fight them after all.

It was now the turn of Fox to employ Gorst. In mid-December the Premier rode with him into Upper Waikato to meet the chiefs face to face in order to try to come to an understanding with them. He also bore fresh proposals from Grey about the old Waitara land dispute. Finally he would be telling the chiefs about Gorst's forthcoming appointment as resident magistrate at Upper Waikato, although he did not seek the chiefs' consent to this move.

The two men spent Christmas at the Ashwells' mission station at Taupiri where other Europeans in the area were congregating. This was Gorst's first Christmas in the New Zealand bush. In his brief account of the festivities he makes no reference to his family, who presumably were languishing perforce in Auckland.

After Christmas the Premier went to distant Hangatiki where he and Gorst met Rewi, the leader of the war party, whom they found to be in silent mood, and Wiremu Kingi from Waikata. This was in the heart of the Ngatimaniapoto country, probably the most anti-European part of the Waikato. Nevertheless, the visitors were received with honour by the Maori King's bodyguard of 40 young men who lined both sides of the road and presented arms. This body – to the disgust of old Maoris – was modelled, in terms of uniform and drill, on the British army. Fox's discussions there achieved little. The Premier had wanted while in the Waikato to talk as well to Tamihana, but the chief proved elusive and the two did not meet. It also seemed as if the Maoris were preventing Matutaera, the young Maori King, from meeting Fox – not that Matutaera, who had become King after his father's death in 1860, carried much political clout. When Fox suggested a meeting, the King's secretary replied by saying that 'Mattie is too ill to come – rather do you send us some pork and a little pepper.'[7] The next morning the messenger begged for tobacco but avoided any commitment to a meeting.

One evening during this visit Gorst found himself sitting next to Rewi at dinner. The Maori chief said he regretted Gorst becoming a magistrate. Why couldn't he be just a trader or missionary? He, Rewi, was bored with listening for twenty years to Mr. Morgan's sermons at Te Awamutu and would gladly exchange Morgan for Gorst. Tamihana was another who did not take kindly to Gorst 'defecting' to the government side. He condoled, almost mischievously, with his English friend. The chief was sorry that the new magistrate's fellow countrymen had such a low opinion of him. Tamihana, as was his wont, quoted the scriptures: 'Does not St Paul say, set them to judge who are least esteemed by you?'[8]

The time had come – it was January 1862 – for Gorst to take up his appointment as magistrate in Upper Waikato. He therefore had to collect his family and move them from Auckland into the heart of the King country, a distance of some 80 miles as the crow flies. A house, called Te Tomo, had been rented from a settler for the Gorsts at Otawhao. This house, set in thirty acres of grassland and half a mile from the Rev. J. Morgan's mission station at Te Awamutu, would be home for the Gorsts for the next six months.

John, Mary and the baby were to be accompanied into the Waikato by a Scottish couple and their 12-year-old daughter; they had come out on the *Red Jacket* and had agreed to go up country as servants to the Gorsts. Also a young woman engaged to a captain in the army begged to come as a companion for Mary, for John would often be away to attend meetings with the Maoris. Finally, there was Marsden Clarke, who was to act as clerk and interpreter.

Transporting the baby through the bush and into the Waikato was described by Gorst as 'arduous'. Fortunately it was midsummer so the weather was fine. The journey took a long six days. To begin with, Jack did not mind the cart which carried the party along the military road being cut through the Hunua forest. Indeed the rougher the road and the more he was shaken the more Jack enjoyed it. But the river stage by canoe was not to his liking, and his good humour deserted him. 'Whether', wrote his father, 'it was the heat or the sand-flies or the mosquitoes which covered his fair skin with spots and hillocks or the exceeding slowness of the canoe's progress, for some reason he roared all the way.' From Taupiri he was slung in a blanket and suspended from the pommel of Clarke's saddle. His humour returned and the motion pleased him so much that he was either in fits of laughter or else slumbering soundly.[9]

Te Tomo was of a simple wooden construction. The house was fronted by a verandah which led into the main living-room; this also did service as dining-room and nursery. From this main room, doors opened on to three bedrooms. At the back there was a kitchen, usually full of blinding smoke and cats to keep down the rat population, plus a pantry and storeroom. No mention is made by Gorst, in his description of the house, of washing and lavatorial arrangements – too delicate a subject for Victorians. The Gorsts could not have been unpractical, for they 'painted and papered' the house themselves. The Scottish couple had their own little wooden house nearby and another house was being got ready for Clarke. Behind the main house was a yard and a well-stocked garden with fruit trees.

Housekeeping presented some difficulties. But the boycott of the magistrate, which, as we shall see, was about to occur, did not mean that the local Maoris deprived the Gorst community of food. This would have been quite repugnant to Maori tradition. For instance, some years before, at the time of a small fracas between British soldiers and a Maori tribe, a sympathetic European suggested to a chief that he should cut off the supply of oxen being sent to the army's camp. The chief replied indignantly: 'But if the soldiers get no beef they will not be able to fight.' One local Maori, a strong advocate of expelling Gorst, regularly sold the family fowls at 6d or 1s each and live pigs at 1½d per lb. The Gorsts and their entourage lived at Te Tomo mainly on dairy produce, bread, pork and chicken, with mutton sometimes and beef rarely. There was usually no shortage of fruit and vegetables.

What, though, of Gorst's work as a magistrate? This was of course the reason he and his young family were now living remotely in the middle of a Maori community. When Gorst went to Otawhao he was full of optimism, and expected that 'a reconciliation and alliance might be effected between the government and the leaders of the King party'. And further he even hoped that the King's officers might be employed in the new district organisation of the colonial government. Unhappily Gorst's hopes were to be dashed.[10] Gorst was not the first European magistrate to be stationed in the Waikato. There had been two men before him. An able lawyer and former Native Secretary, F. D. Fenton, had arrived in 1857 as a touring magistrate, although not living in the area. His court was ill-attended and his short tenure was not successful.[11] You might therefore say that there was writing on the wall for Gorst before he ever set foot in Otawhao. Nearly four years on, times had of course changed. The Maori King was now well established. The Maoris' attitude to the government and Europeans had hardened especially as a result of the Taranaki war, and nowhere was this more evident than in the Waikato. Gorst's time as magistrate in the Waikato was – sad to relate – even more unsuccessful than Fenton's.

Gorst rode all over the Waikato, with a Maori lad to accompany him, getting to know the district and people. As Gorst perceived it, Fenton had failed as magistrate to conciliate the chiefs, so he made a special point of meeting and talking to them. He carried his kit in the saddle and slept and ate in the villages. The people soon became used to him, everywhere receiving and entertaining him as a friend. They talked freely before him, and when they were ill he had medicines for them. It is no surprise that he warmed to the Maori people. But as a magistrate he never in six months heard a single case involving a Maori. His guns had been spiked, so to say. For the runangas in the Waikato had already decided that British magistrates were not to be allowed to exercise jurisdiction within their areas, and specifically forbade any Maori bringing a suit before a magistrate. One Maori did try to bring a case to Gorst, but his attempt was nipped in the bud with a heavy fine imposed by his local runanga.

Nevertheless Gorst did exercise on occasion some influence with the leading Maoris. When a knotty point arose at a runanga about which the chiefs thought they might benefit from legal advice, one of them 'would slink down' in the morning to Gorst and extract a legal opinion from him. Sometimes this was done by a frank recitation of the actual facts and at others, to Gorst's amusement, the question would be put as in a hypothetical case.[12] Once Gorst was approached by the losing side in a case heard before the King's runanga. It was all to do with rights to an eel fishery at Paetai. A small tribe just 50–60 men strong was challenging the King and predictably lost. They were aggrieved and, as a tribe, defected from the King as a result of the decision. Now, having changed sides, they wanted to do all they could to help the colonial government and accordingly demanded the appointment from their number of no less than ten salaried government officials. They were disappointed when Gorst told them this would not, with the best will in the world, be possible.

Only a few weeks after Gorst had arrived at Otawhao, one over-enthusiastic chief, Patene, decided to take action on his runanga's decision to forbid British magistrates in the King's dominions. These dominions extended far afield, to the north as far as the Mangatawhiru river and to the south even, some said, to the Cook Strait. Patene, with something of a flourish, gave notice that he was going to expel Gorst from the Waikato. A large body of people, including some Europeans and a crowd of scampish young Maori boys, assembled by the European mission station to see the fun. There was much joking and laughing among the audience. Gorst and Clarke sat on the church steps awaiting Patene's arrival. Eventually he appeared attended by a troop of Maori soldiers in their smart uniform of white trousers and blue coats plus a cap with a red cross on it. Patene then proceeded to read out a declaration signed apparently by over 2,000 people, and ordered Gorst to leave the Waikato. Good-humouredly, he refused. Again Patene ordered him to go and again he refused. Stalemate. The populace, not knowing quite what to make of all this, looked on expectantly, while the crowd of boys poked fun at the soldiers for not intervening. Finally, in the face of the magistrate's obstinacy, Patene gave up and, threatening he would return, marched his soldiers away, first reprimanding them for allowing the boys to jeer at them. Later, to Patene's mortification, Tamihana and other influential chiefs condemned him for what he had tried to do. For the time being no other attempts were made to drive Gorst away.[13] Patene admired Gorst's unyielding stance and the men became friends. Later on, as we shall see, Patene rendered stout assistance to Gorst at a time of crisis.

On the other hand, Gorst as magistrate did hear a few civil disputes between European settlers, although he described this work as being more akin to that of an arbitrator than a judge. The parties, after they had each had their say, would comply with his decision and there was no need for a formal judgement or legal process. It also fell to Gorst to take up cases where Europeans had had their goods or cattle seized by the Maoris or had been threatened with violence by them. When this happened he would usually, as a first step, visit the local runanga to discuss the matter. He was almost always well received, but no one was anxious to help him. During a visit to Kirikiri on account of a European suffering at the hands of the Maoris, he had a verbal altercation with the pugnacious Rewi. In the middle of this the chief caught sight of Mary Gorst who had ridden over with John to buy some quinces. Rewi asked why she was there. On being told, he turned to the people sitting around and told them to give Mary as many quinces as she needed as a present from the tribe.

On another occasion Gorst rode 150 miles all told, to try to rescue a flock of 500 sheep belonging to a European, which had been stolen by a handful of Maoris who alleged trespass and demanded £200 before releasing the sheep. Gorst complained about this to the runanga of Ngaruawahia. He was referred to Kihikihi where, in the absence of their chief Rewi, two young Maoris in their twenties truculently told him, rather untypically, to mind his own business and leave the matter for them to settle. Later when the chief returned, action was in fact taken, the sheep rustlers being threatened by the local runanga with a 'war-party'. The result was that most of the sheep were released.

Social welfare matters with a legal angle would sometimes arouse Gorst's interest. For instance, he had been struck in Auckland by the plight, by no means unusual, of destitute children, both European and those of mixed race, who had been abandoned by their parents. In the Waikato an English boy, 11 years old and apparently an orphan, had been found being brought up by Maoris. Gorst wrote to the Attorney-General about the problem, and suggested that resident magistrates be given powers to place such children in schools and, where possible, order putative fathers to support them.

It must have been a frustration to Gorst that as a magistrate he was ignored. 'The monotonous occupation of pretending to be a magistrate' as he described it, while being 'deprived of all real power and authority' was once varied for him by a 60-mile journey with Premier Fox through primeval forest to Taupo. In every village they were hospitably welcomed. On another journey he was coming one evening up a river by canoe paddled by a Maori; he was wet through, cold and hungry. On the bank an old woman called out inviting him to land. She wept at his forlorn condition and took him to her house. There she tied an eel to a split fern-stick and roasted it over the embers of a fire. It was 'the most delicious morsel' he had ever tasted. Refreshed, he continued on his journey.[14]

Gorst wrote regular reports on events in Upper Waikato addressing them to the Native Secretary or to the Attorney-General. He also kept an 'official' diary or journal, extracts from which he passed to Auckland.[15] At the beginning of June 1862 after five months at Otawhao and at the suggestion of Dillon Bell, quite soon to become Native Minister, Gorst put together a full report for the government. This aimed to give 'a plain account of the present state of affairs in the Upper Waikato districts and especially about the King movement'. Bell had a motive for his suggestion for he anticipated the report would show Gorst's disillusionment with the Maoris and so provide him, Bell, with a means of attacking Fox's policies. He had confided to the former governor, Gore Browne, that Gorst was a 'conscientious, just, truthful and highly educated man' who would carry weight with the Assembly.[16]

Bell was correct in his assumption, for the report indeed struck a despondent note and its reader in Auckland or London (where it was eventually printed officially) might well have despaired – given the accuracy of the author's reporting – at the virtual absence of progress being made in implementing Grey's administrative reforms in the Waikato. And this was not all. The story it told of the deteriorating economic and social conditions in the Waikato districts must have made equally dismal reading. Thus there was obviously going to be a food shortage in the winter. Nor had the Maoris been planting much wheat in this important corn-growing area. Also, they had sold nearly all their horses and cattle and their houses were in disrepair. As a sign of the times European traders were now leaving the Waikato. As poverty was increasing so also was disease, especially among the young. Furthermore, education of Maori children, as we have already seen, was more and more being neglected.

Nevertheless from his observations Gorst considered that the greatest peril confronting the colony came from 'the utter lawlessness and anarchy of the native population'.[17] Gorst instanced that the younger men who had fought in the Taranaki war roamed the Waikato country with their guns, taking horses and cattle from Europeans. They were indifferent to the authority both of the colonial government and of their own people. Many chiefs, in Gorst's view, had lost their hold.

The main instrument of Maori government as has been mentioned earlier was the runanga. Gorst was critical both in his report and later in his writings of how the runangas exercised their powers. The laws they passed could include regulations, covering almost every facet of private life as far as Gorst could see, and this he felt sometimes bordered on the tyrannical. For instance they laid down what constituted defamation (one could not take exception to this); what the people could or could not do on a Sunday; the selling price for corn, potatoes, pigs and so on. They would also pass wide-ranging resolutions: thus requests were made to the government to send a blacksmith to repair their ploughs, and to provide them with a gift of bullocks. One runanga required the Governor to send them a doctor, preferably an elderly man, who would not misconduct himself with women or drink rum.

On the judicial side Gorst considered most runangas – for he made some exceptions – failed to 'administer substantial justice'; this could happen when they were prejudiced against defendants or litigants. As for Maori magistrates, they acted, as Gorst saw it, essentially in a detective-cum-prosecutor role.

But above all, Gorst reported, the runangas were not succeeding as institutions of government, since they had no police force at their command or any other means of enforcing their laws and judicial decisions. As a consequence their laws and decisions were not being obeyed, and law and order was not therefore maintained.

One tribe in the far Ngatimaniapoto country south of Hangatiki seemed to have found some kind of answer to this vexed question. As Gorst approvingly wrote:

> a chief called Reihana had organised the best system of law and order in the country. He kept a force of 80 strong lads, clothed and equipped by the fees and fines of the court … two days were allowed [the man fined] to obtain some money; but on the third day if the money was not forthcoming the fine was increased.[18]

If a man was too poor to pay, his kinsmen apparently had to stump up for him. Reihana's judgements in court were said to be just and there seem to have been no complaints mentioned of strong-arm tactics being employed by the 80 lads. It was their success as law-enforcement officers which caught Gorst's eye, and later, because of Gorst's report, the Governor's too.

Over this generally unpromising situation in Waikato presided the young Maori King, Matutaera. But he had little to do with affairs of state, being mainly a figurehead. That was left to the King's Council, in effect the runanga of Ngaruawahia. Gorst attended many sessions of this Council, but never once was the King in attendance. Contrary to the opinion he expressed about many other runangas, Gorst was lavish in his praise for the wisdom and acuteness of the King's

Council. They argued calmly and usually came, he believed, to the right decision on Maori law. Unfortunately their sensible decisions were often not carried into effect. Gorst's presence at the Council did not seem to cause the councillors undue concern. He recalled with wry amusement one session of the Council when he stayed with them late. In reflective mood they grew confidential and revealed their troubles, especially those concerning the disobedience to their injunctions of distant tribes. At length, the Council members started up and said how foolish they were to talk in this way before the Europeans had gone to bed. Everyone laughed, shook hands and then said good-night.[19]

There was one practical way in which individual tribes were supposed to support the Maori King. Each tribe had to furnish a company of soldiers to guard the King. They called themselves the King's soldiers or bodyguard but, perhaps misleadingly, did not come under his command, or either, it seems, come together for training or military duties. Their uniforms have already been described. For arms they relied on muskets, fowling pieces or a few rifles acquired in the Taranaki war. Their discipline was strict and their drill, as observed by Gorst, excellent. They were said to be paid 3d a day and were the only King's officers to receive a wage. But the King's cause was always short of money and funds in due course began to dwindle.

Gorst, as a result of the information which came his way, was able to make an estimate for the government in his report of how the King's movement was funded. It relied heavily on donations and a share of fines paid to local runangas. Maoris in government employment were supposed to give the King a share of their salaries. Another modest source of revenue came from dues taken by ferries. The Maoris had once contemplated putting a tax on produce exported from their districts and a toll on ships entering their harbours, but these ideas were discarded as impracticable. Gorst was always deeply interested in the financial side of government, as will be seen when he became well established as an MP at Westminster, and kept a close eye on estimates and expenditure, particularly those for the navy.

In the Maori kingdom the influence of the centre was weak, tribes being unwilling to surrender their independence. What held the Maoris together, as seen by Gorst, was their common distrust of Europeans and their consequent antagonism to the government. As Tamihana said to Gorst: 'I like your laws, it is your men I do not like.' But for some time after the establishment of the Maori King, much affection was felt for Queen Victoria and Maoris were ready solemnly to repeat prayers that she might 'vanquish and overcome her enemies'. At a service, Gorst once shared a prayer-book with King Matutaera, who said a loud 'Amen' after prayers for the Queen.[20]

At the end of his report Gorst concluded that in terms of creating a Maori government the King's movement was a failure. Nevertheless it posed a 'formidable danger' to the colonial authorities. He acknowledged that it 'originally may have been a movement for law and order' but 'had altogether lost that character now'. Although he did not precisely say so in his report, the shocking implication was there: the Maoris wished to supplant British rule with their own. He still of course averred that the King should be put down, but not by force. His remedy was vigorous colonial government to remove the causes of distrust and regain the confidence of the Maoris.

At the same time as he produced his report Gorst wrote a private letter to the Governor. The nub of this was: given the situation in Upper Waikato among the Maoris and Gorst's inability to sit effectively as a magistrate, should he not, as an 'honest man', resign?[21]

The colonial government wanted Gorst to go to Auckland to discuss his report. But Gorst was reluctant at first to go, asserting he had nothing more to say. If the government did not agree with his views and proposals it would be better if they accepted his resignation at once. This is the first time we have evidence of Gorst retorting sharply to those above him. Grey now stepped in and summoned Gorst to see him. The Governor was not lucky, apart from Gorst, in the quality of his magistrates and commissioners. Rutherford, Grey's biographer, states that these officials were often men of neither education nor good manners; three of them turned out to be drunkards. Gorst himself was critical of the poor quality of government 'agents', comparing them unfavourably to the fine men sent out by the missionary societies.[22]

Grey recognised Gorst's talents early and did not want to lose him. The Governor agreed with Gorst both in his assessment of the Maoris' general condition and also in his report's conclusions, but disclaimed responsibility for the present situation; he had of course, he could maintain, handed over the day-to-day running of the native department to the colonial government. Also, perhaps wickedly, he hinted to Gorst that he, Grey, agreed with him in thinking that 'Mr Fox and his ministers [were] a set of old women'.[23] Gorst went into the interview wishing to resign. Owing to Grey's remarkable powers of persuasion and personality, he came out renewed and ready to continue in government service. Gorst was now appointed as Civil Commissioner over both Lower and Upper Waikato taking his instructions direct from Grey. And with a new mandate.

In the week that followed this important interview with the Governor, Gorst had a series of meetings with him. He then wrote a memorandum, dated 28 June, to the Governor setting out what they had decided to do and how these plans were to be implemented.[24] At first Grey had wanted to establish at Otawhao a kind of flying-squad force to police Upper Waikato, taking as a model Reihana's force of 80 men. Gorst told him 'this was madness', as Rewi would suppress it. So instead it was proposed to build at Te Awamutu, near Otawhao, a technical school for big lads and young men to teach them trades. In course of time, Gorst thought, the school might grow into a police station. The trades were those of carpenter, blacksmith, wheelwright, shoemaker, tailor and later on printer, while some pupils would be involved in agriculture on the school estate. A European schoolmaster would teach the three Rs, and various kinds of games would be taught and encouraged. Marsden Clarke, who had relevant experience, was to manage the school at an enhanced salary. There were already school buildings at Otawhao together with 200 acres of land owned by the Church Missionary Society. Bishop Selwyn gave up this property to the government so work could begin at once on renovating the buildings.

It was also decided to build at Kohekohe in Lower Waikato a police station served by a native police force of 60 men. Their duties would include the arrest of dangerous offenders, the enforcement of magistrates' decisions and the protection of the district from the incursions of the lawless. The men, to be drawn from a number of tribes, would be well lodged and fed, uniformed and properly trained. Their pay would be 6d a day (twice that of the King's pay). They would also receive schooling and be paraded for prayers. Their barracks would be built next to the court-house being constructed in the same village.

As soon as the rough plan of the police station at Kohekohe was put in front of him, the Governor set off with Gorst to see General Cameron and ask him that his engineer officers modify the plan so that the building could be converted into a military block-house. Gorst, years later, commented that he had 'never met another man [than Grey] in my life so cool and quiet in conversation and so energetic in action'.[25] Grey was also a man to hedge his bets.

Grey lost no time in putting Gorst in charge of both projects but never consulted his colonial ministers about them. Just how much the putative schemes owed to Gorst it is hard to estimate, but he certainly made a contribution. The idea of setting up a police force in Lower Waikato, the more amenable part of the Waikato, was sound, for

Upper Waikato was, administratively, a tougher nut to crack. However, the Maoris, ever suspicious and perhaps with some cause, thought any scheme dreamt up by Grey had a concealed purpose. Nonetheless some of them grudgingly recognised that the technical school might have its uses. As for Tamihana, he sang its praises. According to the author James Cowan, the King's runanga at Ngaruawahia told Gorst that if some local government plan of the kind Grey was trying to promote had been introduced five or so years before, there would never have been a Maori King.[26]

NOTES

1. NZR, 142.
2. Sinclair, *History*, 134; MK, 234–6, 316; NZR, 166, 239.
3. MK, 212.
4. Ibid., 215.
5. MK, 64; NZR, 175-6.
6. NZR, 185.
7. MK, 241.
8. NZR, 193.
9. NZR, 194-5.
10. General report by J. E. Gorst, 5 June 1862, AJHR, 1862: E-9, Section III, 9–19; A. Ward, *A Show of Justice: Racial Amalgamation in Nineteenth Century New Zealand*, Auckland, Auckland University Press, 1973, 133.
11. MK, 98-129.
12. NZR, 197-8.
13. Report by J. E. Gorst of proceedings of Patene and Ngatimaniapoto natives, 8 Feb 1862, AJHR, 1862: E-9, Section III, 3–4.
14. NZR, 302.
15. General report by J. E. Gorst, 9.
16. Daglish, 'How half-civilised people ought to be managed', 139; also see A. Ward, *A Show of Justice*, 148–9.
17. MK, 261.
18. MK, 272; General report by J. E. Gorst, 16.
19. MK, 275.
20. MK, 284; NZR, 221.
21. NZR, 209, 223.
22. Rutherford, *Sir George Grey*, 467; MK, 43.
23. NZR, 225.
24. Memorandum by J. E. Gorst on the establishment of a Police Station at Kohekohe and an Industrial School at Otawhao, 28 June 1862, AJHR, 1863: E-4, 35–6.
25. NZR, 226; also see Dalton, *War and Politics in New Zealand*, 163.
26. Cowan, *New Zealand Wars*, 227.

5

Expulsion from the Waikato

Back at Otawhao, Gorst now had to move his family out of their comfortable cottage into a large and rather tumble-down house where the Rev. J. Morgan, the missionary and postmaster, had lived for 20 years and where he had his school. Morgan, angry at not being consulted, rather resented this move. He had a large family and Gorst's cottage was poky. But generously enough he decided to put no obstacle in the way of the changes if these would help the Maoris.[1] In the meantime, work on the technical school proceeded apace, helped by Gorst's enthusiasm. The house was in need of considerable repair but the school buildings were sound and could be adapted for their new purpose. About 20 pupils were selected and the teaching staff arrived. The General Assembly meeting at Wellington voted ample funds for the new work and then agreed as well to the building of a hospital on Crown land at Te Awamutu (this had been promised before). There were to be two doctors, one attached to the hospital and the other, the Rev. A. Purchase, acting as a 'Medical Commissioner'; he was to travel around the Waikato to attend to the sick and to improve public health.

In theory at least, and for a time, things were 'looking up' in the Waikato. Relations too between the races must have been tolerable, at least on the surface. To commemorate the accession of the Maori King, the local chiefs at nearby Rangiaowhia gave a dinner to which all Europeans were invited. Gorst was asked to take the chair and was supported in this role by Te Paea, the King's sister, a woman of strong personality and well-disposed to Gorst. He wrote:

> The dinner was excellent: roast beef, preserves, tarts and bottled ale were in the bill of fare and everybody behaved in the most decorous manner. After dinner there were races, and other athletic sports. I ran a race with the General in the King's army and was beaten by a head ... [2]

What Gorst was trying to do in the Waikato was not universally popular in the colony. The news of these festivities was ill received in

Auckland by one newspaper, which declaimed that 'if ever a man deserved to be hanged for high treason, Mr Gorst was that man'. But Grey, and this was the important thing for Gorst, expressed his approval of the celebrations and even admired the young commissioner's tact in allowing himself to be beaten by the General in the race.

Nevertheless, storm clouds continued to drift around the political sky. In October an important Maori convention was held at Matamata to discuss the Waitara dispute and the Governor's offer of a judicial inquiry. But while British troops continued to occupy the disputed land the Maoris refused arbitration and continued to hold settler land at Tataraimaka, also near New Plymouth, as their security. Gorst later wrote critically about the government's handling of its offer. He believed Grey should have gone ahead with a public inquiry as this would have shown the justice of the Maori case and therefore would probably have averted the second Taranaki war from breaking out in May 1863.[3]

Gorst was due to attend the convention but the Governor changed his mind about this. Bishop Selwyn did attend and made, but with no success, an impassioned plea to the Maoris to accept the government's conditions for an inquiry. After the meeting the Bishop came and stayed for a week with the Gorsts at Te Awamutu. He was an exemplary guest, making his own bed, cleaning his boots and even washing his clothes. Fond of children, he would often be found by the Gorst parents with young Jack riding on his shoulders.

Some months later two major events of a political character occurred, both of which profoundly affected John Gorst's career. First, in January 1863 the Governor made an unheralded visit to the Waikato. During its course he met Tamihana at Taupiri. Familiar political ground was raked over in discussion, especially the Waitara problem. Grey was reported as having made one observation which reverberated round the Waikato when he said: 'I shall not fight against the King with a sword, but I shall dig round him with spades until he falls of his own accord'. The Maoris looked about them and ominously decided that John Gorst was the principal 'spade' digging in their district. Moreover, the Governor's metaphor would presently be flung back in his own face by Rewi.

The other political event would directly lead to Gorst's expulsion from the Waikato. For some time the Waikato Maoris had been producing at Ngaruawahia on behalf of the King their own newspaper *Te Hokioi*. The name meant in Maori a mythical bird. It was edited by a clever man, Patara, a cousin of the Maori King, and was being read and enjoyed all over New Zealand for its witty articles coming from the editor's own hand. As a counterweight the Governor – or was it Gorst, we can't be sure – considered that a government newspaper must be produced putting the official point of view. As editor Grey chose Gorst. The new paper – to be written in the Maori language – would be called *Te Pihoihoi Mokemoke* ('the lonely lark on the housetop'). The paper would be distributed free and be printed at Te Awamutu on a press purchased in Sydney.[4]

In the first issue published on 2 February there was an article entitled 'The Evil of the King Movement'. It caused a sensation among the Maoris, many of whom were very angry about its mocking style and content. The article, forcefully expressed, was highly critical of the Maori King for not punishing crime in the Waikato. If the King, its author declaimed, had power to put a stop to evil deeds, it was 'wicked' of him not to exercise this power. We cannot be sure who wrote the article but Gorst was likely to be the author helped by Miss Ashwell, the missionary's daughter who spoke idiomatic Maori. Gorst tells us that he composed some articles for the five issues of the paper but edited them all. Grey, we know, 'revised' the whole manuscript for the first issue, so he too might have had a hand in this all-important article.[5]

The new paper and its leading article were discussed at the King's Council, where regret was expressed that the editor did not follow the calm reasoning used by the editor of *Te Hokioi*. Demands followed for the new press to be suppressed. Rewi now saw his opportunity, and began in secret to organise an attack on the press at Te Awamutu and, at the same time, laid his plans to expel the commissioner. For his part Gorst took the precaution of warning Bell, now Native Minister, about a visit he had received from his former enemy and now his friend Chief Patene. A letter, said Patene, had been sent out by certain chiefs to Rewi and others advising that the technical school, the magistrate and the press should be 'driven out' for their work was 'like Satan's'. Gorst, in somewhat flippant vein, commented to Bell that, if anything more was heard of this, the best course would be to demand a payment for being compared to Satan.[6] Gorst later admitted he was thrown off his guard that anything unexpected was going to happen because Rewi had been 'peculiarly civil' to him and to the visiting interpreter, Angus White, during a visit they made to Kihikihi soon after Patene's warning.

On a more auspicious note, there was one other event early in the year which we should note but which Gorst, rather characteristically, does not mention in his books. It was the birth on 27 January of the

Gorsts' first daughter, Constance. It is likely, but we cannot be sure, that Constance was born in the Waikato with Purchase in attendance as Mary's doctor. Early in the year Mainwaring arrived in Upper Waikato. Another visitor was one of Mary's brothers. The Gorsts were not short of support from friends and relatives at this time.

In March the pace of events in the Waikato quickened. While the technical school at Te Awamutu was distinctly finding its feet as a useful institution for training apprentices, there had been no progress over the building of the police barracks at Kohekohe in Lower Waikato; also no policemen had yet been recruited. One cause of the delay in building was the shortage of timber. Wood and workmen had been needed for a military redoubt for 500 troops being built on crown land at Te Ia some eight miles downstream. The carpenters would move to Kohekohe only when the redoubt was finished. On 7 March local Maoris demanded that the building of the barracks at Kohekohe be abandoned, for the project would be 'death to the nation'. Consequently, timber stocked on the banks of the Waikato river just above the site was mischievously thrown into the river and as a result floated on downstream past the building site, eventually being fished out of the river at Te Ia. This, though, was a minor setback compared with what soon followed in Upper Waikato.

The technical school farm needed bullocks, and on the morning of 24 March Gorst rode over with his friend Mainwaring and Angus White, the interpreter, to Kopua to inquire about the availability of the animals. He had heard some rumour that an 'army' from Kihikihi would visit Te Awamutu but paid no attention to it. In fact the rumour was only too true. A body of some 80 armed men from Ngatimaniapoto arrived at the door of the printing office in Te Awamutu at 3 pm that day. They were led by Aporo, a henchman of Rewi's and a noted firebrand. Rewi himself had come too, but to begin with kept in the background. Inside the office Mr von Dadelszen, the printer, and his Maori assistant were busy printing the fifth issue of *Te Pihoihoi*. The noise of Aporo's men brought them to the door. They came out to see what was afoot, locking the door behind them, whereupon an assault force of 50 men, having said a prayer, proceeded to batter down the door and enter the building. They then dragged outside the printing press, the type and various boxes. Every single article they found in the office, except for an iron bedstead, was loaded into two bullock drays already parked outside and then driven away. While this was going on, Chief Patene came storming in dressed as if for a levée in smart pantaloons, a light summer coat and waistcoat and a new black silk top hat. He was incensed by what was happening and, helped by a Maori employed at the station, forcibly ejected half a dozen of the assailants, seizing each by the collar and the seat of his trousers. But the damage was done. Once the office had been emptied, Aporo and his men deliberated whether to burn it down. There was fear, too, at this time that the men might now attack the nearby mission buildings, but good sense prevailed and no move in this direction was made.

At about this moment two chiefs from Rangiaowhia, Taati and Te Oriori, both well-disposed to Gorst, arrived on the scene, and remonstrated with Aporo telling him and his men to do nothing until the next day.

Gorst and his companions, unaware of what had been happening at Te Awamutu, arrived home at 8 pm. Gorst was unmolested and walked past the sentries posted round his house without saying a word to them. That evening it was being spread around that Gorst would be expelled in the morning and, if he did not go, he would be shot. We have no idea how Mary fared during what must have been a frightening ordeal for her.

As for the boys at the school they behaved 'splendidly', Gorst reported. They all said that they would stand by him and the next day they kept working at their lessons and trades as if nothing had happened. In the meantime, that morning, a great crowd of people gathered by Gorst's house. Rewi, accompanied by Wiremu Kingi, now took charge of operations. Taati and Te Oriori, back on the scene, vehemently protested at the action taken as did Patene who, in a great passion, tried to knock Aporo down. Gorst wrote about the scene: 'The intervention of my little son who was running about clasping the angry men by their legs . . . averted a conflict.' Also Mainwaring calmly offered tobacco all around, and this, Gorst said, also helped to reduce the tension.[7]

Eventually Gorst was invited onto the road outside his house and offered a stool to sit on. For what happened next we turn to Gorst's official report to Bell about these events.[8]

> Aporo asked me to get up and go away from Te Awamutu; I said I should do no such thing. This was repeated several times. I then asked Aporo what he had come to my land for and robbed me of my property [sic]. He said because I had trampled Mr Morgan's work. Mr White read out a proclamation of Matutaera's dated 22 January about abstaining from molesting Europeans ... Aporo invited me to disobey my master by leaving Te Awamutu; I again quietly refused ...

This 'catechising' with the same questions and answers went on for some time, Gorst insisting that only orders from the Governor would induce him to leave his post. At length Gorst went inside his house. Presently the impasse was to an extent resolved when the Rev. A. Reid, the Wesleyan missionary from Kopua, went to see Rewi and brought back to Gorst a proposal from the chief. Rewi agreed to withdraw his men if he, Gorst, would write to Grey informing him of what had taken place and seeking his permission to leave Te Awamutu. Gorst, concerned about what the 80 armed and 'sulky' men might do, felt compelled to agree to do this; but added the stipulation that a period of three weeks should be allowed for the Governor's answer. Rewi accepted this, saying to Reid that if Grey left Gorst at the technical school 'he left him to his death'. The attacking force was then withdrawn.

So Gorst did as he was bidden and told the Governor that 'the natives had beaten him utterly' and explained the consequences of his remaining at Te Awamutu.[9] Gorst with a remarkable show of goodwill invited Rewi into the house where the chief sat down at the writing-table and wrote his own letter to the Governor beginning: 'Friend Governor Grey – greeting! This is my word to you. Mr Gorst has been killed [has suffered] through me. The press has been taken by me ...' Rewi went on to say that Gorst was being driven away because of the 'great darkness' caused by his being sent to Te Awamutu and because the Governor said 'he would dig around the King till he fell'. Rewi ended by saying if Gorst stayed 'he will die'.[10]

Grey refused to take any notice of Rewi's letter but sent instructions to Gorst that 'in the event of there being any danger whatever to life then he was to return at once to Auckland with the other Europeans in the employment of government on the station.'[11] On 11 April Gorst wrote to Rewi telling him he had heard from the Governor who did not want the commissioner 'to fall a victim to Rewi's blade'. The same day Rewi briefly acknowledged receipt of Gorst's letter, interpreting the exchange of correspondence correctly, as meaning that Gorst would leave.

According to Maori usage Gorst was now technically 'dead'. This was borne in on him for when he travelled by canoe there were cries from the bank: 'How are you and your corpse?'[12] When the news of Rewi's violence reached him, the Maori King, on the advice of Patara, the editor of *Te Hokioi*, wrote to Rewi condemning his conduct and telling him to send back the press, pay for the damage done and leave the question of Gorst's removal to his Council to decide. Tamihana and other chiefs agreed with these instructions. Rewi complied with the first two instructions but on the last injunction he was not to be moved. Gorst, he insisted, had to go. When Tamihana came to see Gorst, the chief found his friend adamant about not leaving until word arrived from the Governor. Tamihana, anxious to do his best for Gorst, decided to try to get the King's soldiers to come to Te Awamutu with the object of protecting the Europeans there against a possible further attack. The two men shook hands and parted sorrowfully. Gorst never again saw Tamihana, who in a few short months was to join the fighting party.

To look ahead for a moment, Tamihana survived the conquest of the Waikato by British troops but died soon after he and his people made peace with the government in 1865. Rewi too survived the war and, many years later, would even write to Gorst in England seeking his advice on Maori affairs. As for Aporo he was recognised and arrested in Auckland just before the start of the war. He had gone there on a visit to sell pigs. He was found guilty of theft for what had happened at Te Awamutu and sentenced to two years' hard labour. Gorst did not think this was just, since Aporo was not in his view a common criminal and he had respected private property at the time of the raid on the press.

As a last hope Gorst now went with Purchase to Ngaruawahia to appeal against his expulsion to the King's Council. The pair were lodged hospitably by Te Paea, the King's sister. She was indignant at what had happened and, tears running down her cheeks, she addressed the Council on Gorst's behalf. It was to no avail. What Gorst wished to discover was whether it was the will of the King and his chiefs that he should go. So – it was 14 April – he wrote a letter to the Council, who dithered and sent Patara to tell Gorst that they could not make up their minds. Finally the next day a written reply came, which was what Gorst wanted. It was short, and, signed by Matutaera, it ended by saying he 'must go'.[13] The King, counselled Patara, was just the mouthpiece of his people and could no longer give Gorst his protection. Another brave effort was made by both Patara and Te Paea who came to Te Awamutu to induce Rewi to abstain from further violence. The good Te Paea wanted to do one more thing for the Gorsts. She had also come to take charge of Mary and the children to ensure their safety. She was mightily relieved to find that John, so serious did he now consider the situation, had despatched them to Auckland some days before.[14]

At this juncture Rewi received news from Taranaki that the Governor had marched with his soldiers to reoccupy the Maori enclave at Tataraimaka. Immediately, Rewi mustered his men and, with the pugnacious words 'strike the pakeha', set off to Hangatiki to gather together all his men for the impending struggle.[15] He and his war party had become without doubt the dominant force in the Waikato.

Gorst now had no choice but to abandon Te Awamutu, being as he said 'without arms and at the mercy of the first assailant'. He left on 18 April being followed by most of the settlers. The boys at the technical school split up. A few remained at the school-house. Two returned home. The rest found their way to Auckland,[16] where the Governor wished to see them continue their training or find work. Unhappily his intentions were frustrated by events and the increasing anti-Maori feeling among the colonists, and it was left to Bishop Selwyn to take charge of those boys finally left in Auckland.

Gorst's last few months in New Zealand were unsettled ones. After the debacle at Te Awamutu he hurried back to Auckland, being given shelter for a night on the way at Ngaruawahia by Patara his rival editor – a chivalrous gesture. He had only a moment to see that his family were safe in Auckland before travelling off by sea with Bell, the Native Minister, to report to the Governor who was in New Plymouth. It was probably on this trip that Bell recruited Gorst as his private secretary. On landing, Bell and Gorst found the situation tense; an attempted Maori ambush – with the Governor as the probable target – had just failed. During the week he was in New Plymouth Gorst acted as secretary in preparing memoranda for Alfred Domett, the new Premier, and Bell on the Waitara controversy.[17] Both Grey and Domett agreed that the disputed land should be given back to the Maoris but, rather absurdly, neither of them could agree who should publicly take responsibility for making the necessary declaration and restoring the land. Here Gorst saw at first hand the fatal duality of government he so disliked.

Gorst left Taranaki on 3 May. The next day a Maori ambush against British soldiers ordered by Rewi succeeded this time and seven men were killed. This was the spark which reignited the Taranaki war.

Grey had directed Gorst to collect together all those driven by Rewi from the Waikato and take them temporarily to the island of Kawau,[18] 30 miles north of Auckland. The island was privately owned by Grey who, an early conservationist, had stocked it experimentally with deer, kangaroos, wild cattle, emus and other forms of wild life. The party was to await the Governor's return to Auckland before being repatriated – at least this was the unlikely plan – to the Waikato. For some weeks the party was left practically marooned on the island, since in the developing crisis the schooner delivering supplies to

Kawau was needed elsewhere. For a man of Gorst's energy to be stuck on Kawau with little to do, and at such a time, must have been galling. There were compensations for him, although he may not have seen it in this light, such as enjoying the succulent oysters, the tranquillity of the place after the turmoils of the Waikato, and watching his 2-year-old son playing with the deer and feeding by hand an enormous kangaroo.

Back in Auckland with the Kawau party dispersed (but not returning to the Waikato), Gorst again had work to do and spent in his own words 'many unhappy days' as an official in a government office. Rumours were circulating: Auckland was going to be attacked by the Waikato Maoris and there was a conspiracy to murder Europeans. The populace was in some terror. Gorst himself, then and in retrospect, was inclined to discount these particular rumours.

To forestall any attack on Auckland by the Waikato Maoris and to punish them as a whole for the acts of Rewi,[19] Grey decided in July to invade the Waikato, a decision which must have been painful to Gorst. Unfortunately, the military preparations of General Cameron were completed before the Governor's proclamation was distributed to the Maori people as a whole explaining the reason for government action. After the troops crossed the Mangatawhiri river into the Waikato territory on 12 July the war became general.

There were several villages around Auckland inhabited by relatives of the Waikato tribes, many of whom were old and infirm. Rather callously the government issued an order expelling these Maoris, unless they took an oath of allegiance. Gorst was strongly against the issuing of this order, and vainly protested about it to the colonial ministers.[20] He pointed out that these people were mainly the elderly and were unlikely to harbour dangerous characters; a handful of police, he considered, could have kept an eye on them. The order caused much distress. These Maoris, dispossessed of their houses and belongings, became refugees. As they moved out so the looters – both troops and settlers – moved in, ransacking the empty buildings. James Fulloon, a highly intelligent man of mixed parentage in government service, told Gorst that the conduct of the white population made him ashamed of being partly English.

Finally, the government were forced into doing something about the plight of the refugees who, as they fled south, were caught in the Hunua ranges between Maori skirmishers and British troops. The Governor turned to Bell and his private secretary Gorst, and on 13 July sent the two men, unarmed, to Drury to find out what was happening to the refugees, and to make arrangements for them to escape from the perilous confines of the Hunua forest. The pair were also charged with supplying them as necessary with food and promising them safe conduct. In the circumstances it was, Gorst wrote, his 'most dangerous service' in New Zealand; already two Europeans had been found killed by the Maoris on the road beyond Drury. At last the refugees were located at Kirikiri. The old people, together with women and children, gratefully accepted the offer of food and safe conduct. Unhappily, owing to some mix-up over orders, they were then arrested by troops just after Bell and Gorst had set off to return to Auckland. Gorst described this as having the 'unfortunate appearance of a gross breach of faith'.[21]

Grey now found he was desperately short of troops. To help remedy the situation he decided to recruit 5,000 military settlers in Australia. After doing a stint of three years military duty in New Zealand, these men would be given land to farm in the Waikato as compensation for their service. A fruitful source of supply for the robust manpower needed would, it was hoped, be found in the Australian goldfields. In August, therefore, anticipating the approval of the imperial and colonial governments, Grey sent off the same pair as before, Bell and Gorst, to Sydney to find the first 2,000 settlers.[22]

Gorst took his family with him to Australia. He felt that Auckland, vulnerable to attack and with only a few militiamen and volunteers to defend it against a possible Maori incursion, was too dangerous a place in which to leave his family. Gorst must have expected to return to New Zealand when his work in Australia was completed, for he later wrote that when he left Auckland that August he 'little imagined it would be 43 years before I should see New Zealand again'.[23]

We have to conclude that while he was in Australia something happened to change Gorst's mind about returning to New Zealand. We do not know what it was. Certainly he was out of sympathy with Grey's war policy, for he never believed the colony's differences with the Maoris should be solved by force. More specifically he thought it wrong to punish the Waikatos for the 'evil' deeds of Rewi. It has been said he had ambitions to enter the General Assembly and make himself heard there, but this possibility, if it was one, did not materialise. So he may well have felt he wanted to challenge imperial policy about New Zealand on a wider stage at home.

His career in New Zealand must have been a disappointment to him. He had dabbled in missionary work and tried his hand at a bit of teaching. Then, embracing the work of the public service, which had undoubtedly caught his attention, he found himself shunned as a magistrate and rejected, humiliatingly, as a civil commissioner. These set-backs would have unsettled the most resilient of men. Yet Gorst was no quitter as his long years at Westminster would show.

While he had made friends among the Maoris and some of the European humanitarians, there were people critical of him. For instance Sewell, the Attorney-General, noted a 'want of judgement' in Gorst[24] and blamed him for a substantial amount of the Waikato trouble. Whatever the view of those on the spot about Gorst's judgement, attaching blame to him does not look fair insofar as Gorst was trying to carry out government policy in difficult circumstances.

Morgan, the missionary, well placed to observe him in the Waikato, said Gorst was 'soon elated and soon depressed'.[25] The well-known journalist W. T. Stead wrote years later that when Gorst finally left Te Awamutu a feeling of great despair overwhelmed him, and he wept like a child.[26] Stead almost certainly had this information from Gorst himself. These vignettes of his character as a young man appear to conflict with his later reputation as a cool parliamentarian who never lost his self-control. But as we shall see, he remained an emotional man who disguised his feelings.

Nevertheless, when Gorst came to look at the problems of the colonists and Maoris from the other side of the Tasman sea, his impatience and underlying mood of despondency may have got the better of him. His reaction may have been 'a plague on both your houses, my adventure in New Zealand is over. It is time to go.'

At any rate, for whatever reason, and some mystery remains, this complex man decided during the few weeks he was in Australia to return to England. For Mary this may have been a tough decision, for by now her parents and two brothers were living and working in New Zealand. The Gorsts sailed from Australia in September and arrived home on 14 December 1863. John Gorst had been away nearly four years.

NOTES

1. NZR, 227; Daglish, 'How half-civilised people ought to be managed', 140.
2. NZR, 230.
3. NZR, 246.
4. MK, 336–7; NZR, 240–1.
5. NZR, 254–6.
6. Civil Commissioner, Otawhao, to the Honourable Native Minister, 25 Feb. 1863, AJHR, 1863: E-1, 3.
7. There are various descriptions to be found on the events in Te Awamutu in March 1863, e.g. MK, 339-55; NZR, 260–77; J. Cowan, *The Old Frontier*, Te Awamutu, Waipa Post, 1922, 27–30.

8. Civil Commissioner, Otawhao, to the Honourable Native Minister, 28 March 1863, AJHR, 1863: E-1, 8–9.
9. Cowan, *The Old Frontier*, 29.
10. NZR, 268.
11. MK, 347.
12. NZR, 268.
13. MK, 353.
14. NZR, 277.
15. MK, 354.
16. Ibid., 367.
17. NZR, 49-50.
18. Ibid., 25.
19. MK, 371; Sinclair, *Origins*, 267; Dalton, *War and Politics in New Zealand*, 176–7.
20. NZR, 324.
21. MK, 384–8.
22. Rutherford, 493.
23. NZR, 326.
24. Daglish, 'How half-civilised people ought to be managed', 142, quoting H. Sewell's journal.
25. Ibid., 140, quoting the Gore Browne papers.
26. *Review of Reviews*, 4 Aug. 1891, 578.

6

The Lure of Politics

When the Gorsts arrived home in England just before Christmas in 1863, John decided he would resume his legal studies and become a barrister. He would be following in the footsteps of his late uncle and of his younger brother who was about to be called to the Bar; also two of Mary's uncles were barristers. Quite soon he took a suburban villa in Tooting, which was between six and seven miles from the Inner Temple.

But there was something else on Gorst's mind. He had determined to write a book on the Maori rebellion, and he needed to get the work completed while events in New Zealand were fresh in his memory and before he turned his energies to pastures new. No doubt he began planning the book, or even writing it, on the long journey home.

Gorst wasted no time. The book was published by Macmillan in 1864 with the title *The Maori King: The Story of Our Quarrel with the Natives of New Zealand*. Now regarded by many as a very useful and perceptive account of the early stages of the Maori King movement, the book reflects Gorst's admiration for the Maoris. One of his main reasons for writing the book was his conviction that the Maori case had not been properly appreciated nor even fully understood in Britain. Further, he felt that, as he put it, 'the story of how a deadly quarrel arose between a race and its rulers cannot be unimportant or uninteresting'. There was another reason, he stated, why this episode of history should be examined:

> New Zealand has been recently quoted as a proof of the impossibility of civilising barbarous races. It is urged that, wherever the brown and white skins come in contact, the former must disappear, and that the old fashion once pursued by our forefathers in the backwoods of America was a more merciful, because a more speedy, way of doing the inevitable work than the lingering modern method which has superseded it.

His book, he proclaimed, was a protest against a theory which 'despairs of justice and humanity'.[1] At the same time, he hoped to convince his readers that the quarrel had come about through avoidable errors. He laid these essentially at the door of the Governor, colonial government and colonists, although he was ready to criticise the Maoris too. There was another matter which disturbed him. He was alarmed that the war might be fought to the bitter end, and the Maoris exterminated.

In his book Gorst was at pains to cover in some detail the reasons for the rise of the Maori King movement, which is regarded today as having been nationalist in character. He argued there was no single reason for the rise of the movement and gave three causes which led to its establishment as a dominant anti-government force. They were:

1. The desire among Maoris for law and order owing to the failure of the British to supply proper government in Maori districts;
2. The need to prevent the further sale of Maori land to the Crown;
3. The mortification felt especially by the younger Maoris at being regarded by a large majority of their white neighbours as an inferior and degraded race.[2]

He also made the important point that the character of the movement was continually changing.

Gorst, therefore, considered that the Maoris had legitimate grievances over their treatment and that the government had been unable to remedy these. This had led the Maoris to wish for 'separation and independence' as Gorst put it. He may not have described the movement as a 'nationalist' one – the term was not then in vogue – but he was effectively saying something very similar.

At the end of *The Maori King* Gorst turned to the future. How, after the war was ended, he asked, should the Maoris be governed? Constructively he put forward several proposals. Dual government had to be abolished – an old chestnut of his. Either the Maoris should be ruled by the imperial authorities or by the local colonial ones, but not by both. He was against the colonial government being put in charge. The Maoris would get, he believed, a fairer deal from the imperial government. He then proposed a system of administration run by imperial officers, somewhat similar to the model operating in parts of British India. The Maori districts would come under powerful British residents, who would be advised by a Maori council of chiefs, but be responsible directly to the imperial government. The council of chiefs would also have law-making powers. A native police force would be established responsible to both resident and chiefs, although in Gorst's scheme the former would have the final say. He considered that only a small English staff would be needed to govern the Maori districts and this contingent plus the police would cost the government just £50,000 a year, a charge to be shared between imperial and colonial governments.[3] Some of these proposals are reminiscent of what Grey was trying belatedly to do in the Waikato.

Finally Gorst thought that if he had made in his book a sufficient *prima facie* case for a government inquiry into the relationship between the races, then a special commissioner should be sent to New Zealand to take evidence directly from the Maoris about their grievances, and then, presumably, to make recommendations. We do not know whether this particular proposal of Gorst's, which had some merit, was ever considered by the British Government. It remains to be said that the Maori war dragged on and on but without discernible benefit to the Maoris. Although the Waikato was subdued by British troops in 1865, the war flared up, often with savagery on both sides, in other parts of North Island, including Taranaki, until as late as 1872 and after British regiments had left the colony. It was not until 1881 that the Maori King submitted to the government's rule.

Gorst wrote again about New Zealand in the middle of 1865 and this time in *Macmillans* periodical.[4] In chronicling recent events there he reminded his readers that it was the British and not the Maoris who had actually started the series of Maori wars. He described the war in the Waikato as a 'national' one, and one in which the Maoris were fighting to defend their independence. One obstacle to peace, he saw, was the 'mistaken' government policy of confiscating Maori land as a punishment measure. He also saw a withdrawal of the imperial troops as being a first step towards peace. Above all he urged the government to deal with the Maoris as an 'independent' people. The Maoris, for their part, seemed to have recognised from his writings that Gorst saw himself as their friend, for they gave him a warm welcome when he revisited New Zealand in 1906.

Gorst's experiences in New Zealand left him with a life-long sympathy for the well-being of the native peoples of the Empire. His time as an MP bears testimony to this. At least until he became a minister he frequently intervened in the House to draw attention to what we would call today 'human rights' problems. At some stage as he became immersed in the Maori problems of the Waikato, he realised he was not cut out to be a missionary and so gave up all thought of a career in that field. As a politician he would show a keen interest in the affairs of the Church, particularly over religious instruction in schools, regarding himself as a middle of the road Anglican. But there is no evidence to show he was a deeply pious man.

Gorst was called to the Bar on 1 May 1865, his sponsor being Kenneth Macauley, a Bencher of the Inner Temple and MP for Cambridge until July that year. In those days to qualify for call, a student must have attended, over a year, certain lectures given by readers appointed by the Inns of Court, or have passed an examination. Another requirement for call, an ancient one, was that a student had to have kept 12 'terms' (there were four in the legal year) at his Inn. This involved dining in Hall on six occasions during term, although for members of certain universities these occasions were reduced to three. Gorst had begun eating his dinners before he went to New Zealand, so he now only had to keep the balance of the terms outstanding.

In due course Gorst joined the Northern circuit where, so he presumably argued, he would be more likely to pick up work than he would in the south. At the same time he found a place in chambers in the Temple. A young barrister, then as now, would have to struggle to find work. Gorst was lucky insofar as he was able to 'devil' for an experienced and successful barrister, John Holker, about whom we shall have more to say presently. Devilling consisted of doing work for a barrister who was too busy with his other cases to undertake it all himself. In those days a young barrister might not be paid for devilling, the remuneration for which was entirely a matter for his principal. Gorst was by no means well off, and we assume that essentially he had to make his living from his work at the Bar and from the odd article he wrote. Money from *The Maori King* would hardly have paid for more than a few months' rent and groceries.

But Gorst's career at the Bar was now, at least to some extent, side-tracked, even before it had quite begun. Politics were responsible. Not yet 30, he was invited to stand in the Conservative cause in the general election of 1865 for Hastings, a borough which then returned two members. The election had been called for July by the Liberal Prime Minister Lord Palmerston, who was at the very end of his career and would die a few months later. Gorst, as we have seen, had always been drawn to matters political, so it is no surprise to find him hankering for a seat in parliament. Whether Gorst was wise to go for a parliamentary career before he had established himself at the Bar is a moot point. Parliament was then very much what you made of it and MPs were not required to attend much to their constituents. There was, therefore, time to spare for other activities. The Bar, however, was for a junior a demanding profession. There was thus a danger that Gorst would fall between two stools.

The Conservative Party had been having a difficult time ever since the repeal of the Corn Laws in 1846. Sir Robert Peel's decision to adopt free trade policies had fundamentally split the party, which consequently had to face a lengthy time in the political wilderness. Indeed, over a period of 20 years the Conservatives were in office for a total of just 26 months, both times under Lord Derby who, although a scholarly man, was reputedly more interested in racing than in politics. It was the Whigs and Liberals together with a few Radicals, often in a series of loose coalitions, who dominated a confused political scene with a rather free and easy approach to party discipline in the Commons. For instance, Lord Aberdeen abandoned his high-Tory principles and led for just over two years a coalition ministry consisting mainly of Whigs and Peelites. Benjamin Disraeli, having broken with Peel over the free trade issue, then changed his mind about protection and, by now leader in the Commons of the still split Conservatives, made it clear he now accepted free trade. William Gladstone, on the other hand, began his long parliamentary career as a traditional Conservative supporting protection and served in Peel's last cabinet. But, after the repeal of the Corn Laws and at a time of rising prosperity, he became increasingly unhappy about the social system. Accordingly, he gradually shifted his stance towards the Liberals until he became Palmerston's Chancellor of the Exchequer in his two administrations.

This, then, was the background to the politics of the age as Gorst prepared to enter the electoral fray a few weeks after his call to the Bar. Politics could be rough. Bribery and corruption were still rife in elections in the 1860s and for some time after. Also there was no secret ballot until 1872. A prospective candidate at Taunton in the 1865 election found, during a preliminary canvass of 900 electors, that between 260 and 270 of them were resolved to vote for no one unless they were paid for doing so. Richard Glass, the pioneer manufacturer of submarine cables, announced when he arrived at Bewdley, where he stood in the 1868 election, that he was prepared to lay out £4,000 for the 1,000 electors; consequently his agents opened 20 public houses to all comers. Professor Hanham lists no fewer than 64 boroughs, including Hastings, which had a record of corruption between 1865 and 1884. In the 1880 election, 28 magistrates were found guilty of corrupt practices.[5]

In his election address Gorst confined himself to just five topics: the franchise, the church, foreign affairs, the military forces and corruption. Thus:

> he was opposed, having 'witnessed' the results of democratic government in the colonies, 'to the lowering of the franchise, though not to its extension in other ways';

he was in favour of religious freedom as long as this was consistent with the safety of the constitution. But the Church of Rome should not be allowed 'to acquire political power within the realm under plea of religious liberty'; the government should abstain from 'irritating foreign nations by officious meddling and empty threats';

the country's 'honour and safety' required the maintenance of the army, navy and volunteers in a state of efficiency;

he looked upon 'corruption in the discharge of a public office as a grave crime ...'[6]

This was all fairly traditional stuff. The franchise and the church were both matters of great public concern at the time. In a speech reported on 9 June he disarmingly told his audience that he had not 'a set of cut and dried opinions on any subject, but he had principles'. Turning to colonial legislatures he claimed that the colonists' power to elect these were lodged with the labouring classes, which was 'a great and monstrous evil'. Further, he found there were people in England who wanted 'to pull down our constitution' by lowering the franchise so that the labouring class could have the vote. This would turn the country, he unflatteringly suggested, into a 'sort of second-rate Australia'. Rather than lowering the franchise, he considered, moving away from his somewhat reactionary views and being more constructive, that the country should try to 'raise the working man'. The idea of improvement would be a recurring theme with him.

He described himself as a 'sincere and attached' member of the Church of England, but he was by no means ill-disposed to nonconformists, considering for example that they should be allowed to obtain university degrees. But, harking back to his more severe views on the Roman Catholic Church, he re-echoed what his Conservative running mate had said about the need to inspect nunneries and convents to ensure that the inmates were not there against their free will. Once he referred to New Zealand, criticising the war there as being 'expensive and disgraceful'; Gorst never liked to see what he considered wasteful public expenditure. This address prompted an editorial in the *Hastings and St Leonards News* which gave Gorst a pat on the back, saying that he made the best speech of the evening because it was the most political, but then going on to state that the paper could not endorse the 'extreme anti-democratic sentiments' he had expressed.[7]

There were occasions during this campaign where Gorst showed good humour on the hustings and an ability to poke fun at himself. He thus once referred to three distinct 'names' he had been called. One reflected his physical condition because he had been called a 'g(h)ost'. The second affected his character for he had been called 'a returned convict'. The third name called into question his religious character for he had heard with some 'horror' that he had been called a 'Puseyite'. He had been hurt by being thought of as a member of this very high church movement, and wondered what he had done to deserve it. Then he had suddenly discovered the reason. He realised that he had recently been the guest of Mr 'Pope' Hutchings![8] These sallies were greeted by his audience with loud laughter.

That Gorst displayed plenty of confidence about the result of the election is clear from a short report about his bullish outlook which was sandwiched between an exciting account of the Bexhill v. Hastings and St Leonard's cricket match (it was low-scoring and ended in a draw) and an article on a serious balloon accident in Ulster.[9] But Gorst was to be disappointed for he did not win his seat. Defeated for the first but not the last time, Gorst returned to the law. But not for long. The following year another opportunity, an unexpected one, came his way to get into parliament. He took it eagerly.

At Cambridge two Conservatives had been returned for the borough in the 1865 general election, but one of them, by name Forsyth, was eventually disqualified on petition. A fresh election was called and the leader of the local Conservatives hurried up to London in April 1866 to obtain a suitable candidate, wanting as he put it, 'the best man in England'. In the meantime Gorst was on his way from Holyhead to Dublin for a visit to Ireland. It was a rough crossing, and Gorst was dreadfully sea-sick. On arrival he could manage no breakfast but gradually began to thaw out sitting down, as he described it, 'to some well-selected luncheon . . . to restore my shaken nerves'. Just then a telegram was handed to him stating that a parliamentary seat was vacant at Cambridge and that he had been selected as the candidate. There was no time to be lost and so once more he had to face without respite 'the terrors' of the Irish Sea. With some trepidation he travelled on to Cambridge, where he was given, to his relief, a most cordial welcome by the Conservative fraternity.

It was a short campaign, due to conclude before the end of the month. Gorst began it by addressing a Conservative meeting at the Lion Hotel. He confided to them that on his return from New Zealand he had thrown in his lot with the Conservatives for three reasons.

First, venturing into the field of foreign affairs, he did not like the way the Liberal government had behaved towards Poland (the Russians had ruthlessly crushed a rebellion by the Poles in 1863), Denmark (the Germans had invaded the Duchies of Schleswig and Holstein in 1864) and the Confederate States in the American Civil War. The government had held out hopes of giving assistance to the losing side in each conflict but in the event and in the interest of non-intervention, had done nothing. Gorst said that although he was not in favour of war he did not like leaving friends in the lurch. Second, he believed the Liberals were trying to destroy the Church of England and third, he did not favour the Liberals' view on reform, which issue he thought would decide the election.[10] On the subject of parliamentary reform his opinions had not changed since Hastings, and he told voters that, if elected, he would oppose Liberal measures to lower the franchise.

Gorst made a number of speeches which were fully reported in the local press. As a reading of them shows, they were anything but dull. Opinions, comments, ideas and proposals all seemed to tumble from his lips. Some of them may have been a trifle ingenuous, as when he dealt with the 'working classes', which he did at considerable length. For instance at a speech at the Bell public house on the Newmarket road he said that he thought the term was wrongly applied if it only meant labourer, insisting that he himself was a working man. He thought he ought to know something about this subject for in New Zealand he had travelled, sat, eaten and smoked with 'carpenters, blacksmiths and manual labourers'. He accepted that the condition and especially the education of this class needed improving. What was wanted, though, was not political reform but social reform, which he believed would come about as a result of education.

At the same time he could not forbear from pointing out that the labouring class was prone to drunkenness. He was not a teetotaller himself, he assured his audience, and did not want to deprive a working man of his beer, but nonetheless far too much money, which could be put to better use, was being spent on drink. For instance, if money destined for drink went instead on better housing, then the working man might find himself enfranchised. An agricultural labourer, whom Gorst saw at the bottom of the pile, could not support a 'wife and little ones on eight bob a week'. The only remedy he saw – a stark one maybe – was for these people to emigrate. In the colonies there was good work and money. He did not think Acts of Parliament would 'mend the condition of the labouring class'. The change must come from them and their own manners and habits. He then instanced how legislation had not improved the lot of chimney-climbing boys. It was true, of course, that the series of Factory Acts passed between 1833 and 1850, undertaken under the leadership of Lord Shaftesbury, had alleviated many of the problems concerning child labour. Nevertheless this did not stop Gorst from alluding to the cruel employment of young girls and boys in the mines, the potteries and lace industry, practices which needed, he believed, reforming.[11] No doubt he was referring in particular to the early age at which children were required to work. The time would come – but this would not be for some 25 years – when Gorst would harness his formidable energy and restless spirit to campaigning earnestly for reforms in the fields of social welfare and employment.

Gorst seemed particularly anxious to be regarded as the working man's friend and promised at his meetings that, if elected, he would give a great part of his time to this particular class of constituent. Displaying some early political skill, he was careful not to commit himself too specifically on issues, and stressed not for the first time that he would be an independent kind of Conservative. Despite his inexperience, Gorst sufficiently impressed the voters to be elected by the narrow margin of 24 votes, receiving 776 votes to the 752 votes given to his Liberal opponent.

The new MP's arrival at the House of Commons in May 1866 came at a critical moment. On the death of Palmerston the previous year, Lord John Russell had become Prime Minister. Now, aged 74, Russell wished to give his name to a second reform Bill before time ran out for him. Accordingly, a Bill was introduced. But the Liberals were split over qualifications for the franchise and in June 1866 were defeated. There was no dissolution and the Conservatives took office with a minority government for the third time under Derby, who early in 1868 was to hand over the reins to Disraeli. Gorst bided his time and did not speak in the Commons until he had given himself a reasonable period to absorb its atmosphere.

Gorst began his active career in the Commons by putting a question on 12 February 1867 to Charles Adderley, the Under Secretary for the Colonies (the Secretary of State, the Duke of Buckingham, was in the Lords). He asked what was the present number of British troops in New Zealand, the size of the force to be left there permanently and who was to pay for this force.[12] It was eminently sensible for the new MP to start with a subject about which he knew something. He was told in answer to his question that the number was 3,190, that one infantry regiment would remain in New Zealand to be paid for by the imperial government, and that for their part the New Zealand government would find £50,000 for 'native purposes'. Further papers on the situation in New Zealand, Adderley said, would soon be laid before the House. A month later, and before the promised papers had materialised, Gorst was able to make some further 'observations' on the same subject, although this apparently did not count as his maiden speech. He now pointed out – giving notice of how vigilant he was to be in matters relating to public expenditure – that a sum of between £60,000 and £70,000 appeared in the Estimates for the support of the single regiment. He regarded this sum as 'both unnecessary and positively injurious' to the colony.[13] This prompted Adderley who, even though Disraeli promoted him to the Cabinet a decade later, was never regarded as a successful minister, to explain at tedious length the detailed arrangements made between the two countries. The following year Gorst would again cross swords with Adderley but next time more vigorously.

For many years the problem of church rates had been picked over in the Commons. It was still simmering in the 1860s. Until 1811 there had been no difficulty with these rates, which churchwardens were empowered to levy for the upkeep of the church and for the proper maintenance of services.[14] Then the nonconformists, especially in the towns, began to refuse to pay the rates. A draper even went to prison for their non-payment. This was not too surprising as nonconformists, after all, had their own chapels and did not attend the Anglican church. Earlier attempts by the Whigs to abolish church rates were unsuccessful, and now once again a Church Rates Abolition Bill, introduced by J. A. Hardcastle, the MP for Bury St Edmunds, had come before the House. Gorst decided that this would give him the opportunity to make his maiden speech. So on 20 March 1867 he seconded an amendment opposing the Bill. In his speech he took the line that in country districts the money collected for the rates was often distributed among the rural poor thus relieving misery. These needy people would be the first to suffer if the rates were abolished. The speech, while having a valid point to make, reads a trifle oddly for towards the end of it he began to digress, saying that dissenters were better educated than members of the Church of England over the habit of 'giving', and that this fact was 'peculiarly visible . . . in the colonies'.[15] Gorst may well have been nervous – even if this was not in character – for his son Harold stated that making this speech was the 'most terrifying ordeal' in his father's recollection. As for the Bill, it finally made the statute book, but not until Gladstone's administration arrived on the scene the following year.

In early May Gorst attended a meeting held at the Freemasons

Tavern in London organised by a group of young Conservatives, many of them barristers, including H. C. Raikes, later to be a minister under Lord Salisbury. Its object was to consider the expediency of forming some sort of union which would serve as a means of both uniting and communicating with the Conservative associations already in existence in various parts of the country. During these proceedings, Gorst asserted that the next election would be won by the party possessing the best organisation. It was decided to hold a further meeting inviting every Conservative association to join what was to become known as the National Union of Conservative and Constitutional Associations (National Union for short) and to draw up plans for a committee, rules and so on.[16] Disraeli was kept informed about these developments by Colonel T. E. Taylor, the Chief Whip, and Lord Nevill, an influential party manager. This is the first we hear of Gorst's interest in party organisation, but he was a man who liked to keep plenty of balls in the air at the same time.

When next he made a speech in the House, Gorst again chose to be on familiar ground. In a debate in June he intervened on a motion that British troops should be withdrawn from the Cape of Good Hope. He agreed with the government that the troops should go, and was able to work into his speech a warning of the dangers of having a divided authority between imperial and colonial governments. He ended by saying that he hoped for the day 'when not one imperial soldier would be left in the colonies'.[17] This did not sound like a traditional Tory, more like Gladstone or one of his followers. Gorst's position seems to have been that the colonies should stand on their own feet and also should not be an undue financial burden on the home government. But he believed too – and he made this clear in his speech – in resolute government, for this was something subject peoples understood and respected.

The most important measure, it can be safely said, passed by the Derby/Disraeli government was the Reform Bill of 1867, which increased the electorate by 700,000 by giving the vote to the urban artisan (the population of England, Wales and Scotland was some 26,000,000 in 1871, an increase of something like 60 per cent over the figure for 1831). Anyone worth his salt would have been expected to speak in the debates on the Bill, or so it would have seemed to the ambitious Gorst, for a man without views on the franchise might not count for much in politics.

Looking back for a moment to the first great Reform Act of 1832, we are reminded that the Whigs effectively enfranchised the urban middle classes by regularising the borough franchise, giving the vote to every adult male occupant of a house with a rental value of £10, and to leaseholders with properties worth £50. In 1867, the Conservatives adopted a different criterion, relying on a rating and not a rental qualification for the franchise. Among the main provisions of its final form, the 1867 Bill gave the borough vote to all rate-paying occupiers of separate dwellings and those occupying lodgings of £10 value, and the county vote to those occupying houses rated at £12. In addition, 45 seats were redistributed. This then was Disraeli's 'great leap in the dark' as he expressed it. The debate on the Bill, both in Cabinet and in Parliament, had flowed back and forth, for Disraeli's approach was always pragmatic and he had no preconceived views on the ultimate shape and content of the Bill.

Where did all this leave Gorst? On the hustings, it will be recalled, he was loath to lower the franchise. Yet here was. the party he espoused aiming to carry through a radical measure – indeed more radical than the Liberal one he had opposed – purporting to enfranchise some of the very people whom he considered did not deserve the vote. He was faced therefore with a problem as to what line he should take. At the committee stage of the Bill, as each clause was taken, he voted on almost every occasion in favour of the Bill. But when he finally spoke at this stage he was unable to conceal his disquiet that the party was 'in great danger of getting rid of the best part of its principles' by giving the country 'an extreme democratic measure'.[18] To Gorst's dismay, various proposals he saw as safeguards, such as a second vote for those with educational or property qualifications or for those paying direct taxation (these were known as the 'fancy franchises'), were dropped by Disraeli for tactical reasons during the passage of the Bill.

On 15 July during the third reading, Gorst spoke out forcefully and said he proposed to vote against the Bill. He believed that in its final form the Bill 'greatly disturbed the balance of political power' and would imperil the future. The Bill, he said, went against what had been stated in the Queen's speech, by giving to one class a 'preponderating power' over the rest. Thus in the boroughs the current non-tax payers – he was referring to those about to get the vote – would be in a majority and the current tax payers in a minority. So he could not join in the 'rejoicing' of the party over the measure. He 'might have held his tongue on the subject but he thought it manlier to speak out, though he knew he could have changed his coat in silence with the crowd'. When the Conservatives, he opined, went to the country they would be rejected by the people for being 'clad in the false cloak of Liberalism'.[19] Gorst was proved to be correct about losing, although whether the Conservatives lost for the reason he was suggesting is open to argument. Gorst's views on parliamentary reform, held on rational and not emotional grounds, would evolve under the influence of Disraeli.

In the meantime progress had been made by the group of young Conservatives who had called the meeting at the Freemasons Tavern the previous May and with whom Gorst was associated. Their ideas had now developed, and they had determined that one of the main objects of the National Union would be to assist in the revival of Conservative working men's associations and clubs, which had existed at an earlier time in Lancashire and Yorkshire. The plan was to affiliate these associations to the National Union and then through them to woo the newly enfranchised urban voter.[20] The National Union held its first full meeting, again at the Freemasons Tavern, on 12 November 1867. The meeting, attended by delegates from 65 associations and branches, was chaired by John Gorst. The choice of chairman was surprising because Gorst had all along been opposed to lowering the franchise and therefore might have been supposed to be hostile to working men's associations. But this was not so. As we have noticed already, he wanted to be known as the working man's friend. At the same time he was quick to spot that the Conservative Party had to improve its organisation if it was to win the next election. The Reform Act was now a *fait accompli* with the urban voters enfranchised. So in Gorst's view the Conservatives had to make the best of the situation if they were going to achieve their electoral aims and objectives. He did not consider that there was any inconsistency between his views on reform and the objectives currently being thrashed out by the promoters of the National Union.

This of course still does not answer the question of how this junior MP, with not quite orthodox views on reform, came to be chairing the meeting. As it happened, Gorst was a last-minute stand-in. For some reason Raikes, the organiser and not then an MP, was not willing to take the chair. In fact he had been upstaged to an extent by a large gathering of Conservatives, 2,000 no less, at the Crystal Palace held the previous day. That meeting had the blessing of the party leadership, while Raikes and his meeting were snubbed,[21] although at least Markham Spofforth, the principal agent, attended it. In his opening remarks as chairman Gorst said:

> I am very sorry in the absence of better and more distinguished men that it has fallen to my lot to take the chair on this occasion. It was hoped that Lord Holmesdale would have been able to take

the chair or Lord Dartmouth ... [but] Lord Holmesdale has been obliged at the last moment to send an excuse because it is perfectly impossible for him to disappoint some friends with whom he has another engagement ...[22]

This of course says little for Lord Holmesdale, but the peer's absence gave Gorst a chance to show his paces.

Gorst then turned to the objects of the meeting, which were not, he stressed, to discuss the principles of Conservatism but to consider by what organisation they might make those principles 'effective among the masses'. He asked those who were going to speak 'to be short and to the point'. He had to recommend 'that precept by my example and by making a short speech myself'. With that he immediately sat down. The secretary of the meeting then read, at the chairman's request, a statement – possibly drafted by Gorst – referring to how the 'working classes of England' might be supported in maintaining the 'fundamental principles of our ancient constitution'.

A long discussion then followed about the name, the rules and electing the officers of the new association. Gorst proved to be a firm chairman, ready to rule speakers out of order. At one stage a man rose to speak and admitted he was not a Conservative at which there was 'hissing'. At once Gorst as chairman said that 'hissing is a very unparliamentary proceeding and I cannot consent to remain in the chair if it is repeated'. The speaker continued and there was no more hissing.[23]

Members of the council were then elected but Gorst was not one of them. Finally, votes of thanks were proposed, among others one to the chairman. The seconder of this, a Mr Sapwell, said he had never in his life met with a chairman who had conducted a meeting so well as Mr Gorst had done that day. He deserved their warmest thanks.

A vivid contemporary description of Gorst has been handed down by his fellow barrister and associate in the National Union, Edward Clarke. 'Gorst was short, thick-set, bustling, abrupt . . . incurably prosaic, with no pretensions to oratory, and a total lack of humour ... Gorst had a genius for organisation; was a keen judge of men, with an inflexible will and an untiring diligence.'[24]

The National Union, though not at its start, was destined to play – with Gorst on stage – an important part in Conservative Party history. But this comes later, and the story will be told in its place.

The last long speech Gorst made in the Parliament which would be dissolved at the end of 1868 was an important one for him, because it caught Disraeli's attention. The Prime Minister must have been aware of Gorst's involvement with the National Union and may have spotted his potential. The speech was on Ceylon (Sri Lanka), in those days a crown colony ruled by a Governor with a Legislative Council (Legco) consisting of ten officials and six non-officials. Seeing himself as someone specialising in colonial affairs, Gorst rose on 20 March to draw the House's attention to a petition received by the Queen from the people of Ceylon; it was signed by 2,000 Cingalese (Sinhalese) and 500 Europeans. The petition, Gorst claimed, indicated a depressed state of things in Ceylon. Further the people were 'very angry' with the government of the country. The accompanying despatch by the Governor showed, in Gorst's view, that the Governor had quite misunderstood the precise nature of the complaint, which had arisen out of an original question concerning military expenditure in respect of British troops stationed in Ceylon and who should pay for them.

But this question, Gorst asserted, had developed into a much wider one concerning whether Ceylon was to be ruled from London or from the colony. He explained that Downing Street had in effect peremptorily ordered Ceylon to increase its share of this expenditure, and the officials on Legco, voting to orders, had quickly complied. The petitioners, while being ready to meet the £24,000 requested, objected to these matters being settled in London and asked in addition for parity of representation on Legco. The colonists, Gorst pointed out, were less concerned about the settlement than about the way it had been arrived at.

For good measure Gorst pointed out that there were also complaints by the petitioners against the police, the administration of justice, the state of education and about incompetency in the management of public works. What, asked Gorst, did the government propose to do?[25] Mr Watkin, the member for Stockport, concurred with Gorst's views.

Adderley, the Under Secretary for the Colonies, answered Gorst at some length. The nub of his argument was that the position in Ceylon was fine. The petitioners were mainly rich planters who wanted more power. The education department had been increased in size, the police reformed, public works improved, and so on. He denied the grievances and said the remedy sought was 'inadmissible'. Only Edward Cardwell, a previous Colonial Secretary, rallied to Adderley's cause.

A month later Watkin moved for a Select Committee to inquire into the condition in Ceylon, and was supported by a number of other members. Adderley once again – perhaps he was not good at catching the mood of members – refused to admit anything was wrong, and said that the matter had been fully discussed a month before and that there was no need for an inquiry. At this point Gorst intervened. He thought the House had failed to dispose of the grievances of Ceylon and failed to understand them. It was 'ridiculous' to say that the matter had been fully discussed before, because only four members had taken part in that last debate. Further, the Under Secretary for the Colonies and the member for Oxford (Cardwell) had 'misconceived the real ground for complaint'. He ended by saying that the House took no interest in colonial matters and that some machinery should be devised for effectively controlling the expenditure in this field.[26] If Gorst had intended to try to lay the blame for this state of affairs on Adderley he seemed to have succeeded.

Disraeli had been listening to this debate without saying anything, and presumably sphinx-like as ever. Gorst's energy and independence, however, must have struck a chord with him, or maybe caused him to recollect his own early rather rebellious days in parliament when he was trying to make a name for himself. At any rate after Gorst had sat down, Spencer Walpole, the Home Secretary no less, came round to his seat and remarked: 'I thought you would like to know that Mr Disraeli was extremely pleased with your smart attack on Mr Adderley.' The appreciation was as unexpected as it was unconventional, but this extraordinary incident gave Gorst great encouragement.[27]

By the middle of 1868 the Conservatives had run their course. Gladstone now declared that the time had come to disestablish the Church of Ireland and carried a resolution to that effect. The Conservatives were opposed to this policy and Disraeli announced he would dissolve the House in the autumn when the new voters' register would be ready.

On the hustings in November Gorst, standing again for Cambridge, referred to the Reform Act stating that he did not approve of all that was in the measure. This created 'uproar' among his audience. The party to which he belonged, he went on, 'deserves the credit and I do not claim to share in that credit'.[28] At least he was being consistent as well as honest. But the subject about which he was clearly most passionate and on which he wanted to stand or fall was the question of the Irish Church. He was utterly opposed to disestablishment, seeing it as being a first step down the road to sundering the union between Ireland and Britain. The Conservatives did badly in the election, and Gorst, bottom of his poll, lost his hard-won seat.

It is not surprising that during his quite short spell as an MP Gorst did not make any special impact on the House, except for once attracting the attention of Disraeli. The historian J. R. Vincent sees Gorst at this time as a 'convinced anti-democrat' with his attitude to the franchise.[29] His 'reactionary' phase did not last long for his ideas were to change under the influence of Disraeli. Also he came to realise that the extension of the franchise to the urban working class would give the Conservatives an opportunity to gain new voters. Gorst was always to regard himself as an independent Conservative. His views, as we shall see, moved inexorably during his career from right to left. As a progressive Conservative he began, aged 55, to devote much energy to campaigning for social reforms and improving the condition of the people. Disillusioned by the failure of the Conservatives to act, he eventually became a Liberal.

And what, during these last five years, of Mary? She too had been very busy. In the period she had borne her husband three more children. Violet was born in January 1865, although she would not live to see her eighth birthday. Then Hylda, the author's grandmother, was born in 1867 to be followed the next year by Harold, born just after John Gorst had lost his parliamentary seat. The family continued to live in London, moving in 1868 from Tooting to Kensington. Once John took a house for some months in Worthing so they could all benefit from the bracing Channel air. While there is information on record about John the budding politician, on John the family man with a wife and five children, hardly a word has been handed down. There is, though, more than a sneaking suspicion that he preferred the Commons to the joys of his hearth and home.

NOTES

1. MK, 11. The book runs to some 100,000 words. Unfortunately it lacks an index, but such is its stature that it was reprinted in 1974, thereby reflecting the continuing significance of Gorst's contribution to the development of New Zealand. Indeed to this day there are roads named after him in Auckland and Te Awamutu, and at the latter a House at the local school also bears his name. The historian Keith Sinclair regarded *The Maori King* as a valuable secondary source when he wrote his *Origins of the Maori Wars*.
2. MK, 10, 60, 65, 79.
3. Ibid., 403–7.
4. *Macmillans* (periodical), June 1865, 168–75.
5. H. J. Hanham, *Elections and Party Management*, London, Longman, 1959, 64, 263, 268.
6. *The Hastings and St Leonards News*, 23 June 1865.
7. Ibid., 9 June 1865.
8. Ibid., 16 June 1865.

9. Ibid., 7 July 1865.
10. *Cambridge Chronicle*, 21 Apr. 1866.
11. Ibid.
12. 3 PD 185, 12 Feb. 1867, 282.
13. Ibid., 15 Mar. 1867, 1932.
14. L. Woodward, *The Age of Reform 1815–70*, Oxford, Oxford University Press, 1979, 511; Clark, *Making of Victorian England*, 39.
15. 3 PD 186, 20 Mar. 1867, 225.
16. *Cambridge Chronicle*, 4 May 1867; H. E. Gorst, *The Earl of Beaconsfield*, 127.
17. 3 PD 187, 4 June 1867, 1598.
18. Ibid., 188, 5 July 1867, 1073.
19. Ibid., 15 July 1867, 1557.
20. Hanham, *Elections and Party Management*, 105–7; R. T. Mackenzie, *British Political Parties*, London, Heinemann, 1963, 147.
21. R. Shannon, *The Age of Disraeli 1868–1881*, London, Longman, 1992, 20–1.
22. Minutes of National Union of Conservative and Constitutional Associations, 12 Nov. 1867.
23. Ibid.
24. E. Clarke, *The Story of My Life*, London, John Murray, 1919, 96–8.
25. 3 PD 190, 20 Mar. 1868, 2021.
26. 3 PD 191, 20 Apr. 1868, 978.
27. FP, 31.
28. *Cambridge Chronicle*, 21 Nov. 1868.
29. J. R. Vincent, '"A Sort of Second Rate Australia": A Note on Gorst and Democracy 1865–8', *Historical Studies (Australia and New Zealand)*, 15, 1973, 539–44.

7

Summoned by Disraeli

The Conservatives' cries of 'no Popery' and 'Church and State' had not carried the day with the electorate, and Gorst was now out of parliament. With his growing feel for the political scene, he may not have been surprised by the Liberals' victory. However the size of its margin – they gained a majority of 112 – must have been unexpected by most people. Oddly enough, Gorst had told the electors of Cambridge that it would not be a 'source of great mortification' should he be rejected by them.[1] Nonetheless he had become infected by the political bug and would make a come-back as soon as an opportunity arose; as it was he would have to wait over six years. Then he would sit continuously in the House of Commons for 30 years.

For the time being Gorst returned to his practice at the Bar. But he continued to have other irons in the fire. He kept his political hand in with his work as secretary for the London and Westminster Conservative Association where 'his immense capacity for organisation was of the greatest value'. This association, which later changed its name to the Metropolitan Conservative Alliance, had valuable links with many other Conservative associations and was influential in the party.[2]

By the end of 1869, with his developing social conscience, he had become interested in the work of the newly founded Society for Organising Charitable Relief and Repressing Mendicity (COS for short). In November of that year he was elected to its Council, on which he then served for a number of years. London in the 1860s was a city, in places, of much poverty and degradation, and home to an army of beggars. The COS saw its committee as being 'in the ultimate resort sources of relief for cases that cannot be properly dealt with by any other agency'. In cases of destitution bread might be given to a starving applicant but, unbelievably, had to be eaten in the presence of the charity's officer.[3] The COS also aimed to maintain the family as the basic unit in the community, as it still does today under its present name of the Family Welfare Association. In 1870 the COS was trying to do something about the high level of unemployment and founded an employment enquiry office in Greek Street, Soho – in effect the country's first labour exchange.

In October 1870 Gorst wrote from Lancashire to C. B. P. Bosanquet who was to be the COS's first general secretary. By this time Gorst was a local secretary of the COS. In his letter Gorst regretted that various plans for the COS's committee were to be decided before his return to London. He then urged Bosanquet not to employ in the office two particular women, Miss D and Miss M, both of whom he thought 'impractical', adding they would do 'more harm than good'. There quickly followed another letter with a more urgent tone:

> In every executive there must be subordination; if two men ride a horse one must ride behind … [Miss D and Miss M] must do as they are bid. I am quite ready to resign at any moment although there is not the same reason for my resignation now that there was in the Spring. All I shall stick out for is so much subordination on the part of the ladies as appears to me essential to the due working of the office. If the committee won't give me proper authority I won't be secretary.[4]

As we shall see Gorst had already acquired in the spring a demanding administrative post in the political field, and this is what he is presumably alluding to in his letter.

Besides his work for the COS, Gorst also became a Poor Law guardian. The COS and the Poor Law guardians had different functions in the relief of distress. Broadly, the COS undertook inquiries into the causes of poverty and publicised its findings. Subsequently the charity played a prominent part in promoting legislation to reform the Poor Law. *Per contra*, the guardians administered locally the system set up by the state and had as well a central supervisory role. Gorst clearly wanted to have a foot in both camps. Seeing how the infamous workhouses were run, he rightly, no doubt, estimated that he would be better placed to assist the COS in its reforming aims.

There was one other revealing slant on Gorst's activities, mentioned by Sir George Grey, the former governor of New Zealand, who had been in England trying, unsuccessfully, to enter parliament in a by-election. Grey 'encountered his old friend' John Gorst conducting evening classes in the slums of Lambeth.[5] Here was Gorst again teaching, this time to the most underprivileged in the community. Gorst's association with COS and his work in Lambeth must have opened his eyes, if indeed that was necessary, to the needs of the poorest classes.

The Conservative Party, in the meantime, was licking its electoral wounds as a result of its defeat at the hands of the Liberals, but not doing very much about it. The National Union was not prospering and indeed was becoming somewhat moribund. For example in 1868 only seven people attended its annual conference. Disraeli himself, now freed from the toils of office, had decided to the detriment of his political work to write another novel. This he did in secret all through 1869. In May the following year *Lothian*, a thriller involving a Fenian conspiracy, was published and was an instant success.

Once he had got his new novel out of the way, Disraeli turned his attention to the question of party organisation which was in urgent need of reform. For many years the Carlton Club had been in effect the Conservative Party headquarters. The party's principal agent, Markham Spofforth, was a partner in a firm of London solicitors, Baxter, Rose, Norton and Co. For 15 years this firm had been entrusted by Disraeli with running the affairs of the party, and employed for the task an army of clerks. The firm had benefited from its work before the courts, hearing petitions regarding disputed elections and related matters. There was now some criticism of Spofforth's general management of party affairs; also unfavourable comparisons were being made with the Liberals who some years before had formed what was in effect a central party organisation. On Spofforth's retirement Disraeli began to look around for an ambitious young Conservative who would be willing to devote his time to working out a scheme for reorganising the party.[6]

On 2 April 1870, Gerard Noel, the Conservative Party Chief Whip, wrote to Disraeli asking him for his 'opinion of Mr Gorst as Spofforth's successor'. A few days later Noel was telling Disraeli that he thought Gorst had the necessary qualities for the job: 'he is a Gentleman with a good manner, an excellent temper . . . and is also very energetic in all he undertakes'. On 22 April Noel reported back to Disraeli that he had seen Gorst who, he thought, would take Spofforth's place. The only thing apparently that made him hold back was the idea of giving up the House of Commons for some time.[7] In the event Gorst accepted the post but, slightly surprisingly, refused the salary offered. This may have had something to do with his taking the job part-time. Also thinking about his practice at the Bar he may have felt – and this would be in line with his character – that he would be more independent and have more freedom of action if he were unpaid. In fact so busy did he become, at least in the first years he worked as principal agent, that his legal work was neglected.

From the information available, which is sparse, it looks as if Gorst was talent-spotted for this party job, and that he did not, as he had once done in New Zealand, offer his services. He would almost certainly have preferred to find and win another seat in Parliament than become a party administrator, although he saw the new post as offering him an avenue of political advancement which he would do all he could to exploit.

The party did not, as far as is known, give Gorst any special mandate on his duties or on how he was to reorganise the party. But what was most wanted, Disraeli told his new manager, was that every constituency should have a candidate ready to fight an election.[8] This, then, was a priority facing Gorst. Another was to find an office. In due course he and his staff moved into new premises at 53 Parliament Street, Westminster, which would become known as Conservative Central Office.

In the constituencies Gorst found the position highly unsatisfactory. With a few exceptions such as in the enlightened manufacturing centres in Lancashire there was no permanent local party organisation. When an election took place a paid secretary or agent, often a solicitor, had to be found together with paid canvassers to help obtain the votes. Afterwards this *ad hoc* arrangement was discontinued. Parliamentary candidates had always been selected by Spofforth and his firm, to whom someone interested in standing in the Conservative cause would apply. The candidate obtained the backing of the Chief Whip and then presented himself at the constituency which had little or no say in the selection process. This Gorst changed so that the constituency was made as far as possible to choose its own candidate from an approved list maintained by Central Office. The choice was made easier because emphasis was placed on the candidate's background so as to facilitate matching the candidate to the constituency.

The county constituencies, being in the hands of big landowners, country gentlemen and superior farmers, caused the party little trouble, for they mainly voted Conservative. But the boroughs, at least the larger ones, and municipalities were often Radical, and therefore had to be fought, as was the custom, with bribery. This, though, was not Gorst's way. He insisted that Central Office steered well clear of anything to do with bribery.[9] Gorst himself would later take a strong stand in parliament in trying to stamp out corrupt electoral practices.

Gorst told Noel within a few months of taking his new post that 'we shall never attain stable political power till the boroughs are conquered'.[10] It was in the boroughs, especially the larger ones, that he felt the next election would be won or lost, and so it was here that another priority task faced him. The principle on which Gorst and his team worked, as he was in due course to remind Disraeli, was:

> to find out in each borough the natural political leaders to evoke their zeal and active co-operation and throw upon them the responsibility of selecting their own candidates and organising their own machinery. We helped but never interfered.[11]

The practice was to set up party committees in the towns and cities and to a lesser extent in the counties. All this involved Gorst in much travel visiting constituencies. He was ably supported by Major the Hon. Charles Keith-Falconer, who had been secretary of the National Conservative Registration Association, a body which had a responsibility for overseeing the registration of electors and which canvassd during elections. The Association also managed elections through a system of ward managers who had been highly successful in contested elections. The two men spent some time in Scotland trying to overcome the prevalent feeling of defeatism there, with the result that Conservative morale improved and some gains were made in the next general election.[12] Once set up, the local committees grew into permanent Conservative associations. When constituencies were sluggish then it was up to Central Office to stir them up into taking action.

Central Office itself under Gorst's methodical leadership became a repository of political information and data vital to the party's proper functioning. Apart from the list of candidates, this included in course of time lists of all Conservative associations and their chairmen, records on the registration of voters and the results of revisions made in registration courts, draft model rules for local associations, publications and leaflets for distribution, statistics about parliamentary and municipal elections, and relevant information about forthcoming parliamentary Bills. Inquiries from all over the country on key political matters were dealt with and answered by Gorst's staff.[13] All this sounds dull stuff. But it was vital for the proper functioning of party electoral machinery.

Disraeli gave Gorst a fairly free hand in carrying out his reorganisation. Gorst for his part kept his chief in the picture, often with a wealth of detail about personalities, issues and party prospects in individual constituencies, seeking his advice as necessary. The new system was tested to some extent in by-elections, in which Disraeli took an especially keen interest. When one was lost he wanted to be fully informed of the reasons for the defeat. There was in September 1871 a success in Truro prompting Disraeli to write a letter to Gorst stating the 'great victory ... is entirely owing to your energy'.[14] Moreover, Disraeli had told his young lieutenant early on in his spell at Central Office that if the party came into power 'you can look with certainty for some substantial gratification of your laudable ambition'.[15] Gorst was to remember these encouraging words from his chief.

In contrast to Disraeli's keen interest in following what was going on in Central Office, other leading Conservatives disliked the new policies and held back from assisting Gorst. According to Gorst's journalist son Harold, the only ones to help were Lord Cairns, the future Lord Chancellor, the successive Chief Whips Colonel Taylor and Gerard Noel, and to an extent Lord Derby. 'The rest of the party', wrote Harold Gorst, 'held aloof under the impression that the Conservatives were hopelessly defeated for many years to come'.[16] This apparent lack of interest on the part of much of the leadership and the hostility often shown by the squirearchy could not have made life easy for Gorst.

There was, Gorst found, some duplication of effort going on between his Metropolitan Conservative Alliance and the National Union. Leonard Sedgwick, the secretary of the latter which mainly had been used in the 1868 election to distribute electoral literature, was also in correspondence with local associations and agents asking the same kinds of questions as Gorst. This was not calculated to create confidence in party headquarters. Happily the problem was resolved with Sedgwick's retirement in 1871; his place was taken by Gorst and Keith-Falconer who became joint honorary secretaries of the National Union, the offices of which were then transferred to the premises of Central Office at 53 Parliament Street. For the next few years Central Office and the National Union, their identities being to all intents and purposes merged, worked in close harmony. This arrangement, importantly for Gorst, ensured a measure of discreet control by Central Office over local associations. For a time Gorst and Keith-Falconer also worked together as editors of the Conservative Central Press Association which acted, in effect, as a Conservative news agency for provincial newspapers. This association was formerly a business in the Strand purchased by the party in 1871.[17]

The original idea, going back to 1867, was to foster Conservative working men's associations and clubs, and to encourage them to affiliate to the National Union. While Gorst continued to pay close attention to the need to attract the urban working-class voter to the fold, the National Union became in due course and at Disraeli's instigation a federation of *all* local Conservative associations and not just of those run by working men.

The growing number of these associations thus affiliated bears witness to the combined efforts made both locally and by Central Office. For instance the figure of 289 associations in 1871 had risen to 420 in early 1873. When Gorst reported this to Disraeli, he was able to state that 69 new associations had been founded in 1872 and that the great majority of all associations were in good working order. In 1874, the year of the next general election, the number was 472, no less than 150 being working men's associations.[18]

Gorst had long been trying to persuade Disraeli to visit Lancashire where support for the Conservatives was well founded, particularly among the working class. Thus he wrote to Disraeli as early as December 1870 to say the desire for a visit was 'strong and universal'. Moreover, in the north of the county, he continued, the men who had helped to carry the boroughs there wanted a working men's meeting in Blackburn or Preston because

> they want to see and hear you and they want you to see the newly enfranchised electors of your own creation. Amongst them at least you would receive genuine thanks for the Reform Bill of 1867 and in their quaint and old-fashioned way, with guilds and strange customs and medieval ceremonies, they would give you a reception that would I think please you.[19]

There was logic in what Gorst was suggesting. At the same time he would have seen that a successful visit would be a feather in his cap. Eventually as a result of pressure from the constituency associations and of Gorst's own efforts, Disraeli paid a visit to Lancashire in April 1872. This was unusual because leaders of political parties, perhaps with the exception of Gladstone, were not then accustomed to delivering important speeches outside parliament or their constituencies.

Gorst played an essential part in making arrangements for the visit, and provided Disraeli with detailed speaker's notes in respect of the different constituencies and the local party officers to be encountered. In Oldham, for instance, Gorst noted that most employers were radical: 'The borough is organised by the workmen themselves who have about 20 most admirable ward associations. Almost every man in the register is canvassed and his politics known... ' Disraeli saw that the visit was very much Gorst's work for on the back of a hostile letter telling him not to come to Lancashire he had scribbled: 'This is not agreeable – what will Gorst say?'[20]

The climax of the visit came on 3 April when Disraeli addressed a vast audience collected together by the National Union in the Free Trade Hall in Manchester. Fortified by brandy, Disraeli made a fiery speech and kept going for no less than three and a quarter hours, presenting the Conservatives as a party having a broad-based appeal to the working class on the one hand as well as to the forces of property on the other. The occasion has been described by one of Disraeli's biographers as being 'brilliantly stage-managed' by Gorst.[21] The Manchester meeting was followed by another huge rally, also under the auspices of the National Union, at the Crystal Palace in London. This time the organisation was in the hands of Keith-Falconer to whom Gorst, in a letter to Disraeli, later paid a handsome tribute.[22] This rally was the occasion when Disraeli said the Tory party was nothing unless it was a national party and that it was a party formed of all the numerous classes of the realm including the working class. These two successful mass meetings helped to consolidate Disraeli's position as leader of the party, for there had been some murmuring in high places against him and his direction of affairs.

Gorst would have benefited to an extent from these successes because he had hitched his wagon to Disraeli's star and, in so doing, had come under his chief's magic spell. That a man from a non-traditional Tory background and without family influence could have reached the top of the 'greasy pole' must have been a source of inspiration to Gorst. Disraeli's political beliefs were essentially free of doctrine. One of his strongest themes, that the Conservative Party was a national one pledged to defend the great institutions of the country such as the monarchy, the church, parliament and the people in all their guises, appealed to Gorst. In addition there were two particular manifestations of Disraeli's programme which impressed Gorst. One was his chief's efforts to rebuild the Conservative Party machine along, as Gorst perceived it, democratic lines with all classes, including working men, represented in the process. The other was the importance apparently attached to social progress, a principle to be revealed in fuller measure in 1875 when Disraeli's government introduced a number of far-reaching social and welfare reforms. Gorst shared in the one, and became in due course convinced about the need for the other.

A decade later, Disraeli's principles were more fully manifested through the promotion by Gorst and Lord Randolph Churchill of the concept of what became known as Tory democracy. Undoubtedly the years Gorst spent at Central Office when he was close to Disraeli were critical to the evolution of his own pragmatic political philosophy, and contributed to his emergence as a more liberal kind of Conservative than he had been when MP for Cambridge.

Inevitably there were problems and sometimes friction between Gorst and the party leaders. Gorst was not always tactful and, with his strong personality, wanted his way. One difficulty arose after Gorst, against his will, had been persuaded by Noel to act as the party's official political contact with the *Standard*, a newspaper founded as a Tory evening paper in 1821 and relaunched in the 1860s as a morning daily, becoming a competitor to *The Times*. It survives today as *The Evening Standard*. When, during the ministerial crisis of 1873, Gladstone temporarily resigned, Gorst's guidance to the paper – in the absence of any line given to him by the party leadership – was that the Conservatives would be willing to take office. This was, unfortunately for Gorst, not so (Disraeli was too canny to accept office with what would have been a minority government). The *Standard* was disturbed to be given an incorrect steer by the Conservative Party's principal agent. Gorst was obliged to apologise to Montague Corry, Disraeli's close friend and private secretary.[23] The *Standard* could not have been too troubled by Gorst's error, for he was to become one of the paper's leader-writers.

The same problem arose in February 1874 when Gorst was denied information given to *The Times* about Lord Salisbury's willingness to take office under Disraeli, a subject of immense interest in the political world. Salisbury, having resigned from the Cabinet in 1867 over franchise reform, was now becoming a formidable figure on the right of the party. Again Gorst wrote to Corry. He was clearly put out, and asked if in future he could be given as much information as was given to other papers or, say, to *The Times*. He claimed no 'right to exceptional treatment' but wished to act with the *Standard*'s proprietor in 'a manner consistent with my own honour'.[24] It was fairly obvious that the party would choose whichever newspaper it desired to provide the public with important political information but Gorst thought the channel should be the *Standard* although, interestingly, he did not write direct to Disraeli about it. The truth is that Gorst's position as principal agent did not admit him to the inner counsels of the party. In fact he never quite overcame the suspicion in which he was held by many party grandees and by the whips. The value of his energetic efforts to secure the votes of working- and middle-class voters were not always appreciated by the landed interest, whose views he was not sufficiently prepared to conciliate.

In 1873 the Conservatives won a series of striking victories, especially in Lancashire, in the municipal elections. Professor Hanham has drawn attention to the importance of municipal elections which was 'fully recognised by the pioneers of party reorganisation in the seventies, John Gorst and Joseph Chamberlain ...'[25] He goes on to note how Gorst 'carefully collected' the results of the 1873 municipal elections and urged party leaders to take a greater interest in these elections which he considered provided a barometer of changing public opinion. Unfortunately Gorst's warnings, including one made specifically to Disraeli after he had left his position as principal agent,[26] went unheeded, and the party steadily lost ground in municipal elections from 1874 onwards.

As a propagandist, a job he relished, Gorst prepared various political pamphlets and surveys of current and previous parliamentary sessions. He told Disraeli at the end of the summer in 1873 that he would have ready a handbook for Conservative candidates for use at the next general election.[27] This must have been one of the first such handbooks produced.

Litigation about elections, usually involving the Reform Act 1867 and to a lesser extent the Ballot Act 1872, which introduced the secret vote, gave Gorst timely work as a barrister in the courts. With his party political work ensuring practical experience of problems in the field, he seemed ideally placed to handle these kinds of cases, which were not in short supply. Our knowledge of them is derived from reported cases heard on appeal in London from decisions of revising barristers in the provinces. Electoral petitions, often highly technical, might come of course from anywhere. Thus Gorst appeared as counsel when the question arose before three Judges of the Court of Common Pleas as to whether a particular corporation life tenant in Stafford was entitled to vote. The same sort of question arose in Lancashire where there was an objection to a minister, living in a parsonage and entitled to pew rents, being on the register of voters. A petitioner in Barnstaple claimed to be the winner of a municipal election, alleging he was entitled to a greater number of votes than those given him, and so on. These were not the kinds of cases which were likely to grab newspaper headlines, but they were often heard before senior judges and helped Gorst to earn a living.

The next general election came sooner than was expected (in those days the life of a parliament lasted for up to seven years). Gladstone suddenly decided to dissolve parliament at the end of January 1874, choosing as his main platform a proposal to abolish income tax. Gorst liked being at the centre of affairs. As soon as he heard about the dissolution he hurried off to tell Disraeli, finding him at his house 'coming down to breakfast in his dressing gown'. Disraeli at once issued Gorst with instructions: 'Find out where Cairns and Derby are and get them to come and see me immediately ... you need not trouble anyone else unless you want help in the elections. In that case send for Taylor.'[28] These were the kinds of instruction he liked. He was to get on with the matter in hand and to use his own initiative. In the event he did have the help of an election committee of whips and party managers similar to that set up for the 1868 election.[29]

This time the party succeeded in fielding far more candidates than in any previous election. In 1868 no fewer than 213 Liberals were unopposed. Now the figure was reduced to 150.[30] On the eve of the general election Gorst made an estimate of what the results might be, which showed the Conservatives with a majority of 50. When this was produced at the Carlton Club it was greeted with a roar of derision. The prophetic paper was christened 'Gorst's Champagne Estimates', the authorities at the club declaring the estimate could only have been drawn up after liberal libations of the wine! So Gorst, to mollify his critics, cut the number to 25. Another source has Gorst predicting an overall majority of just three.[31]

At the polls the Conservatives won a resounding victory, gaining 352 seats to the Liberals 243, with 57 seats going to Irish 'Home Rulers'. In the all-important middle-sized boroughs where Central Office and the party organisation elsewhere had put in a great effort, the Conservatives won 23 seats which had been Liberal in 1868, thereby contributing notably to the swing against the government. Despite this great achievement the Conservatives had in fact won a smaller share of the popular vote than the Liberals: 1.09 million to 1.28 million.[32]

The general opinion of historians is that for this victory Disraeli owed a significant debt to Gorst and his reorganised party machine. Gorst himself felt he had made a signal contribution and therefore looked forward to receiving his reward from the party for what he had achieved.

NOTES

1.　*Cambridge Chronicle* (supplement), Nov. 1868.
2.　H. Raikes, *The Life and Letters of Henry Cecil Raikes*, London, Macmillan, 1898, 63; R. Blake, *The Conservative Party from Peel to Churchill*, London, Arrow, 1970, 145; Shannon, *Age of Disraeli*, 23, 118 .
3.　Minutes of COS council, 18 Jan. 1870.
4.　*Bosanquet Papers*, MS Autogr. d 41, Gorst (G)–Bosanquet, 18 Oct. 1870.
5.　Rutherford, *Sir George Grey*, 584.

6. H. E. Gorst, *Earl of Beaconsfield*, London, Blackie, 1899, 125.
7. HP, 137/4, Noel–Disraeli (D)2, 14 and 22 Apr. 1870.
8. Gorst, *Earl of Beaconsfield*, 125.
9. Hanham, *Elections and Party Management*, 277.
10. HP, 137/4, G–Noel 22, Sept. 1870.
11. HP, 129/2, G–D, 3 Mar. 1878.
12. Hanham, *Elections and Election Management*, 115–16, 160–2; Shannon, *Age of Disraeli*, 15.
13. HP, 129/2, G–D, 24 Feb. 1881.
14. D–G, 15 Sept. 1871, in author's possession; also see Shannon, *Age of Disraeli*, 123–4 on results of by-elections in early 1870s.
15. FP, 32.
16. Ibid.; also see E. J. Feuchtwanger, 'J. E. Gorst and the Central Organisation of the Conservative Party 1870–1882', *Bulletin of the Institute of Historical Research*, 32 (1959), 192, who concurs but excludes Derby .
17. Blake, *The Conservative Party*; Shannon, *Age of Disraeli*, 121; HP, 129/2; G–D, 23 Sept. 1871.
18. R. Mackenzie, *British Political Parties*, 159; HP, 129/2; G–D, 12 Feb. 1873.
19. HP, 129/2, G–D, 22 Dec. 1870.
20. Feuchtwanger, 'J. E. Gorst', 199 .
21. S. Bradford, *Disraeli*, London, Grafton Books, 1985, 415.
22. HP, 129/2, G–D, 6 Feb. 1874.
23. HP, 129/2, G–Corry, 17 Mar. 1873.
24. HP, 129/2, G–Corry, 19 Feb. 1874.
25. Hanham, *Elections and Party Management*, 388.
26. HP, 129/2, G–D, 2 Dec. 1874.
27. Ibid., G-D, 11 Sept. 1873.
28. FP, 33 (Noel, the chief whip, was ill).
29. Feuchtwanger, 'J.E. Gorst', 199.
30. Blake, *The Conservative Party*, 115; Hanham, *Elections and Party Management*, 197 gives different figures.
31. W. T. Stead (ed.), 'Coming Men and Coming Questions', 310; Gorst, *Earl of Beaconsfield*, 151; also see W. Moneypenny and G. Buckle, *The Life of Benjamin Disraeli*: vol. 2, London, John Murray, 1910–20, 617; R. Blake, *Disraeli*, London, Eyre & Spottiswoode, 1966, 537 and E. J. Feuchtwanger, *Disraeli, Democracy and the Tory Party*, Oxford, Clarendon Press, 1968, 122.
32. M. Pugh, *The Making of Modern British Politics 1867–1939*, Oxford, Basil Blackwell, 1982, 45.

8

Back in Parliament

Central Office, which, as we have seen in the previous chapter, had been successful under Gorst in preparing for the general election, now faced changes after the Conservative victory. To begin with, Keith-Falconer, an important member of the party's machine, left Central Office in the early part of 1874 to become a commissioner of the Inland Revenue. Gorst wrote a letter of appreciation about his work to Disraeli. In it he said that 'Keith-Falconer shares equally with Mr Noel and myself any credit due for the organisation in the constituencies … of which you have so kindly spoken in terms of commendation.'[1] He went on to say that he and Keith-Falconer had worked for four years 'without an unpleasant word between us. I shall grievously lament the loss of a colleague who has proved himself of the highest value in our work and to whom I am most sincerely attached'.

Gorst's own contract as principal agent ended with the return of the Conservative party to power. Curiously, though, he stayed on in Central Office, still unpaid, in a somewhat anomalous position, which was to prove unsatisfactory. A few years later he was to describe it when writing to Disraeli in these terms: '… I consented at Sir W. Dyke's request out of personal regard for him to remain in a sort of undefined position until some fresh arrangement could be made.'[2] William Hart Dyke was a baronet and had just become Chief Whip; he would supervise the work of Central Office. Gorst professed, at least early on in their relationship, to get on well with him but the two men did not in the longer term achieve any real rapport. Clearly, Dyke thought Gorst came under him, a view not shared by Gorst. Dyke probably correctly felt that he needed, at least to begin with, Gorst's intimate knowledge of the party machine, and, perhaps incorrectly, felt he could control Gorst.

For Gorst the previous four years had been successful ones. Now he was to suffer a set-back, one which was to colour his attitude towards the party's hierarchy still controlled by the grandees and landed interests. It happened when a vacancy came up for a parliamentary candidate at Midhurst, a safe Conservative seat, a few months after the general election. In May, Gorst was writing to Disraeli saying 'an opportunity occurred yesterday for the fulfilment of the promise originally made to me by Noel and recently confirmed by you'. He continued by referring to the seat at Midhurst in respect of which, to his obvious disappointment, 'Dyke had offered the party interest in accordance he said with your wishes to Mr Ward Hunt for Admiral Hornby'. (Ward Hunt was First Lord of the Admiralty, and Hornby was soon to become C-in-C Mediterranean fleet.) He concluded his letter by saying that he

> would have given way in a moment to Admiral Hornby if I had been asked to do so for the good of the cause, but I think my claim to the consideration of the party should have been recognised and not ignored.[3]

We do not know what precisely Noel's promise to Gorst was but it must have been to do with smoothing Gorst's passage back to the Commons at an early date.

Gorst was certainly ambitious to be an MP again. Apparently an opportunity to stand had occurred in 1872 at the safe seat of his native Preston, but at the request of the party leaders, who probably wanted it for John Holker, a future Attorney-General, he had turned it down.[4] He now found, despite the promises of advancement made to him by Disraeli and Noel, that the party leadership was not going to be helpful in finding him a seat. Gorst was not in the mould of a phlegmatic philosopher willing to await his turn. He was an impatient man and believed he deserved early preferment for the services he had rendered the party. The negative attitude of the party towards him, as he perceived it, made him discontented.

By the end of the year this discontent is evidenced in complaining letters he wrote to Dyke and to W. H. Smith, the successful newsagent and bookseller and now Financial Secretary to the Treasury. Dyke in turn wrote an interesting letter to Disraeli about Gorst. These letters are important for they show Gorst's state of mind, and how Gorst was perceived by Dyke.

Gorst told Dyke that the party's most faithful adherents were becoming disenchanted with their leaders' handling of matters to do with patronage.[5] Nothing, Gorst insisted, was being done to reward good party work. He gave an example of a worthy barrister from North Wales who applied for a county court judgeship. He did not get it, the post going, undeservingly in Gorst's view, to a 'private friend of a member of the Cabinet'. There was quite a lot in this vein. Dyke was as unimpressed with what Gorst had to say on patronage as he was with Gorst's gloom about the results of the municipal elections. Although Gorst was ready to complain about the use of patronage by the party, this did not prevent him, as we shall see in a moment, from trying to use the system to help his own family. When he wrote to Disraeli, Dyke accused Gorst of using 'strong' and 'violent' language in his letters[6] although the truth of this assertion is not discernible from the surviving correspondence. There were two other points about Gorst which the Chief Whip made to his chief. Apparently, Gorst, citing a promise made, had been seeking help through Dyke and Smith to obtain for his – of course deserving – younger barrister brother, Tom Gorst, a Treasury post as Examiner of Bills. The historian E. J. Feuchtwanger suggests Lord Cairns, the Lord Chancellor, may have somehow been involved in raising false hopes with John Gorst about this post.[7] At any rate Dyke expostulated to Disraeli that the post of Examiner was one for a solicitor, and that Tom was a barrister, moreover 'without chambers or brief'. On a more positive note Dyke admitted that John Gorst was working cheerfully and was of great use 'with all his crotchets', and that he intended to keep on Gorst 'crotchets and all'. The word crotchets, or crotchety, applied to Gorst, has stuck, and been repeated by various writers. In the dictionary sense crotchet, a word used more then than now, is defined as a 'whimsical fancy'. The novelist Thomas Peacock clearly saw the word as being connected with odd behaviour, as in his book *Crotchet Castle* in which a number of very odd characters assemble in a country house. Somehow the term applied to Gorst has come rather to indicate a certain perverseness or prickliness.

The fact that Gorst could on occasions display a prickly side to his character is borne out by the contents of Gorst's letter to Smith. In it he complained to Smith about 'being so accustomed to the refusal of every request I make to the Conservative government whether on political or personal grounds, I am neither surprised nor mortified at the announcement that the promise made to me on my brother's behalf is not to be fulfilled.'[8] While unhappy about the outlook for the party he assured Smith that his own attachment to the cause remained unaffected by these disappointments.

We must here complete the saga of John Gorst's efforts on behalf of Tom. Ever persistent, a notable characteristic of the man, the older brother tried in March 1875, this time directly to the Prime Minister, to obtain for Tom the post of Clerk to the Parliament of the House of Lords. He made the point in doing so that Tom had performed services, presumably in the general election, for the party. He further told Disraeli that 'both my elder brother and I are most anxious for his advancement'[9] and that they would be grateful for favourable consideration by the party. For this post Tom's claims, whatever they might have been, were overlooked. John, displaying something of a thick skin, was still undaunted in trying to promote Tom. Eventually he was successful and in 1877 Tom was appointed Solicitor to the Commissioners of HM Woods, Forests and Land Revenues. Almost certainly the job had been secured with help from Disraeli.

Gorst often went too far in his efforts to obtain jobs for those who had served the party well. Professor Shannon sees him as having assumed 'an almost emblematic role as a kind of shop steward of the deprived Conservative classes'. For instance, Gorst had appealed to Disraeli for a post for the Chairman of the Conservative association at Cambridge. He confessed that he could not see how the party could be kept together unless '… those who have made sacrifices for the cause while in adversity are to share in the advantages of success'. Disraeli told Corry, his secretary, that he had 'snubbed' Gorst in replying to his 'insolent epistle', although he let him down gently.[10]

Gorst continued to correspond with Disraeli, so far as we can tell, fairly regularly, even though he was not naturally as close to his chief as he had been when principal agent. Gorst was worried, he told Disraeli in December 1874, that 'in the boroughs we are grievously deficient of Tory leaders' and that electors once having made their point at the polls in 1874 against a government that had become unpopular would now return to their former allegiance. Pessimistically Gorst considered little had been done to strengthen Conservative supporters in the boroughs and much to alienate them. For instance he had hoped that, following the example of the opposition, the power and patronage which the possession of office had given the party might have been used to create a permanent Tory faction. Dyke, he believed, was of the same opinion although here he was wide of the mark. Gorst's judgement was not always reliable as far as other people and their opinions were concerned. At least, though, Gorst was right in his general assessment of the political situation and of the party's need to foster middle-class leadership as well as working-class support. Sadly for the party he was ignored.

Nonetheless there was better news for Gorst round the corner. Early in 1875 he was adopted as Conservative Party candidate in a by-election at Chatham, where the sitting member, Admiral Sir George Elliot, was standing down on being appointed Commander-in-Chief Portsmouth. As might be expected, Gorst had made much play during the campaign with the importance he attached to the dockyard and its workers, and reminded his audiences how the Prime Minister saw the improved condition of the working classes as one of his cardinal aims. If returned to support the government, Gorst warned that he would always be sufficiently independent to say what he thought. Gorst was elected on 16 February by 215 votes out of a poll of 4,131[11] and so was able to get back into the House of Commons, only just over a year after the general election. Gorst's son Harold was to comment, maybe echoing his father, that influential members of the party had done their best to prevent Gorst from re-entering Parliament and his success at Chatham was accomplished 'in spite of active opposition at headquarters'.[12]

Gorst found some notable changes in the House since he had been there six years before. For one thing the Conservatives had a large working majority. And then Gladstone had retired – temporarily as it turned out – as leader of the Liberals, his place being taken by Lord Hartington. The latter would become in due course the eighth Duke of Devonshire, and, having effectively changed sides over Irish Home Rule, would in 1895 be Gorst's immediate chief. One thing that had not changed was the kind of men of whom the Conservative leadership was composed. The Prime Minister had chosen as members of his Cabinet seven men who were peers or sons of peers, and four commoners, thus reflecting the influence still wielded by Tory grandees.

Coinciding with Gorst's arrival in the Commons came a flurry of legislation involving domestic reform introduced by the Home Secretary, R. A. Cross, a lawyer, who was born near Preston and whose family had once been tanners. For instance there were passed: a Conspiracy and Protection of Property Act, which allowed among other things peaceful picketing; an Artisans' and Labourers' Dwellings Improvement Act giving local authorities powers to pull down slums; a consolidating Public Health Act, and an Employers and Workmen Act, which decriminalised most breaches of contract. Except for some minor contributions on the last-named measure, Gorst did not speak on these matters. But then he had other things on his mind. He was now the member for a constituency which contained a great naval dockyard. This turned his energies and interest at once to matters naval and maritime.

For a long period after the intense activity of the Napoleonic wars the navy had been in a state of neglect. With no other country threatening the command of the seas there had been a reduction in the navy's strength while its ship design and equipment had stagnated. The launching in 1858 of the French battleship *La Gloire*, the world's first iron-clad, sounded alarm bells in the conservative Admiralty, and slowly the long process of changing from wood to iron and from sail to steam was begun. Quite apart from the navy's ships, the state of its personnel had been for some time a cause of concern. A Select Committee of the House of Commons had in 1863 considered the question of naval promotion and retirement. Many senior officers were far too old and had to be compulsorily retired. Problems over the breakdown of discipline which had led to desertion, riots and near mutiny had to be addressed. Action had to be taken to remedy discontent among engineers. The first Naval Discipline Act was passed in 1861 and, as a result, flogging was reduced. Monthly pay was introduced and leave was granted on a more reasonable basis. Despite improvements and the opening in 1873 of the Royal Naval College at Greenwich, Oscar Parkes, the naval architect and writer, has called the decade 1872–82 the 'Dark Ages of the Victorian Navy'.

There was therefore plenty for Gorst to do as a dockyard MP, and he lost no time in entering the parliamentary fray. Within three weeks of winning his seat he had put down a question about the safety and design of HMS *Volage* following an accident she suffered. This corvette had taken a party of scientists to the Kerguelen, a plateau in a remote part of the Indian Ocean, to observe the transit of Venus. The seas were partly uncharted, and bumping over a shoal *Volage* had damaged her hull. Design problems of naval ships were still a matter of public concern after the disaster in 1870 to the new 7,000-ton battleship HMS *Captain*. This ship, constructed with an iron hull, had been advertised as the warship of the future but this did not stop it from tragically foundering during trials in the Bay of Biscay with a huge loss of life, which included the son of the First Lord of the Admiralty. Its design was accepted as being a failure. Gorst was determined to be vigilant in this field.

The same day as his question on the *Volage* was answered (the First Lord, Ward Hunt, was quite satisfied with the safety and design of the ship) he was up on his feet making a long speech on the unsatisfactory promotion prospects of officers in the marine corps.[13] In the next five months of the parliamentary session that year he asked questions or made speeches in the House on: discontent among dockyard workers, uncompleted building work in the dockyard, the conditions of service in the navy of engine-room artificers, improving the methods of paying merchant seamen, why marine light infantry officers were paid less than marine artillery officers, and the navy estimates. To many of these matters he would return again and again, never accepting what he saw to be an unsatisfactory answer. Whether grievances related to officers, NCOs or ratings, or to the navy or merchant marine, seemed to matter little to him provided there was a case to answer.

In particular he spoke frequently during the passage over the next two years of the Merchant Shipping Bill, one of the purposes of which was to attempt the regulation of over-loaded and over-insured ships, which endangered seamen's lives. Gorst was of course very much on the side of the angry Radical Samuel Plimsoll, who gave his name to the Plimsoll line, the load line painted on the side of a ship indicating the limit of submergence allowed by law.

But Gorst did not concentrate exclusively on naval and maritime matters. In May 1875 he drew attention to grievances of the ratepayers which had come to light in Lancashire (a county which always drew the man's sympathies) and the effect of this on the administration of the criminal law. Apparently, Treasury officials had disallowed expenses incurred by witnesses in prosecution cases at Quarter Sessions in the county; these expenses would therefore fall on ratepayers. This, so argued Gorst, would cause magistrates in future to send cases to assizes, where the Treasury met the full cost of prosecution. The result would be, perfectly logically if Gorst was correct in his contention, that assizes would become overburdened by work. He did not fail to point out that a judge had advised that these Treasury disallowances were anyhow illegal. Gorst must have been somewhat gratified to provoke the Chancellor of the Exchequer, Sir Stafford Northcote, into admitting in reply that the Treasury up to 1874 might well have been acting illegally.

Gorst would not leave this question alone. Some weeks later, on 6 July, in a debate on the Civil Service estimates – for many, a boring subject, but for Gorst a fruitful field to be ruthlessly exploited – he brought a motion under the heading 'law and justice' to reduce the total amount to be voted (some £131,000) by the paltry sum of £3,874. This was the amount set aside for the salaries and expenses of Examiners of Criminal Law Accounts. As the Treasury, Gorst submitted, had now ended the arbitrary way these Examiners disallowed expenses, these officers no longer had a function to perform. He could not in addition stop himself from referring to the problems of ratepayers in Lancashire which he had highlighted the previous May. 'The cost of justice', he declared, 'was an imperial affair and should be defrayed by the imperial exchequer.'[14] The reader may be forgiven for imagining that these phrases were delivered in ringing tones. Not so. Gorst was never a thunderer. For he was developing, as his parliamentary style, a cool, quietly spoken manner, cutting if necessary, but not ranting. He believed on this occasion he was saving the country £4,000 odd. So he divided the House – presumably to the irritation of the Conservatives – but without success: the ayes had 39 and the noes 266. Two years later he returned to this very subject in trying to get counties and boroughs repaid from the Exchequer for the cost of criminal prosecutions.

As his parliamentary career developed so did Gorst's ability to surprise the House from time to time with his occasional quirky interventions and rather deadpan sense of humour. We may give just two examples. The first occurred late in the 1875 session when he asked the First Commissioner of Works whether his attention had been directed to the dilapidated condition of the statue of Queen Anne opposite St Paul's cathedral and, further, who was responsible for keeping the statue in a proper state of repair.[15] Lord Henry Lennox, the minister concerned, was unable – probably to Gorst's delight – to answer the question fully. To restore the statue, he said, would cost around £5–6,000. But no one knew, he was forced to admit, who had put the statue there or whether 'she' had ever been repaired. In any case there were no funds available for repairs and no one claimed ownership. Finally, Lord Henry said, almost triumphantly, that as the statue was not within the metropolitan police district he had no power to take Her Majesty under his charge!

In 1878 Gorst referred the Home Secretary, R. A. Cross, later to be Gorst's chief at the India Office, to the case of a Mr Harman. This unfortunate man came to be arrested by the police during the Eton v. Harrow cricket match at Lords on a charge of stealing an opera glass which proved to be his own. With a series of interrogatories Gorst went on: was it not a fact that on arrest Mr Harman had been able to give most satisfactory evidence of his name, address and position? And was he not detained from Friday to Monday without being able to contact his wife and friends? And had not another gentleman, no, definitely not Mr Harman, been arrested the previous year at the same match under similar circumstances for stealing an opera glass, which turned out to be his own? And was this man not confined to bed for three or four months as a result of this experience? Further, Gorst asked the Home Secretary to cause inquiries to be made and compensation to be paid to Mr Harman, and lastly whether – adding a touch of humour – he would take steps for the future to protect those attending the Eton v. Harrow match and prevent them from being arrested and sent to prison on grounds of suspicion. The answer Cross gave was disappointing and showed no disposition to humour. No mention was made of the prisoner's sobriety, but Cross did refer to how the magistrate was struck by the prisoner's silence in court as if this explained a great deal. There were of course no grounds for compensation. On a more positive note, Mr Harman *had* been allowed to write to his wife.[16] A curious episode which must remain a minor mystery.

Towards the end of 1875 Disraeli offered Gorst a junior appointment in his government, as Under Secretary of the Local Government Board. While this was obviously a recognition of Gorst's parliamentary talents it may also have been meant as a reward for his past services at Central Office. Gorst wrote back to the Prime Minister:

> ... as I have never before contemplated such as step as giving up [my] profession and accepting a political office I hope you will not think me unreasonable in asking to postpone my answer till tomorrow in order to have the opportunity of thinking the matter over and consulting with my elder brother.[17]

The next day, 20 November, he wrote briefly to Disraeli declining the offer made.

So why did Gorst not seize the chance of getting his foot on the bottom rung of the ministerial ladder? Was he generally piqued by the party's treatment of him, cavalier as he perceived it, and did this offer not sufficiently make amends? On the other hand, he could scarcely have expected to be offered a more senior post. Some years later Gorst told Disraeli in a letter that he should have asked for an interview before turning down the offer. 'But then I believed that for a person like myself without social interest the acceptance of such an office meant political extinction: and I turned to the Bar as the only avenue in public life that was open to me.'[18] Some further light is shed on the matter when in July 1880 Gorst gave an explanation to W. H. Smith. If he had accepted Disraeli's offer he would, with the President of the Local Government Board, G. Schlater-Booth, also being in the Commons, have been practically 'shelved'. He had wanted a post which would not have denied him the chance, he said, of showing his own ability and which would lead to further promotion.[19]

The slight puzzle still surrounding this episode is not exactly solved by what Gorst wrote in March 1876 to Disraeli about a rumour suggesting that Colonel Stanley was to vacate the post of Secretary of the Treasury. He went straight to the point:

> If this rumour is true will you consider me in the choice of a successor to Colonel Stanley. You were good enough some years

ago to encourage me ... that the work I [did] for the Conservative Party would enable me at a future time to work in the Public Service. I am the only person engaged in the party management in 1874 to whom our access to office has brought no political advancement as yet.[20]

One might forgive Disraeli if he had retorted in answer to the last observation: 'and whose fault is that?' In fact, maybe to Gorst's private disgust, Stanley was replaced by Dyke.

A character sketch of Gorst appeared some years later in the *Review of Reviews*, a journal edited by the prominent reformer and journalist W. T. Stead who was an admirer of Gorst. The article related how just before the dissolution in 1880 Lord Beaconsfield, as Disraeli had become in 1876 when he went to the Lords, sent for Gorst, and expressed in his handsomest manner his regret that his services had been overlooked. Stead then quoted Beaconsfield as saying:

Why did you not come to see me? To remind me of your existence. It is impossible for me to keep everybody in my mind, especially when so many are pushing.[21]

Harold Gorst quotes the same story in *The Fourth Party* and has Beaconsfield adding to John Gorst '... you have been very badly treated, and I am extremely sorry for it'.

Harold Gorst also refers in his book, without giving a date, to an occasion when there was some talk in the party of a dinner for his father and 'the presentation of some plate', although nothing came of this. From the context, this idea may have been mooted soon after the Conservative election victory in early 1874.

While Gorst had certainly found his feet in the Commons, his present relationship with Central Office was drawing to a close, although it would be renewed, a shade surprisingly, some years later. W. B. Skene was made principal agent in 1876, an appointment not considered a success. Then early the following year Gorst was told by Dyke with no reason being given that, with the concurrence of party leaders, he, Gorst, had been replaced as a party electoral manager. Without much doubt this had come about on account of the steady bickering between the two men. Finally, at the end of 1877, and making the break with party administration appear complete, Gorst resigned as secretary of the National Union. Earlier there had been differences over policy between Gorst and Raikes on account of the former's wish to see the functions of the National Union expanded and also its representation broadened, proposals which Raikes was able to defeat at the Annual General Meeting.[22] When matters came to a head, Gorst at first resisted the move to get rid of him from his position as secretary. Proper notice was not apparently given him, and Northcote the Chancellor of the Exchequer had to send him a conciliatory letter, regretting that 'your feelings should have been in any way hurt'.[23] Gorst's feelings, as we are increasingly seeing, were quite easily ruffled.

At about the time of his departure from Central Office, Gorst wrote a valedictory letter to Beaconsfield giving his views on party organisation and the management of elections. He explained that he had found himself

> without power and with continually decreasing influence having little or no voice in the selection of candidates and the management of elections. I have had the misfortune to witness the whole system, to establish which so much trouble was taken, gradually fall into decay. Our organisation in 1877 is greatly inferior to what it was in 1874 … [24]

The chief cause of what Gorst described as the 'mischief' was the system of having Dyke manage elections from the Treasury. Local leaders, Gorst told Beaconsfield, had been interfered with and offended. Also money had been spent against Gorst's advice. He made some suggestions for improvements and while doing so stressed that he did not 'covet' any new position as manager for he was 'far too much engaged in other pursuits'. He warned the Prime Minister about the need for energetic remedial measures. But by now Beaconsfield had lost interest in party organisation. Furthermore, the government was showing signs of running out of steam on social legislation. In addition, the passage of government business was now being affected by the obstructionist tactics of Irish Nationalist members under Charles Parnell. Also Beaconsfield had begun to concentrate his mind on foreign and imperial affairs, such as the purchase of Suez Canal shares and making the Queen Empress of India. Later he would become enmeshed in the problems of the Balkans and attend the Congress of Berlin.

All through the 1870s Gorst saw himself in the House as, to use his own term, an independent supporter of the government, never beholden to his own front bench and with the self-appointed task of keeping them up to the mark on various maritime and colonial matters, as well as keeping a sharp eye on various aspects of public expenditure. He was always ready to challenge the government on issues which he thought needed airing. Twice he went into the lobbies with the Liberals when he believed the rights of subject peoples had been infringed or ignored. When, on the other hand, he thought the government acted fairly, he said so. For instance the Peruvians had taken into custody the crew of the British steamer *Talisman* believing them, wrongly, to be gun-running for a gang of revolutionaries. Ultimately, after representations had been made by the Minister in Lima, the crew were all released except the captain and mate. In a debate in the Commons in 1876 Gorst stated that he thought the government had acted throughout with admirable judgement.[25] Nonetheless, when there was no further news of the two imprisoned men, Gorst took up the cudgels on their behalf putting down questions in the House in April, May and June of that year.

In the same way and year, in a debate on the treatment of fugitive slaves, Gorst attacked the policy of the previous Liberal government who had reversed the traditional anti-slavery policy of the British on grounds of cost. He gave instances of several occasions when naval captains had been censured – here he pointed the finger at the late Lord Clarendon, the former Foreign Secretary – for receiving on board their ships runaway slaves seeking protection against ill-treatment from their owners. He wished to see naval officers continue to have discretion to deal with fugitive slaves on the merits of each case. The only fault he could find with the present administration was that they had been too cautious in undoing the mischief caused by their predecessors.[26]

In the celebrated *Franconia* case, a German vessel had collided with a British ship two miles off Dover. Lives had been lost. In the British courts it had been held after lengthy argument that there was no jurisdiction to try the German master for manslaughter. This Gorst felt was quite unsatisfactory and the law needed reforming since justice was not being properly administered. Therefore, with Sir Henry Drummond Wolff, with whom he was soon to be so closely associated in the Fourth Party, and C. T. Ritchie, a future Chancellor of the Exchequer, Gorst introduced a two-clause Bill to extend British jurisdiction to a distance of three miles from the coastline. In a speech moving the second reading of his Bill, Gorst went to inordinate lengths to enlighten the House on the niceties of international law, making the fundamental point that writers on international law had long held that territorial waters were part of a state's dominion, although there was a difference of opinion on the exercise of jurisdiction. History does not relate how patiently the House received

Gorst's long lecture which included 15 lines of quoted Latin from two academic authorities. Ultimately, after the intervention of Holker, the Attorney-General, Gorst agreed to drop his Bill.[27] But his aim was ultimately achieved, for the Territorial Waters Jurisdiction Act was safely passed in 1878 extending British jurisdiction in the way Gorst had desired.

The interest Gorst showed in the Pacific and its remote islands might, though perhaps mistakenly, be attributed to the fact that he had once been destined to preach the Word in Melanesia. More likely he was manifesting what he perceived to be the need for vigilance concerning the rights of all subject peoples. It was entirely in character therefore for him to support the Radical John Bright who had drawn attention in a Supply debate to 'the execution of some savages' in Fiji following an outbreak of tribal warfare there. They were guilty, it was reported, of a crime because some Fijians had taken prisoners and then eaten them. Gorst hoped the committee would insist on having further information on the execution of these 'unfortunate people' whom he accepted were undoubtedly cannibals. But he continued 'we had no right to execute men because they did what their ancestors had done for generations.'[28]

In another episode involving Pacific islanders Gorst became involved in outspoken exchanges with his friend Holker. Gorst had begun by asking the Attorney-General in January 1878 whether he was aware that the Commanding Officer of HMS *Beagle* (not the ship Darwin sailed in) had held a court on board his ship by which someone was tried for an offence not committed within Her Majesty's jurisdiction, found guilty and sentenced to death. The prisoner, a native islander, had then been executed on board the *Beagle*.[29] In his reply, arguably an inadequate one, Holker referred to the *Beagle* lying off the coast of a land – it was the island of Tanna (now part of Vanuatu) – inhabited by savages, where no law prevailed.

Dissatisfied with the government's response, Gorst moved a Resolution in August of that year that instructions should be issued to Officers commanding HM ships 'to define and regulate their authority to put persons to death not subjects of Her Majesty'. What he particularly objected to, Gorst said, was the system by which naval officers were turned into 'Judges of Assize and HM ships into a sort of itinerant gallows'.[30] What was unfortunate in this case was that the wrong man might have been tried and executed. Briefly what had happened was this. An English trader had been murdered on Tanna after a quarrel with an islander over coconuts and a woman. The navy was sent to arrest the murderer, who could not then be found. Instead they detained his brother, who, while he had witnessed the murder, had not fired the shot. Yet it was the brother who was tried, found guilty and hanged.

Sir Charles Dilke, a leading Radical, sympathised with Gorst's motion and rebuked Holker for making 'merry' at Gorst's expense. Indeed, it has been said that Holker lost his temper with Gorst during the debates over the *Beagle*, although, if this is true, it did not affect Gorst continuing to appear with the Attorney-General in prosecutions in the courts. Gorst had certainly stirred up a hornet's nest. The long debate involving three ministers of the Crown was wound up by Smith, the First Lord of the Admiralty, who regretted what had happened but refused to censure the officers involved. In the end Gorst did not press his motion to a division.[31]

While there was no sign in that year of any let-up in Gorst's pursuit of naval and maritime matters, he also participated in debates on, for instance, contagious diseases, the criminal law, customs matters, the national debt, parliamentary privilege and women's disabilities. He spoke too in 1878 on numerous occasions during the committee stage of the Factories and Workshop Bill, which sought to improve conditions in factories. Besides demonstrating a wish to protect young children in the workplace such as the neglected match-girls, he was also keen to point out, as a result of his diligent research, the anomalies in the law. Thus the minimum age at which children might begin work varied confusingly; for instance in the textile trade it was set at 10, in the coal mines 12, in many other trades it was 8, and in agriculture there was no age-limitation at all. Gorst the humanitarian was evident during the passage of the Bill. He seemed to show an equal interest in the plight of the children and in the legal technicalities of the Bill.

In the following year Gorst showed himself to be alert to a failure by the government in its handling of events in South Africa. This happened when Beaconsfield and his government ran into problems with the Zulus. Sir Bartle Frere, the new High Commissioner, was fearful of the menace posed by the Zulu military system. To Beaconsfield's dismay and contrary to official instructions, Frere, through an ultimatum disregarded by the Zulus, had committed Britain to a serious war. Lord Chelmsford, the military commander, invaded Zululand in January 1879, and there followed the disaster at Isandlwana. Surprisingly, neither Frere nor Chelmsford was recalled. In Parliament Beaconsfield defended them both. A motion of censure on the government moved at the end of March by Dilke was defeated by 60 votes, but with no thanks to Gorst, who, after making a long speech, voted with the opposition against the Conservative government.

The motion – and its precise terms were important for Gorst – was that the House 'regrets the ultimatum which was calculated to produce immediate war should have been presented to the Zulu King without authority … and that an offensive war should have been commenced without imperative and pressing necessity and adequate preparation …' This was an implicit censure of Frere. But was it also a censure of the government?

The war, Gorst began by saying, was similar to what had happened in New Zealand. He always felt 'the presence of a number of imperial troops in a colony invariably engendered a war fever'. Perhaps he was right. Gorst went on to point out that the Zulu side of the story had not been heard; similarly he had believed years before that the Maoris' story had not been told. One of the central issues of the Zulu war for Gorst had turned on the instructions – 'hesitating advice' he called it – sent out by the home government. First, as he reminded the House, the government in a despatch on 18 October had absolutely refused to send reinforcements to South Africa. Then in another despatch five weeks later the government stated that in sending more troops they were not disposed 'to furnish the means for a campaign or conquest but only for preserving the lives and properties of the colonists'. Why, asked Gorst, did not this despatch stop Frere from starting the war? He blamed the government for the second despatch which approved of what they had before disapproved.

Almost thinking aloud, and appearing to wrestle with his conscience, Gorst did not consider that the motion, if passed, would be a vote of censure on the government, although it would be one, he opined, on Frere. Yet – and this is where Gorst seemed to be wanting to have it both ways – he 'had no wish to condemn Frere'. Nonetheless he made it plain 'he wished to enter a protest against a course of action which was calculated to involve the country periodically in ignoble wars'.[32] Bravely for an ambitious politician he therefore went into the lobby with the Liberals, an act, even in those days, not calculated to endear him to his own side. Indeed, his local party were angry with him and as a result he was summoned to appear before his constituency committee at Chatham. But the reasons he gave for condemning the Zulu war found favour, particularly with working-class members of the committee, and he came out of this episode with 'flying colours'.[33] But Gorst continued to have difficulties at Chatham, as he told Lord Salisbury. The influential Mr Thomas Winch, Chairman of the Conservative Association and described by Gorst as a 'vulgar young brewer', would have been glad with his friends to see Gorst replaced 'by a richer and younger candidate'. Winch was telling everybody at the end of 1881 that their MP did not have the confidence of local party leaders. It also looks as if Gorst and Winch fell out over election irregularities (the nature of these is unknown), for which Gorst blamed his Chairman unequivocally.[34] In the event Gorst survived at Chatham and it was not for another ten years that he changed constituencies.

NOTES

1. HP, 129/2; Gorst (G)–Disraeli (D) 26 Feb. 1874.
2. Ibid., G–D, 3 Mar. 1877.
3. Ibid., G–D, 7 May 1874.
4. Salisbury papers, G–Salisbury, 4 Sept. 1891.
5. HP, 125/3; G–Dyke, 19 Nov. 1874.
6. HP, 125/3; Dyke–D, 8 Dec. 1874.
7. E. J. Feuchtwanger, 'J. E. Gorst and the Central Organisation', 200–1.
8. HP, 125/3; G–Smith, 11 Nov. 1874.
9. HP, 129/2; G–D, 12 Mar. 1875.
10. Shannon, *The Age of Disraeli*, 240–1.
11. *Chatham and Rochester News and North Kent Spectator*, 13 and 20 Feb. 1875.
12. FP, 35.
13. 3 PD 222, 11 Mar. 1875, 1617.
14. 3 PD 225, 6 Jul. 1875, 1012–14.
15. 3 PD 226, 2 Aug. 1875, 371.
16. 3 PD 242, 5 Aug. 1878, 1172.
17. HP, 50/2; G–D, 19 Nov 1875.
18. Ibid., G–D, 4 Apr. 1878.
19. Feuchtwanger, 'J. E. Gorst', 204 .
20. HP, 129/2; G–D, 30 Mar. 1876.
21. *Review of Reviews*, 4 Aug. 1891, 580; the story no doubt originated with Gorst himself. Of course his services had not exactly been 'overlooked'. There is, however, no reason to doubt that Disraeli did say something along these lines to Gorst.
22. Hanham, *Elections and Party Management*, 366; Mackenzie, *British Political Parties*, 166.
23. Feuchtwanger, 'J. E. Gorst', 202.
24. HP, 129/2; G–D, 3 Mar. 1877.
25. 3 PD 228, 21 Mar. 1876, 410–2.
26. 3 PD 227, 24 Feb. 1876, 827–32.
27. 3 PD 233, 18 Apr. 1877, 379–87.
28. 3 PD 235, 17 Jul. 1877, 1416.
29. 3 PD 237, 28 Jan. 1878, 533.
30. 3 PD 242, 5 Aug. 1878, 1183-5.
31. Ibid., 1204.
32. 3 PD 245, 31 Mar. 1879, 72–6.
33. *Review of Reviews*, 4 Aug. 1891, 580.
34. Salisbury Papers, G–Salisbury, 5 Dec. 1881.

9

The Mysterious Death of
Charles Bravo

During the 1870s Gorst's practice at the Bar began to gather some momentum. In the summer of 1875 he took silk, just ten years after call, and from then onwards for some years he kept his two careers, those of barrister and politician, running in parallel with tolerable success. It is difficult to assess whether becoming a QC helped or hindered his practice. It is often argued that a busy junior counsel can make more money than a run of the mill QC, who is always obliged to have a junior with him. In summing up Gorst's legal career at that time, the *Dictionary of National Biography* states that 'he consolidated his reputation as a lawyer of note'.

Gorst's practice was varied. Criminal work apart – and we do not know its precise extent on the rapidly expanding Northern circuit and elsewhere – this was broadly in the common law field. Also, as he became more experienced and better known, he had a fair amount of appeal work including appearances in the House of Lords and before the Privy Council. Gorst had a long association in the courts with Sir John Holker which must have given him considerable help in his career. The earliest reported case of this association seems to have been in 1869 when Gorst appeared as Holker's junior in a libel case. Holker, known for some reason as 'sleepy Jack', was a highly successful barrister said to have been earning £22,000 a year (*c.* £946,000 now), much of his work coming from patent cases. His rise was meteoric. He became MP for Preston in 1872, Disraeli's Solicitor-General in 1874 and Attorney-General the following year. The greater part of his professional life had been spent in chambers in Liverpool and on the northern circuit. Consequently he found himself sometimes ignorant on the more obscure niceties of legal practice in London. Gorst on one occasion was more knowledgeable, and came to Holker's aid. In the Court of Exchequer there were two ancient offices filled by barristers, known for reasons lost in the mists of time as 'Tubman' and 'Postman', each with a separate box in court. Counsel occupying them had a right of addressing the judge even before the

Law Officers of the Crown. The new Solicitor-General, Holker, knew nothing of this, for when he rose to address the court, the judge, Lord Chief Baron Kelly, interrupted him telling him to give way because 'Postman' was present. Holker sat down totally mystified and it fell to Gorst his junior to enlighten him on his error.[1]

To give just a flavour of Gorst's work at the Bar we may cite a few cases in which he was involved. Occasionally, these came from the colonies. Thus Gorst appeared before the House of Lords for the Crown in an appeal from New Zealand in a maritime case. A ship laden with coal had entered Westport harbour and, striking the submerged stump of a tree, had sunk. Gorst needed to argue – he was unsuccessful – that the harbour authorities were not negligent in failing to remove this underwater hazard.[2] Another case relating to New Zealand must have caused quite a stir in that country at the time. This case came before the Queen's Bench Division a little ahead of the time we are mainly talking about. The defendant was an author named Rusden, who had written a history of New Zealand in which he was alleged to have libelled John Bryce, the Minister for Native Affairs in the New Zealand government. The book's publication in London had been stopped pending the outcome of the trial. Sir Richard Webster and Gorst, who until two months before had been the Law Officers in Salisbury's first administration, appeared for Rusden, while Sir Henry James, then Attorney-General in Gladstone's second administration, represented the plaintiff. The first passage complained of referred, in discussing the Maori war years, to Lieutenant Bryce of the Kai Iwi cavalry. It described how he and a sergeant had dashed upon some women and children who had emerged from a fortified Maori village to hunt pig. In a charge the two men had 'cut them down gleefully and with ease'. Consequently, so the author stated, Bryce had become known among the Maoris as a murderer. The other offending passage described Bryce as being 'brutal' and much else besides, as well as again referring to his exploits with his troopers against little children.[3]

The defence team were badly handicapped when they had to admit, as a result of the evidence that emerged, that much of what had been written by Rusden in connection with Bryce was inaccurate. Thus there were no women present at the incident of the charge, nor was Bryce himself there. Clearly, the historian had not checked his facts properly. Defence counsel argued that what was written was fair comment, and that the passages were written in the honest belief that they were true and not malicious. These arguments did not carry the day. Although he was on the losing side, Gorst emerged with some credit, as the judge referred to his 'admirable and candid speech'. Later Gorst said the defence had been 'hopelessly defeated'. Unusually heavy damages, £5,000, were awarded against Rusden. Gorst asked for a stay of execution on the grounds the damages were excessive, but the judge did not allow this. When Gorst was in New Zealand in 1906 he met Bryce, then a school manager, 'who seemed very glad to see me again'.[4]

Cases with an Empire flavour did not all come from New Zealand. Once Gorst appeared in an appeal heard in the House of Lords brought by a widow from Ceylon. In a lower court she had succeeded in a suit to recover property due to her. On appeal, the Supreme Court in Ceylon had reversed the lower court on the basis that the widow had never been married. In the Lords, having presumably mugged up his Roman-Dutch law (on which the law in Ceylon was based), Gorst was able successfully to argue for the widow that there was a presumption in favour of marriage and not one, as had been held in Ceylon, in favour of cohabitation.[5]

There are a number of instances in the reported cases of Gorst being involved in what we should call today family law. Not infrequently he appeared in matrimonial and divorce cases on behalf of the Queen's Proctor, the officer who intervened when fraud or collusion was suspected. For instance Gorst, representing the Queen's Proctor, once attended a case in the Probate Division involving an unfortunate woman who had obtained years earlier a decree *nisi* on the grounds of her husband's cruelty. Her solicitor told her, wrongly, that she need not now make another appearance in court, and so she went through a ceremony of marriage with another man. The decree *nisi* had never been made absolute by the court as was necessary, so the new 'marriage' was invalid, a matter she only discovered some years later. The court sensibly decided to make the decree *nisi* absolute and Gorst, perhaps we could say equally sensibly, made no move to intervene on behalf of the Queen's Proctor.[6]

A periodically fruitful field for Gorst was provided by rather mundane cases, usually from Lancashire, about the maintenance of the highway. It seems that the local authorities could never decide who should take the responsibility for the upkeep of turnpikes and so on. In one such case Gorst showed himself to be perhaps over-confident in arguing what an earlier case had decided, for the judge, Mr Justice Matthew, rebuked him saying 'having taken part in that decision I was astonished at [Mr Gorst's] gloss on it for I am sure it was not my intention nor that of Mr Justice Williams to decide anything like that which Mr Gorst understood the case to determine'. However

– and we cannot tell whether Gorst remonstrated with the judge – Mr Justice Matthew may somewhat have mollified counsel by stating that the language of the judgment could not have been clear as Mr Gorst misunderstood it.[7]

In the 1870s there was a steady stream of cases about mineral rights and mining, especially safety aspects. Gorst had his share of these. For instance he appeared for the Crown before the Privy Council in 1879 in an appeal from the Isle of Man. The Crown was claiming rights to minerals but it was held, the case going against Gorst, that in this context clay and sand were not minerals.[8] He had been more successful earlier in a case from Flintshire when appearing with the Attorney-General on behalf of a government inspector of mines. The question arose on appeal as to whether the lessee of a lead mine, now disused, still had an interest in the mine and was therefore guilty of an offence under mining regulations in not properly fencing it. Gorst argued that the respondent did have an interest and the judges agreed.[9]

Examples taken from Gorst's case-book might have come from other legal fields in which he plied his craft such as tax, contract, patent law (why should he appear in this very specialised field unless Holker had had a hand in it?), fraud and so on. The reader might possibly ask whether Gorst won more cases than he lost, or *vice versa*, even if this is to misunderstand counsel's role in the courts. But as a matter of interest, an examination of 29 reported cases in which he appeared over about a 16-year period shows that he was on the winning side 14 times and on the losing side 15 times. However, his record as an advocate certainly cannot be judged solely in this way.

Inevitably in his career at the Bar, Gorst was counsel in some cases which came to be regarded as 'leading' ones, or which achieved a degree of notoriety. We will refer to just two cases. Both had unusual features. In *Nichols v Marsland*, heard in 1876, Gorst appeared on appeal before the Court of Exchequer Chamber for the defendant in a civil case commonly cited as illustrating the special defence of Act of God. For many years the defendant had on her land some ornamental lakes formed by damming a natural stream. An extraordinary rainfall the previous year, more violent than any within living memory, caused the banks of the dam to burst and the escaping water to rush onto the plaintiff's land carrying away four bridges. The plaintiff argued the defendant had been negligent. But judgment was given for the defendant in the lower court, the jury finding no negligence. On appeal the lower court's decision was confirmed, after Gorst had successfully argued that the defendant should not be liable for an extraordinary act of nature which she could not reasonably anticipate, that is an Act of God.[10] The term is not of course a theological one, but is merely concerned with the operation of natural forces.

The notorious case we are going to mention in which Gorst was closely involved is still picked over today. In the exceptionally hot summer of 1876 the country was riveted by a sensational inquest beginning in July. Every day for a month the proceedings, with a series of scandalous revelations, made headline news. The inquest was into the death by poisoning on 21 April that year of 30-year-old Charles Bravo, a barrister who lived in Balham. There had in fact been an earlier inquest at the end of April. At this first inquest an open verdict had been returned, but its finding was quashed as unsatisfactory by the Lord Chief Justice.

The July inquest turned into what some saw as a trial of Bravo's young wife Florence, who was suspected in certain quarters of doing away with her recently married husband, or else of being an accomplice to his murder. Florence, a widow before her marriage to Bravo the previous December, had inherited a large sum of money from her first husband, who had died of drink. Between marriages she had conducted an affair, until she dismissed him, with the elderly Dr James Gully. This, when revealed, was very shocking for Victorians especially as the doctor was a celebrated physician specialising in hydropathic treatment (the application of water externally and internally), who counted among his patients people such as Dickens, Tennyson and George Eliot. The other principal player in the drama was Mrs Jane Cox, Florence's companion of four years' standing. She, a widow in her late forties with three school-age sons to support, was handsomely paid £100 per annum with all found. Her position, until Florence's marriage to Bravo, had been comfortable and secure. After the wedding, as companion to a young married woman, her job was in effect redundant. Not surprisingly, Bravo was keen to see her go. For her part, she did all she could to stay. Both Bravo's stepfather, Joseph, and Florence's father were rich and successful men, and could afford to retain some of the top lawyers.

Into the billiard room of the Bedford Hotel in Balham a great crowd of people had gathered for the inquest. They included press, public and a galaxy of legal talent. The presiding coroner, William Carter, was a man of no great ability who would find it hard to keep the lawyers and public in order. The Crown was represented by the Attorney-General, no less, although he did not appear until the eleventh day of the proceedings, by John Gorst and by Henry Poland, destined to become a notable criminal lawyer. Florence was represented by the distinguished Sir Henry James, who had been Attorney-General in Gladstone's government. James was present on each of the 23 working days the inquest lasted. Besides receiving a heavy retainer, he charged the then huge fee of 100 guineas (*c.* £4,400 now) a day for his services. He also had a junior. The accomplished George Lewis, a solicitor later to be knighted, represented Joseph Bravo (Charles' stepfather) and was said to have been paid 1,000 guineas as his fee for the case. John Murphy, the fourth QC present, who charged just 50 guineas a day, and his junior, represented Mrs Cox. Finally, Dr Gully retained the services of a senior lawyer from Serjeants' Inn, Serjeant Parry, also at 50 guineas a day.

This time the jury returned a verdict of wilful murder by the administration of tartar emetic (antimony) although there was insufficient evidence to fix the guilt on any person. The facts were briefly these. On the evening of Tuesday 18 April, Charles and Florence Bravo and Mrs Cox sat down to dinner at about 7.30 pm at the Priory, a biggish house built in gothic style and set in ten acres of grounds. Florence was recovering from her second miscarriage. That afternoon Charles' horse had bolted with him and shaken him up badly. Florence and Mrs Cox drank, according to the butler, two bottles of sherry at dinner while Charles confined himself to several glasses of burgundy. Florence went soon after dinner to her bedroom which – on account of her recent miscarriage – she was sharing with her companion rather than her husband. She prepared for bed and was soon slumbering. Charles had followed his wife upstairs and after a brief conversation with her had gone to his room. Before retiring it was his practice to drink from a water bottle placed by his bedside.

At about 9.30 pm Charles suddenly emerged from his bedroom in his night-shirt screaming for his wife and calling urgently for hot water. The maid, Mary Ann Keeler, heard him and rushed into Florence's room where she told Mrs Cox, still dressed, that the master was ill. Charles was violently sick and in a state of collapse. He then became unconscious for a time. Doctors were summoned – no less than six in the next three days including Sir William Gull, one of the most eminent in the land – but none of them could understand his symptoms or do anything for him. All Bravo would do was to admit that he had taken laudanum for toothache or neuralgia. After suffering terrible agonies Bravo died on Friday 21 April.[11] His widow appeared devastated.

No one was ever arrested in connection with Bravo's death. The police investigation, which culminated in a report by Inspector Clarke, began too late and is generally regarded as having been inadequate. The case has continued to fascinate and baffle writers, students of crime and others. Many books have been written on the tragedy, Agatha Christie pronounced on it, and the BBC's contribution to the mystery was a series of TV factual dramas produced in 1975. Did Florence murder her husband, and if so why? Was Mrs Cox involved in the death? Or was Dr Gully, who lived nearby, implicated? Or was it suicide? Or was it, somehow, accidental death? Most commentators regard suicide as very unlikely but an ingenious theory on the possibility of accidental death was produced by Sir Arthur Channell, a retired High Court judge. He thought that Bravo was trying to cure his wife's overfondness for alcohol by dosing her with small quantities of tartar emetic to make her sick. This was not an unknown practice. The writer Yseult Bridges went further and believed that Bravo was trying to murder his wife for her money. Both the retired judge and Bridges found explanations for how Bravo, possessed of tartar emetic, had accidentally poisoned himself. Probably the soundest book to date is Taylor and Clarke's study of the tragedy with its convincing exposition of how Mrs Cox had at the inquests lied and twisted the evidence, and, to suit her own purposes, had suggested that Bravo had committed suicide. She had the motive, means and opportunity to kill Bravo, argued the authors, who proceeded to reconstruct the crime in detail.[12]

And what of Gorst's part in the inquest? He was, as we might expect, prominent in the proceedings. His role is well brought out in a lively exchange he had with Serjeant Parry. This began when Parry rebuked Gorst for laughing in court. It is true that there had been laughter among the public because Gully's butler Pritchard, so it was related, had been ordered by his master the previous year not to admit Florence or Mrs Cox to the house. But Gorst denied he was laughing. Parry then accused him of smiling on two occasions. To this Gorst said: '. . . I certainly do plead guilty to having smiled . . . this is not a prosecution and I am not here to prosecute. I certainly smiled as my friends opposite have smiled as Mr Parry has smiled and I hope he may smile several times during the course of this investigation' (renewed laughter and applause). Gorst, warming to the subject, went on to say that he would not be able to sit through the long inquest 'with an impassive and wooden face . . . I shall certainly smile if evidence is given which is amusing'. The coroner was incensed at all this and threatened to clear the room; he was backed by Parry, who accused Gorst and Poland of being there for the purpose of fixing the guilt upon three individuals; no doubt he meant Florence, Mrs Cox and his client Dr Gully. At this point George Lewis leapt to Gorst's defence, saying Parry's observation was unjust to Gorst, who, he asserted, had 'acted most impartially on the part of the Crown and had fairly brought out evidence telling on both ways'. Gorst, determined in this exchange to have the last word, said that he had been instructed to lay before the coroner and jury all the evidence and to elicit the truth , 'and these instructions are not to bring any charge against any person'.

Another example of Gorst's demeanour and sharpness in court occurred when he was cross-examining Mary Ann, the maid. Sir Henry James interrupted, requesting Gorst to clarify a question he had put to the witness. Gorst retorted that *he* was the best judge of the 'intelligence' of his questions, and further that he objected to being called to order by Sir Henry who had no position in the court entitling him to interrupt.

The wide press coverage of the inquest whetted the public's appetite for more and stimulated the imagination of readers. Hundreds of letters were received by newspapers, jurymen and counsel in the case. Of the barristers involved, the most popular recipient of this influx of mail was Lewis, closely followed by Gorst and Poland.

Some writers have made play with the 'grave charge' said to have been made by Florence against her husband, an issue which seems to have had its origins in Gorst's cross-examination of Florence. As early as the second and fourth days of the proceedings Gorst had been putting questions to the doctors called as witnesses about the effect on the human body of receiving small doses of tartar emetic. Although Bravo had died of a huge dose of the fatal poison this was, of course, a line of questioning to be expected of counsel, especially of someone such as Gorst who, as we saw in our first chapter, had a knowledge of chemistry.

On the twenty-first day Gorst was subjecting Florence to a lengthy questioning about events on 18 April, when he suddenly changed tack and, using information he had found in the police report, asked her: 'Did you ever make a grave charge against your husband to Inspector Clarke at Brighton?' Florence, who had gone to Brighton to recuperate after Bravo's death, deflected the question. She had told the inspector, she said in reply, that he could consult her doctor in Brighton if he wanted to pursue this. Although Gorst persevered in trying to get to the bottom of the grave charge issue he met with no success. Nor, perhaps out of consideration for Florence's feelings, did he suggest to her what the charge might have been. On the last day of the inquest a juror insinuated that Bravo may have been suffering from venereal disease. Taylor and Clarke reject this theory, pointing out that the inspector used in his report the words: '. . . he was very persistent in that line of conduct'. They consider accordingly that Florence was referring to buggery (or sodomy). Bridges concludes in her book, making rightly or wrongly a link with Gorst's questions to the doctors and the grave charge issue, that Florence's husband was trying to poison her by giving her small doses of tartar emetic.

We have unfortunately no way of knowing what Gorst himself thought about the mystery, and whether he considered the grave charge was after all a red herring. His questioning of witnesses did not appear especially to indicate where he thought the truth might lie. Interestingly, when Mrs Cox came to be called as a witness it was the Attorney-General, Sir John Holker, and not Gorst who examined her on behalf of the Crown. Intelligent and self-possessed, she never appeared to deviate from the view she made every effort to promote, which was that Bravo had committed suicide. There is of course no reason to suppose that Gorst, if he had been questioning her, would have been any more successful than the other counsel in testing her evidence.

When the long inquest was over the three principal players went their separate ways. James Gully, his reputation in tatters yet regarded by most as wholly innocent, died seven years later. His son, William Gully, became Speaker of the House of Commons 20 years later. It has been said that when he took his seat he was greeted with cries of 'Bravo, Gully!' Florence and Mrs Cox had, maybe significantly, already separated in early May. Florence, broken by her ordeal, became an alcoholic and died, aged 33, just 14 months after the inquest. Mrs Cox appears to have vanished. She remains the great enigma of the tragedy.

The events at Balham had taken place a stone's throw away from where the Gorsts had lived at an earlier date in Tooting and before they moved to Kensington. By 1875 they were back south of the river in a house on the edge of Wandsworth Common. There they lived in a road today called 'Gorst Road', named after John. Then in 1881 they would be living in St George's Square, Pimlico, conveniently not much more than 20 minutes' walk from the House of Commons.

The Gorst family was complete by the middle of the 1870s, Mary having endured continual pregnancies for over 15 years as normally happened to women in those days. Three more girls had been born: Edith in 1871, Eva in 1874 and Gwendolen in 1876. For the little and patchy information about Gorst's family life we have to rely on John's two sons. Jack left behind him, after his career in the Foreign Office ended with his premature death, some autobiographical notes as well as a diary. Harold, as we have seen, wrote books, and his last one, written as late as 1936, gives us some glimpses of his boyhood.

Jack proved to be a clever child. While at Kensington Grammar School and at the age of ten he developed a terrible abscess in the pelvis. Several operations were performed to get at an apparently infected bone but without success. The doctors then tried applying an acid treatment which was tormentingly painful. After a year or two Jack persuaded his parents to abandon this treatment, the remedy, as he described it, being worse than the disease. He had been taken away from school and, not surprisingly, he had got well behind with his lessons. As a result he had to have a tutor. Now better but wearing an iron shield to protect his back, Jack was sent in January 1875 to Eton, his mother Mary taking him to the school. Interestingly, John Gorst's bachelor brother Edward paid for Jack's school fees. This, if indeed confirmation is needed, shows that money in the Gorst household must have been tight at this time.

Gorst had a significant influence on his elder son while he was growing up. Jack did well at Eton, displaying drive as well as brains; in his notes he confided that the credit for his progress 'is entirely due to my father who by well-timed severity kept me up to the mark'. When Jack did badly his father treated him in a 'cold and distant manner', and said little.[13] However, this typically stern Victorian father decided in the long vacation in 1879 to take his son abroad for a tour of Europe before the young man went up to Trinity College, Cambridge. Also John, anxious that his son should do well at university, coached him, and Jack took his degree in the mathematical tripos as 20th Wrangler.

Harold Gorst was talented in a different way from his brother Jack, being musical and having a literary bent. But he was not to turn out to be as amenable to his father's outlook on life as Jack had been, and over the years relations between the two would not always be smooth. It was not perhaps a good start when this sensitive boy was despatched at the tender age of 7 to a preparatory boarding school in Cheltenham, run by a Miss Briggs. Mary, wrote Harold, protested to her husband about the plan to send Harold away, though to no avail. Again it was Mary who had to perform the unenviable task of taking her small son to Gloucestershire and leaving him there among strangers. Harold suffered agonies of homesickness at being, as he put it, thrust out of a loving home. For this act of 'cruelty' he blamed his father. His mother, on the other hand, he described as having 'the tenderest heart and the most affectionate disposition in the world' but as not given to public displays of feeling.[14]

A curious tale is told by Harold about Miss Briggs and his father. Apparently, she had paid a visit to New Zealand at about the time the Maori war broke out. Somehow she was captured by a band of Maoris, and was tied to a tree while her captors debated her fate. In the end she was released without any real harm coming to her. She then appealed to John Gorst, who must at this time have been working in Auckland as private secretary to Bell, stating that the Maoris who captured her should be punished. But Gorst, perhaps realistically, refused to do anything, saying that the Maoris had acted with forbearance considering they were at war with the government. When Miss Briggs returned home she wrote to the papers about the incident and denounced Gorst for his 'callous indifference' to her fate.[15] Miss Briggs's earlier complaint against him did not, however, perhaps to his credit, prevent Gorst – assuming he realised who she was – from later entrusting his younger son to her care.

As for the Gorst girls, we have little knowledge of their upbringing and schooling except that we do know Hylda went for a time to a good school in Putney and later to a German school for a few months. The pity is that Gorst's views on how his girls should have been educated are unknown, as indeed are his feelings towards them. His views on schooling for the nation's children and on the welfare of those children, boys and girls, are well known, fully documented and in advance of his time. Moreover, his contribution to the reforming of the late Victorian educational system constitutes an important part of his story.

NOTES

1. Lord Alverstone, *Recollections of Bar and Bench*, London, Edward Arnold, 1914, 30.
2. *R v. Williams PC* (1881), 9 App. Cas. 418.
3. *Bryce v. Rusden* (1886), 2 TLR 435.
4. NZR, 101.
5. *Sastry Velaider v. Sembecutty* (1881), 9 App. Cas. 364.
6. *Wickham v. Wickham* (1880), 6 PD, 1.
7. *Newtown Improvement Commissioners v. Justices of Lancaster* (1884), 13 QBD, 623.
8. *A–G for Isle of Man v. Mylchreest* (1879), 4 App. Cas. 294.
9. *Evans v. Mostyn* (1877), 2 CPD, 547.
10. *Nichols v. Marsland* (1876), 2 EXD, 1.
11. A contemporary and illustrated broadsheet on the case, *The Balham Mystery*, gives a detailed record of the inquest.
12. Among books written about the Bravo case are: B. Taylor and K. Clarke, *Murder at the Priory*; Yseult Bridges, *How Charles Bravo Died*; Elizabeth Jenkins, *Six Criminal Women*; *The Poisoning of Charles Bravo* by Ken Taylor was transmitted on BBC 2 on 18 and 25 June, and 2 July 1975.
13. JG AN vol. 1, 13.
14. MLL, 28.
15. Ibid.

10

Enter Lord Randolph Churchill

In April 1880 the Liberals were returned to power at the general election with a sizeable majority. Gladstone came out of his semi-retirement obeying what he regarded as a divine call and, although now past 70, became prime minister for the second time, presiding over a mixture of Liberals and Radicals. His ministry would prove to be a divided one assailed by a harsh sequence of events abroad in South Africa, Afghanistan, Egypt and the Sudan. But perhaps above all he would be beset by problems in Ireland, where disorder at times amounted almost to civil war.

Gorst, who had been re-elected at Chatham by the fairly narrow majority of 90 votes out of a total poll of 4,887, now stood at a somewhat critical moment in his political career. He was 45 and saw himself as a progressively minded and still independent Conservative ready to judge and challenge issues strictly on their merits. A decade before, under the eye and tutelage of Disraeli, he had had success in party administration, but his early promise somehow had not been fulfilled. His outspokenness about the old order, whose dominion over the party he resented, had not helped. His talents in the House of Commons had been recognised by Disraeli, but when he had refused an offer of a junior ministerial post, his seniors may well have begun to wonder what to make of this clever, sometimes prickly, no longer so young member for Chatham.

Now in opposition, there was to begin for him a period of nearly five years when his parliamentary gifts would be given full rein. At heart a rebel, he would always be better at opposing than supporting the government of the day. His sharp mind was well suited to exposing incompetence or weakness displayed by ministers in the handling of events as well as pointing up the flaws in a policy or argument. Furthermore, as a lawyer with a passion for detail, he had mastered the intricacies of parliamentary procedure. Like him or not, these skills, it might be supposed, would be welcomed by the opposition's front bench. But in this new Parliament things did not quite turn out as might have been expected. Before we turn to examine the dramas that were about to unfold in the spring of 1880 on the floor of the Commons, we must take a look at how the Conservative Party managers reacted to their second heavy defeat in a dozen years.

In May, Beaconsfield summoned a meeting of Conservative peers and MPs. He told them that a committee under W. H. Smith, known to all as a genial and sensible man as well as being one of the very few middle-class leaders of the party, was being set up to investigate party organisation and how it might be improved. Out of the investigation there soon emerged a powerful Central Committee chaired by Smith.

One of the first acts of the party managers had been to call for Gorst and then to re-employ him as a successor to the undistinguished Skene as party agent. Gorst, as readers will remember, had been naggingly critical of the failures of the party organisation in the second half of the 1870s and had issued warnings, which went unheeded, about what might happen in the next general election. For this he was credited with some prescience. Now it was optimistically thought that he might for a second time pull the party's electoral chestnuts out of the fire. In a way it was surprising that Gorst was willing to become once again a party functionary beholden now to the Central Committee, as he could hardly have forgotten the unsatisfactory period he spent at Central Office after the 1874 general election. His acceptance of the job may be explained by the fact that it was Beaconsfield who asked him to undertake the work.[1] Also, he would have been pleased to be at the centre of party affairs, as he was made a member of the Central Committee. The other members, besides Smith, were the Hon. Edward Stanhope, a future Cabinet minister, Lord Percy, chairman of the National Union (a post created in 1869), and Rowland Winn, soon to be the Chief Whip.

This time round Gorst, in his executive role, was not to have the powers or room to manoeuvre which he commanded in 1870. His terms of reference charged him primarily with responsibility for finding parliamentary candidates.[2] He was also tasked with reorganising electoral machinery in the constituencies. These tasks were described by Sir Stafford Northcote, the Conservative leader in the Commons, as 'outdoor' management. Presumably, the 'indoor' side was Central Office, where Gorst was expected to conform to the wishes of the leadership. He was not, however, given any powers to spend money, only to put up proposals for expenditure. There was also an effort made to spell out more clearly than previously the demarcation line between Gorst and the whips. Soon Dyke was replaced as Chief Whip by Rowland Winn, whom Gorst saw as a

11

The Fourth Party: Heyday

Ireland was the cause of the first split in the Fourth Party. The Liberals had decided, on taking office, not to renew the Peace Preservation Act, originally passed in 1870, by which the government was given special powers, though not draconian ones, to rule in that country. The government now determined that Ireland should simply be governed by the ordinary provisions of the law. This was a bold departure in view of agrarian crime and general unrest there. Government efforts in July to enact legislation compensating evicted tenants failed when the Lords, to the anger of the Irish, threw out the Bill. There followed a grave escalation in violence with a spate of Fenian and other outrages. Troop reinforcements were hurried to the island. Finally, the government decided to recall parliament in January 1881, six weeks early, to introduce a Coercion Bill which would suspend *habeas corpus* and lead to imprisonment without trial. It also looked as if powers of arrest would be increased and other tough measures introduced. This was, of course, an admission of the failure of William Forster's rule as Chief Secretary since the previous May, and would thus provide a ready field for the Fourth Party to stir up trouble for the government.

The four friends dined with Wolff at the Garrick Club on 26 December 1880 to decide what line to adopt over the new measure. During the years he had spent in Ireland as his father's secretary, Churchill had travelled widely, mixed with all classes of people and studied the problems facing the country. In so doing he had developed a sympathy for the Irish. Subsequently, with his knowledge of the country, he had won some acceptance in the Commons as an authority on Ireland. It is not surprising, therefore, that Lord Randolph hated the idea of coercion, and he suggested the Fourth Party should move an amendment proposing to limit the duration of the proposed Act to one year, not an unreasonable proposal. The other three were sure they should consult Northcote or Beaconsfield. To this Lord Randolph concurred. Gorst had earlier in the month written to Beaconsfield on behalf of the four friends seeking advice generally on Conservative Party tactics on Ireland in the next session. He was therefore the obvious one to be entrusted with the task of seeing Beaconsfield about this particular plan. At first their chief was not unfavourably inclined to the idea, but wanted to mull it over. On the eve of the new session Beaconsfield gave his answer which was that '… the proposal however good in itself as a parliamentary manoeuvre was not practicable for a Conservative opposition'.[1] The Fourth Party, bar Lord Randolph, accepted this. He wanted to go ahead despite Beaconsfield's advice. Churchill was in no mood to listen to argument and accused his friends of deserting him. There were hot words and a quarrel ensued. Churchill angrily stumped off. Ultimately, he was only persuaded not to proceed with his amendment by his father, the Duke, who made a special visit to the Commons.

The consequence of all this was that the Fourth Party, to the satisfaction of the government (and no doubt Northcote), in effect ceased to exist for a while. There were no more dinners, no more councils and no more combined action in the House, although Balfour, Gorst and Wolff supported each other at times. Thus during the long and stormy passage of the coercion legislation the Fourth Party played, quite uncharacteristically, no part in the proceedings.

Then, on 14 March, Bradlaugh made another appearance in the House to present a petition. Gorst immediately rose on a point of Order to object that Bradlaugh was not a member and could not do this. The Attorney-General and others followed Gorst. Then quite unexpectedly Lord Randolph rose in support of 'my hon. and learned friend', and suggested that Mr Gorst would be satisfied if Bradlaugh withdrew and considered his status *sub judice* pending a decision by the House on the question of issuing a new writ for an election at Northampton. When he sat down he whispered to his old ally: 'Make it up, Gorst?'[2] From that moment friendly relations between the four were restored. Soon the same cordiality existed as before. The Fourth Party, to the discomfort of both front benches, was once more in business. It all perhaps went to demonstrate how important among the four was the relationship between Churchill and Gorst.

The death of Lord Beaconsfield on 18 April 1881 led to a serious problem over the leadership of the Conservative Party. Was the leader to be Northcote or Salisbury or someone else? The Fourth Party, as we shall see, became in due course deeply involved in this issue. Balfour, from the outset, naturally enough favoured his uncle Lord Salisbury. Despite his aversion to Northcote, Lord Randolph, according to his son, was in doubt for some time over whom to back. The same source reported that Gorst was quite well disposed to Northcote, although Gorst himself, writing notes on the Fourth Party 20 years later, said that 'of the two I should have preferred Lord Salisbury. Randolph was actively hostile to Northcote as leader of the House of Commons. I always deprecated this ...'[3]

Anyhow, for the moment Northcote led in the Commons and Salisbury in the Lords, and the Conservative Party had to do without an acknowledged leader, not by our standards today a viable position at all.

Beaconsfield had been puzzled by Gorst and had said of him that he was the 'only really dangerous member of the Fourth Party'. Moreover, he confessed that he was 'quite unable ever to guess at the motives which guided Gorst'.[4] If anything is needed to underline the complexities of this man's character it is the apparent inability of the shrewd Beaconsfield to fathom him.

For his part Gorst admired Beaconsfield and believed strongly in what he thought Disraeli stood for. Yet he did not attend his funeral. Perhaps he was repulsed by the great wave of emotion which swept the country on the old man's death and the eulogising which took place in the press. When he was asked at a dinner party by the woman sitting next to him whether he had attended the funeral, he replied: 'No, I was not invited, and I am not one of those people who invite themselves.'[5] She thought this reply was characteristic of the man, uncompromising and ever certain of himself.

The history of the Fourth Party is well documented. Apart from works by various historians the sons of both Lord Randolph and Gorst have written about it, as did Balfour. Wolff on the other hand was disappointingly frugal in his autobiography over this episode in his life; for him it may have been less important than it was for Churchill or Gorst. We have nonetheless some vivid glimpses of the four friends at work and play. They all liked to entertain. Lord Randolph would gather the others 'in festive council round the dining-room table amid the haze of countless cigarettes ...'[6] at his house in St James's Place. Unbelievably this was next door to Northcote's, although the walls were thick. Wolff and Balfour would give dinner parties at the Garrick Club. All these men liked the company of other leading politicians, and their dinner parties became quite famous. As for Gorst, he would take the others down to dine at his house on the edge of Wandsworth Common, or to play tennis there at weekends in the summer. Once at the close of a session the four men dined at *The Ship* at Greenwich and had a convivial whitebait dinner. Their guest was the Radical MP Henry Labouchère, who was the standard bearer of their antagonist Bradlaugh and editor of the political journal *Truth*.

Lady Jeune, a Conservative hostess of her day, describes how Lord Randolph, Gorst and Wolff used to come to tea with her at her house in Putney on Sundays at four o'clock. They were on their way to Gorst's to dine. They made, she said, a remarkable trio. She described Lord Randolph as their 'ring-leader, a great school-boy full of fun and mischief', concocting schemes. As he lay in a deck-chair under a tree the other two would look on with 'cynical approval'. Gorst, she said, was 'serious and industrious', and these characteristics, when added to Lord Randolph's 'audacity and ambition', made them a powerful combination.[7] The Liberal lawyer, Sir Henry James, used a sporting metaphor to describe them. For him the two men were a poacher's combination: a pointer to find the game, and a greyhound to run it down.[8] Another political hostess, Lady Dorothy Nevill, had an eye for celebrities, and often asked the Fourth Party to small lunch parties in the early 1880s.[9] The four were thus in much demand socially.

It has been suggested that Gorst was on the one hand priggish and on the other humourless.[10] These are harsh judgements. There is no denying he was precise, liked preaching and did not suffer fools gladly. But he had wit and sometimes showed a distinct sense of fun. For instance, once Gorst accompanied Lord Randolph to a magistrate's court to answer a minor summons. To support his friend Gorst dressed up in all his finery as a Queen's Counsel which caused consternation in the court and a rapid dismissal of the charge. On another occasion the four friends found themselves, after a festive evening, on Westminster Bridge. One of them – the suspicion must be that it was Gorst, acting as a pointer, though it might as well have been the cavalier Wolff – wagered it was impossible to run across the length of the bridge and back while Big Ben was striking midnight. At once with typical bravura Lord Randolph accepted the challenge. Breathless, he arrived back at his starting point as the twelfth stroke boomed out.[11] One day Gorst, in semi-conspiratorial mood, suggested to Lord Randolph that they should meet at a deserted spot like Didcot to discuss a burning issue. He told Wolff, with whom he often adopted a joking relationship, that their deliberations would be known as the Didcot convention.

Lord Randolph and Gorst were drawn together by politics. They came from different backgrounds but their ideas on what direction the Conservative Party should take were very similar. Each had a strong streak of idealism in his make-up, but this was tempered by a pragmatic approach to affairs in and out of the House. As we have already seen, Churchill was sometimes volatile, although squalls did not usually last long. Gorst though, less generous than his friend, could let himself become embittered by harbouring grudges. Among many others, the problems of Ireland concerned both men. Gorst visited the country in October 1881 and went there again just after Christmas to stay in Dublin with Lord Randolph. Each returned home disgusted with the coercion measures and the miseries they perceived to be caused by them. Evictions were usually of poor tenants by well-off landlords. Sometimes it was the reverse. Thus Gorst was present when an enforcement order was executed on a rich tenant on behalf of an impoverished landlord. Payment of a year's rent was required. To effect the order 40 constables and 50 soldiers, armed to the teeth, were mustered. The party then proceeded to expropriate 14 fat bullocks to pay for the £100 due. The magistrate, also there, had the Riot Act pasted in the crown of his hat ready for an emergency. On this occasion it was not needed.

The next year Gorst stayed with Churchill, again in late December, on the Riviera where the latter had gone for health reasons. Nearer home, Gorst once invited Churchill to watch some torpedo-firing off the south coast. On another occasion they tramped together over Hampstead Heath one Sunday morning, no doubt immersed in plotting against their Liberal opponents. Undoubtedly, in these years the two were close friends.

Gorst had an interest in music and sometimes in his speeches he referred to characters in grand opera. During his Fourth Party days he brought in a Bill to amend, of all extraordinary subjects, the law on musical copyright, because recently people had been prosecuted – he believed unfairly – for singing songs at 'penny readings' without permission of the song-writer (he succeeded in having the law changed). Lord Randolph could not have cared much for music. So Wolff and Gorst, both middle-aged, found themselves not infrequently escorting the delectable Lady Randolph to concerts. They must have made an unlikely threesome.

If in the House of Commons Northcote saw the Fourth Party as a major nuisance to his leadership of the Conservatives, the acute Gladstone had been quick to discern the threat they posed to his government with their debating skills and procedural knowledge. Gorst seemed to relish taking on the grand old man across the floor of the House. Indeed, it was said there was no one who ever irritated Gladstone more than Gorst.[12] In the midsummer of 1881 the Irish Land Law Bill was, at its committee stage, in full flood. This was a measure genuinely aimed at helping tenants and giving them fixity of tenure, fair rents and free sales. At one moment Gladstone gave his opinion that five hours had already been spent debating 'one of the smallest points which had been discussed'. Gorst jumped up and said – slightly inaccurately – that he was astonished to hear the Prime Minister describe this as 'one of the smallest points in the Bill', and that four speeches had been made by ministers on this 'smallest point'. In fact, Gorst continued, goodness knows how much longer the Attorney-General for Ireland would have gone on had not the Prime Minister 'pulled him down'. Gladstone, annoyed, told Gorst to be more careful in the accuracy of his statements. He had not referred to one of the 'smallest points in the Bill', but one of the smallest points 'of the subject under discussion', a totally different matter.[13] Splitting hairs appealed to both Gladstone and Gorst.

A fortnight later, with the Bill still in committee, Gorst asked, slightly mysteriously, for the words 'schools, churches and hospitals' to be inserted after the word 'cottages' in a particular clause of the Bill. Gladstone asked Gorst to withdraw his amendment which was in the wrong place. Gorst could be stubborn, and declined, saying the words he had suggested were necessary as 'an earnest and proof' of the government's intention. Gladstone took this, it seems, as impugning his integrity. Icily he thanked Gorst for wanting such 'proof' in order that his, Gladstone's, veracity might be believed. Northcote went to Gladstone's aid, and in doing so persuaded Gorst to withdraw. But Gladstone, now on his high horse, objected absolutely to the withdrawal unless Gorst gave a more 'explicit explanation' with reference to the words he had used. So Gorst, ready to oblige now he had nettled the Prime Minister, begged unreservedly to withdraw any 'insinuation that he had the least doubt in the world as to the right honourable gentleman keeping every promise and pledge to the committee'.[14] Gorst had not in any way let flag his interest in supply matters or in naval and imperial affairs. He raised a typical objection in 1881 to the Secret Service vote. During a debate on the estimates there was a motion to grant £10,000 up to the end of March 1882 for 'Her Majesty's Foreign and other Secret Services'. He disliked the idea of a block vote, and anyhow why it was necessary to spend this sum? He took a swipe at Harcourt, the Home Secretary, another of his sparring partners, who 'lectured' the House and often 'entirely misunderstood the point being made'.[15] He was not the only Member dissatisfied with this vote.

Frequently, Gorst spoke about the Pacific Islands and various parts of southern Africa, especially the Transvaal where war had broken out in December 1880 (the first Boer war). Gorst was never an unalloyed imperialist and had confided to Lord Randolph a few days after the start of hostilities that the annexation of the Transvaal in 1877 had been a 'very foolish acquisition'.[16] The following July, just before the Convention of Pretoria was signed, he told the House that 'the part of their policy which was most likely to be condemned hereafter was their entire disregard of native interests'.[17] The following year he spoke on Borneo when he introduced a resolution whereby he sought to revoke the Charter just given to the British North Borneo company, or alter it insofar as the Charter gave an implied sanction to the maintenance of slavery under the British flag. Taking his information from a Blue Book produced in 1878 by an agent of the company, Gorst stated that slavery in Sandakan harbour was rampant and that slaves were used in the 'most atrocious way'. The agents of the company would become officers of the Queen and be required to regulate and protect the institution of slavery. To cries of 'Why?', he explained that the Charter was 'bound to observe existing customs'. He was supported by Balfour, and provoked a lively debate in which Gladstone and James, the Attorney-General, spoke. Better still, he succeeded with his resolution.[18]

The session of 1882 saw the Fourth Party still pulling together in their efforts to make life difficult for ministers while at the same time opposing the often over-conciliatory attitude of their own leaders to the government. Their effectiveness, however, had been reduced by the long illness of Lord Randolph, who had been absent at the time the Chief Secretary for Ireland, Forster, resigned and when Lord Frederick Cavendish, the new Chief Secretary, and T. H. Burke a senior official, were assassinated in May in Phoenix Park, Dublin. In the summer Gorst commented to Churchill how dull the House was without him. While Churchill's magnetism and sparkle helped to stimulate him in the political arena, Gorst always had a wide circle of associates among the Radical fraternity: men like James, Labouchère, the once avowed Republican Charles Dilke, the Irish nationalist Callan, and H. N. Hyndman the ex-Conservative Marxist and one-time stockbroker. Dilke said of Gorst: '[he was] dangerously frank, a nominal Tory, in fact a Radical, ever battering his own side for the mere fun of the operation, old in years, young in activity of brain and body ...'[19]

Dilke's asssessment of Gorst may come close to the truth. One thing is clear. It is certainly a mistake to try to attach too precise a political label to Gorst. With his intellectual curiosity and abhorrence of party discipline, he liked the freedom to mix with a broad spectrum of political opinion. Only in this way could he maintain the room for manoeuvre and the freedom of spirit which he arrogantly claimed for himself.

In the meantime a crisis had arisen in Egypt. The navy shelled Alexandria after 50 Europeans had been killed there in riots. Gorst put down a motion in the House condemning the bombardment but was induced to withdraw it by Northcote. Subsequently, an expeditionary force, sent out to Egypt under General Wolseley, inflicted a heavy defeat on the Egyptian army at Tel-el-Kebir in September. Arabi Pasha, leader of the nationalist movement, was arrested and Khedive Tewfik's regime survived. The Fourth Party was against what they saw as the un-Liberal intervention by Britain, and, with Lord Randolph now back in the House and restored to health, made many speeches with the object of embarrassing the government. Churchill sent £50 towards the cost of Arabi's defence before the Egyptian court, while Gorst asked repeated questions on the situation in Egypt. Concerned always about the forms of justice, Gorst wanted to know in particular what law Arabi had broken and under what code he was to be tried.

It was towards the end of 1882 that an article appeared in the influential *Fortnightly Review* entitled, 'The State of the Opposition'. It was signed by 'two Conservatives'.[20] Gorst has always been credited with being one of the authors, and there is no reason to doubt this. Once historians were divided as to whether the other author was Lord Randolph Churchill or Wolff. It seems to be now accepted that it was Churchill.

In the article Gorst – and we shall assume that its words came principally from his pen – first expatiated on the disorganisation prevailing within the party and then criticised the shortcomings of having a dual leadership. He did not mince his words about those who controlled the party, asserting that they belonged solely to one class and were a 'clique ... surrounded by sycophants ...' In retelling recent Conservative Party history (about which he knew as much as anyone) he praised the great manufacturing towns of Lancashire for building up after 1868 political organisations 'not blighted by the patronage of lords and landowners'. This of course was pure Gorst. But he regretted that, as soon as the Conservatives had achieved their victory in 1874, the old guard 'had rushed in to share the spoils'. Furthermore an earlier distinction between county and borough members was revived so that the latter were made to feel an inferior class. Moreover the legislative 'interests of boroughs were subordinated to those of the counties'.

The members of Beaconsfield's Cabinet, excepting the leader himself, whom Gorst was careful to exonerate, had learnt nothing from the defeat of 1880, nor were there grounds for supposing they

1. Winckley Square, Preston. [*Source:* Horace Halewood, *Preston, a Pictorial History*, Timmins & Phillimore, 1992]

2. The grammar school, Preston. [*Source:* Horace Halewood, *Preston, a Pictorial History*, Timmins & Phillimore, 1992]

3. *The Red Jacket* clipper ship. [*Source:* lithograph published by Carrier and Ives, 1855]

4. John Eldon Gorst (hereafter JEG), *c.* 1863. [*Source:* Auckland Institute and Museum]

6. Rewi Maniapoto [*Source:* John E. Gorst, *New Zealand Revisited*, Pitman, 1908]

5. Wiremu Tamihana [*Source:* John E. Gorst, *New Zealand Revisited*, Pitman, 1908]

8. Sir George Grey. [*Source:* Thomas Gudgeon, *Defenders of New Zealand*, 1887]

7. Right Revd Bishop Selwyn. [*Source:* Thomas Gudgeon, *Defenders of New Zealand*, 1887]

9. A. J. Balfour. [*Source: Review of Reviews*, August 1891]

11. Randolph Churchill. [*Source: Vanity Fair*]

10. Benjamin Disraeli. [*Source: Vanity Fair*]

12. Royal Commission on Labour, 1891 (with JEG standing up and Lord Hartington, later Duke of Devonshire, sitting at the head of the table).
[*Source:* Sir John M. Gorst]

GORST, ET PRÆTEREA NIHIL!

13. JEG as Minister of Education. [*Source: Punch*]

15. Harold Gorst. [*Source:* Christina Gorst-Ellis]

14. Jack Gorst. [*Source:* Paul Lysley]

17. Edith Sykes (*née* Gorst). [*Source:* Paul Lysley]

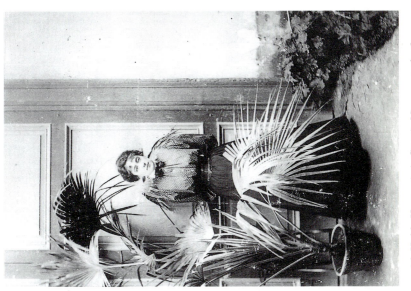

16. Hylda Hunter (*née* Gorst). [*Source:* author]

18. Eva Gorst [*Source*: Paul Lysley]

19. Gwendolen Herbert (*née* Gorst). [*Source*: Paul Lysley]

20. JEG with General William Booth of the Salvation Army, his wife Mary and daughter Constance *c*. 1903. [*Source:* Paul Lysley]

21. JEG in 1899. [*Source:* Birmingham Central Library]

22. JEG with Maori friends, 1906. [*Source:* John E. Gorst, *New Zealand Revisited*, Pitman, 1908]

23. JEG with Eva in Maori canoe, 1906. [*Source:* Te Awamutu and District Museum]

24. Castle Combe Manor House, Wilts. [*Source:* G. Poulett Scrope, *History of the Manor and Ancient Barony of Castle Combe in the County of Wiltshire*, 1852]

had learnt anything since. He then laid into the present organisation, which needed to undergo a 'radical revolution', making it clear that he disliked the managing role played by the Central Committee. The National Union, of which he was a Vice Chairman, on the other hand, was representative, but had no funds and was impotent. The state of local Conservative associations he castigated, believing them to be corrupted by patronage. Oddly, for he was still closely involved in this field, he asserted that the 'provision of a candidate to fight the next election does not come within the scope of their activity'. This was all extraordinary stuff, coming as it did from the hand of a paid party functionary, and one who was a member of the powerful Central Committee.

The concept of dual party leadership came badly out of the article's critical analysis. The authors – and this is where the hand of Lord Randolph is discernible – considered the party to be in fact leaderless. The article took a dig at certain peers and, naming some commoners, did not much approve of Cross and Smith (Lord Randolph's Marshall and Snelgrove). To Northcote the authors were quite kind, although it was suggested he was too amiable for the job he was doing. Lord Salisbury they tended to handle carefully.

On the party's approach to Irish affairs, Churchill and Gorst could not resist writing critically. The dual leadership had succumbed, they said, to the influence of an 'injudicious Irish coterie'. At issue was the passage of the Arrears of Rent (Ireland) Bill, whose double object was to compensate landlords for loss of rent and to reduce the liability of tenants for arrears of rent. What Lord Salisbury and his 'band of Irish barons' had failed to take proper account of, the authors opined, was the British taxpayer, who would have to foot the bill. In fact Gorst had spoken at length in May (Lord Randolph was then ill) on various defects in the Bill as he perceived them to be, describing the measure as profligate. In this instance he was concerned more with the interests of the taxpayer than with the merits of the legislation as it might affect the land problem in Ireland.[21] Gorst certainly must be regarded as the principal author of this part of the article. Thus the reference in it to the Conservative element in Ireland as being 'one of Protestantism of the hottest type, fanaticism of the deepest orange' is Gorstian. His dislike of certain Ulstermen was to surface a few years later to his disadvantage.

Looking ahead, the authors suggested, with much good sense, that the leader of the party might be chosen 'by a common suffrage of both Peers and Commons who may guide the policy, command the confidence and enlist the loyalty of politicians both inside and outside the Houses of Parliament'. Here the authors were 80 years and more ahead of their times.

After this remarkable effusion, what of Gorst's position as a party functionary? In fact his re-employment by the party had not been going well for some time. Between Gorst and Smith there was discord over Gorst's position as agent. Smith regarded himself as being in charge of the party organisation in which Gorst was simply an employee. Gorst, though, did not see matters this way, for he did not brook interference with the work he was required to do and had little respect for the Central Committee. As a party manager he was accused of aiming at absolute autocracy, wanting all important questions on organisation and funds entrusted to his discretion. Also there were complaints that Gorst was not giving enough time to party affairs, allegations he stoutly denied.[22]

After he had been serving in his new post a year or so, the question arose of the remuneration he should receive for his services. It was agreed that he should be paid a thousand guineas for the period June 1881 to June 1882. He then claimed the same sum retrospectively for his first year in office. Smith, and the other leaders, would not accept this. Instead they gave him 500 guineas (*c*. £23,500 now) as a general recognition of services rendered. For his part Gorst eventually waived his claim for the balance.[23] All this haggling could not have been dignified. Perhaps both parties were to blame for not properly clarifying the question of salary when Gorst was reappointed. Probably, with his various commitments, Gorst had less time available for his practice at the Bar and therefore badly needed the money.

Gorst's finances remain something of a mystery. Balfour, who kept his uncle Lord Salisbury closely posted about what was going on both in the affairs of the Fourth Party and regarding party administration, said that Gorst '*has* been and perhaps *is* embarrassed by poverty.'[24] Lord Randolph similarly referred a year or two later to his friend's 'poverty'. It may be that it suited Gorst's purposes for his patrician friends to think of him in this way.

Unhappily Gorst's relations with the Whip's office were not too cordial. One disagreement arose over corrupt practices at elections. Gorst, and the Fourth Party, wanted very properly to see these eliminated, and a strong Bill introduced in the House. But alas, J. C. Shaw, a protégé of the Chief Whip Rowland Winn, was prone to the very failings Gorst was trying to stamp out. The man, as Gorst told Smith, was much sought after in corrupt constituencies.[25] These were matters in which Gorst was not prepared to compromise. His strained relations with Central Office did not prevent Gorst from giving his views, as sharply analytical as ever, to party leaders on electoral prospects. These, at the time, he did not rate as good.

In October 1882 he went to Scotland on party business, travelling via North Berwick and Edinburgh to Glasgow, where he heard Northcote make a dull and rambling speech, and then finally on to Inverness. 'Our position in Scotland is hopeless', he told Lord Randolph. He attended a highland gathering which he described as 'curious and interesting'. The seven pipers made an agreeable substitute for a band. The pipes would make, he suggested, a grand instrument for Mr Speaker to call upon to stop a 'tedious oration' in the House of Commons.[26]

After the publication of the article in the *Fortnightly Review*, of which Gorst must have admitted co-authorship, it is difficult to see how Gorst could continue as a paid official of the party. On 17 November, in answer to a letter he had received from Northcote, he wrote resigning from what he described to Northcote as his 'demi-official' position in the party in order to relieve him, Northcote, 'of all further embarrassment.'[27] It has been suggested that Gorst's resignation was precipitated by a resolution passed by the Chelsea Conservative Association condemning Gorst's disloyalty towards party leaders.[28] Whether this resolution was prompted by the contentious article or by something else is not certain. Showing that he respected the Conservative dual leadership, Gorst wrote, also on 17 November, to Lord Salisbury telling him of his resignation and adding, 'Arthur Balfour will explain the circumstances'.[29]

Thus finally ended Gorst's connection with Central Office. His first four years as a party administrator had been, by most judgements, a great success. Indeed, Coleman comments that the choice in 1870 of giving Gorst the job of improving party organisation was an inspired one.[30] His two further stints at Central Office were not successful. His reputation would have benefited if he had avoided hanging on too long after 1874 or going back in 1880. Probably he twice misjudged the situation, and did not recognise that the recipe for further success was not then present.

NOTES

1. Churchill, *Lord Randolph Churchill*, 161.
2. FP, 178; 3 PD, 259, 14 Mar. 1881, 892–9.
3. MLL, 141.
4. Shannon, *The Age of Disraeli*, 405.
5. T. E. Kebbel, *Lord Beaconsfield and other Tory Memories*, London, Cassell, 1907, 137.
6. Churchill, *Lord Randolph Churchill*, 141.

7. Lady St Helier, *Memories of Fifty Years*, London, Edward Arnold, 1909, 282.
8. FP, 175.
9. H. Lucy, *Diary of a Journalist*, London, John Murray, 1923, 113–4.
10. Shannon, *The Age of Disraeli*, 105, 405.
11. R. V. Rhodes James, *Lord Randolph Churchill*, London, Weidenfeld & Nicolson, 1959, 92, 94.
12. *Saturday Review*, 18 April 1916, 345.
13. 3 PD, 262, 16 June 1881, 744; B. B. Gilbert, 'Sir John Eldon Gorst: Conservative Rebel', 153, quoting the *Saturday Review, Historian*, vol. XVIII, no. 2, 1956.
14. 3 PD, 262, 1 July 1881, 1905.
15. 3 PD, 264, 2 Aug 1881, 658.
16. Correspondence of Lord Randolph Churchill (Ld RC); Add. 9248, Gorst (G–Churchill (C), 30 Dec. 1880.
17. 3 PD, 264, 25 July 1881, 1833.
18. 3 PD, 267, 17 Mar 1882, 1148–71.
19. R. F. Foster, *Lord Randolph Churchill*, Oxford, Oxford University Press, 1982, 30, 71–2, 78, 85.
20. *Fortnightly Review*, xxxii, Nov. 1882.
21. 3 PD, 269, 22 May 1882, 1322–27.
22. Raikes, *Life and Letters*, 158; Hanham, *Elections and Party Management*, 364; Feuchtwanger, *Disraeli, Democracy and the Tory Party*, 152–3.
23. Feuchtwanger, *Disraeli, Democracy and the Tory Party*, 154–5.
24. Harcourt Williams, *Salisbury–Balfour Correspondence*, Hertfordshire Record Society, 76–9.
25. Shannon, *Age of Disraeli*, 398.
26. Ld RC, G–C, 6 and 14 Oct. 1882.
27. Iddesleigh, Add. 50041; G–Northcote, 17 Nov. 1882.
28. Feuchtwanger, *Disraeli, Democracy and the Tory Party*, 156.
29. Salisbury Papers, G–Salisbury, 17 Nov. 1882.
30. B. Coleman, *Conservatism and the Conservative Party in the Nineteenth Century*, London, Edward Arnold, 1988, 145.

12

The Fourth Party: Bid for Power

No man had a more powerful and direct influence over Gorst than Lord Randolph Churchill had for a few years in the 1880s – not Bishop Selwyn 20 years before, nor even Disraeli, although both of these men exerted considerable influence over him in their different ways. And Disraeli's political philosophy, as perceived by Gorst, was a long-lasting influence. We have mentioned how for two years running Gorst went off over the Christmas period to stay with Churchill, the personal magnetism of the younger man drawing the older away from his family. Churchill combined the flair and intellectual power which Gorst sought in a friend and close political associate.

After Gorst had returned from his three-week holiday with Churchill in France he enjoyed writing a succession of letters to his friend early in 1883, giving him the Commons gossip and other news. For instance, Smith apparently was 'really most hostile to the goat [Northcote] and likes us very much' (was this just wishful thinking?). Gorst showed impatience with both front benches because no franchise reform was to be brought in during the coming session. Although Gorst himself was in favour of further reform of the franchise, he also saw a tactical opportunity here for the Fourth Party to attack both front benches for their failure to act.

That 'wretch' Wolff, as Gorst jokingly put it to Churchill, he had not yet seen. In fact, Wolff was out of circulation for a bit on account of his son's serious illness; Gorst wrote with concern to Wolff about this and sent thoughtful messages to Wolff's wife and daughter. Gorst also told Churchill that he had seen Lady Randolph, now convalescent after being seriously ill with typhoid, who was looking 'rather pale and thin in the face but seemed bright and cheerful'. She had expressed 'the most lively horror of Torquay and Bournemouth'.[1]

Churchill himself wrote to Wolff referring to what he and Gorst had been talking about on the Riviera. He was anxious to give notice to Winn, the Chief Whip, that the three of them should now decline the Conservative Whip.[2] But Churchill must have had second thoughts about this on his return from France in February, or else the other two persuaded him against the course. His disenchantment with the party led him in March to reply testily to a letter from Northcote who complained that steps taken to 'mark out a separate party within the general body of the Conservatives must be prejudicial to the whole ...'[3] Churchill's relations with his party's front bench entered a new period of strain.

In the meantime Gorst was immensely busy. In the House he was in the thick of it, making in a mere fortnight three big speeches lambasting the government about their failures in different parts of the world. So busy was he in his researches in the Commons library that he complained in the chamber, and was supported by Lord Randolph, about the quality of the lighting in the House, comparing it unfavourably with the law courts where the Swan Company had successfully installed some new lighting.

On 2 March Gorst attacked the government for their mistakes in Egypt, telling them that the Khedive Tewfik was only kept in his position by the bayonets of British troops.[4] He was almost certainly correct. Next, a week later, he raised in a long speech the government's failures over the seizure in a Jamaican port some six years before of the cargo ship *Florence*. In brief, the Governor of Jamaica had prevented the sailing of this ship with its cargo of arms and ammunition until its captain entered into a bond for £1,000. In an action for damages and costs against the Jamaican government for wrongly detaining the vessel the owners of the ship were awarded £8,000. The Colonial Office then tried to get the Legislative Council in Jamaica, in opposition to the wishes of its unofficial (that is local) members, to charge half this sum against the revenue of the colony.[5] Gorst was filled with indignation concerning 'this grave scandal'. This was a typical example of how he liked to fight on behalf of a colonial people whom he thought had been shabbily treated. To score party-political points at the same time would of course be a bonus.

In similar vein, but without censuring the government, he moved a resolution on 13 March drawing attention to the complicity of the Boer Transvaal government in attacks made on two chiefs in neighbouring British-run Bechuanaland (now Botswana). He asserted that lawless 'freebooters' had crossed the border and the Transvaal authorities had turned a blind eye to their exploits in breach of the Convention of Pretoria. The chiefs had been loyal to the British Crown in the first Boer War and were now the object of Boer vengeance.[6]

Gorst's resolution created something of a brouhaha. This was because Hicks Beach, an opposition front bench spokesman later to become Chancellor of the Exchequer, had plans to put down a motion on the same subject. When Gorst heard this he offered to withdraw his in favour of Beach's, but the offer was refused. This did not stop some Conservatives grumbling about what they saw as Gorst's insubordinate behaviour. Immediately Gorst flared up, as was his wont, and wrote to Northcote about the 'calumnies' being spread abroad about him. With another swipe he referred to the 'persecutions' to which he had been subjected in the Conservative ranks since 1874 against which he had 'vainly looked for support from the leaders to whom I have always been so loyal …'[7]

This did not end the affair, for Gorst finally wrote to *The Times* a letter, published on 3 April, stating that twice in the session his actions in the House had been cited as examples of 'insubordination'. This he hotly denied. On the first occasion – to do with an Irish controversy – an amendment he had moved had been, he insisted, warmly approved of by Northcote. The second was concerning his Transvaal resolution which, he knew, had the 'entire approbation' of Northcote.

This incident reflects on Gorst's perception of his conduct. As far as loyalty to the party went he clearly considered that up to this time he, and the Fourth Party too, had shown no disloyalty to the party leadership, even if in private he mocked them. It is true that Gorst was more careful in what he said than Lord Randolph, but at the same time he must be open to the charge of either misjudging the situation or else of a tendency towards hypocrisy.

More dramatic events, however, were about to unfold which would in due course drastically affect the relations between the Fourth Party and the Conservative leadership. Lord Randolph was now determined to grasp the nettle of the leadership issue. First he wrote to *The Times*, a practice much favoured by the two most militant members of the Fourth Party. The letter, which was simply signed 'a Tory', denounced the fact that Northcote was to play the principal part in the forthcoming ceremony of the unveiling of Beaconsfield's statue in Westminster Abbey Green, while Lord Salisbury had only a secondary role. Four days later Churchill followed up this letter with another one over his own signature. This time, going to the heart of the matter, he appealed to the party to choose a new leader forthwith. Northcote, Lord Salisbury and Lord Cairns all had good qualifications, he pointed out. But, having laid at Northcote's door a catalogue of failures on the part of the opposition, he then came down firmly in favour of Salisbury as a leader.

This letter went down badly with the party. Northcote received an enormous ovation in the Commons when he next rose to speak. 'Even

Gorst publicly signified his allegiance to Northcote', wrote the biographer Winston Churchill,[8] presumably referring to a testimonial raised by colleagues in support of Northcote which Gorst (and Wolff) had signed.

Lord Randolph was not discouraged and against the advice of various friends (not necessarily his Fourth Party ones) proceeded to send yet another signed letter to *The Times* on the same subject, this time asserting that there was now a need for the party to have a leader who was not afraid of meeting the working class and who by the influence of an ancient name could 'move the hearts of households'.[9] For many, Churchill could have been referring again to Lord Salisbury. But many others believed that Churchill was, audaciously enough, throwing his own hat into the ring. This, indeed, was his intention. The political excitement occasioned by these two letters was further increased by an article which appeared on 1 May in the *Fortnightly Review* entitled 'Elijah's Mantle'. It was written by Lord Randolph after discussion with Gorst and Wolff,[10] and bore the unmistakable imprint of the Fourth Party.

Elijah was of course Lord Beaconsfield. The theme of the article was that there was a need for his mantle to fall on someone capable of carrying forward his policies on imperial rule and social reform. For the first time Churchill used the term 'Tory democracy' and outlined the kind of social progress he envisaged it would bring. For him the central proposition of Tory democracy was that the Conservative Party was competent to deal with the needs of democracy and the multiplying problems of modern life.[11] Furthermore, the Constitution, so far from being incompatible with the social progress of the great mass of the people, was itself a flexible instrument by which that progress might be guided and secured.

The term Tory democracy has been discussed backwards and forwards by historians of the period. No one seems quite sure what the two words taken together precisely mean. There does, however, seem to be some common ground in that the term became prominent through its promotion by Lord Randolph Churchill and the Fourth Party. Further, its origins are somehow related to the supposed political principles handed down by Disraeli.

Shannon states that the term is 'doctrinally notoriously problematic ...' and that it 'has often meant different things to different men'. He goes on to refer to the radical W. S. Blunt, who had quoted Lord Randolph as not knowing himself what Tory democracy was 'but I believe it is principally opportunism'. For Coleman, Disraeli did little to reshape Conservatism significantly in either thought or policy, and was largely indifferent to the opportunities offered by Tory democracy. Nor were the Tories in 1880 'a social reform party and indeed had never been one'. Foster, in his biography of Lord Randolph, emphasises Gorst's one-time influence over Churchill who, he considers, was in 1882 'borrowing ideas of Gorst and [Edward] Clarke and dressing them up in the language of Tory Democracy'. However, Foster does not attempt a definition of the troublesome term.[12]

There are strong grounds for believing that of the Fourth Party friends it was Gorst who really took the lead in pushing for a redefinition of Conservatism. He had long sought to mobilise middle-class Toryism, and to attract support from the working class to the cause. In this way the party would become a popular one. During Churchill's illness in 1882 Gorst wrote to him as follows:

> The time seems ripe for the rise of the Democratic Tory party which was always Dizzy's dream at the head of which you might easily place yourself. I want to write an article on the feebleness of the Conservative Party as a political organization, pointing out it is led by and in the interest of a narrow oligarchic and land-owning class and that the people in whom the real Conservatism of the nation resides have no voice in the matter.

There followed quite soon the two articles to which we have referred: one was 'The State of the Opposition' and the other 'Elijah's Mantle'. In the early 1880s Gorst had seen an opportunity of using the aristocratic Churchill to front for him in promoting his ideas. But Churchill, no front man as Gorst was to discover, had his own goals.[13]

Many years later Gorst propounded in a well-known passage what he believed was meant by Tory democracy as follows:

> The principle of Tory Democracy is that all government exists solely for the good of the governed; that Church and King, Lords and Commons, and all other public institutions are to be maintained so far, and so far only, as they promote the happiness and welfare of the common people; that all who are entrusted with any public function are trustees, not for their own class, but for the nation at large; and that the mass of the people may be trusted so to use electoral power, which should be freely conceded to them, as to support those who are promoting their interests. It is Democratic because the welfare of the people is its supreme end; it is Tory because the institutions of the country are the means by which the end is to be attained.[14]

When Gorst wrote these words in a letter to *The Times* published in 1907 he had had time of course to reflect on and to distil his own political philosophy, which was based, as he always believed it to be, on sound Disraelian principles. The probability, however, is that this definition of Tory democracy did not differ so very much from the beliefs he held in the heyday of the Fourth Party. For Gorst, the father of Tory democracy was undoubtedly Disraeli. If, on the other hand, Disraeli was indifferent to the concept of Tory democracy as Coleman, and others, contend, and indeed was not even enthusiastic over social reform, where did this leave Gorst? Either he misread Disraeli or else, in pursuit of his own aims, he decided to promote his ideas in Disraeli's name. Could this have been what Disraeli meant when he described Gorst as the only 'dangerous' member of the Fourth Party?

The principal purpose of the Fourth Party in its first three years of existence had been to supply an energetic opposition to the government, even though this meant at times revolting against the weak tactics adopted by Northcote. Now it seemed as if a quite new objective was discernible. The Fourth Party was to spearhead a campaign to make its dynamic chief into the party leader.

Balfour now stood aside and dropped out of the counsels held by the other three. He wanted his uncle Lord Salisbury as leader and wished to take no part in any plan which ran counter to this aim. The others understood this. Although there is no direct evidence, Balfour's departure might have been a relief to Gorst. Later Gorst had strong reservations about Balfour and his motivation for being a member of the Fourth Party. He would write that Balfour 'though acting with us was all the time a spy upon us reporting to Lord Salisbury that we were trying to upset both Northcote and him'.[15]

And what of Gorst and Wolff? How did they respond to Lord Randolph's plan? Winston Churchill writes that after the publication of his successive letters in *The Times* his father sat in the Commons 'alone and abandoned hunched up in his corner seat' and remained 'silent and solitary' for a week.[16] It does not, therefore, look as if his two comrades were very obviously supportive at this stage. This must have been for Gorst a critical time. According to his son Harold, he had misgivings about departing from the original principles which guided the Fourth Party. In John Gorst's own words, he urged Lord Randolph that he 'should look to succeeding and not supplanting Northcote'.[17] This prudent advice was disregarded. Gorst was not, however, a man to dither. Hanham states that Gorst had gone too far with Churchill not to go the whole way, and 'by the end of April he was committed to supporting Lord Randolph's bid for party leadership'. Certainly, Gorst was soon reconciled to Churchill's new ambitions whatever the cost to his own political prospects. The upshot was that both he and Wolff stood loyally by the younger man.

At this moment an unexpected blow befell Lord Randolph. Early in July 1883 his father, the Duke of Marlborough, died suddenly at home. This happened when the Fourth Party had been combining together – for the last time – over the Parliamentary Elections (Corrupt and Illegal Practices) Bill, which sought to prevent abuses at elections by setting maximum expenditure limits in a constituency, and imposing on a designated agent the responsibility of making a full return of a candidate's expenses. This was a measure about which they all felt strongly; Gorst for instance, ever in the forefront as an advocate of such reform, was on his feet no less than 33 times during the Bill's committee stage.[18]

Churchill was profoundly shocked by his father's death and retired to Blenheim to read his father's letters preserved from boyhood. Nothing would persuade him to return to the rough and tumble of the Commons for the rest of the parliamentary session. But this did not prevent him from thinking and scheming about how he was to make his bid for the leadership.

According to his elder son Jack, it was John Gorst who suggested to Lord Randolph using the National Union as a vehicle for obtaining power.[19] This sounds right, for Gorst had an unrivalled knowledge of the party machine, and was in many ways the ideas man of the Fourth Party. Gorst had chaired the meeting in 1867 when the National Union had been formed, and then in the 1870s had been the organisation's secretary. He was a regular attender at the National Union annual conferences and was a Vice Chairman. Churchill had been co-opted onto the Council in 1882 and was in the process of winning for himself by his oratory and personality great popularity in the country as a speaker and progressive politician.

The National Union, although a representative body with half of its Council elected, had no real authority in the party and no funds at its disposal. Real control over the party organisation lay, as we have seen, with the Central Committee. The plan worked out by Churchill and Gorst was as follows. The first step for the conspirators – for that is what they were in effect – was to get delegates to the National Union conference, due to take place at Birmingham on 1 and 2 October 1883, to register a strong protest against the impotence of their organisation and its Council and to demand reform. Then it would be necessary to win over to their views a majority of the members of the National Council. This meant canvassing among candidates for the Council during the elections which were held during the conference. This was not the end, for they had to ensure that they also had a majority among those co-opted onto the Council after the conference. Then they would be ready to try to obtain financial independence from the Central Committee and to wrest power from that body.[20]

The Churchill-Gorst plan was ambitious but not unrealistic as there was considerable backing in the National Union for the Fourth Party's wish to broaden the democratic base of the Conservative party. Obtaining a majority on the Council was crucial to the plan's success. Against all this, Northcote and Lord Salisbury were the men in possession of the party machine; they disliked the Fourth Party and what it stood for.[21]

The outline of the plan must have been hatched before Gorst left for his holiday in mid-August, for in a letter to Churchill dated 7 August he wrote on how they must both be at the conference 'if we mean to carry out our scheme'.[22] Wolff, though, Gorst said, must not be put up for the Council at the conference but be co-opted later. Clearly Gorst, already working hard behind the scenes on selecting the right candidates for the Council, did not want the exercise to look too much like a put-up job by the Fourth Party. Their designs should not be developed until they had their majority on the Council.

A week later he was writing to Churchill from North Devon telling him that 'I am quite ready to help you to develop a new Tory party, which already exists in embryo and with which your name is identified'. He was against 'leaning on Salisbury who is a broken reed.'[23] Gorst could not have been more wrong in his last observation, as Salisbury would be Prime Minister for nearly 15 out of the next 19 years.

Every year Gorst spent part of the summer holiday with his wife and children. For instance in 1881 they had all been in Castle Combe at his brother's, the next year they were in the Lake District at Grasmere, and in 1884 they would be in the Isle of Wight. Much later on we shall see Gorst happily bicycling with some of his grown-up children in northern France.

Now it was Croyde, Gorst told Lord Randolph, that had been selected by Mary as the 'summer residence of her children'. He described it as a kind of 'ultima Thule' (end of the world). The house they had taken was half a mile from the village, situated on the 'most dismal and desolate shore'. Gorst was an urban man and never really a countryman at heart. Croyde was too cut off for him, with no telegraph and the London papers not arriving till noon. He did, though, say that the 'fine hard sand, pools, shrimps, shells and the open Atlantic [was] to the children ... a paradise'.[24] There was, alas, no indication of whether this somewhat austere-looking heavily bearded man, probably dressed in rather sombre colours with jacket and tie, ever rolled up his trousers to paddle or build sand castles to satisfy Eva and Gwen, still both under ten. Perhaps he did not. More likely he spent much of his time getting his book, boringly entitled *An Election Manual*, ready for the printer. This treatise for election managers paid special attention to the Corrupt and Illegal Practices Act recently enacted and a subject close to Gorst's heart. For secretarial assistance Gorst sometimes used the services of his daughter Hylda, now 16. The father was not above blaming the daughter, to her indignation, for spelling mistakes.

When Gorst left Devon at the end of August he was off to spend a short time in Germany. His destination was Halle but he also made stops at Frankfurt and Weimar, and on his way home he would stay in Brussels. During these travels he had time to write to Lord Randolph discussing the forthcoming Birmingham conference and what their aims should be, and proposing soon a 'real Cabinet' with Wolff. He never hesitated to set out clearly his views. Thus:

> The great thing to work upon is the desire of the associations [of the National Union] to have their importance recognised and we must persuade them that they ought to have more voice in the management of affairs ... [25]

Gorst was ever tactically minded. There can be little doubt that Churchill relied on his friend's knowledge and acute mind to pick a way for them through the labyrinth of the party machine during this exercise.

The conference, attended by over 450 delegates from all parts of the country, went well for Churchill and Gorst, although they did not have it all their own way. Churchill told the delegates that he would like to see the control of the party organisation taken out of the hands of the self-elected body, the Central Committee.[26] Gorst lent all his support to Churchill although when he told the conference there was no danger of a party split over Churchill's proposals he was over-optimistic. Of course Gorst was most anxious at this delicate stage to be conciliatory. Churchill at any rate got his way and a resolution was passed that the Council should take steps to secure for the National Union 'its legitimate influence in the party organisation'. This was enough for the Fourth Party, and Gorst wrote on 3 October to tell

Wolff of their 'triumph' and how Randolph, who was received by the delegates with loud cheers, made a 'capital speech attacking the Central Committee and carried all before him'. The elections to the Council, Gorst went on, were not so successful and 'undesirable men got elected'.[27] According to Hanham, Gorst and Churchill overplayed their hands at first in preparing too thoroughly for the conference because their list of approved candidates leaked out to Northcote. Accordingly, the pro-Northcote camp was able to prevent Churchill from winning an overwhelming victory.[28]

On 2 November the newly elected Council members met for the purpose of choosing the 12 co-opted members. As a result of the lobbying, those supporting Churchill and his Tory democracy platform gained, to Gorst's relief, a small majority on the Council. Overall Gorst, as chief organiser of what amounted to a coup by the Fourth Party, had excelled.

There was one other piece of Fourth Party business taking place at the time of the National Union campaign. The previous spring, at the time of the unveiling of the late party leader's statue, Wolff had hit upon the idea of founding a society in memory of Lord Beaconsfield. Churchill was enthusiastic and Gorst joined the other two in promoting that autumn the Primrose Tory League, as it was first known, a new political society 'embracing all classes and creeds except atheists and enemies of the British nation'. A declaration was drawn up by Gorst whereby every member undertook to devote his, and later her, best ability to 'the maintenance of religion, the estates of the realm, and of the Imperial ascendancy of the British Empire … consistently with his [or her] allegiance to the Sovereign'. The three friends plus Sir Alfred Slade, a senior civil servant, became the Ruling Council of the League. The new society had a slow start in gathering members, and by the end of 1884 a mere 957 individuals had enrolled. But the pace began to accelerate and by 1891, after the official Conservative Party leadership had reluctantly given its approval to the project, the number had passed the million mark. The League's success was in due course assured as it became a unifying force within the party, helping with canvassing and providing social occasions when different classes mixed.[29]

Now in November 1883 there was a disappointment for Churchill. At this still crucial moment Gorst had to go to India to give legal advice to Raja Narend who was aspiring to become the Chief Minister to the young Nizam of Hyderabad. It was a long-standing commitment which Gorst felt he must honour. He would be away for over three months. Churchill was 'terribly upset' at hearing this news from Gorst and tried to make him change his mind about going.[30] Gorst told Churchill it was 'very flattering to my vanity to think I shall be missed as much as you say but reason tells me the Fourth Party movement will go on very well without me'. Perhaps more interesting than this snippet, Gorst commented rather sadly on the outlook for him as he saw it, as follows:

> I have not much political ambition left ... there is not much prospect of my ever rising to any eminence either in the law or in the state, and I only keep on in Parliament partly from habit partly from obstinacy and partly because it will be pleasant to think hereafter that I have been the early colleague of a man who will rise so high as you will in the political world.[31]

This sounded very much like a swan song, and one moreover which seemed to acknowledge a lack of success in his career. Before his ship sailed for India Gorst passed a valedictory note to Churchill beginning as usual 'My dear Randolph', and ending, unusually and touchingly, 'ever your sincere and faithful friend, J. E. Gorst'.[32]

We will now leave the Fourth Party and Lord Randolph's further efforts to pursue his ambitions, and follow Gorst to India.

NOTES

1. Correspondence of Lord Randolph Churchill (Ld RC), Add. 9248; Gorst (G)–Churchill (C), various letters 8–29 Jan. and 5 Feb. 1883; G–Wolff, 7 Feb. 1883.
2. FP, 216.
3. Ibid., 219.
4. 3 PD, 276, 2 Mar. 1883, 1319.
5. Ibid., 1939.
6. 3 PD, 277, 13 Mar. 1883, 413.
7. Iddesleigh, Add. 50041; G–Northcote, 13 Mar. 1883.
8. Churchill, 194.
9. Ibid., 196.
10. FP, 240; also see Churchill, *Lord Randolph Churchill*, 199.
11. Churchill, *Lord Randolph Churchill*, 230.
12. Shannon, *The Age of Disraeli*, 1–2; Coleman, *Conservatism and the Conservative Party*, 157, 159, 160; Foster, *Lord Randolph Churchill*, 60, 96.
13. Ld RC, G–C, 10 Sept 1882; *Review of Reviews*, 4 Aug. 1891, 581; see also Foster, *Lord Randolph Churchill*, 60, 114–15.
14. *The Times*, 6 Feb. 1907.
15. MLL, 141.
16. Churchill, *Lord Randolph Churchill*, 194–5.
17. MLL, 140–1.
18. 3 PD, 280, 12 June 1883 696.

19. JG AN vol. 1, 1885, 22.
20. Churchill, *Lord Randolph Churchill*, 239; FP, 251.
21. Churchill, *Lord Randolph Churchill*, 237.
22. Ld RC, G–C 7, Aug. 1883.
23. Ibid., G–C, 15 Aug. 1883.
24. Ibid.
25. Ld RC, G–C, 22 Sept. 1883.
26. McKenzie, *Political Political Parties*, 170–1.
27. FP, 257.
28. Hanham, *Elections and Party Management*, 367.
29. Churchill, *Lord Randolph Churchill*, 203; Foster, *Lord Randolph Churchill*, 132; Pugh, *The Making of Modern British Politics*, 55.
30. FP, 260.
31. Ld RC, G–C, 9 Nov. 1883.
32. Ibid., G–C, 21 Nov. 1883.

13

Interlude in India

It was in late November 1883 that Gorst hurried by train to Brindisi in Italy to catch the boat for Port Said and onwards to Aden and Bombay. He may have been relieved to leave behind him for a while the Fourth Party's demanding manoeuvres to seize power. He had in fact suggested to Lord Randolph, in one of his last letters written before leaving for India, that Churchill's path in the National Union vis-à-vis Northcote and others would now be easier. For Stanhope, a member of the Central Committee, 'will capitulate to you far more readily than he would to you and me conjoined'.[1] This may have been meant as a crumb of comfort to Churchill who was upset by Gorst going to India.

The journey to Bombay took some 20 days and was described by Gorst as 'pleasant and prosperous'. On board as far as Port Said was the cultivated Nubar Pasha who had formerly been the Prime Minister of Egypt. Some years before he had, in company with the British finance minister, been attacked in Cairo by Egyptian army officers armed with swords. This minor mutiny was a precursor of Arabi's revolt of 1882 over which the Fourth Party had fulminated regarding Gladstone's military intervention. Gorst and Nubar Pasha got on well together and the Egyptian asked Gorst to stay with him on his way back from India[2] – an invitation he could not accept.

But we must turn to the reasons which were taking Gorst to India and, in particular, to how he came to be involved in the affairs of Hyderabad, the largest of all the princely states, in which the Nizam, a Muslim, ruled over 9,000,000 people, mainly Hindus.

About a fifth of India's population was ruled by princes, who numbered 675 at the beginning of the twentieth century. The political status of princely states was the result of treaties made between their rulers and the East India Company. While these agreements acknowledged British paramountcy over a state's defence and relations between its neighbours, the prince was expected to govern his people even-handedly and with the guidance of a British resident or agent. If a prince broke faith he could be deposed by the Viceroy, who also had a final say in any disputed succession.

Hyderabad had a long history of maladministration and had consequently become deeply in debt to the East India Company which had governed much of India until the Mutiny in 1857. By way of liquidating this debt, certain valuable districts of the state comprising a region known as Berar had in 1853 been made over by treaty to the Company, although the Nizam retained over it some nominal sovereignty. In addition, this assignment of Berar was a security for the payment of the 'Hyderabad contingent', a force officered by the British and maintained in the state for internal security reasons, for which the Nizam paid. Berar, well governed and prosperous, became something of a bone of contention between the Nizam, who did not accept he had permanently lost the region, and the Indian government which was represented in Hyderabad by a British Resident.

In 1874 the Nizam was a minor and one of his two Regents, Sir Salar Jung, who was the Chief Minister (Dewan) for the state of Hyderabad, made a claim to the Resident for the return of Berar. The Resident, however, refused to pass this claim on to the Viceroy in Calcutta. After much fencing, a despatch was sent by Jung direct to Lord Salisbury, the Secretary of State for India. Even though this procedure was irregular, Salisbury looked into the matter and asked Gorst for his legal opinion on the whole 'Berar Question'.

Salisbury was five years older than Gorst. The two men, with their bushy beards and domed foreheads, were somewhat alike in looks although Gorst did not have Salisbury's physical presence. Even temperamentally they had some similarities. At this time Salisbury had just begun his second stint at the India Office, having been Secretary of State for a year in 1866 before resigning over the Reform Bill. Several times he had clashed with Disraeli who famously described him as 'a great master of gibes, flouts and jeers'. At this period in the mid-1870s Salisbury and Gorst appeared to have cordial relations. Unhappily, within a decade strains between them were apparent, as the Fourth Party challenged the Conservative Party leadership for power.

In the opinion Gorst gave Salisbury in July 1875 he argued that, if the Nizam ceded or assigned territory in perpetuity, the principal debt would be cancelled in accordance with his interpretation of the treaty. But as the debt had not been cancelled, the region had not been assigned in perpetuity. He also pointed out that under the treaty a perpetual transfer of the management of Berar was allowed without a transfer of sovereignty.[3] One other complication was the Hyderabad Contingent, which, Jung alleged, had not been employed by the government of India in accordance with the treaty and was ruinously expensive for Hyderabad to maintain. In any case these troops were no longer needed for the security of the state, which was tranquil.

Gorst – and we do not know whether he was asked first – also typically enough gave his opinion to Salisbury on wider matters. He considered for instance, writing in November 1874, that Sir Salar Jung as Regent offered the state stable government. On Berar, which he held to have been improperly acquired by the Company, he believed the time was favourable for the restoration of the region to the Nizam. This surely was a political, and not a legal, matter. For good measure he also indicated to Salisbury his disapproval of the way the Resident had handled the Berar question.[4] Salisbury, in the event, postponed making any decision on the matter until the Nizam came of age in 1884. In the meantime, Gorst continued to have dealings with Hyderabad, where he must now have been regarded as sympathetic to Sir Salar Jung and his views. In September 1875 he had received telegrams from the Dewan about the Indian government's proposal that the Nizam, a delicate and nervous child, should go to Bombay to meet the Prince of Wales at the start of the first royal tour of India. But the Dewan, under pressure to agree to this, wanted to reserve the right for the Nizam not to go if he were ill. In passing this on, Gorst told Salisbury that there was a danger that Jung might think he could appeal to Salisbury over the head of the Viceroy.[5]

There is one other instance of Gorst doing work for the India Office when in 1877 he advised Salisbury that certain letters patent on the appointment of bishops would be 'null and void' if left as drafted by his department.[6] Apart from this, there is no further evidence that he discussed Hyderabad again with the India Office. It does, though, seem that Gorst remained in touch with Jung, for in November 1883 he was telling Lord Randolph that he had been 'consulted by a succession of Ministers of the Nizam about the Berar question for the last 10 years'.[7] It is curious that, having started his connection with Hyderabad by advising the Secretary of State for India, Gorst seems to have continued it by advising the Nizam's Chief Minister. Presumably he saw no conflict of interest here.

In February 1883 the long-serving Jung died of cholera. The British government, faced with the prospect of the Nizam not attaining his majority for another year, appointed (at the suggestion of the Resident) a Council of Regency. Executive power was for the moment shared between Liak Ali, the eldest son of the late Dewan, and the elderly Raja Narend, whose title was the Peshcar and who had himself been a long-time colleague of the Dewan.

At the very time that Gorst was travelling out to India these two men – the Peshcar and Liak Ali, a generation apart – were becoming locked in a power struggle as to who would become the Dewan. While the authority of the Viceroy, Lord Ripon, loomed large over the choice, it was nonetheless both in theory and in practice the Nizam himself who chose the Dewan. Gorst's services had been retained by the Peshcar who required the English lawyer's advice on the current situation over the Dewanship and on the governance of Hyderabad. The Peshcar's friend and legal adviser in India was Thomas Palmer, a Eurasian barrister. Palmer met Gorst off the ship and would soon accompany him to the seat of the government in Calcutta. To Gorst's evident pleasure he was accorded while in Bombay the 'kindest hospitality' from the Governor with whom he stayed for his first two days in the country. Slightly hypocritically, Gorst praised Northcote to the governor, and blamed for all 'his errors' the hapless Cross, a regular butt of the Fourth Party.[8]

That we know something about Gorst's progress in India is principally due to six surviving letters he wrote while there to Lord Randolph. These letters were full of wit and comment, often pungent. Early on he pretended to have fallen victim to the Indian climate:

> I am stretched in an indolent attitude upon a luxurious chaise longue smoking a cheroot after tiffin (observe the Indian phraseology), quite unable to rouse myself to write a letter; so my friend … (who) is not so lazy has kindly consented without the slightest pressure to write from dictation.[9]

But the writer makes it clear in a footnote that he had only consented to write after the 'strongest' pressure had been applied. In fact, during his two-month visit, Gorst appeared to be full of energy and took abundant notice of all he heard and saw.

In Calcutta, where Gorst stayed in an hotel, were gathered the Nizam of Hyderabad, Liak Ali, the Peshcar, two other less significant men hoping to become Dewan and other Hyderabad luminaries. They were there primarily to see an exhibition. Gorst had countless interviews with them all. The air was always thick with intrigue (a word much favoured by Gorst – he always spelt it 'intreague'), and round the Nizam and his entourage swirled, to Gorst's delight, a crowd of jesters, astrologers and soothsayers.

The Nizam, Gorst found, was intelligent but shy. He was, of course, not yet 18. Gorst had little time for Liak Ali, a fat youth of 20, born of a slave concubine of low caste. The young man, Gorst said, was 'tipsy and depraved'. He had reputedly great influence over the Nizam because he supplied him with liquor and got drunk in his company. In later letters Gorst said that Liak Ali, a 'clown' of no ability, used violent language against the British government quoting him as saying, somewhat mysteriously, that 'he would not take the trouble to smite the Resident on the mouth with his shoe ... '[10] Gorst found it hard to believe this youth might be entrusted with the post of Dewan.

At first Gorst misjudged the Peshcar, assessing him to be like the 'goat' (Northcote) at home: that is, he was swayed by his advisers. He revised this opinion on better acquaintance and described him as 'a shrewd and clever man, a great judge of character and has a strong will of his own'. Gorst thought he should be left alone by the government and he would govern the state well. Maybe Gorst was premature in making this judgement because he had not yet visited Hyderabad. When he did in January 1884, he saw to his amusement that the Peshcar was undoubtedly eccentric and did his business in a strange way. Gorst described a visit to his palace in the city of Hyderabad:

> After penetrating several streets crowded with bullock carts, horses, natives dressed and undressed, Arabs armed to the teeth, Rohillas with lighted matchlocks, elephants and other perils, we went down a narrow lane just wide enough for the carriage to pass and emerged in a courtyard crammed with every sort of picturesque rascal you can imagine. Thence we penetrated into a large open space with rooms all round and gardens in the middle, occupied by people who had the entrée, very pretty and charming. Finally I was taken down some narrow steps into a dark cellar not 6 feet high, tiled and floored with white calico. There my Prime Minister was seated on the floor with his official documents strewn about, governing the state ...[11]

As far as the Raj went, Gorst described India as a 'paradise of permanent officialism'. The government, he conceded, was benevolent and well-intentioned. It collected a vast amount of information on material facts but everything was 'ingeniously contrived to keep [those governing] wholly ignorant of the feelings and character of their subjects'. He singled out as 'preposterous' the transfer of power, for climatic reasons for nine months of the year, from Calcutta to Simla where officials were cut off from communication with the outside world. It was as if, he said with nice exaggeration, the Cabinet was governing Britain from the Caucasus.[12]

Surely, he suggested, this was something that the Fourth Party should attack in Parliament.

At the head of the pyramid was the Viceroy, Lord Ripon, a former Liberal politician, appointed in 1880. He was a Roman Catholic convert, a fact which gave Gorst the opportunity for making digs at the proconsul. Ripon had taken no notice of Gorst who could not therefore go to Government House and 'bully' him as, he told Lord Randolph, 'you would have done …' However he, Gorst, 'had been very kindly received by many members of the Council'. Gorst was not entirely without humility for he added that Wolff with his 'immense knowledge of men and talent for intreague' would have 'worked' the Council a hundred times better than he, Gorst, had done. On his own, and away from his Fourth Party friends, he admitted to feeling lame and incompetent.[13]

The talk of the town among Europeans at the end of the year was about the 'Ilbert Bill'. A problem for the Raj – Gorst did not consider it an important one – had arisen in the field of criminal jurisdiction. Until 1883 an Englishman could demand to be tried in court by another Englishman. But by the 1880s some Indians had become judges. Ripon proposed to sweep away racial distinction in the courts by means of this piece of legislation. Despite the justice of the measure, the Bill ran into trouble from the European community and the Viceroy had to make a compromise whereby Europeans facing trial could opt for a British judge and demand juries composed of at least six Europeans.[14] Gorst in his sharply critical way told Churchill that Ripon was partly to blame for all this as he had mishandled matters. Another source of irritation to Gorst was that Ripon was toying with the idea of dissolving all connection between the government of India and the Anglican and Presbyterian church establishments. Something, he suggested, might be made of this. Wolff, 'our champion of religion', might frame some 'poisonous questions' on the subject in parliament. All this had come to light in the press, perhaps, as Gorst mischievously suggested, through the Viceroy's Jesuit confessor.[15]

A journalist, Seymour Keay, had been writing, Gorst reported, 'scurrilous' articles in the *Statesman*. Keay, it seemed, was supporting Liak Ali for the Dewanship and presumably wished to discredit the Peshcar and his various advisers. Among other things Keay had accused Gorst of robbing the Nizam's treasury of 75,000 rupees (some £5,300). This, Gorst told Churchill, was simply not true.[16] His legal fees amounted to a mere £1,000 a month (*c.* £48,000 today).[17] In an article written in Simla in June 1884 by Grattan Geary, to which we will refer in more detail presently, it was stated that the sum of 82,000 rupees had been withdrawn by the Hyderabad treasury for payment to the lawyer Thomas Palmer. The Peshcar, on being asked about this sum, said rather opaquely that it was needed 'to make large purchases for the Nizam in Bombay'. But the newspaper *Pioneer*, quoted by Geary, maintained that money was drawn as 'a fee for Mr Gorst' whose advice was sought by the Peshcar, and that this statement had never been contradicted.[18] Of course, there was nothing wrong in Gorst accepting a fee for his legal services. He would not have gone to India in the first place unless the visit had been made financially worthwhile for him.

On 5 January Gorst went to Hyderabad, where he stayed at the Residency in Bolarum outside the capital. He was there for just over a month and attended the investiture of the Nizam on 5 February. Gorst spoke well of his host the Resident, whose influence 'prevented acts of cruelty and oppression' in the state. Affairs in Hyderabad Gorst regarded as being in a mess, the government operating a system of 'robbery and plunder' at the expense of the peasants. No one thought about the wretched condition of the millions of Hyderabad's cultivators of the soil, which was far worse, he opined, than that of their neighbours administered by British officials. The previous much-vaunted Dewan, Sir Salar Jung, for whom Gorst had once acted, had been, in his revised view, a rank failure as an administrator, and was therefore largely responsible for the present poor state of affairs. Gorst may have taken away an exaggerated picture of the miseries in Hyderabad but, he told Churchill, he had been careful to get the views of all parties there.[19]

The Berar question might have been expected to loom large during Gorst's visit. Instead it failed to surface. In fact, the question had receded into the background as the leading men in Hyderabad did not want to muddy the waters while the Dewanship was still undecided. Far more important for the Peshcar was his apparent need to obtain Gorst's advice on the running of the state.[20] In this he seemed to be picking Gorst's brains not so much as a lawyer but rather as a politician-cum-administrator. Whether Gorst, with his basic ignorance of Indian affairs, was the right person to advise is another matter. Geary refers to a report of two-and-a-half printed sides which was handed by the Peshcar to the Viceroy with proposals for the future government of Hyderabad. He implies this was the work of Gorst. The report recommended that there should be no consultative council in the state, that the Dewan should have sole and undivided authority and that to counter the impulsive temper of youth the Dewan should be a person of 'mature age'.[21] It is a pity that more is not known of this report so that we can judge the full sense of its author's arguments and recommendations.

Although some 5,000 miles away from London, Gorst did not neglect keeping abreast of affairs at home as far as he could through the newspapers and letters sent to him by Lord Randolph and others, even if his information was well out of date by the time it reached him. In fact the later letters he wrote to Churchill seem to show more interest in what was happening in the National Union and in respect of forthcoming events in the Commons than to what went on in 'this benighted and heathen land', as he put it. On 22 January he was earnestly requesting Churchill to protect his position in Parliament and to see, for example, he was not left off the Public Accounts Committee. There is an amusing postscript to this letter which reads:

> Please tell Wolff that when the Viceroy arrives here [at the Residency] next week I am to be turned out of my room into a tent in order to make room for Father Carr, Lord Ripon's popish confessor, and that a room in the Residency is being fitted up as a chapel in which Mass will be said and Lord Ripon will go daily to confession.[22]

Gorst could not resist picking on this kind of incident which pleased his puckish sense of humour.

While Gorst did not leave us with a full description of the Nizam's installation by the Viceroy on 5 February, he does refer to the occasion in an article entitled 'The Kingdom of the Nizam' which he wrote for the April 1884 issue of the *Fortnightly Review*.[23] In this article Gorst, as anyone reading thus far might anticipate, was highly critical about certain aspects of the governance of the country he had just visited. In Hyderabad's rural districts there was no proper administration of justice, and persons were thrown into 'loathsome' prisons on 'frivolous charges'. Although the system in place was fair, the revenue collectors were in practice corrupt and they stripped the peasants 'of everything except the cloth round their loins'.

Gorst criticised too the disposal of the revenue, the absence of an independent audit and the total indebtedness of the state which, he calculated, was £2,000,000 (*c*. £96m today). Also Hyderabad was 'infested with salaried officers with absolutely nothing to do', and the Resident at the time of Jung's death was ignorant of the real condition of the people and the disordered state of Hyderabad's finances. Gorst suggested, and here he may have been rather chancing his arm, that Hyderabad – whose Nizam was one of the leading Muslim princes in the land – was well fitted to become a 'centre of disaffection to the British power'. Although he did refer to Hyderabad's loyalty during the Mutiny, Gorst was worried that the chief posts in the Nizam's government were occupied by men from outside Hyderabad.

Gorst then had some fun at the expense of the Indian Foreign Office which was responsible for relations with the princely states and, as he saw it, its over-zealous regard for ceremonial. Its voluminous pages of printed instructions issued for the Nizam's installation caught his eye with, for instance, details of how a train with two sleeping Hyderabad noblemen was required to meet at the state frontier in the dead of night a train containing 'his slumbering Excellency' and how the two noblemen had to greet H.E. when he awoke at 8 am to inquire after his health. He noted too how it was laid down precisely how many steps down his carpet the Nizam should take in order to meet the Viceroy. All this was of course the very stuff of which Imperial protocol and pageantry was made, but for Gorst it was 'childish'. He did not fail to observe that Lord Ripon had, at the durbar, succeeded in attaching the sword of honour to the Nizam's wrong side. The attendant nobles were horrified and regarded this as an evil omen, ascribing the attack of cholera with which the Nizam was seized after the ceremony to the Viceroy's blunder.

Towards the end of the piece Lord Ripon took some heavy punishment from Gorst's acerbic pen. The Viceroy, 'bewildered by his own ignorance, and frightened by the violence of the conspirators', had 'yielded to clamour' in approving the appointment of Liak Ali as Dewan. In doing so he had gone against the advice of the Residency who favoured the Peshcar. Finally, in defence of his client, Gorst accused the Viceroy of 'dismissing with the greatest discourtesy' the experienced Peshcar at the installation.

The Indian government or someone close to it could hardly not respond to what Gorst had written. An article, already referred to, entitled 'Hyderabad Politics', was published in Bombay and written by Grattan Geary.[24] His response was far longer than Gorst's piece. While Geary called Gorst's contribution clever, he baldly stated that it had 'no particular relation to the state of things as they existed in Hyderabad'. He then went on to repudiate much but not all of what Gorst had said. He considered that Sir Salar Jung had been a model reformer, that the Peshcar was old, feeble and an opium eater, and that Liak Ali was not dissipated. He admitted that the peasants were in a depressed condition in some areas but the main cause for this was the prohibition of the lucrative cultivation of the poppy. To represent the officials in Hyderabad as constituting – as Gorst said – an agency for seditious intrigues was 'wild and mischievous'. There was much more besides. The views expressed by the writers of the two articles were poles apart. But who was right? Taking account both of the history of maladministration in Hyderabad and of Gorst's powers of penetration, uncomfortable as these might sometimes be, we might guess that Gorst was not so wide of the mark in his main allegations about the governance of the State.

For the moment, but not for long, the affairs of India slip down below our horizon. There was a certain irony in what followed. Little did Gorst realise that in only two and a half years' time he would again be plunged into the affairs of the sub-continent, responsible in the Commons, as Under Secretary of State for India in Lord Salisbury's government, for dealing with that huge and complex land. At least he had been to the country, even if his visit was only a fleeting one. Fortunately by 1886 there was a new Viceroy, for Lord Ripon, after Gorst's strictures, would hardly have welcomed him as one of his political masters.

NOTES

1. Correspondence of Lord Randolph Churchill (Ld RC), Add. 9248, Gorst (G)–Churchill (C), 9 Nov. 1883.
2. Ibid., G–C, 14 Dec. 1883.
3. Salisbury Papers, G–Salisbury(S), 27 July 1874.
4. Ibid., G–S, 30 Sept. and 19 Nov. 1874.
5. Ibid., G–S, 13 and 25 Sept. 1875.
6. Ibid., G–S, 14 Dec. 1877.
7. Ld RC, G–C, 9 Nov. 1883.
8. Ibid., G–C, 14 Dec. 1883.
9. Ibid., G–C, 1 Jan 1884.
10. Ibid.
11. Ibid., G–C, 16 Jan. 1884.
12. Ibid., G–C, 24 Dec. 1883 and 5 Jan. 1884.
13. Ibid., G–C, 1 Jan. 1884.
14. Lawrence James, *Raj: The Making and Unmaking of British India*, London, Little, Brown, 1997, 351.
15. Ld RC, G–C, 1 Jan. 1884.
16. Ibid.
17. *Review of Reviews*, 4 Aug. 1891, 581.
18. BL, *Hyderabad politics*, printed at Bombay Gazette steam press, 6.
19. Ld RC, G–C, 22 Jan. 1884.
20. Ibid., G–C, 24 Dec. 1883.
21. *Hyderabad Politics*, 6.
22. Ld RC, G–C, 22 Jan. 1884.
23. *Fortnightly Review*, April 1884, 522–30.
24. *Hyderabad Politics*, 1–24, an article written in Simla in June 1884. There is no entry for any Grattan Geary in the India Office list of the time. This suggests the author was not an official. He may have been a journalist.

14

Exit the Fourth Party

John Gorst arrived back in England from India on 2 March 1884. There was much to hear about the Fourth Party and its activities. Some of the developments made Gorst uneasy.

Early in the previous December Churchill had succeeded in setting up, with himself as chairman, an 'organisation committee' reporting to the National Union's Council. It was principally composed of his supporters. Its purpose was to consider the best means of carrying forward the proposals of the conference held during the previous October[1] about seeing 'its legitimate influence in the party organisation' realised. This of course meant, for the Fourth Party, effectively relieving the Conservative Party's Central Committee of its power and transferring that power to the Council of the National Union.

In February Churchill had got into a dispute with Lord Percy, who objected to Churchill chairing the Organisation Committee, the result being that Lord Percy resigned as chairman of the Council. Churchill was promptly elected in his place. As promised at a meeting with Churchill the previous month, Lord Salisbury wrote on 29 February a formal letter to the Organisation Committee setting out the fields in which the Council could usefully operate. He stressed the National Union 'is and must remain in all its essential features local'. This letter was received with delight by Churchill and his friends who – calling it their 'charter' – considered they had been given all they were seeking.[2] This was unfortunately a serious misinterpretation of what Salisbury had said. Next the Organisation Committee proceeded to draft a report on the way ahead, as they now saw it, which *inter alia* claimed that funds should be set aside by the party to enable the National Union to discharge its new functions. This report was bound to offend against party orthodoxy.

Somehow Salisbury learnt what was in the wind, and without delay wrote to Churchill telling him there was no question of the National Union's Council taking the place of the Central Committee. Churchill, in his impulsive way, replied vigorously, putting down the Central Committee which in a struggle with a popular body, he was happy to say, would go 'in these days ... to the wall.'[3] The party leadership was now beginning to get irritated. The situation was compounded when the Council on 14 March, with Lord Percy and his cohorts dissenting, agreed to adopt the Organisation Committee's report by 19 votes to 7. In no time the National Union received a notice coming from the party leaders requesting them to quit the premises they had shared with Conservative Central Office since Gorst's day as party agent. This was a tactical error for the leadership had no legal power to eject the National Union, and their action upset Council members, many of whom were men of local importance.[4]

What we cannot be certain of is just how much of a part Gorst played in these events during the first half of March. For instance, with his knowledge of the Conservative Party machine, what interpretation did he place on Salisbury's 'charter letter', and was he a party to the Organisation Committee's report? Certainly he was present at the National Council's meeting of 14 March because he helped to defeat Lord Percy's motion.[5] He also attended a meeting Churchill had with Salisbury, Northcote and the Chief Whip, Winn, on 21 March at which some modifications were agreed to the contentious report. At the end of the month Gorst saw Northcote; he told him that on his return from India he had found some things done of which he did not approve (the ousting of Lord Percy was one). Also he indicated that the Fourth Party, desiring harmony, was anxious to come to terms.[6]

The Conservative leadership, uneasy at the course of events, now decided to state clearly what the limited functions of the National Union were. In a letter dated 1 April Salisbury declared that complete control of the National Union must lie with the Central Committee. Churchill hurriedly called together his Organisation Committee and sent off a belligerent reply, which was described by his son as an 'open declaration of war.'[7] This reply was composed by only four men: besides Churchill there was Gorst, now a member of this committee, a Mr Cotter and Colonel Burnaby. The last-named was a flamboyant and gallant explorer destined to be killed in the Sudan early the following year at the battle of Abu Klea. Some of the Council at its next meeting disapproved of the 'disrespectful and improper tone' of the Organisation Committee's letter. But Churchill, the bit firmly between his teeth, survived an acrimonious debate and vote of confidence. For the rest of the month intrigue was followed by counter-intrigue with a whiff of compromise in the air. In all this Gorst loyally supported Churchill. Even if there had been any doubts in his mind about the Fourth Party's tactics, his commitment to the cause was now firm, and he wrote to Churchill about 'our fight with Salisbury'.[8]

The next landmark was not long in coming into sight. At the Council's meeting in early May, Churchill, with several of his friends away, found himself unexpectedly outvoted and at once resigned the chairmanship of the Council. In the heat of the moment he said that he would retire from politics and the Fourth Party would be dissolved. Gorst and Wolff had heard this before and took no notice. The next day Churchill, in high good humour, acted with his friends as before and as if nothing had happened.[9] In the country, however, there was consternation at his resignation. A groundswell of support for him came flooding in and on 16 May he was unanimously re-elected chairman, with the result that his position was strengthened.

At about this time Jack Gorst, John's elder son, accepted against his father's advice an offer by Churchill of becoming the honorary secretary of the National Union. Jack, down from Cambridge, was undecided, like his father before him, on what career to choose. John Gorst strongly urged his son to learn from his own experience of the hazards of following a political career without benefit of powerful friends or money,[10] advice to which Jack only half listened. Jack would stay on with the National Union until the following year when Churchill asked him to be one of his private secretaries. This job he did for several months before finally joining the Diplomatic Service. As we shall see in the next chapter, Jack's association with Churchill was to prove of some use to his father.

During the Fourth Party's battle to capture the party machine, John Gorst never neglected his parliamentary work. Indeed, if anything he seemed to have been reinvigorated by his time in India and by his sea voyage home. Hyderabad was still on his mind and one of the first things he did on his return was to seek an interview with Lord Kimberley, the Secretary of State for India, to give him information about the 'cruel oppression' practised on the peasants there by the revenue collectors.[11] Typically, he followed this up with parliamentary questions in the House on this and other matters concerning Hyderabad.

In March Gorst quickly became involved in a whole series of interventions in the House of Commons on maritime and naval matters. Thus on 13 March he was asking whether parliament would make some effective provision regarding the over-insurance of unseaworthy vessels; a week later he made a speech on the state of the navy, aiming a shaft towards governments past and present at the 'supineness of successive Boards of Admiralty'; again in the following week he expressed his unhappiness at why workmen in Chatham dockyard were placed on piecework without being informed about their rates of pay. Later he would make his usual contribution in the debate on naval estimates and would then push the worthy cause of shipwrights, who, he thought, were being invited unfairly at the age of 40 or 50 to pass a qualifying examination for admission to the royal corps of constructors. If bishops, judges or ministers of the government had to pass qualifying examinations, few would come out with credit, he suggested.

Wearing his 'human rights hat' – what anathema this must have been to Tory diehards – he asked a question about the jurisdiction of the High Commissioner in the Western Pacific over British subjects. The sting was in the tail. And had the government received any complaints about acts of cruelty committed in the area by officers and men sailing under the British flag? The reply was rather squashing. The first point had been answered the previous month when the honourable and learned member was not in his place but on the high seas. And on the second point the answer was 'none'.[12] Gorst's continuous and diligent interest in all matters maritime was recognised at the end of the year when he became a member of the Royal Commission on merchant shipping.

The military position in the Sudan had now deteriorated and General Gordon was bottled up in Khartoum by the Mahdi and his forces. In May the Conservative opposition introduced a motion of censure against the Government's mismanagement of the situation there. The Fourth Party had made a speciality of goading the government over its handling of events in Egypt and the Sudan. Both Gorst and Churchill spoke to good effect. Gorst could not hope to match his friend's oratory, but his was a well-informed and telling speech, for once not conflicting with the party line. Prophetically he stated that the government's policy in the region had been marked 'by misfortune at its beginning and would probably be marked by misfortune at its end.' Moreover, Gorst went on, there was a feeling abroad that despite the perils facing him, Gordon had been 'abandoned ... most shamefully and disgracefully by the government.'[13]

Gorst was not a popular man in his party and had been seen by some as the 'evil counsellor' behind Churchill in the battles for the control of the party organisation.[14] For the part he and Churchill had played in the ructions the previous autumn and winter, there had been talk of 'ostracising' them both.[15] This did not happen. Balfour – a man already becoming influential – apparently advised against this course. Gorst, though, was wondering what the future might hold for him, and on 4 June he wrote to Wolff:

I believe Salisbury and the old gang are at last opening their eyes to the force of Tory democracy. The effect will be that they will try to place themselves at its head and oust us from our legitimate position. Their efforts at conciliation are to be viewed with suspicion ... Seeing that Randolph is too strong and popular to be crushed, they will now make you and me the object of their attacks ... [16]

The climax in the affairs of the National Union was, as usual, the annual conference, due to take place that year in Sheffield. This was the occasion the Fourth Party had been building up to. Much groundwork had been done by the activists of the two rival factions, and their struggle 'was assuming heroic proportions. Neither side left a stone unturned to ensure the discomfiture of its rival ...'[17] When the usual host of delegates assembled in the Cutlers' Hall on 23 July, Lord Randolph took the chair. Neither he nor the other two members of the Fourth Party had attended Lord Salisbury's pre-conference meeting that day for the simple reason they were not asked. Churchill had in fact shortly before given Northcote, who wanted to consult him on various party matters, the brush off. It looked therefore, on the face of it, as if the two factions were as far apart as ever.

With an eye on the all-important elections to the National Union's Council, Churchill made a conciliatory speech to the delegates and urged on them the need to modernise the party's organisation. Gorst supported his friend sturdily. A key issue he felt was how to influence people outside the party. He denounced country landowner MPs as being removed from the people, and pleaded for the election of a more representative Council. Lord Percy, speaking with official authority, attacked Churchill for breaking away from the party leadership.[18] But it did him no good. At the head of the poll and well out in front came Churchill. Out of 30 candidates proposed by him, 22 were voted onto the Council while Lord Percy secured 18 out of 36. The victory was Churchill's, and Gorst's too, although the margin was not overwhelming. Reforms in organisation, including the abandonment of control of elections by the party leader and enhanced powers for the elected Council of the National Union, were conceded by the Central Committee and were adopted by resolution at the conference. There was no doubt Churchill would be re-elected chairman.[19] It looked as if the Fourth Party had triumphed.

After the conference was over there was a sudden and totally unexpected turn of events. Gorst had gone down to Freshwater Bay in the Isle of Wight to be with his family. To his astonishment he received a message on 26 July from Lord Randolph announcing that he had arranged a reconciliation with Lord Salisbury.[20] Back in London Wolff and Churchill had talked over the implications of their victory at Sheffield. Wolff had urged on Churchill a settlement with Salisbury to which he had reluctantly consented. Wolff therefore went off as an intermediary and made contact first with Balfour and then with Salisbury. Consequently a meeting took place between Salisbury and Churchill – just the two of them – at a garden party at Marlborough House. Terms were agreed although nothing was put in writing. Broadly these were that the Central Committee was abolished and the democratic reforms to the National Union were confirmed. Sir Michael Hicks Beach, a neutral figure, was nominated by both sides as chairman of the National Union's Council with Gorst as one of the vice-chairmen. The Primrose League was formally recognised. Finally, to cement what is sometimes referred to as the 'concordat', Salisury was to give a dinner in a few days' time to all the members of the new council. More intangibly, there was an understanding that Lord Randolph and his friends were to be treated in full confidence by Salisbury and the leading members of the party. Just as Churchill had acted off his own bat – although with Wolff's full approval – so had Salisbury.[21] He never consulted Northcote and sent him a letter on 27 July containing the terms of the concordat presented as a *fait accompli*.

Where did all this leave Gorst ? Isolated, yes. Also hurt and angry at never being consulted. Never mind whether the settlement did or did not make political sense. His two close comrades had, without any reference to him, taken decisive and presumably irreversible action which fundamentally affected the work they had been engaged in together for over four years. In fact, the settlement, as it was meant to do, rang the death knell for the Fourth Party.

Giving himself only a short time for reflection, Gorst picked up his pen and wrote on 27 July a longish letter to Churchill. From a general reading of this letter one might assume that Gorst was in agreement with what Churchill had ordained, supposedly in the name of the Fourth Party. For instance he approved of the demise of the Central Committee, although the difficulty would be putting something in its place. He thought Churchill's declining to take the chair was a 'good stroke of policy'. He himself, though, would not serve as a vice-chairman to anyone other than Churchill, and he commented that they would both have more power as 'independent' members of the council. He was now 'tired of organisation of which I have done a fair share'. He believed, moreover, that the next election would be disastrous to the Conservative cause and he did not 'care to be mixed up with certain defeat'.

On an even more pessimistic note he also wrote that he had no hope of being able to carry out his ideas, and added darkly: 'the leaders I can never trust again; I cannot like you throw myself on the Tory Democracy. With you the thing was difficult: without you it becomes impossible. After the experience of the central committee and W. H. Smith I know the forces are too strong to contend with and I am not disposed to recommence a fruitless struggle.'[22]

This letter is not altogether easy to interpret. Parts of it have an almost despairing note. The terms of the reconciliation did not refer at all to Tory democracy and it did look, therefore, as if these principles, by which Gorst set much store, had been thrown overboard. By 'forces' in the above quoted extract we must assume Gorst meant 'the old guard' and considered, moreover, that they had triumphed. To understand this episode it must be recognised that the letter was as important for what it did not say as for what it did. In his preface to *The Fourth Party* John Gorst stated that 'written as well as spoken words are sometimes used to conceal thoughts'. As his son seems to suggest, John Gorst in writing these particular words was referring to his response to the settlement, one of the most painful moments in his career.[23] One of Churchill's biographers, R. F. Foster, commenting on Gorst's muted response, suggests that he had a 'private reason' for giving way. This was because Churchill had agreed with him that when the Tories came in he would insist on Gorst being made Solicitor-General.[24]

There are two other points to be examined. First, why did Churchill suddenly – and Wolff's account certainly suggests the decision was sudden – decide to throw in the sponge? Second, why did Churchill not consult Gorst? There is something of a puzzle about Churchill's motivation, and historians and politicians seem divided over it. Churchill's son Winston offers no real solution to this conundrum. Balfour considered that Churchill, perceiving he might not be so far away from the actual Conservative leadership, and therefore thinking as a potential leader, had second thoughts about transferring power to an independent body, that is the National Union for which he had no further use.[25] Rhodes James, on the other hand, thinks that Churchill never aimed to do anything more than democratise the National Union, and, now in a strong position, saw there was 'no point in continuing the wearying internecine conflict' within the party. Foster supports this view. Shannon holds that Churchill settled on grounds beneficial both to himself and to the party, and had conceded that further aggressive campaigning would have served no useful purpose.[26]

About the failure to consult we can only speculate, while bearing in mind Foster's suggestion. In addition, Wolff has given us a clue, for years later he stated that the negotiations in that July were conducted in a hurry. The election for the chairman of the National Union was pending and there was, therefore, no time, he avers, for discussions or telegrams.[27] This is not entirely convincing, with Gorst only 70 or so miles away in the Isle of Wight. There is another aspect to the problem. Had Gorst been consulted he might well not have agreed to a reconciliation unless the terms, in his view, were right. He could, for instance, have pointed to an absence of any commitment to Tory democracy in them. In this case, better not to consult him at all, so his two friends might have argued.

Harold Gorst in his *The Fourth Party* makes an important point:

> There was a definite compact between Lord Randolph Churchill and my father that the former, in return for his colleague risking everything for his (Lord Randolph's) advancement, would consider himself pledged to take no important political step involving their interests without that colleague being consulted. This was, no doubt, a private arrangement between them.[28]

Given that there was such a compact, and there is no reason to doubt it, this author considers that Gorst was badly let down by Churchill. It is difficult not to agree with Harold Gorst's conclusion that '… Lord Randolph, having pledged himself as described, should not have acted on the advice of one partner [Wolff] without consulting the other.' Harold Gorst calls the settlement a 'surrender', and this is what it must have seemed to his father.

In the event John Gorst did not go to Lord Salisbury's dinner. It is easy to criticise him for his failure to attend, but Gorst was only human and sometimes over-sensitive. Later he was to write: 'I was too angry with Randolph. Lord Salisbury never forgave this.'[29] This admission seems to militate against Foster's suggestion about the 'private reason' Gorst had for reacting in the way he did to the settlement.

It might be supposed by his non-attendance at the dinner that Gorst was signalling his disagreement with the settlement. Certainly not everyone saw it in this light. For instance Wolff, possibly disingenuously, was to write to Harold Gorst in 1903 saying that 'until now I had always understood that he [Gorst] concurred in the course taken.'[30]

On the other hand Gorst's real feelings, despite the smoke-screen type of letter he had written on 27 July, were discerned by Churchill according to his son Winston. As a result a 'coolness ensued between them, diversified by occasional heats.'[31] This coolness is reflected in a well-known incident occurring in November in the House of Commons during the passage of Gladstone's Reform Bill, a measure which gave the vote to the country constituencies – notably to the agricultural labourer and miner.

Lord Randolph's approach to reform had been somewhat equivocal. At first he opposed the idea, partly on tactical grounds. Nor did he relish seeing the extinction of his small agricultural borough of Woodstock. But when the government's measure was introduced in May, Lord Randolph spoke vigorously in its favour in accordance with the principles of Fourth Party Tory democracy, attacking an official Conservative Party amendment moved by Colonel Stanley which sought to delay the Bill's progress on the basis that its provisions must be accompanied by a proper arrangement of electoral areas.

During the second reading in November Gorst, who had not wavered in his support for Tory democracy, spoke against an entirely new Conservative amendment proposing the Bill should be accompanied by a Redistribution Bill. This amendment appeared similar in intent to the one put forward by Stanley the previous May. This November amendment, following strictly the party line, was proposed by Edward Stanhope on behalf of no less a person than Lord Randolph who was absent that day at a funeral. Gorst in his speech explained why he wanted to see the Bill passed without being opposed rather than suffer delays, and in doing so had attacked Stanhope's amendment in the manner in which Churchill had attacked Stanley's the previous May. Whether Gorst realised the amendment was Churchill's is not clear. Certainly times had changed, and there was no longer any pre-debate discussion by Fourth Party members as in former days. Churchill's biographer son Winston described Gorst's speech as 'very able and perfectly consistent' with the line he had previously adopted.[32]

Lord Randolph, having read about Gorst's speech in the newspapers, went down to the House the following day expressly to castigate his friend, having angrily said that Gorst 'must be punished'.[33] What particularly enraged him was that Gorst should have ignored the approved Conservative Party line and in so doing had compromised, as he thought, his own new and immaculate position. Beginning his speech by referring to their close friendship, 'not only political but private', and what a 'very painful surprise' Gorst's speech had been to him, Churchill went on to repudiate in scathing and sometimes sarcastic terms just about everything Gorst had said. For instance he referred to how, with 'his finely legal mind', Gorst did not understand the current political situation, accused him of 'prostrating himself to the Prime Minister' and of 'counselling his fellow-comrades to an ignominious surrender' to the Bill. He then went on to mention how Gorst came in the autumn 'to prance off to the Western Highlands and stir up among the crofters of Skye a great amount of bittterness and discontent with their position …'[34] This was a reference to a visit Gorst had made to Scotland in August in company with Professor Blackie, the Scottish lawyer and scholar. At Portree in Skye he told crofters that the land belonged to the people and that it must, therefore, be held for their greatest good. We may assume that, while wanting space after the Fourth Party debacle, Gorst wished to do his bit for the crofters who 'had suffered grievously from the "clearances"' (a Crofters Act was passed in 1886 giving security of tenure at a fair rent).

Gorst may well have been maladroit in his speech but could hardly have expected Churchill's blistering attack. Charles Russell, a Liberal lawyer and later Lord Chief Justice, who followed Churchill in the debate, was not unsympathetic to Gorst. He thought the House had only been witnessing 'a lovers' tiff' (it was more than this) and went on to suggest that Gorst was only 'following the lead and teaching of the noble Lord',[35] and was amply justified in what he had said. One sad consequence of this so-called 'tiff' was that Gorst's correspondence with Churchill over the years now more or less fizzled out. Churchill may of course have been suffering from strain or even illness, for a few weeks later he sailed to India for health reasons and was away many months. As his ship disappeared over the horizon he sent via Wolff messages of amity to all his friends, 'even the erring Gorst'.

What would Gorst have thought of the long Fourth Party episode when he took stock that winter? In its first phase, until about the end of 1882, the Fourth Party had essentially constituted a ginger group of four talented men. The journalist Stead saw Gorst as the 'wire-puller-in-chief' at this time.[36] Gorst himself would probably have agreed with this, and considered too that the Fourth Party had played its hand well and made a notable impact on the parliamentary scene.

It was the second phase, when the remaining three friends were challenging the party leaders for control of the Conservative organisation, which would surely have caused Gorst to ponder hard. Just what had the Fourth Party achieved, if anything, in the last two years? Here it is relevant that Gorst's own political objectives differed from Churchill's. Gorst wanted to see the party organisation reformed in accordance with Tory democratic principles. This was to an extent an end in itself. But Churchill was using the National Union as a means to an end, for he was seeking power for himself and on his own terms. On the merits of Churchill's settlement Gorst could hardly have been satisfied. It was not that he eschewed compromise, but, as he already suspected and would discover in the years ahead, the 'old gang' still ruled the party. Neither Salisbury, by now emerging as the putative leader of his party, nor Balfour had any time for his concept of Tory democracy. Salisbury had always distrusted democracy, Tory or otherwise, and had argued in his writings against enfranchising the working class. He had been unable to support the Reform Bill in 1867 and had considered writing a pamphlet against reform before the passage of Gladstone's measure in 1884. While Salisbury never sought to conceal his opinions on democracy – they were anathema to Gorst – the views of his nephew Balfour on the subject were more equivocal. In his autobiography published in 1930 referring to events over 45 years before, Balfour wrote that he had 'mildly resented' what was being said about Tory democracy. It was as if the concept were a 'racy invention of the Fourth Party'. To him the idea was a 'familiar truth under an unfamiliar name'.[37]

Where were Gorst's ambitions now left? He had told Churchill only a year before that he was no longer politically ambitious. This was not true, although he may have been deceiving himself. He was indeed intensely ambitious – even if this was not always obvious – and would remain so for many years. But he must have realised that his unpopularity with party leaders was now likely in the normal course of events to prevent him from achieving office. For advancement, therefore, he would have to rely on Churchill. There was a certain irony in this, for Gorst was not a person who usually felt a sense of loyalty to people. He was too much his own man. Yet until 27 July, one could almost say he had been very loyal to Churchill. Now, feeling let down by his friend, he would henceforth more than ever fight his own corner. At the same time, however distasteful it might be, he would still be obliged, if and when opportunity arose, to hang onto Churchill's coat-tails to satisfy his own underlying ambitions. Perhaps, not surprisingly, the cynical streak in his character became more noticeable.

NOTES

1. Churchill, *Lord Randolph Churchill*, 244.
2. Ibid., 245–6.
3. FP, 269.
4. Churchill, *Lord Randolph Churchill*, 248–9.
5. FP, 272.
6. Rhodes James, *Lord Randolph Churchill*, 146–7.
7. Churchill, *Lord Randolph Churchill*, 250.
8. Correspondence of Lord Randolph Churchill (Ld RC), Add. 9248, G–C, 14 April 1884.
9. FP, 287–8.
10. JG AN, vol. 1, 1885, 24.
11. Kimberley Papers, Eng. c. 4247, G–Kimberley, 10 March 1884.
12. 3 PD 285, 13 Mar. 1884, 1340, 1354; 3 PD 286, 20 March 1884, 350.
13. 3 PD 288, 12 May 1884, 74.
14. Feuchtwanger, *Disraeli, Democracy and the Tory Party,* 169.
15. Rhodes James, *Lord Randolph Churchill*, 141.
16. FP, 294.
17. Ibid., 293.
18. Churchill, *Lord Randolph Churchill*, 275; Shannon, *The Age of Salisbury*, 41.
19. Churchill, *Lord Randolph Churchill*, 276.
20. FP, 303.
21. Churchill, *Lord Randolph Churchill*, 276–7; FP, 303, 305, 319–20.
22. Ld RC, G–C, 27 July 1884.
23. FP, viii, 312.
24. Foster, *Lord Randolph Churchill*, 157–8.
25. Balfour, *Chapters of Autobiography*, 168–9.
26. Rhodes James, *Lord Randolph Churchill*, 154–5; Foster, *Lord Randolph Churchill*, 158; Shannon, *Age of Salisbury*, 43–4.
27. FP, 307, 320.
28. Ibid., 321.
29. MLL, 142.
30. FP, 308.
31. Churchill, *Lord Randolph Churchill*, 278.
32. Ibid., 288–9.
33. Ibid.
34. 3 PD 293, 7 Nov. 1884, 1247–54; Foster, *Lord Randolph Churchill*, 158.
35. 3 PD 293, 7 Nov, 1884, 1261–2.
36. *Review of Reviews*, 4 Aug. 1891, 581.
37. Andrew Roberts, *Salisbury: Victorian Titan*, London, Weidenfeld & Nicolson, 1999, 46, 57–9, 299; Balfour, *Chapters of Autobiography*, 157.

—15—

Ministerial Office at Last

When the parliamentary session began in 1885 time was running out for Gladstone. With Wolseley's failure to relieve Khartoum, and the death there of the nation's hero General Charles Gordon, the government was doomed. The Sudan apart, various imperial matters commanded Gorst's attention. In the Commons for instance he seemed worried that part of British New Guinea might be taken over by private German colonisers. A few days later, inconsistently some thought, he was suggesting that Heligoland, British since 1807, should be handed over to Germany; the island, he said, was of no 'mercantile or strategic value to Britain' and cost the taxpayer money to maintain.[1] A few eyebrows were raised at this proposal, which was not as outrageous as it seemed for the island was ceded to Germany five years later.

When in April Gorst asked in his independent way how the detention in Gibraltar of the powerful Sudan slave-baron Zebehr Pasha was authorised,[2] Harcourt, the Home Secretary, hit the nail on the head. Had Gorst been in the Commons at the time, he commented, he would have asked the Attorney-General under what law Napoleon was detained at St Helena.

In early June a group of six Conservatives, including Gorst and his former friends in the Fourth Party, framed at a meeting in Balfour's house an amendment to the budget in the name of Hicks Beach which was approved by both Salisbury and Northcote. The amendment, cleverly drafted, condemned the proposed increase in beer and spirits duties and succession tax, and was designed to unite the opposition while claiming the support of the Irish. The plan worked and Gladstone was defeated in the vote. On that night of nights Gorst remained in his seat characteristically calm and unmoved while Churchill jumped up on his seat cheering, a witness said, like a schoolboy.

Gladstone, perhaps surprisingly, resigned and Lord Salisbury proceeded to form a minority government. Northcote went to the Lords (as the Earl of Iddesleigh) and Lord Randolph became Secretary of State for India with a seat in the Cabinet. Balfour got the Local

Government Board, and Wolff became a Privy Councillor. Gorst waited anxiously to see if he would be offered a post. Churchill wrote to Salisbury pushing Gorst's claims and adding '... it makes me perfectly wretched to feel that it must occur to his [Gorst's] mind that his failure to obtain that for which so many persons of knowledge consider he is fitted in every way is due to lukewarmness on my part'.[3]

Jack Gorst, who was keeping his father informed of developments, noted: 'At this juncture my position as Lord Randolph's private secretary was very useful to my father. Lord S wished to buy him off with the Judge-Advocate Generalship but he stuck out for being one of the Law Officers of the Crown ...'[4] At last, after a longish wait, Gorst received a letter dated 27 June from Salisbury offering him the post of Solicitor-General which he accepted. As pleased as Punch he wrote thanking Churchill effusively for his help, saying he owed the post '... entirely to your persistent and obstinate friendship for me.'[5] Interestingly Gorst was also grateful to Churchill for the offer of a 'place at Madras'. From this it looks as if Churchill promised Gorst the governorship there, presumably if he did not become a minister. Churchill wrote back to Gorst on 1 July:

> ... you owe nothing to anybody for anything which you have got. You have to thank your own pre-eminent talents and parliamentary knowledge which could not be passed over with decency or security.[6]

A month later as the newly appointed Junior Law Officer Gorst was knighted, for the appointment always carried this honour. He had first sat in the House 19 years before, and must now have felt as if he were standing on the threshold of great things. The job of Solicitor-General must be seen as quite a plum. Together with the Attorney-General, Sir Richard Webster, Gorst would be responsible for representing the Crown in the courts as well as acting as legal adviser to the government in important matters. It has been calculated that in those days the post was worth £10,000 to £12,000 a year (*c.* £490,000–588,000 now),[7] for Law Officers drew substantial fees for Crown litigation, though private practice was not allowed.

What are we to make of this sudden, and perhaps improbable, twist in Gorst's fortunes, and what of his qualifications for his new post? In the House Gorst had shown regular interest over the years in legal and procedural matters. In 1877, as we have seen, he had introduced a Bill to extend jurisdiction in territorial waters. When speaking in 1882 on the Criminal Law Amendment Bill, he had put forward a number of detailed proposals for improving the administration of justice which included the removal of certain anomalous penalties in the criminal law, the rationalising of the bail system, the exclusion of a possible right of the Home Secretary to order a new trial and the possibility of allowing appeals as of right.

Certainly, in legal circles there was surprise at Gorst's appointment. Asquith, a rising barrister at the time, later wrote, maybe unkindly: 'his professional claims [to the post] were of the slenderest kind'.[8] Other well-informed contemporaries made the same kind of comment. For instance, Arthur Godley, the Permanent Secretary at the India Office (later Lord Kilbracken), believed 'he never had any legal business worth mentioning'.[9] Two obituarists in legal journals made the point in 1916 that he had not attained any real position as an advocate.

Yet Holker had regarded Gorst highly as a lawyer. And again Webster, who as Lord Alverstone was later Lord Chief Justice, and who ought to have known, said that Gorst was 'a very distinguished lawyer' and 'a man of great ability and learning who had not met with that success at the Bar which his merits deserved.'[10] Winston Churchill, more in the political context, paid tribute to how 'his knowledge of the law proved on repeated occasions of inestimable value' to the Fourth Party. Even Balfour, not one given to praising Gorst, thought him a good lawyer.[11] The truth is that, while Gorst's abilities as a lawyer were not in doubt, he had never given the time to his profession to become a leading counsel.

As there were others, like Edward Clarke, who had a better claim than Gorst to being Solicitor-General, it is fair to say that he was fortunate to secure the office. Almost certainly he owed his elevation to Lord Randolph. In the event he was only Solicitor-General until January 1886, when Salisbury's minority government was turned out of office after losing the general election held in the previous November.

As for Gorst's performance as a Law Officer in those seven months there is little for a biographer to record. Since parliament was prorogued on 14 August and did not meet again until the following January, this did not give him long to make any sort of mark. His first appearance at the despatch box was on 14 July on a minor matter to do with electoral law, over which he got his way in preventing an increase in the security needed for uncontested elections. Later on, in debating the Criminal Law Amendment Bill under which, *inter alia*, the age of consent was raised from 13 to 16, Gorst made it clear that he did not wish to see the definition of the word 'brothel' expanded. Leave it to the 'common sense of the judge and juries' he suggested. When Gorst was challenged sharply on this, the distinguished Liberal lawyer Sir Henry James came to his defence saying there was no reason to treat him 'roughly',[12] as if Gorst was not capable of looking after himself. But he did speak once while Solicitor-General on an important occasion. This was during the debate on the horrific Maamtrasna murders in Ireland when he made a foolish error, though not a legal one, upsetting some members on his side of the House.

Three years before, six members of the same Irish family had been shot or bludgeoned to death as they slept in their remote windowless cottage in County Mayo. Only a boy of eleven survived the attack. Thirteen men were soon arrested for the crime and brought to trial in Dublin. Three were executed and six sentenced to life imprisonment. The motives for the crime were obscure and doubt existed as to whether justice had been done. An inquiry had been held by the Lord-Lieutenant, Lord Spencer, who decided the verdict and sentences had been right. In the House of Commons in a debate in 1884 the Liberal government had defeated a motion – not one supported by the opposition – for a further inquiry. Lord Randolph and Gorst had both voted with the Irish Nationalists against the Liberals and their own party. After the debate the Liberal lawyer Charles Russell and Gorst had made a suggestion in *The Times* that it might be possible to re-try the men still in prison, who claimed to be innocent, on a different charge. Gladstone had consulted his Attorney-General who ruled out the idea on account of the state of excitement prevailing in Ireland at the time.

When the Conservatives came into power Parnell moved for a fresh inquiry, his resolution being opposed by the government. However the new Lord-Lieutenant, Lord Carnarvon, promised to look into the matter and consequently Parnell withdrew his motion, agreeing to await the Lord-Lieutenant's decision. The Conservatives were content to await developments. The stance adopted by the government, nevertheless, offended Ulster MPs, who saw it as a concession to Irish nationalist feeling, and it fell to Hicks Beach, Lord Randolph and Gorst to defend the government's position in the House. At one moment in his speech Gorst appealed to the 'party opposite to make some better use of the time of the House than applauding speeches of reactionary Ulster members'.[13] 'Reactionary'? It was an unfortunate slip – or was it deliberate? Hart Dyke, the Chief Secretary for Ireland, wrote to Carnarvon saying that Gorst's speech had given 'immense dissatisfaction to our supporters'.[14] There was apparently a feeling that Gorst's speech, as well as the one made by Churchill, might be construed as indicating that the government, when they thought Irish nationalists should be humoured, were ready to condone crimes of violence. The worst was that Gorst had registered another 'black mark' with Salisbury, who regarded Gorst's speech as 'quite indefensible'.

The new electoral register was finally ready by November 1885 (there were two million new voters and a redistribution of boundaries to take account of), and so Salisbury was not able to seek a dissolution until November. In the general election, which opened on 23 November and took three weeks, the Conservatives won 249 seats and the Liberals 319. The 86 Irish Nationalists held the balance. In the event, Salisbury did not resign until the end of January when he was defeated on a vote in the new House. Gorst himself produced a pithy election address for the Chatham electors. In it, apart from stressing the need for a strong navy and for the Established Church to be maintained, he underlined the importance of local authorities whose powers were to be extended (this happened three years later with the setting up of elected county councils). A decade later Gorst was to be a keen advocate of local government, which, he believed, understood the interests of local people better than a department in London. He himself was re-elected this time with a much more comfortable majority than he had in 1880.

Gladstone was thus back in power for a third time in February 1886, though it was not to be for long. He had now become convinced that if the Irish problem was to be solved the country must be given home rule. His new policy split his party fatally. Chamberlain and Hartington were against him, and the Home Rule Bill was defeated. Before parliament was dissolved in July we may note in passing Gorst's views on the death penalty for murder during a debate for its abolition in May. He favoured the introduction of a criminal code and wanted the death penalty limited to certain classes of case where the penalty was 'appropriate' without specifying what the classes should be. Further, he wanted the sentence of death carried out 'in the most decorous and humane way that the resources of knowledge and science could devise.'[15] Above all, there must be no 'bungling' of executions, a demand which struck a positive chord with the House. He may have been thinking of the incompetence attending the hanging of one of those convicted in the Maamtrasna murders.

These murders were responsible for another passage of arms between Gorst and Gladstone during the 1886 election campaign. This occurred when Gorst's opponent at Chatham published a telegram purporting to come from Gladstone in which the Grand Old Man had said that Gorst had 'run down Lord Spencer for his brave and manly government in Ireland'. Gorst at once hotly denied this in a letter to Gladstone. Swiftly Gladstone came back, standing by what he said after checking Gorst's speech as Solicitor-General a year before. In reply Gorst pointed out that he had taken the line that the inquiry ordered by Lord Spencer into the Maamtrasna murders was 'unsatisfactory and unreliable'. This was because the inquiry had been conducted by the officials 'whose conduct had been inculpated by the Archbishop of Tuan'. Other matters had also needed investigating. This, Gorst continued, was very far from running down Lord Spencer. Gorst then had the correspondence published in *The Times*.[16]

On the hustings once again, Gorst confined himself exclusively to the Irish question. He made it clear he was a strong supporter of the Union and rejected Gladstone's Home Rule proposals. He gave various reasons for his stance: for instance, he wished to preserve the unity of the United Kingdom and was against two parliaments, one in London and one in Dublin, because collisions between them would take place; he feared law and order problems because Ireland, unlike Scotland or Wales, was a country of two races and two religions, in which religious animosity had not died out; he believed there was no certainty that Parnell would pay the £6,000,000 promised to the British exchequer, and was also doubtful of the Irish ability to shoulder its fair share of the national debt. But he was not against a measure of self-government. Gorst would take a similar sort of line when Gladstone made his second and last bid for Home Rule seven years later.

The Liberals lost the election in July and a fourth government in 13 months was in office. Salisbury was again Prime Minister. This time the Conservatives had a healthy majority, which included Liberal Unionists opposed to home rule in Ireland. Gorst wrote to Salisbury on 29 July about a conversation they had had that day, saying he hoped to be offered the post of Solicitor-General again. He also referred to Churchill's promise to use his 'good offices with you'.[17] According to Harold Gorst the offer of the Solicitor-Generalship was made but only on the condition that Gorst took the first vacancy for a puisne judgeship.[18] This may sound a curious condition but most Law Officers in those days became judges using their posts as recognised stepping stones for elevation to the Bench. But Gorst refused the offer on these terms, and Edward Clarke became Solicitor-General. Gorst's ambition, we must remember, was to be a Cabinet minister rather than a judge. In any case Gorst's dedication to his legal career, and for that matter to the law, was never absolute. Years later, on the pitfalls of litigation, he gave his family some advice: 'Put up with any insult. Put up with any injustice, but NEVER go to law.'

Churchill, about to become Chancellor of the Exchequer and Leader of the House though only for five short months, was in the thick of government-making, and at one moment suggested to Salisbury that Gorst be made 'Education' minister.[19] In fact Churchill could not have done Gorst's cause much good when almost in the same breath he told Salisbury, rather disparagingly, that Gorst had come to him for help in somewhat 'crawling terms'. He seemed impatient with his former friend, who 'was too impractical for anything. He ought to have jumped at a judgeship.'[20] The perceptive Jack Gorst noted that his father was unpopular with the leaders and that Churchill made a 'dead-set' against him.[21]

It was touch and go as to whether Salisbury would now find a place at all for Gorst. We know this from Balfour who was soon to be brought into the Cabinet. He wrote on 1 August to Salisbury:

> Our prime object in giving Gorst office is to prevent a coalition between him and Harry [Chaplin]. It is therefore no use in offering him a place which he will not accept ... R [Lord Randolph] seems to have no doubt ... Gorst would accept India.[22]

In other words both nephew and uncle seemed to agree it was safer to have Gorst inside the government than outside it. Chaplin, known as 'The Squire', became President of the newly created Board of Agriculture in 1889.

As it was, the post of Under-Secretary of State for India was worth only £1,500 (c. £75,000 now) a year, so from the point of view of income and prestige Gorst had suffered a political demotion by accepting it. His chief would be Cross, now promoted to the Lords. Unhappily Gorst did little to conceal his poor opinion of Cross, whom the historian Penderel Moon described as 'an undistinguished and irresolute figure'.[23]

According to Jack Gorst, who by then was in the Diplomatic Service, there was talk towards the end of 1886 of John Gorst being made Governor of the Cape. Had he been, Jack would have gone to South Africa as his father's private secretary.[24] This shows the government still hankered after finding Gorst employment away from Westminster.

There is one other little episode to record about this period. When he was making the 'farewell distribution of places' on leaving office back in the winter of 1885/86, Salisbury wrote to Churchill about the need to pay debts in the way of judgeships. In this general context he said that 'G [Gorst] lies heavy on my soul; I dare not look C [Edward Clarke] in the face ...'[25] That winter some early copies of *Whitaker's Almanac* for 1886 carried the name of Sir John Gorst printed among the names of the judges. This confusion seems to have arisen because a Conservative MP William Grantham, in a safe seat, was made a judge at about this time, and Gorst's name was mistakenly printed instead of his. Nonetheless, the judges themselves had been thinking of putting forward Gorst's name for a judgeship. Thus Lord Chief Justice Coleridge had written to the Lord Chancellor, Lord Halsbury, mentioning Gorst's name in this very context.[26] It is a nice point whether the judicial Bench's loss was the front bench's gain – though we can guess what Salisbury's view would have been. As a postscript on this we might note that an obituarist was to write that Gorst, a man of 'first rate mental calibre ... would probably have made a good judge'.

NOTES

1. 3 PD 296, 30 Mar. 1885, 1011.
2. 3 PD 297, 30 April 1885, 23.
3. Churchill, *Lord Randolph Churchill*, 323.
4. JG AN, vol. 1, 1885, 29–30.
5. Correspondence of Lord Randolph Churchill (Ld RC), Add. 9428, G–C, 29 June 1885; also see Clarke, *Story of My Life*, 242 on Gorst's appointment.
6. Letter in author's possession.
7. *Solicitors' Journal and Weekly Reporter*, 15 April 1916, 422.
8. *Law Journal*, 8 April 1916, 186; The Earl of Oxford and Asquith, *Fifty Years in Parliament*, 117.
9. Lord Kilbracken, *Reminiscences of Lord Kilbracken*, London, Macmillan, 1931, 186.
10. Lord Alverstone, *Recollections of Bar and Bench*, London, Edward Arnold, 1914, 136, 164.
11. Churchill, *Lord Randolph Churchill*, 114, Balfour, *Chapters of Autobiography*, 135.
12. 3 PD 300, 7 Aug. 1885, 1507–8.
13. 3 PD 299, 17 July 1885, 1123.
14. Sir Arthur Hardinge, *The Life of Henry Herbert, 4th Earl of Carnarvon*, vol. 3, London, Humphrey Milford, 1925, 170.
15. 3 PD 305, 11 May 1886, 447.
16. *The Times*, 5 July, 1886.
17. Salisbury Papers, G–Salisbury, 29 July 1886.
18. FP, 317; also see DNB 1912–21, 219, although this may have relied on FP as a source.
19. Churchill, *Lord Randolph Churchill*, 494.
20. Rhodes James, *Lord Randolph Churchill*, 251–2.
21. JG AN, vol. 1, 1886, 1.
22. Harcourt Williams, *Salisbury–Balfour Correspondence*, 155.
23. P. Moon, *The British Conquest and Dominion of India*, London, Duckworth, 1989, 893.
24. JG, AN, vol. 1, 1886, 7.
25. R. Heuston, *Lives of the Lord Chancellors 1885–1940*, Oxford, Clarendon Press, 1964, 37.
26. Ibid., 41–2.

16

The Manipur Massacre and Lord Salisbury's Rebuke

John Gorst's tenure at the India Office coincided with a mainly tranquil period of prosperity and some complacency on the sub-continent. In fact, the Viceroy, Lord Dufferin, perhaps a shade optimistically, told his successor Lord Lansdowne when handing over in 1888 that there was not a 'cloud in the sky'.[1] While Burma had in 1885 been incorporated into the Indian Empire it was still in the process of being settled. Also, the Indian National Congress had just appeared on the scene but happily for Gorst had not yet begun to make its political presence felt. There was, though, one serious episode with which Gorst had to deal in his time. We will come to this presently.

Had one been an attentive listener in the Commons at parliamentary question time over the next few years one would have learnt from Gorst's answers at the despatch box a lot about India: both its darker side, such as the traffic in liquor, the opium trade, forced labour, child marriages and dacoits, as well as the more constructive side, with vaccination programmes, the expansion of the railways, progress in agriculture and forestry and so on. The list of subjects handled by Gorst was endless. A ready questioner was the Radical Charles Bradlaugh, now rapidly gaining respectability as an MP, who saw himself, Gorst-like, as a guardian of the rights of the Indian people. For Gorst the boot was now on the other foot for he had to defend what the government was doing. He seemed to take particular pains in trying to satisfy Bradlaugh who often asked probing and no doubt sometimes irritating questions. Prudently, to try to avoid being caught out, Gorst took the precaution of asking the Viceroy to send him reports of vitally important events as soon as possible.[2]

Undoubtedly, Gorst was not unduly stretched in his new post. On the front bench he was of course shackled, no longer able to range widely and at will over the leading issues of the day. Sometimes he stood in for the Under-Secretary of State for the Colonies and so kept in touch with the more global imperial picture. He seemed perfectly at home in dealing with facts and figures given him by his civil servants, invariably master of his brief, even if it was usually not too demanding a one. It is no surprise that with his knowledge of parliamentary procedure he was appointed in due course Chairman of Committees, and then in December 1889 was made a Privy Councillor. It might be supposed that Gorst had settled down to become a conventional team player. Any such supposition would be mistaken.

About Gorst's five-year spell at the India Office Lord Kilbracken has some interesting comments. Gorst, he considered, was one of the 'very ablest men' among the Conservatives of his day. His chief, Lord Cross, was in Kilbracken's view:

> ... obviously rather afraid of him and although there was no breach of the peace this was only because Gorst was allowed to do pretty much as he liked ... Gorst was very industrious and worked long hours at the India Office but he was a dark horse with many undisclosed interests and undertakings which occupied probably nine tenths of his time.

Kilbracken was right about his outside interests. We have already had a glimpse of his involvement in charity work.[3] Soon he would acquire a deep concern for the plight of factory workers and the poor in the East End of London, which would lead to his passion for social reform. In addition he had business interests in sugar and, having maintained his links with New Zealand, he was the chairman of the New Zealand Shipping Company besides being a director of both the New Zealand Loan and Mercantile Agency and of the Waikato Land Association. Some years earlier he had proposed setting up a building society with the object of attracting working-class voters to the Conservative cause. The idea was to convert tenants into owners of property.[4] As if these interests were not enough, he was in addition an active freemason.

Did this multifarious range of activities and the restless energy that went with it leave John Gorst any time for his family? It is a nice question and one for which we do not really have a proper answer. For Gorst as a family man in this period we have to rely almost exclusively on what has been handed down by his two sons. Jack Gorst was now launched on what was to be a highly successful career, tragically cut short by his death at the age of 50. He was a dutiful son and his autobiographical notes and diary have references in them to his father but usually they are brief and not illuminating.

Harold wished to follow a musical career as a cellist, and clashed over this with his father who, conventionally enough, wanted him to be a lawyer. Harold's ambitions were not surprising, for music was important in the Gorst family. His father had an interest in music and his mother Mary, an artistic woman, was highly musical. She played the piano with a very delicate touch, especially Beethoven's sonatas. His eldest sister Constance had a fine singing voice, while Hylda and Eva both loved music, and Eva played the organ. But Harold described his father as 'inflexible' when it came to discussing his career. Eventually, and even unexpectedly, John relented about his second son's career and allowed Harold to study the cello in Leipzig. About the same time he sent Hylda to school in Weimar for a few months.

John Gorst was a lover of Germany and all things German. As a young man he had lived in the country and had learnt to speak its language. He enjoyed its literature and had pleased his younger son by translating for him some German fairy stories. He had travelled in Germany and probably, although we cannot be sure of this, had German friends. From the 1860s Germany had begun its transition into a powerful modern state and Gorst would soon be in thrall to Bismarck's social welfare system. Always he admired what he saw to be German order and efficiency.

The Gorst children had always enjoyed dressing up. Harold was a practical joker and this combination could be fairly deadly. Once John Gorst's patience and temper were seriously embarrassed by his younger son. This happened when Harold and his sister Hylda, both in their teens, disguised themselves as itinerant musicians. They then proceeded to perform their music up and down the road outside their house in St George's Square, Pimlico. The next day there arrived a letter of complaint about the inferior quality of their music. This letter purported to come from an old lady and her sister living nearby, but in fact Harold recognised the writing as being that of a Mr Macauley, their next-door neighbour who was entering into the joke. In the same spirit Harold and Hylda wrote back to Macauley recommending that the old lady and her sister retire to a lunatic asylum and declaring further that her brother, a General, whose name the complainant had used to intimidate the young Gorsts, might go and be hanged. Harold put the letter in an envelope and, in a moment of aberration, addressed the envelope to the old lady before posting it through Macauley's front door. The footman picked it up and seeing the addressee's name took it round to the old lady's house. Three days later Harold encountered his stupefied father reading a letter from a distinguished General, whom he did not know, threatening legal action unless an ample apology was received for the insulting letter written to his sister. 'The explanation which followed', wrote Harold, 'hardly abated my father's wrath'.[5] Happily, Macauley, at once consulted, agreed to go round to the General with Harold to explain matters. Angry at first, the wounded General then saw the funny side of the situation and exploded into laughter at the nonsense. One hopes that eventually John Gorst, who was not without a sense of fun and perhaps in response to Mary's intervention, also saw the humour of the episode.

In the winter of 1887 John had most of his family with him in Switzerland for Constance's marriage in Berne to a young naval officer, Edmund Paston Cooper. (Why the marriage was held there is a mystery.) Afterwards the Gorst family repaired to Grindelwald for winter sports where John hugely enjoyed toboganing and skating. He 'never had such fun in his life', he wrote in a newsy and cheerful letter to Richmond Ritchie, his private secretary in the India office. 'Sliding down the mountains in snow', he declared, 'is one of the most fascinating and exciting amusements I have ever tried.'[6] Also on this holiday Gorst chartered for his family a small steamer to cruise on Lake Thun. Presumably, he was for once flush with funds.

By the late 1880s the Gorsts had left their home in St George's Square and apparently had for a while, as described by Jack, no 'settled abode'. They lived for a time at Tunbridge Wells and then at Ascot before finally taking Lawford House, a large Georgian house in spacious grounds, at Manningtree, Essex, where they lived for a number of years. Why the Gorsts thus peregrinated we do not know. There is no reason to ascribe these removals to any desire for change on Mary's part. Far more likely, they reflect John's restlessness.

There now occurred an event which had a profound influence on John Gorst and on his later life's work. Germany, politically unified only some 20 years before, was seeking to play an increasingly prominent part in the affairs of Europe. In the very month, March 1890, in which the new and vigorous young Kaiser Wilhelm II chose to dismiss his Chancellor Bismarck, an international labour conference opened in Berlin. Its object was to improve conditions in factories and mines. Salisbury, a man not known to be particularly interested in this subject, selected Gorst to head the British mission to the conference.

Gorst saw from his fortnight in Berlin that, in some of the provisions they made to protect their workforces in factories, a number of west European countries were ahead of Britain. He was determined to address this problem when he came home. We shall see what action he took in the next chapter. For the present we may simply note that Gorst, through his endeavours, had a significant influence on the setting up in the following year of the Royal Commission on Labour.

Back in the India Office it may have been something of an anti-climax for Gorst, after being fired up by the cosmopolitan atmosphere and deliberations of the Berlin conference, to have to respond to the more routine matters which arose concerning his great parish. He had no trouble heading off a perennial issue about the treatment of coolies in the tea gardens of Assam, for he was able to quote to the Commons the opinion of the peripatetic Rev. Isaac Row, secretary of the Anglo-Indian Evangelisation Society. Conveniently enough, Row had written to an Indian newspaper with his findings on conditions among the coolies. As a rule, he said, the tens of thousands of men he had seen were remarkably well fed, cared for and housed by their employers. The House seemed satisfied by the views of the cleric, judging by the 'hear hears' and 'cheers' punctuating the statement made by Gorst.[7]

Gorst faced a more weighty matter in July when Bradlaugh, in moving the adjournment of the House, called for an inquiry into the way the Indian government had taken away from the Maharajah of Kashmir his powers of governing his state. Unlike Hyderabad, Kashmir was a state in which a Hindu chief ruled over his predominantly Moslem subjects. Amusingly Gorst referred to the 'irony of fate that the Radical member for Northampton [Bradlaugh] should be pleading in this House the Divine right of an Oriental despot to deal with his people as he pleased, and that I, a humble but reactionary Tory, should be pleading the right of these poor Moslems … to cultivate their own lands.'[8] The House agreed with Gorst who spoke with authority that Kashmir had been misgoverned for years by a 'band of corrupt and mischievous men', and the motion was defeated by a large margin.

But a year later Gorst was in political trouble. In the remote princely state of Manipur in north-east India a palace revolution had taken place in September 1890. The ruling Maharajah was replaced by a younger brother in a bloodless coup, led by yet another brother, the able but villainous Tikendrajit, who as the Senapati was the commander of the Manipur army. Grimwood, the British political agent, was not unduly disturbed by what had happened and recommended that the government should accept the change of Raja. In no hurry, the Indian government at Calcutta took a leisurely six

months in deciding what to do. At last, believing the Senapati to be a
bad influence and taking a different view to Grimwood, it insisted in
the following February that he was arrested and exiled. Quinton, the
Chief Commissioner for Assam, had no alternative but to comply with
this decision. Taking with him 400 Gurkhas under Colonel Skene he
went to Manipur himself arriving there on 22 March 1891. Outside the
city Quinton held a preliminary meeting with the Senapati, who was
required to be present at a durbar the next day. But the Indian,
suspecting something was wrong from the presence of the Gurkhas,
refused to attend the durbar, thinking – probably correctly – that he
would be arrested. Early the following morning a detachment of
troops stormed the Senapati's house, now turned into a fortress. The
attack went wrong and was beaten back. Whereupon 5,000 Manipuri
troops surged forward and invested the Residency.

Consequently Quinton, Grimwood, Skene and two other British
officers agreed to parley with the Senapati and the Raja, but when
they entered the palace a soldier speared Grimwood, who was
mortally wounded. Seeing what had happened, the Manipuri leaders
at once decided to kill the other four British. These unfortunate men
were at once beheaded and their dismembered bodies put on display
in the city. The Residency, now set on fire by the besiegers, was
abandoned and its survivors beat a hurried retreat. Retribution was
swift. Manipur was occupied by British troops. Those responsible for
the outrage were arrested and tried. Five men were in due course
executed, the Senapati meeting his fate on a scaffold set up on his polo
field.

At home news of the 'massacre' was greeted with shock. There was
a fear that this might be the start of another mutiny. While there was
of course no resemblance at all to the awful events of 1857, some
people, including the Queen, were worried that vengeance would be
wrought on the same scale as that meted out to the mutineers 34 years
before. Questions rained down thick and fast on the head of Gorst in
the House. There was concern, for instance, that the summoning of
the Senapati to the durbar was somehow an underhand device to
arrest him. Gorst had to make soothing noises and await a full report
on the disaster. It was not until 16 June that a debate on Manipur was
held in the Commons.

Harcourt for the opposition, in a moderate speech, implied censure
on the government on a number of counts. Gorst, in reply and leading
for the government, agreed with him that the Viceroy should have
consulted the Secretary of State in London before sending the military
to Manipur. Also he seemed to be in some agreement with Harcourt's

criticism about the Indian government's long delay in making a decision on recognising the new Raja. Otherwise he considered the government and its officials had acted properly, although without sounding over-enthusiastic in their defence. But in dealing with the Senapati he stumbled. First he described him, perhaps mockingly, as 'not a man of very nice moral character'; this did not quite strike the right note. Then in referring to Grimwood's risky policy of using the Senapati as an instrument of government he rashly said:

> Governments have always hated and discouraged independent and original talent, and they have always loved and promoted docile and unpretending mediocrity.[9]

Gorst then proceeded to illustrate his point by referring to past British action taken against Cetewayo, Arabi and others. The next speaker, Curzon, a Conservative backbencher but in seven years' time destined to be Viceroy himself, then launched a strong attack on Gorst, totally disagreeing with the way, perceived by him as being inadequate, he had defended the government. In particular, he accused him in effect of being soft on the Senapati, whom he described as 'an infamous character.'[10]

When Smith, Leader of the House, wrote to the Queen about the debate he referred to some 'cynical observations' made by Gorst in his speech. Cross too had a go at Gorst when he told the Queen the speech was 'unpalatable', though he tried to excuse his subordinate whom he said had been suffering from influenza and gout.[11]

The opinion of those who counted was that Gorst had not properly supported the Viceroy. There were some who even thought that in his reference to 'mediocrity' he was having a dig at Cross his chief. Two months later Gorst was to admit to Salisbury that he had not made a good speech because he was unwell. The fact of the matter is that Gorst was not in sympathy with the action taken by the government of India, especially over the despatch of the Gurkhas to Manipur, and that this inevitably showed in his speech.

For some time Gorst had been looking for another constituency. Chatham was not congenial to him and he had continuing differences with his party association there. As a seat, Chatham, even if not quite a marginal one, could not be regarded as safe for the Conservatives. He had long had his eye on one of the two Cambridge University seats, and was in touch with the powers-that-be there. The university constituency had a distinct appeal for Gorst. Now past 50 and having fought seven hard elections, he was less in need of stormy weather on such occasions. He saw the Cambridge seats as lying in calmer waters. His chance came with the sudden death in August 1891 of H. C. Raikes, the Postmaster-General, who had held one of the university seats. At the same time Gorst saw an opportunity for political promotion, for the job of Postmaster-General, although out of the Cabinet, was quite important and worth £2,500 a year (*c.* £135,000 now).[12]

Gorst therefore lost no time in writing to Smith and then to Salisbury reminding the Prime Minister of his claims for the now vacant post. The 'mortification' of being excluded from the office of Solicitor-General was somewhat relieved, he wrote, by the making during the last three years of 'very distinct promises of speedy promotion to Cabinet rank ... by the Leader of the House of Commons, and on the strength of them I have given up the governorship of the Cape, Bombay and Madras, any one of which would have satisfied my ambition.'[13] This was all pretty explicit stuff (although we have not heard of Bombay before). He also wrote at the same time to Balfour to obtain support for his candidature at Cambridge University. Although Balfour did not give it, Gorst was finally adopted at the University in time for the election held in July 1892.

Raikes's death had indeed left Salisbury with a problem as to how to fill the position now vacant. Already the Prime Minister had drawn up a 'short' list of 15 candidates with Gorst's name on it. Balfour, consulted by his uncle, thought Salisbury had no option but to offer it either to Gorst or to W. L. Jackson; the latter was his preferred choice. The objections to Gorst, he wrote, were 'the insecurity of his seat and his disloyalty to the party'. (In those days Gorst would have been required on accepting the office of Postmaster-General to resign his seat and recontest it.[14])

Sadly, from his point of view, Gorst misplayed his hand that summer in seeking his promotion. On 4 September he wrote again to Salisbury complaining that party representations were being made to prevent him obtaining the Conservative nomination for the university seat. He went into a long explanation that he had to reckon with his elder brother Edward, who paid his election expenses at Chatham.[15] His brother, he went on, was disappointed that he, John, was still only an Under-Secretary after 25 years as an MP and was unwilling to advance him the funds 'to fight a critical contest' at Chatham, advising him to find a safer seat which would not hinder his promotion prospects.[16] Gorst's allusion to his brother may or may not have been true, but there was something a little whingeing in this somewhat ham-fisted approach. It could not at any rate have gone down well with Salisbury, who was prompted to write Gorst a long and candid letter. He began by denying that he had had any communication with the Cambridge Senate over Gorst's candidature, and then pointed out that Gorst did have 'enemies among the partisans' of the government. Tellingly enough, as we shall see in the next chapter, he then told Gorst:

> You claim a much wider freedom in the expression of your independent opinions than is customary among members of a government ... you have in consequence embarrassed us considerably more than once during the past year. No serious evil resulted from it ultimately but it gave rise to a good deal of angry comment in the party ...[17]

Salisbury continued by lecturing Gorst on the consequences of his independent attitude, and urged him to think dispassionately where this attitude was leading him. As an emollient, no doubt, he stated that he had 'the very highest estimation of your abilities', although he had seen 'with great sorrow the impediments you have thrown in your own way'. It was a remarkable letter and reads somewhat as if written by one schoolmaster to another, especially in the strictures on the need for loyalty.

Gorst could not resist a rejoinder, but in it he made the false assumption that Salisbury had been referring to some embarrassment he had caused on the 'labour question'. He probably irritated Salisbury by also saying that 'many of your colleagues are wholly out of touch both with their party and with public opinion upon the subject'. By return Salisbury rather sharply corrected Gorst's misapprehension. He had not said that the dissatisfaction noted had arisen out of the labour question.[18] Back came Gorst: if it was not the labour question then it must have been the Manipur debate to which Salisbury was referring. The tone as well as the content of this next letter was unfortunate, for Gorst was now complaining about the 'harshness' with which he had been treated over his speech in that debate. The occasion, he admitted, was not a congenial one to him. But he had done his level best to defend the government even though he was unwell, suffering from some nervous complaint. Many times he had extricated the government from difficult positions by successful speeches. (Did he have the Kashmir debate in mind?) Rather bitterly, it seemed, he ended:

> There are plenty of instances of a minister making a fiasco in debate. I doubt if there is one precedent of an old and faithful

servant of the party being so savagely trampled upon for a single failure.[19]

There was no reply from Salisbury.

Gorst was having a bad patch, for once again, at this very moment, he was to upset his party leaders. This happened on account of a visit he made to Ireland that September when he was accompanied by Michael Austin, an Irish nationalist and a fellow member of the Royal Commission on Labour. In Cork Gorst said publicly that he saw no reason for the British government to withhold financial help from a particular Catholic school. Unfortunately this remark was out of step with the policy then being pursued by the Chief Secretary for Ireland, who was now Balfour, a man rapidly climbing the political ladder.

Balfour had not been consulted by Gorst over this remark and he wrote to Salisbury at once. There followed an extended exchange of letters between uncle and nephew on the subject of Gorst. Balfour was pretty angry and one letter he wrote to Salisbury was headed 'Gorst !!' Salisbury agreed that Gorst had played him a 'very ugly trick' and believed it was deliberate. The two men debated, on paper, whether Gorst's resignation should be demanded. Balfour was in favour of dismissing Gorst as 'an impossible colleague', a man not bound, he considered, by the ordinary ties of loyalty. In fact he thought he should have been sacked after the Manipur debate. The more cautious Salisbury, however, decided on balance that this was not a case when dismissal was appropriate. If Gorst were to be dismissed then he thought the party generally might consider Gorst had been ill-treated and the vague discontent existing might crystallize round him.[20] So there the matter rested.

In the meantime the office of Postmaster-General was still unfilled. Gorst had his backers, in particular the Chief Whip Akers Douglas and the party agent Middleton, even if both had doubts about his loyalty. In the event the post went to Sir James Fergusson who was reputedly rather a friend of Gorst's and on the Board with him of the New Zealand Loan and Mercantile Agency.

Ever since his return from the Berlin conference, at which he had been persuaded of the merits of Bismarck's social welfare reforms, Gorst's efforts to rally support for working men and their rights, such as their hours and conditions of work, had gathered pace. He began a campaign in early 1891 on the labour question with a speech in his constituency (we discuss this more fully in the next chapter). This attracted wide attention and must have made Salisbury uneasy. Gorst was also making it clear that the government should become a model employer, and further was proposing a Royal Commission on Labour. Probably the letter Gorst wrote Salisbury on 10 September 1891, with its virtual threat that he might have to pursue an independent course on the labour question, sealed his fate over promotion.

Anyhow, Salisbury decided that it would be quite impossible to put Gorst at the head of a department with a huge workforce and where the labour question was constantly arising, and so give him 'frequent opportunities of driving us into a corner'. Thus had Gorst been excluded from being a candidate for the post.[21] It was a good example of Gorst shooting himself in the foot.

Nevertheless, in early November 1891, Salisbury moved Gorst to the Treasury where he became Financial Secretary and where in Salisbury's opinion he would have fewer opportunities for 'doing mischief' than he had at the India Office. Balfour, also moving to the Treasury as First Lord on the death of Smith, told his uncle that he would not find Gorst difficult to work with as '*He* knows nothing about my views on his Irish and Indian escapades: and the man himself, treacherous as he is, and dangerous as I think him, I have always been able personally to get on with'.[22] It is hard to feel that there was not something two-faced about Balfour in his dealings with Gorst. As it was, Gorst was at the Treasury for less than a year before the next general election intervened. He did though, while there, manage to submit a weighty memorandum to the Chancellor, George Goschen, arguing for the abolition of the doctrine of common employment. The costs should be borne, he considered, by the people who made the profit in the trade concerned and not by the ratepayer. Salisbury, looking ahead to the next election, did not think much of the idea.[23] One thing Gorst did while Financial Secretary was to gain the gratitude of Aberdeen University when he obtained a grant for them of £40,000.

One of Gorst's failings was that he could never make himself a true party man, not even when he was in office. Constitutionally, he seemed unable or unwilling to adapt. Among his peers his loyalty to the party was ever in doubt. About this he was either myopic or plain obstinate. He must have seen that if he did not trim his sails and follow the broad party line he could hardly expect to achieve high office. Nonetheless, the evidence suggests that he always wanted to have his cake and eat it. With a good conceit of himself he felt somehow the party owed it to him to allow him enormous independence of thought and action, and at the same time promote him to the Cabinet. We shall soon see how this attitude of his continued through the 1890s.

NOTES

1. Moon, *The British Conquest*, 892.
2. L. James, *Raj: The Making and Unmaking of British India*, London, Little, Brown, 1987, 34.
3. Kilbracken, *Reminiscences of Lord Kilbracken*, 186.
4. Feuchtwanger, *Disraeli, Democracy and the Tory Party*, 154.
5. MLL, 36–7.
6. Ritchie papers, Mss Eur. 342; Gorst (G)–Ritchie, 17 Jan. 1888. Sir Richmond Ritchie became Permanent Secretary at the India Office in 1909.
7. 3 PD 341, 3 Mar. 1890, 1634–6.
8. 3 PD 346, 3 July 1890, 713–22.
9. 3 PD 354, 16 June 1891, 567.
10. Ibid., 574.
11. G. Buckle (ed.), *The Letters of Queen Victoria 1891–5*, vol. 2, London, John Murray, 1931, 42.
12. Harcourt Williams, *Salisbury–Balfour Correspondence*, 346.
13. Salisbury papers, G–Salisbury (S), 28 Aug. 1891.
14. Harcourt Williams, *Salisbury–Balfour Correspondence*, 346, 348.
15. Hanham, *Elections and Party Management*, 250. In 1880 Gorst's election expenses had amounted to £1,300 compared with his opponent's £3,000.
16. Salisbury papers, G–S, 4 Sept. 1891.
17. Ibid., S–G, 7 Sept. 1891.
18. Ibid., G–S, 10 Sept. 1891 and S–G, 12 Sept. 1891.
19. Ibid., G–S, 15 Sept. 1891.
20. Harcourt Williams, *Salisbury–Balfour Correspondence*, 352–3.
21. Ibid., 353–9; Salisbury papers, G–S, 10 Sept. 1891.
22. Harcourt Williams, *Salisbury–Balfour Correspondence*, 370.
23. Shannon, *The Age of Salisbury*, 361–2.

Social Reformer

We must now go back to the beginning of 1890. Just as he was probably becoming a trifle bored with the India Office, Gorst's life took a new turn. Lord Salisbury gave him the job of leading the eight-man British mission to the international conference on labour in Berlin in March of that year. The conference, with delegations from 15 European countries, was held under the auspices of Kaiser Wilhelm II to find ways of improving the conditions of work in factories and mines. Salisbury did not rate questions to do with labour very highly. If he had done, someone senior to Gorst would have gone to Berlin. Why Salisbury should have chosen Gorst, well known for his often awkward liberal views and social conscience, is a bit of a mystery unless his predilection for Germany was a factor. And certainly had Salisbury anticipated the effect the conference was to have in directing Gorst's energies and ideas into new channels, a development viewed by some as inimical to the party's interests, he might have paused for more thought before making the appointment.

The instructions given to Gorst by Salisbury (who was his own Foreign Secretary) were explicit. Notably he was not 'too readily to accept benevolent projects'. Also he was to refer back proposals to which he was sympathetic and to which he might assent, so that Salisbury could confirm their acceptability.[1] There was, therefore, a firm hand on the tiller at home. Gorst scrupulously obeyed these instructions while at Berlin.

The conference was conducted with the usual German thoroughness, the proceedings specifically covering: work in mines, Sunday labour, child labour and labour of young persons from 14 to 18 years of age, and female labour.[2] The final protocol aimed at laying down, rather modestly, desirable standards in these areas.

Standards of protection given to workers obviously varied widely in Europe, and Britain did not always compare favourably with the countries leading the field. This was particularly the case, for instance, regarding the age at which children were allowed to begin work. In Britain the age was set – cruelly low to us today – at 10 (but 12 in mines). The comparable age in Austria and Switzerland was 14. The conference's proposal was that the minimum age should be 12 (except in southern Europe). Gorst and his team agreed with this, and so specially requested and obtained Salisbury's support for the delegation's view.[3] This did not stop the Conservative government, much to Gorst's impatience, from later dragging its feet in implementing this proposal.

There was another area which caught Gorst's eye. In Germany workers were protected by an insurance system which, thanks to Bismarck, had developed rapidly in the 1880s. German workers, in the lower paid bracket and in a range of industrial occupations, were protected by compulsory insurance on the part of the employer in respect of sickness, infirmity and accident. Provision was also made for them in old age. Nothing like this existed in Britain. While social insurance schemes were not on the conference's agenda, Gorst considered that the German view was essentially the right one, that is the state had a duty to promote the social welfare of its subjects, especially those in need of help.

At the conclusion of the conference Gorst wrote to Salisbury conveying a personal message to him from the Emperor, and at the same time adding his own gratitude for being sent to Berlin as a delegate. His task there had been one of the 'most interesting and instructive' he had ever been engaged on.[4] After his stimulating experiences at this great gathering he returned home determined to do something to improve the lot of working people and children in Britain.

He had, to start with, two particular ideas. The first, an eminently practical one, was that the British government should take the lead itself in labour matters and become a model employer. The second was that a Royal Commission should be appointed to inquire into the conditions of labour to see how they might be improved. Apparently some ministers were in favour of Gorst's proposals, but, as the War Office and Admiralty, the largest government employers of labour, were against stirring up their workmen with 'dreams of Utopian excellence',[5] nothing was done. Neither did his idea of a Royal Commission meet with any enthusiasm. So what then was he to do to advance his ideas? Still at the India Office, he could not make an appeal in the House of Commons. Nothing daunted, he decided to make a speech to his constituents at Chatham about the labour question – not the first time he had spoken to them on this subject. The event, an important one in Gorst's career, took place at the Workmen's Institute on 12 February 1891.[6]

While defining the labour question, he told his large audience that there was a movement throughout the world among working men to secure shorter hours of work, better wages and more leisure so that their lives were 'more desirable and more noble and more worthy of men to live'. No enlightened person would disagree with these idealistic sentiments, although some of what followed would no doubt send a shiver of apprehension down the back of many an employer. In spite of his intellectual gifts Gorst was a down-to-earth man, and he was not going to spend too much time on high-flown thoughts. He preferred to draw his audience's attention to the evils of unemployment such as existed in the East End of London and to the waste of effort which occurred when men had to work unreasonable and exhausting hours. In doing this, he cited the case of certain glass factories in Germany where shorter hours had actually resulted in higher productivity.

Turning to how the present situation might be redressed, ever empirical, he did not think the Eight Hour Bill then before the House of Commons (it purported so to limit the working day) was a panacea. In the Lancashire textile factories, he explained, both employer and employee were against the measure. A reduction of hours would mean a rise in the wages bill for the employer. The effect of this would be to let in competitors, and as a result thousands might be thrown out of work.

Although Gorst claimed that British labour was more efficient – with its mostly higher wages and shorter hours – than other countries in Europe, he still made a whole series of proposals. We have already seen how he wanted the state to be a model employer and to appoint a Royal Commission, and wanted the age of working children to be raised. These demands he repeated, and to them he added new ones as follows:

- Councils of conciliation, to which disputes involving strikes might be referred, should be set up, as well as industrial tribunals with both employers' and employees' representatives to cater for disputes concerning a workman's contract on matters such as the withholding of wages or wrongful dismissal. Perhaps as light relief, he mentioned a case in Austria where a local tribunal heard a workman's complaint that he was being forced to play cards with his employer.
- Trade unions should be free to combine. He did not see these bodies, as some did, as dangerous institutions; but when union members used or threatened violence in pursuit of their aims, they should be punished as anyone else.

- Much more should be done to provide technical education for the working class. In this field the British worker was lagging behind his continental rivals.
- Workers should receive compensation for injuries received arising from accidents at work.
- A ministry of industry should be set up to look after the interests and welfare of the working population.[7]

There were other proposals too, concerning for example the welfare and safety of seamen, sweated workshops in the East End of London and labourers' dwelling houses. Gorst's multifarious ideas reflected his burning desire to change the lot of the working class. This speech was in its way a *tour de force*, and he repeated it with variations up and down the country over the next four years or so.

If we were looking for political watersheds in Gorst's life, his February speech in Chatham was such a one. He was 55, an age when politicians and others tend to become more conservative in their views. Gorst on the contrary was becoming more radical in his outlook. There had always been an element of the crusader in Gorst's make-up, never far from the surface, and his conversion to the cause of social reform now gave full rein to his instincts.

Gorst was a natural propagandist, and by having his Chatham speech printed he ensured it came quickly to the notice of a wide and thinking public. The Conservative agent, alarmed by some of its content, was able to assure party leaders that the speech did not have the endorsement of Central Office.[8] Gorst's speech soon came to the notice of that indefatigable campaigner for social refom, W. T. Stead. A controversial figure, he had in 1885 daringly drawn attention, as editor of the *Pall Mall Gazette*, to the practice of purchasing child prostitutes by openly committing the offence himself. His article 'The Maiden Tribute of Modern Babylon' caused a sensation, and he ended up going to prison for three months. He continued to be an enthusiastic promoter of reform in various fields, however, until, at the age of 63, he was drowned in the *Titanic* disaster in 1912.

Stead now interviewed Gorst at the India Office in the 'little den' from which, as Stead would have it, Gorst 'directed the government of 300,000,000 of the human race'. Smith, the Leader of the House, criticised Gorst for the impropriety of being interviewed. In reply Gorst simply said he needed the publicity.[9] In the Stead interview Gorst covered much the same ground as he had done in his Chatham speech, but had now re-ordered his thoughts and produced, at least as revealed by Stead, a punchier and more refined 'programme'. He was now calling for a further Royal Commission, this time into the subject of Poor Law relief. Questioned on the possibility of a six-day working week – a regime not observed, Stead indicated, in some of the great new industries such as the railways – Gorst agreed that the example set by Belgium and Holland should be followed: a workman should have one day's rest in seven.

Much impressed with Gorst's programme for social reform, Stead published its details in two of his periodicals, first in the March 1891 issue of *Help* and then some months later in the more substantial *Review of Reviews*. Earlier, Stead had sent copies of Gorst's programme to all sorts of people. One of the recipients was David Dale, a mine owner who had been a delegate with Gorst at the Berlin conference. He called it a 'most important and valuable contribution to the most pressing question of the day'. But Michael Davitt, a leading Irish nationalist, found it 'more showy than substantial'. Prominent MPs on both sides of the House were not forgotten and received their copies. One of them, John Morley, who had already served in Gladstone's Cabinet as Chief Secretary for Ireland and was years later to be Secretary of State for India, was another impressed by Gorst's proposals. He said he would move in the Commons for a Royal Commission on Labour, and was confident of carrying his party with him. The government came to hear of this and, according to Stead, decided, as they did not wish to be upstaged by the opposition, that they had no option but to go for a Royal Commission. Things now moved quickly and the decision to set up a Royal Commission was taken on 21 February 1891.

Two months later full details of the Commission, to be chaired by the Liberal Lord Hartington, were published. Its terms of reference were broad, which is what Gorst wanted. In brief it was to inquire into relations between employer and employed, and into the conditions of labour, and then to make recommendations to remedy evils disclosed.[10] Gorst was one of the 27 members of the Commission, although it looked for a time as if membership would be denied him, since he was unpopular in the government on account of how he had in effect got his own way.

As was usually the case with such inquiries, the report of the Commission would not see the light of day for over three years. While Gorst must quite definitely be given his due there were other good reasons for the Commission's appointment, not the least being the wave of industrial unrest which exercised the public's conscience. Thus in 1889 some 50,000 people had marched to Hyde Park in support of the London dock strike when the men demanded a minimum wage of 6d an hour.

Gorst had not been inhibited by his ministerial status from speaking up on labour issues outside parliament. He had explained his ideas still further in a speech in Halifax on 10 November 1891 – he had just 'migrated', as Salisbury put it, from the India Office to the Treasury – when he referred to the importance of making labour more skilled and effective. Warming to the task in hand, he also urged the introduction of a compulsory social security scheme for the working class covering sickness, accident and incapacity to earn a living through debility, disease or old age.[11] The idea to give workers protection against sickness and to provide them with pensions was not a new one, the proposal having been put forward by Canon William Blackley in 1878. Another cleric whom Gorst came to know well, Canon Samuel Barnett, suggested five years later an 8s to 10s a week old age pension for those over 60. Barnett was the founder of Toynbee Hall, the settlement in Whitechapel staffed by enlightened young men from universities, which aimed to promote the welfare of the poor.

Gorst, it seems, was the first politician to espouse publicly the idea of a pension. Professor Gilbert has pointed out that it would hardly have been an accident that Joseph Chamberlain announced his own conversion to the pension idea eight days after Gorst had made his Halifax speech.[12] In a speech at Caernarvon at a labour festival the following May (Gorst was still a minister) he told his audience that he believed social welfare should be regarded as being quite apart from party considerations. Showing a long memory, he declared that he had been impressed as a boy with the misery caused by a damaging strike in Lancashire in 1848 (he was 13 at the time). He then drew the attention of his audience – they included many quarrymen from North Wales – to how the Australians had just set up conciliation and arbitration tribunals to prevent strikes. Some months later during a speech in the Free Trade Hall in Manchester he repeated his call for these tribunals,[13] hoping no doubt to influence by all means possible the sitting Royal Commission on labour.

In pursuit of his cause Gorst had been taking practical steps to inform himself, often through the work of philanthropic bodies, how the poor lived and worked in the East End. He also developed links with other social reformers such as Sydney and Beatrice Webb. From 1890 onwards he became a regular visitor to Toynbee Hall, often staying there days at a time. From this vantage point he was able to familiarise himself with the sweat shops and match factories of the area. He might well have reflected on the remark by the eminent biologist T. H. Huxley, who had once practised medicine in the area, about how the Polynesian in his primitive state 'was not half so savage, so unclean, so irreclaimable as the tenant of a tenement in an East London slum'.[14] Gorst's membership some years later of the Local Government Board's inquiry into Poor Law schools would have given him still more information about the plight of the working class.

While at Toynbee Hall Gorst met Jane Addams, the American social reformer from Illinois, whom he visited in Chicago to see for himself the conditions there.[15] The visit probably took place towards the autumn of 1892. This would certainly have been a convenient moment, for Gorst, unusually, had time on his hands. In the summer of 1892 Salisbury, after his long innings, had gone to the country, lost the general election in July and given way in August to Gladstone who then began his last ministry. Released from office, Gorst was now able to carry forward more freely his plans for social reform, both inside and outside parliament. In the unlikely event of his batteries needing to be recharged, a visit to the USA could have helped him with a new stimulus. Gorst also made a trip over Christmas that year to Egypt to see how his son Jack was faring in Cairo as an under secretary at the Ministry of Finance. For some reason Mary did not accompany him (she was not afraid of long journeys and a year later went to New Zealand to see her aged parents). As a companion he took his eldest daughter Constance, now a widow after the sudden death of her husband. Having seen that Cairo was a proper place for his other daughters to stay with their brother and that Jack was leading a blameless life (in fact, he wasn't), he subsequently allowed Hylda, and in due course Edith, Eva and Gwendolen, to make long visits there. Hylda and Gwendolen – both very good-looking women – found husbands on these expeditions but Eva was not so lucky.

Stead, who was not uncritical of his friends, gave Gorst some advice at this time which throws interesting light on our subject and his character. For Stead, Gorst now stood before the country

> as one of the leading statesmen who has taken up the labour question seriously. He has a great position with untold possibilities for action ... Few things seemed less likely in 1875 than that the astute wirepuller and cynical electioneer of the Conservative party should have become, by natural evolution, the leader of the Labour Movement in 1891.

We may take this last assertion with a pinch of salt. More tellingly, he considered that Gorst with his new social programme had 'reverted to his original type'. By this Stead meant that Gorst had become repossessed by his early zeal and 'philanthropic aspirations' which was apparent when, as a protégé of Bishop Selwyn, his task was to bring the Word to the Pacific islanders and Maoris. Stead went on:

> Like Mr Balfour he [Gorst] would do well to purge himself of the suspicion of cynicism, and to cultivate a little more of that appeal to the moral instinct of mankind which has figured so constantly in the speeches of Mr Bright, Mr Morley and Mr Gladstone ... He is a cool hand who does not let himself go. The emotional enthusiasm which glows in some men seems to leave him comparatively unmoved.[16]

In other words, Gorst should become more of the evangelist when speaking as a social reformer. Whatever Gorst's reaction was to this advice, the reforming image he was projecting must, nevertheless, have been to the liking of the students of Glasgow University, for two years later they elected him their Rector.

In the 1893 session of Parliament Gorst, now MP for Cambridge University, was as busy as he had ever been in the Chamber but this time he was giving pride of place to social questions. He gave notice on 7 February in a debate on the address of the kind of line he would be pursuing. He said:

> The existence of the large bodies of unemployed, half-employed and casually employed in our great cities was a discredit to our civilisation, a standing danger to the maintenance of order and a social evil which urgently demanded the attention of Parliament and of the Government ... no doubt there were numbers of loafers who would not work; but it was equally true that there were a large number of men who were willing to work but who were unable to find employment, and whose wives and families were consequently in a state of semi-starvation.[17]

Gorst went on to say that he hoped that after Ireland – for Gladstone's priority piece of legislation was to be another Home Rule Bill – social reform would take second place instead of what he described as 'gerrymandering' legislation. Later, in June, he would speak against the Bill saying that double government (parliaments in London and Dublin) had always broken down when tried. In fact, Gladstone was to fail with his Irish Bill and the Liberal government's main legislative achievement was in the local government and not in the social field.

A month later a debate on the dockyards provided Gorst with the opportunity he had been seeking. He was now able to make, for the first time in Parliament, all the points he had been hammering home around the country on the need for social reform. We will not repeat them all, but we may observe that he invited the government to pay the same wages in their dockyards as were being paid in private yards, and he commended to the House the German system of old age pensions where the state, employer and employee each paid a third of the necessary contribution.[18] Concerned about safety at work, he urged, during the passage at the time of a Bill on railwaymen's hours of work, that signalmen should not have to work more than an eight-hour day. As usual full of new ideas he made two practical suggestions on unemployment. One was for 'employment registries' to help those seeking work. The other was that the Boards of Poor Law Guardians should experiment in trying to alleviate unemployment by schemes for public works. He cited the Salvation Army as innovators in this field. He could do this with some authority because he had visited a colony of theirs in Hadleigh where unemployed from London were working with success on agricultural projects on derelict land.[19]

Joseph Chamberlain had been looking for an opportunity to amend the Employers' Liability Bill, introduced by the Liberals early in 1893, so that workers received compensation for all injuries received in the course of their employment. In speaking to his amendment he had recourse to German accident statistics. The best speech in support of him came from Gorst, who showed an easy familiarity with these statistics. Gorst also quoted a German authority that 'compensation for injury must be reckoned as part of the cost of production'. In the event the Bill failed. Thereafter Chamberlain and Gorst worked together to try to persuade the Conservative leadership to adopt their proposals for a new Bill. They were not at first successful.[20] But later, under Salisbury's government and at Chamberlain's instigation, a Workmen's Compensation Bill was introduced, and then in 1897 enacted. The Act brought in the principle that accidents to workmen had to be paid for automatically by the employer like other working costs (this was Gorst's earlier point). At first the legislation did not extend to seamen, domestic servants and agricultural labourers; subsequently they all came within its scope. By the time the Bill was introduced Gorst had become deeply involved in educational matters.

Gorst's efforts to obtain better conditions in the dockyards did not slacken. Early in the 1894 session of parliament Gorst was able to ask the Civil Lord of the Admiralty if he was aware that there was now a

48-hour working week at War Office establishments. The reply was opaque, but two months later, and just after Gladstone had been succeeded as Prime Minister by Lord Rosebery, the Admiralty, to Gorst's evident satisfaction, followed the War Office's example.

During these last three years Gorst had put in much time on the Royal Commission on Labour. Its conclusions, published in May 1894 but reached earlier, had been a disappointment to him. It will not surprise readers that Gorst did not associate himself with the report as signed by 19 members, nor even with the 20-page minority report, one of whose signatories was Tom Mann, prominent in the dock strike of 1889. Gorst went one better and wrote his own, mercifully quite short, report.[21]

In the critical field of labour relations the majority of Commissioners had taken a somewhat *laissez-faire* approach, wishing for example to rely on the good sense of employers and employed to sort out their differences. Thus they did not propose statutory boards of conciliation and arbitration, although they did seem disposed towards voluntary boards for this purpose. Gorst was far more interventionist as well as showing a strong tendency to favour the devolution of its powers by central government. He put forward detailed proposals for what he termed 'local boards of industry' set up by County Councils to hear disputes involving an employee's contract and, more significantly, having powers to mediate in trade disputes. Over these local boards would loom a 'central board of industry' beholden to a minister presiding over a powerful Ministry of Industry. The powers of local boards would extend to the framing of local schemes concerned with hours of work which would have to be approved by the minister. It was clear that Gorst did not agree at all with the majority of Commissioners who did not see labour matters as being generally a field for legislation. Gorst also spelt out his views on what employers' obligations should be regarding accidents to their employees. He did, however, agree with the other members on their proposal to increase the number of factory inspectors – he also wanted women appointed to these posts – and on another proposal to institute sanitary certificates for workshops.

Athough unemployment did not come within the Royal Commission's terms of reference, this did not stop Gorst from underlining in his report the urgency of the problem. Here Gorst shared common ground with the view expressed in the minority report. But he obviously did not accept the minority view that the 'present industrial anarchy' was linked to the unsatisfactory relations between employer and employed. Mann and his three colleagues also pointed to the 'demoralising conditions in which great masses of the population are compelled to live'. This was a subject Gorst was to address some years later when he was campaigning for an improvement in the health of working class children.

Gorst's frustration over the paucity, as he saw it, of dynamic recommendations by the Royal Commission is reflected in an article he wrote for *The North American Review*.[22] In it he lamented the low priority being given in the Commons to social legislation. He resented how the Liberals tried to represent themselves as the sole friends of the working class. One day he believed that the working class would find a leader and a policy. From that time he foresaw the emergence of an independent Labour party in parliament. As for his own party, there was a touch of the early 1880s about his scorn for the leaders who 'make no declaration of policy in opposition'. Alas there was no Lord Randolph Churchill with whom to stand four-square. His former friend, now in poor health and no longer a political force, would die in January 1895. Gorst himself was still a vibrant Tory democrat and thus, according to Gilbert, kept alive 'the Disraelian tradition of interest in, and care for, the material welfare of the working classes'.[23]

There was another event in May 1894 which involved Gorst and which must have been disagreeable to him. Mr Justice Vaughan Williams delivered his judgement regarding his examination of the directors and officers of the New Zealand Loan and Mercantile Agency. At the time of the company's liquidation Gorst, a director, had 500 shares in it. The company had been in deep trouble having *inter alia* issued debentures with a misleading prospectus, and had failed to disclose to shareholders its true financial condition. In one transaction a company committee of three, including Gorst, had conferred benefits on the shareholders of the Waikato Land Association (of which Gorst was also a director) while deliberately withholding certain information. The judge considered the committee might have approved the transaction from ignorance of its real nature due to carelessness, rather than showing deliberate intent to deceive. After the case, some rehabilitation of the directors took place. One of them, A. J. Mundella, who had had to resign as President of the Board of Trade, was appointed in November as Chairman of the Poor Law Schools committee and Gorst was made a member of it.[24]

In 1895 Gorst was still concentrating much of his effort on the immediate and worst effect of unemployment: poverty. There was, he urged, a paramount need to relieve distress and not just to talk about it. He reminded the House of Commons in February that in the East End of London according to the reformer and statistician Charles Booth

> ... no less than 35.5 per cent of the population ... were in a condition of chronic and perpetual poverty through being out of work ... the poorhouses in London were never so full as they were at the present time, those sheltered in them having to sleep two in a bed and on the floor.[25]

The next month he made a speech in a debate to bring in a Bill for the better settlement of industrial disputes. In it he made a plea that the tribunals of conciliation and arbitration now at last being mooted by the government, thanks at least partly to his drive, should be given real and not 'sham' powers. Further he wanted these tribunals entrusted to local authorities and not to the Board of Trade. His adherence to the cause of devolving responsibility to local government is significant as we shall see in the next chapter when he was struggling to reform the educational system. At least Gorst had some satisfaction in seeing the passing of a modest Conciliation Bill the following year, the only positive outcome of the Royal Commission on Labour.

The Conservatives' apparent failure to produce a party programme for social reform led Gorst boldly to write one of his own. He published this as an article nearly 7,000 words long in the periodical *The Nineteenth Century* in the summer of 1895.[26] Tongue in cheek, presumably, he called it 'The Conservative Programme of Social Reform'. It was of course no such thing. It was his own programme and no one else's. In putting forward this programme, Gorst saw himself as being consistent in promoting what he saw as the principles of Disraeli.

Gorst made no bones about the political nature of what he wrote, beginning by castigating the Liberal government for failing to deal effectively with the social problems of the day. Conservative policies, he promised, would be guided by 'constitutional principles', and would not imperil past achievements by 'wild experiments with socialism'. In content the article embraced many of the ideas and proposals he had espoused for the last five years. But there were some new matters in the article. In his proposals for dealing with children abandoned by their parents he had some interesting though not novel points to make. These children, he suggested, should become wards of a public authority who should first seek to find them foster parents. The aim, in Gorst's view sensibly enough, should be to give the children as far as possible a family life, and to send them to elementary school. As an alternative he cited the practice in Sheffield whereby guardians, at ratepayers' expense, dispersed children about the town to live under 'mothers' in small rented houses. Approvingly he described the Sheffield experiment as 'a light in the midst of gross darkness'.[27] The worst thing, Gorst said, was to bring children together in their hundreds and place them in great barrack-like schools.

On reverting to a subject of almost equal interest to him, the care of the sick, he considered the state should provide free medical advice and treatment for all who applied for it, thus anticipating the advent of the National Health Service half a century later. At the same time he drew attention to the inadequacy of institutions such as workhouse infirmaries, whose buildings were often antiquated with no hot or cold water supply or sanitary arrangements, and whose staff lacked trained nurses. For this state of affairs he blamed the apathy of government at all levels. As for workhouses themselves he had some ideas on how they might be more imaginatively managed. Turning to the aged he clearly wanted to commit his party – unrealistically – to experimenting with state pensions.[28]

Gorst's programme was truly reformist in outlook. There was one omission. He gave little indication of how his schemes to improve the conditions of the poor and needy would be financed. Nevertheless his ideas and proposals were remarkable when it is remembered they flowed from the mind and pen of a man of 60. He seemed to be just reaching his intellectual prime.

We must assume that Gorst never consulted his colleagues, or those who mattered in the party, on his proposals which must have come like a bolt out of the blue to Salisbury and Balfour. Salisbury, as his biographer Andrew Roberts states, generally did not like change. As for old age pensions, he thought of them as the 'ever-increasing danegold that the haves were forced to pay the have-nots in order to protect their property rights and stave off revolution'.[29] But, as we shall see in the next chapter, even if Gorst had offended the party hierarchy, he escaped retribution. For by the time his article was published he was safely a member of Salisbury's new administration.

NOTES

1. Berlin Conference Proceedings. Parliamentary papers, C 6042, June 1890, item 2.
2. Ibid., annex to Protocol, 7.
3. Ibid., items, 16, 17.
4. Salisbury Papers, Gorst (G)–Salisbury, 31 Mar. 1890.
5. *Review of Reviews*, Aug. 1891, 582.
6. British Library of Political and Economic Science. 'The Labour Question' – a speech by Sir John Gorst at Chatham on 12 Feb. 1891.
7. Ibid.
8. Shannon, *The Age of Salisbury*, 360.
9. *Review of Reviews*, Nov. 1891, 584–5.
10. Royal Commission on Labour. Parliamentary papers, C 7421, June 1894.
11. *The Times*, 11 Nov. 1891.
12. B. B. Gilbert, 'Sir John Eldon Gorst: Conservative Rebel', *The Historian*, vol. XVIII, no. 2, Sept. 1956, 156.
13. *The Times*, 9 May 1892 and 8 Nov. 1892.
14. J. A. R. Pimlott, *Toynbee Hall*, London, Dent, 1935, 6.
15. N. Daglish, *Education Policy-making in England and Wales*, London, Woburn Press, 1996, 34.
16. *Review of Reviews*, Aug. 1891, 586.
17. 4 PD 8, 7 Feb. 1893, 754.
18. 4 PD 9, 6 Mar. 1893, 1120–1.
19. Bramwell Booth, *Work in Darkest England in 1894* (published by the Salvation Army, 1901), 48.
20. E. Hennock, *British Social Reform and German Precedents*, Oxford, Clarendon Press, 1987, 52, 55, 58.
21. Royal Commission on Labour, Parliamentary papers, c 7421, June 1894.
22. Sir John E. Gorst, 'English Workmen and their Political Friends', *North American Review*, Aug. 1894, 207–17.
23. *The Historian* (see note 12 above), 151.
24. *The Times*, 8 May 1894.
25. 4 PD 30, 7 Feb. 1895, 250.
26. J. E. Gorst, 'The Conservative Programme of Social Reform', *The Nineteenth Century*, July 1895, 3–16.
27. Stead papers, 1/29, G–Stead, 24 Apr. 1896.
28. *The Nineteenth Century* (see note 26 above).
29. Roberts, *Salisbury*, 569, 840.

18

Education: The Confusion

Lord Rosebery's Liberal government fell unexpectedly in the summer of 1895 after a chance vote. Sir Henry Campbell-Bannerman, the War Minister who a decade later was to be Prime Minister, had been censured, unjustly as it turned out, for not having procured enough of the new smokeless cordite for the army. Lord Salisbury, the incoming Prime Minister, decided that in forming his third administration he needed the support of the Liberal Unionists. Consequently Joseph Chamberlain joined his Cabinet as Colonial Secretary while the Duke of Devonshire (formerly Lord Hartington) became Lord President of the Council.

With the concurrence of Devonshire, Salisbury offered Gorst the post of Vice President of the Committee for the Council on Education (Vice President for short). This title – mouthful that it was – effectively meant Minister of Education. Salisbury explained to Gorst that, while his nominal chief would be the Duke, he would enjoy an independence 'more than usually complete', because the Duke would have his hands full of other matters. The questions connected with education were 'difficult but urgent and your powers would have full employment in solving the various problems'.[1] The office, he went on, was sometimes included in the Cabinet but at present this would be impossible as that body – with 19 members – was 'swollen'. In the previous Liberal administration Arthur Acland, a successful Vice President, had been in the Cabinet, so this would have been disappointing to Gorst, who nonetheless wrote to Salisbury on 2 July accepting the post.

We do not know what led Salisbury to offer Gorst this post but it is very likely that he with Balfour, First Lord of the Treasury and Leader of the Commons, at his side, would have preferred to keep Gorst out of his government. Probably his feeling was that, as in 1886, it was safer to have him in rather than out. There was, however, no denying that among enlightened reformers Gorst had a certain standing. Thus Stead a few years before had written that in the next parliament Gorst would be 'only second to Mr Balfour in the House of Commons'.[2] In the same vein Henrietta Barnett, the articulate wife of the Warden of

Toynbee Hall, had told Balfour early in 1895 that Gorst, with his knowledge and care about social reforms, was entitled to be considered for Home Secretary in a future Conservative government.[3] Of course both these views exceeded the opinion of Gorst held by the Tory leadership.

When visiting his family in Manningtree that summer while on leave from Egypt, Jack Gorst found everyone delighted with his father's appointment. Jack had had fears that the discreditable affair the year before concerning the laxity of the management of the New Zealand Loan and Mercantile Agency, of which John Gorst was a director, might have been used as 'a pretext to leave him out in the cold'.[4] Also there was Gorst's already mentioned article entitled 'The Conservative Programme for Social Reform' which, with its peremptory definite article, caused irritation to some of his party colleagues.

As soon as he became Prime Minister, Salisbury dissolved the Commons. In the ensuing election the Conservatives won a handsome victory gaining 340 seats and so, with their assured majority, they did not in fact need four Liberal Unionists in the Cabinet. It was, however, too late to exclude them. Gorst was again returned for Cambridge University, and was quite soon to move his family to a house, Howes Close, on the Huntingdon road in Cambridge.

In his earlier years in the Commons, Gorst had not shown any special interest in education. But as his involvement with social reform gathered momentum so did his realisation that education and its organisation were ripe for reform. The education picture in 1895 was certainly complex. Apart from the division of schools into the state and private sectors there was: the distinction between the voluntary schools (predominantly schools owned and run by religious organisations) and the board schools; the multiplicity of bodies responsible for education; the complicated funding arrangements for government grants to schools; the 30 Acts of Parliament dealing with elementary education; the unsatisfactory delivery of secondary education; the shortage of trained, especially female, teachers; the inadequacy of technical education and so on. There was much scope for a clear mind to cut a way through the labyrinth. Gorst had the mind and the ideas too. But how would he manage at carrying through a programme of reform? Would he take his government colleagues, parliament and public opinion with him?

Until 1870 elementary education in England and Wales had been in the hands of the churches, charitable bodies, grammar schools, public schools and other private schools. The government had first intervened in this field in 1833 when it voted the sum of £20,000 (*c*. £840,000 now) for education. Over the years, and spurred on by the developing Victorian conscience, the size of the grant increased until a Department of Education was set up in 1856 to administer the sums disbursed, then amounting to over £500,000 (*c*. £21.5m now). Earlier, as a result of the Great Exhibition, a Department of Science and Art had been established, originally as part of the Board of Trade. To represent these departments in the Commons the new office of Vice President of the Committee for the Council on Education was created. Pressure for a state system of elementary education was maintained, and at last the famous Forster's 1870 Elementary Education Act was passed under Gladstone.

Under this Act, locally elected school boards were set up in England and Wales with power in their 'districts' to levy rates, build schools (the board schools as they came to be known) and provide teachers for children under 13. There was no question at this time of any kind of state education beyond this age. Secondary education therefore remained a privilege limited to middle and upper-class children. Attendance at elementary schools became compulsory only in 1880 (first they had to be built), and was made free in 1891. To obtain government grants the schools had to pass inspections leading to an increasingly unpopular scheme of payments according to examination results. As for the curriculum, this did not in the early years go much beyond the three Rs.

In the dual system which grew up, the board schools and voluntary schools were often in competition. By the time Gorst was Vice President some 4.3 million children (just under 2.5 million of them in voluntary schools) were receiving elementary education. In rural areas Anglican voluntary schools came to dominate the scene, but in the towns it was the rate-aided board schools which did better. In the former category there was of course a great emphasis on religious instruction while schools in the latter had to be non-sectarian, that is no religious dogma distinctive of a particular denomination could be taught in them. This was a source of continuing friction between the state and the different religious groups.

Naturally enough a strong wish developed for the state to provide secondary education, a nettle which governments were unwilling to grasp. Accordingly, some improvisation was necessary, and this public need was partly met by school boards setting up what were known as higher grade schools. At these, older children were offered courses beyond elementary school standards, and subjects such as history,

French, mathematics and some of the physical sciences were taught. These schools turned to the Science and Art Department for funds, and this led in turn to the establishment of schools of science with three-year courses and also evening classes. As we shall presently see, the legality of these schools was to be called into question. This was because the subjects they taught were not allowed for by the Education Department's Code for elementary schools.

There was another development. Under the Technical Instruction Act 1889, the newly created county and county borough councils were empowered to levy a penny rate for educational purposes. These bodies also received for the same use the quaintly termed 'whisky money' originally allotted out of Customs and Excise duty funds to compensate publicans, whose public houses had been declared redundant. Thus yet another breed of school had sprung up, this time under these local government authorities aiming to give a technical education to older children. The historian Eaglesham considers that by the end of the century there was an 'educational muddle' and that, with the Education department vainly trying to administer an outmoded system, reorganisation was imperative.[5]

This deplorably uncoordinated state of education led the Liberal government in 1894 to set up a Royal Commission on secondary education under the lawyer James Bryce, who had known Gorst at the Bar. He was later to be a Liberal Cabinet minister and then ambassador in the USA. Bryce's report was produced quickly and a copy reached Gorst's desk only a few months after he became Vice President.

In elementary education an immediate problem facing Gorst and Devonshire was the future of voluntary schools. A running sore was the concern felt by both the Anglicans and Roman Catholics for their elementary schools. They thought them to be underfunded, and thus at a great disadvantage vis-à-vis the board schools. Anglican and Roman Catholic commissions had separately investigated the plight of their schools and soon the Archbishop of Canterbury, E.W. Benson, would be hammering at Devonshire's door demanding action. Also *The Times* added its voice in the summer of 1895 to the mounting campaign on behalf of the voluntary schools. In a debate on supply at the end of August Gorst was himself made aware of the feeling in some quarters of the House about the 'depressed state' of voluntary schools – they numbered nearly 15,000 in England and Wales – and the 'severe crisis' they were passing through. But he would not commit himself at this early stage about what was to be done.[6] He could be cautious if he chose.

The apparently simmering turmoil sometimes on and sometimes under the surface of the educational scene did not stop Gorst from going off in September for a bicycling tour in northern France. He had been badly bitten by the prevailing craze for bicycling which he regarded as the finest exercise possible. Already as Vice President he was riding to work in London on a brilliant red machine, just possibly being mistaken for an elderly – and rather august – postman.

The fortnight's tour was quite strenuous for Gorst. It began on 5 September at Dieppe where he met his son Jack. Then together with his daughter Eva they all proceeded to ride to St Valery-en-Caux along the coast of the Seine Maritime through Etretat to Le Havre, a distance of 60 miles or more, and then on to Honfleur and Trouville. Although the country is fairly flat the pedalling would have required vigorous effort – their machines would not then have had three speeds – especially if there had been westerly breezes. They stayed at hotels and made a base for a few days at Trouville where they visited the casino in the evenings. Once they went to a concert. On 11 September John and his son rode from Trouville to Pont l'Evêque and back. John was so enjoying his holiday that for a few days more he bicycled round the countryside with the compliant Eva before returning to Dieppe, this time by train, to catch the boat home.[7]

Refreshed by his holiday, Gorst was now ready for serious departmental business. A Cabinet committee on education had been formed comprising five ministers: Salisbury, Balfour, Cross, Devonshire and Gorst. The Duke had asked Gorst to prepare a discussion document with an Education Bill in mind. Here we should remind readers that the Duke was still a considerable figure in politics, twice, as Lord Hartington, having come near to being Liberal Prime Minister. He was intelligent, fair-minded and with the taciturnity associated with the Cavendish family. But by this time he was becoming rather more passive, some said lazy, in his approach to politics. He and Gorst, a strangely assorted pair, got on reasonably well together.

A problem, possibly at first underestimated by those sitting round this particular committee table, was that the views of Gorst on educational policy inevitably differed from those of Salisbury and Balfour. Salisbury, a high churchman, was a strong supporter of Anglican schools in traditional Tory vein, and wanted above all to see them helped financially. He was not much in favour of board schools. His nephew was more pragmatic in approach, while neither of course had the radical reforming outlook of the new and distrusted Vice President. And always over their shoulders loomed the powerful figure of Joseph Chamberlain, champion of the nonconformist cause. The outlook was not exactly promising.

Gorst himself believed that the voluntary schools had an important part to play in the scheme of elementary education, even though some may have been inefficient, but that if they accepted more aid from the state they must at the same time accept an increased measure of state control. As for board schools, Gorst fully recognised the contribution they were making in the urban areas, but was aware, and said, that they often exceeded their function when providing what was in effect secondary education. As Gorst believed that the government's delivery of secondary education was 'ill-designed and ineffective', he was much encouraged by the findings of the Bryce Commission, which recommended sweeping changes. Gorst wanted to see both elementary and secondary education decentralised. He considered that local authorities had displayed more resourcefulness and readiness to experiment than central government in dealing with the problem of the unemployed. They would therefore be the best instrument for carrying forward his reforms. He never wavered from this view. This was not the first time he had felt the centre was too powerful. Gorst, in reorganising the Conservative Party machine 25 years before, had devolved much responsibility to the constituencies. Nor had he much favoured later the powerful Conservative Party Central Committee.

A contemporary educational historian has commented on Gorst's plans as follows:

> Gorst's commitment to the concept of educational devolution, based on the creation of new comprehensive LEAs, ultimately rested on the belief that local bodies, sufficiently large enough to moderate or resist central government – and therefore to act as a buffer for individual institutions – were the only ones which could ensure an effectively harmonious development of the nation's education system.[8]

But Gorst saw progress being barred by party spirit and religious intolerance. His political colleagues, as he perceived it, were often unhelpful. For instance he confided to Stead and to his friends the Barnetts at Toynbee Hall, perhaps with a little exaggeration, that, apart from the Duke and Lord George Hamilton, Secretary of State for India, members of the government were indifferent to education or opposed to it. He even informed his Permanent Secretary about the 'contempt' Salisbury felt for education.[9]

Gorst could never resist having a dig at people or Tories with whom he was not in sympathy. In an article on the prospects for education published only a year and a bit after becoming Vice President, he wrote, in some well-rounded phrases, in the context of the agricultural depression:

> The landowners exhibit that dislike to intellectual development which is characteristic of a territorial aristocracy; the farmers regard the imitation of the methods of their forefathers as the highest agricultural art and scoff at the teachings of science; and the labourers' children are turned out of school to scare crows when eleven years old ...

Part of this statement was to be hurled back at him in a debate in the Commons years later.[10] The trouble was, Gorst never knew when to hold his tongue or curb his pen.

We have seen from his earliest days how Gorst relished speaking up on all issues of the day. Opportunities for speaking to the public and to the teaching profession now abounded for the Vice President. For instance, just before Christmas in 1895 after he had opened a new Pupil Teachers' School in Cardiff (for both board and voluntary school teachers), he addressed an audience in the lecture theatre of Cardiff University College. A particular point he made concerned the need to improve the education of the workforce if the country was to compete with other nations. He instanced Germany, Switzerland and France as having made great strides in the field of technical education. In France there were, he said, 43 schools of agriculture. In Britain there were still only three: at Reading, Leeds and Bangor (had he forgotten Cirencester?). Some years later, this time at University College in Liverpool where he was distributing prizes, he was again referring to the importance of commercial and technical education (which was promoted by local authorities under the Technical Instruction Act 1889) on account of industrial competition from abroad.[11] This was a message he kept driving home.

The Cabinet committee, not unexpectedly given its composition, was somewhat divided on what to put into the Education Bill. To begin with Gorst was responsible, together with parliamentary counsel, for the drafting of the measure. At one moment early on Balfour was critical of Gorst for disregarding in the draft what had been agreed in committee about the contents of the Bill.[12] Importantly for Gorst, the Bill which finally emerged emphasised the need for decentralising the educational system. Indeed, it had the principal aim of creating new local education authorities in accordance with the views of Devonshire and Gorst. But it also contained clauses emanating from Balfour conceding a special 4s grant per child in voluntary schools and limiting the amount of rate aid board schools might levy. In addition there was a clause proposing the repeal of the famous Cowper-Temple clause of the 1870 Act so as to allow denominational teaching in board schools. As a piece of legislation it was cumbersome because of its various purposes. It was also surprisingly radical. For Gorst the Bill was particularly important because it was the first piece of major legislation for which he had been responsible.

With high hopes Gorst introduced the Bill in the Commons on 31 March 1896. He began with a discursive survey of the state of education in all its phases. It was no less than 70 minutes before he began explaining the provisions of the Bill. He was like a Chancellor of the Exchequer keeping his audience on tenterhooks before revealing his budget secrets. At last he came to the main point:

> The principle of the Measure is the establishment in every county and county borough of a paramount education authority. It is to be one channel through which public money is to reach the schools; it is to supplement, and not to supersede, existing educational effort ...[13]

This was a Bill which needed some digesting and we can only guess how impatient Gorst was to move the second reading. This happened in early May. After Gorst had again led for the government, Asquith rose and in a hard-hitting speech attacked many of the Bill's proposals. Others followed suit. Even though the jurisdiction of the school boards was untouched by the Bill, the measure's general direction was too revolutionary for most members. The second reading was only passed after nights of heated debate, too often on matters of detail such as the precise composition of the new education committees. Sensibly enough Gorst tried to have argument on this sort of detail postponed until the committee stage. At length, to the consternation of the government, no less than 1,335 amendments were tabled for that next stage.

An unfortunate incident – a celebrated one – occurred on 11 June when the influential Conservative, Sir Albert Rollitt, the chairman of the Association of Municipal Corporations, moved an amendment in committee. He thought the new education authorities should not be confined to counties and county boroughs. But Gorst did not want an indefinite number of smaller municipal authorities and rejected the amendment. While this was happening Balfour strolled into the Chamber, and when appealed to by another member at once agreed to everyone's astonishment to Rollitt's amendment, thereby cutting the ground from beneath Gorst's feet. The effect of this could only have been to make the opposition press for more amendments.[14] With both sides in a state of uproar about its main provisions the Bill was now doomed and towards the end of June the Cabinet decided to abandon the measure. This was a blow for Gorst, who saw the main plank of the Bill as essentially his brain-child.

The abandonment of this Bill by the Cabinet gave rise to the story recounted by Harold Gorst of how the Duke was given the task of breaking the news to Gorst as tactfully as possible. Accordingly, he walked across Downing Street to the Education department where he went to Gorst's office. There he stood for a while warming his back against the fire (we must assume it was a coldish end to June) without saying a word. Suddenly he blurted out: 'Gorst, your damned Bill's dead!' When Harold taxed his father with this story, John Gorst said there was not a shred of truth in it, although it was typical of the Duke.[15]

The failure of the Bill affected Gorst's standing as Vice President, particularly with Balfour who stated, as if somehow blaming Gorst for this political set-back, that he did not want Gorst introducing any more Bills. It is not too clear why Balfour took this line but it seems to reflect the bad blood existing between the two men, anyhow on the part of Balfour.

Indeed, Balfour was true to his threat when in February the following year he himself introduced the three-clause Voluntary Schools Bill to provide voluntary schools with financial help amounting to 5/- per head per year. This measure the Cabinet thought, erroneously, would solve the education problem. It was of course bizarre that the man charged with responsibility in the Commons for education had no hand in planning this Bill, nor in presenting it to the House. Many expressed surprise that after this slight Gorst was willing to retain office. In the circumstances he made every effort to give his views on voluntary schools a public airing, and in the November 1896 issue of *The Nineteenth Century* there appeared a 12-page article on these schools under his name. Voluntary schools, Gorst opined, were in no danger of extinction in the country even though they might be underfunded. But in the towns they were generally inferior to board schools which counted for income on the ratepayers. To survive they needed, therefore, an adequate and permanent funding arrangement to bring them up to the level of board schools in terms of buildings, equipment and staff. Their managers would have to accept increased public control. Finally Gorst saw no reason why voluntary schools should surrender their liberty to teach the religion of their choice. A reader of this article can only be struck by Gorst's apparent knowledge of his subject and the authority with which he wrote on it.[16]

On 16 February Campbell-Bannerman complained with a nice light touch about Gorst's absence from the Commons at this time:

> They did not speak of the Vice President because they did not know where to find him, either in a physical or in a moral sense. [Laughter] He was now here and now there – now in one part of the House and now in another; now writing in one magazine or in another; but never, until last night, taking any part in the explanation of this Bill to the House. [Hear, hear] He had become, in fact, a sort of parliamentary will-o'-the-wisp. [Laughter][17]

Gorst had in fact supported Balfour's Bill during its second reading in a speech which amused the House the previous day. This had been noted a few days later by Henry Lucy in his column 'Essence of Parliament' in *Punch*. He referred to a certain 'John O'Gorst', who had treated the House to a 'bit of high comedy' not seen for a long time, and whose acting skills the writer obviously admired:

> Everything perfect – the Passive figure, the almost wooden expression on the face as the cheers and laughter rose and fell; the subtle modulation of the voice investing innocent syllables with barbed point. Nothing lacking, not even PRINCE ARTHUR [Balfour], evidently anxious but keenly appreciative, seated close by his docile colleague … The crowning success is that when closely examined there is really nothing in the speech to which exception could be taken.[18]

While we are in descriptive mood, there is a pen picture of Gorst in his mature parliamentary days written by the leading Irish Nationalist MP, T. P. O'Connor:

> … in appearance he was not quite what one would expect. The face was round, the colour ruddy with the health of a good liver – he was an ascetic – and all this, with the long beard and the bald

head, gave a certain benign dignity to the countenance ... But a look at the eyes soon revealed the inner temperament, for their brightness, their coldness, their daring, shone through even the spectacles he always wore.[19]

This time, early in 1897, was one of the low points in Gorst's seven-year tenure of office as Education Minister – he had several. He even came into conflict with the new Archbishop of Canterbury, Frederick Temple, who had accused Gorst of trying to 'undenominationalise' the voluntary schools, in other words of tampering with the religious instruction given in them. An indignant Gorst rejected this accusation, first asking by what authority His Grace was making this statement, and then insisting that he had all his life 'consistently supported the principle that there should be no restriction upon religious teaching in a voluntary school'.[20] Nonetheless, despite various set-backs, Gorst continued to have the support, even protection, of Devonshire.

Gorst often vented his feelings – they could alternate between jubilation and despondency – on the mainly sympathetic Barnetts at Toynbee Hall where there was much intellectual discussion on education and other matters. The Barnetts asked Gorst why he was a Tory, clearly thinking he should have been a Liberal. The worthy Canon and his wife, who fervently believed in government of the people by the people, considered that Gorst's views did not differ very much from theirs in so far as he accepted the need for government to justify itself to the people.[21] In many ways the Barnetts were right. At heart Gorst was a Liberal.

NOTES

1. Lord Salisbury papers, Salisbury–G, 1 July 1895.
2. *Review of Reviews*, 4 Aug. 1891, 575.
3. N. Daglish, *Education Policy-making in England and Wales*, London, Woburn Press, 1996, 34.
4. JG d, 13 July 1895; Daglish, *Education Policy-making*, 35.
5. E. J. R. Eaglesham, *The Foundations of Twentieth-Century Education in England*, London, Routledge & Kegan Paul, 1967, 18.
6. 4 PD 36, 28 Aug. 1895, 1021, 1041.
7. JG d, 5–11 Sept. 1895.
8. N. Daglish, 'Sir John Gorst as an educational innovator: a re-appraisal', *History of Education*, vol. 21, 3 Nov. 1992, 268.
9. Stead Papers 1/29, G–Stead, 19 July 1896; Barnett papers A/FWA, S. Barnett–F. Barnett, 20 Nov. 1896; Kekewich papers, G–Kekewich, 2 Jan. 1897.
10. Sir John E. Gorst, 'Prospects of Education in England', *North American Review*,

Oct. 1896, 427–37; 4 PD 109, 23 June 1902, 1458. The speaker was Dr Macnamara.
11. *The Times,* 21 Dec. 1895 and 29 Oct. 1898.
12. Daglish, *Education Policy-making,* 47.
13. 4 PD 39, 31 Mar. 1896, 538; also see A. S. T. Griffith-Boscawen, *Fourteen Years in Parliament,* London, J. Murray, 1907, 92–3 .
14. 4 PD 41, 11 June 1896, 906–7; Griffith-Boscawen, *Fourteen Years in Parliament,* 103; Eaglesham, *From School Board to Local Authority,* 105–7; Daglish, *Education Policy-making,* 56.
15. MLL, 125–6.
16. John E. Gorst, 'The Voluntary Schools', *The Nineteenth Century,* Nov. 1896, 699–710.
17. 4 PD 46, 16 Feb. 1897, 585.
18. *Punch,* 27 Feb. 1897, 107.
19. *Daily Telegraph,* 5 April 1916: obituary by T. P. O'Connor.
20. PRO ED 24/2099, G–Archbishop of Canterbury, 31 Mar. 1897 and 1 Apr. 1897.
21. Barnett papers, S Barnett–F Barnett, 5 Dec. 1896.

Education: Remedies and People

After the disaster to the Education Bill in the summer of 1896 the Duke of Devonshire asked Gorst to begin work on a new Bill on secondary education, and also to chair an inquiry into the Science and Arts department. On the former task progress was slow. But the latter task, in which Gorst had freedom to choose his own committee, was very much to his taste; for by utilising administrative measures Gorst perceived an opportunity of developing his cherished plan to decentralise education. Progress in this field was relatively swift.

As a result of this inquiry a revised departmental Directory (the administrative regulations for the Science and Arts department) was published in April 1897. Under its new Clause VII, counties and county boroughs possessing an organisation for secondary education under the Technical Instruction Act became entitled to apply to the department for control of science and art instruction in their areas. Thus implementation of Clause VII would permit the effective creation of local education authorities. This new scheme was not popular with the school boards, who saw it as hindering the advancement of their higher grade schools. So they opposed the new regulation. Gorst at first was conciliatory in his approach to the boards, hoping to win them over to his point of view and to ensure they would not try to intervene over the implementation of the new power available to local authorities under Clause VII.

But the school boards showed extreme obduracy and Gorst's efforts were not successful.[1] A major confrontation emerged the following year between the London County Council (LCC) and the influential London School Board (LSB). When the LCC's Technical Education Board decided to make an application under Clause VII in December 1898 for the LCC to become a local education authority its move was vigorously opposed by the LSB. Gorst, annoyed, saw the LSB as blocking his initiative to establish new local education authorities. Eventually he lost patience with the school boards, and determined to have a showdown with them. For some time he had been examining irregularities perpetrated by these boards, whereby public money was being used to provide educational facilities beyond what he, and others, perceived to be the requirements of elementary education. As a test case it was decided to draw the attention of the district auditor, T. B. Cockerton, to particular payments made from its school fund by the Camden School of Art.

Historians are by no means in agreement as to who precisely took the initiative in deciding to involve the auditor. Halévy states the case had been brought 'at the instigation of a committee lately formed to combat the school boards' chaired by Lord Robert Cecil, youngest son of Lord Salisbury, and with Evelyn Cecil his cousin also a member. The Cecils were members of the Conservative High Church party, a defence group formed to protect Anglican church interests in parliament; they were hostile to school boards. Eaglesham, on the other hand, believes that Gorst 'secretly arranged' for the auditor to challenge expenditure. Simon agrees that Gorst was clearly involved although he adds a cautionary rider that the methods used had been the subject of much discussion. A somewhat different view comes from Taylor, who considers that W. Garnett, secretary of the LCC's Technical Education Board, was the prime mover, closely supported by the Cecils with Gorst playing an active but lesser role. Daglish thinks that Gorst's role was a significant one and that he was using Garnett. Whatever the truth of the matter – and it certainly looks as if Gorst was deeply involved – for once Gorst and the Cecil family were working in concert.[2]

The Permanent Secretary at the Department of Education, Sir George Kekewich, had for many years sustained the work of board schools and must have been aware of the irregularities being perpetrated. Presumably, he had turned a blind eye to them. As a result he and Gorst could hardly avoid coming into serious collision on the whole issue.

After examining the accounts of the Camden school in the summer of 1899 Cockerton found that some payments had been made from the school fund which were not within the Education Department's annual Code of regulations. Consequently, as he was entitled to do, he surcharged members of the school board for the sum. The LSB did not accept the auditor's decision and took the case to the courts. Subsequently, in December 1900, the High Court found in what came to be known as the Cockerton case in favour of the LCC and against the LSB. The court held that a school board might not provide instruction out of the rates outside the curriculum for elementary education as laid down by the department's Code and by the 1870 Act. As expected by Gorst the decision was confirmed by the Court of Appeal in April 1901. The Cockerton judgement put the cat among the pigeons because it meant the government would have to take urgent remedial action. For secondary education provided by school boards, including evening classes, now declared illegal, could not continue.

Gorst had followed his Clause VII reform with the introduction in March 1900 of revised rules for elementary education in the department's Code which simplified the system of grants, setting this at a fixed rate of 22s per child per year (the unpopular system of payment by results had been abolished in 1895 by Gorst's predecessor). This increased the money available for education. In addition there was a locally determined liberalisation of the form and content of the curriculum. The new system imposed an age limit of 14 on the children in respect of whom grants were available. This meant that higher grade schools would suffer. The journal *The Schoolmaster* and the Executive of the National Union of Teachers approved of this new Code. Not all the education world approved, and the *School Board Chronicle* denounced the Code as further evidence of the government's hostility to board schools.[3]

There was another important administrative measure brought in by Gorst at this time. It was known as the 'Higher Elementary Schools minute' of 6 April 1900. With this minute Gorst introduced a new type of school called the higher elementary school. The aim was that this sort of school, coming directly under and funded by the Education Department (now known, we shall shortly see, as the Board of Education), would curtail the need for higher grade schools. These new schools would have no pretence of being secondary schools, although their curriculum would be science oriented. Once again Gorst was trying to wrest away from the school boards control of what he perceived to be secondary education. In the Commons it was the Conservative back bencher Sir Richard Jebb who introduced this new measure to the House, commending it as a progressive one. Most commentators and MPs seemed to agree.

Daglish, the educational historian, sees Gorst's various initiatives and measures taken outside the Commons as amounting to a 'pincer movement' against the school boards: the legal challenge on the one hand and the various 'administrative devices' on the other. A strong supporter of Gorst's work in education, Daglish is of the opinion that Gorst's administrative reforms forced his government colleagues into providing by 1902 a solid legislative foundation for the twentieth century in the Education Act based on the concept of partnership between a system of rationalised local education authorities and a unified central government authority.[4]

We shall turn to central government organisation in a moment, and to the Education Act of 1902 later.

When Gorst came to consider whether there were any bodies in existence which might be transformed into the new local education authorities he had in mind, he early on rejected school boards as unsuitable. It was not just that he was critical of them because some of their work was illegal. For he recognised the value of this work, which gave a much needed form of higher education to older children and to adults too. But school boards only covered about two thirds of the country and if they were to be charged with local responsibility for all forms of education then a great number of new boards would have to be created. He did not favour this. Another matter which always bothered Gorst was, as he perceived it, the unsatisfactory calibre of some of those serving on school boards.

While Gorst was considering how he might devolve the responsibility for education onto local authorities, the Duke of Devonshire had turned his mind to reorganising the education machine in central government. His plan was eventually carried through by a Bill passed in August 1899 which resulted in the amalgamation of the Education Department with the Science and Arts Department (the original plan was to include the Charity Commission; this merger was not completed until 1914). A new Board of Education was thus established presided over by a President, to be a minister of Cabinet rank, with a Parliamentary Secretary under him. This Act would come into effect the following spring. This Bill was important for Gorst because, although he had no part in its planning, his office of Vice President – and with it he believed part of his status – was abolished. However, owing to the intervention of the Duke, Gorst was allowed to retain his title of Vice President even if this was now an anomaly. In effect he and the Duke continued in tandem as before.

Through the ups and downs of his time as Vice President Gorst somehow kept his relations with Devonshire on a mainly even keel. Eventually towards the end of 1900 the Duke spoke in quite approving terms of him, and said that he had almost got to like him. There was a nice little ditty penned about the two men entitled 'Gorst's Soliloquy', which went as follows:

Who is my constant friend and true,
Who tells me what I ought to do,
And promises to see me through?
   My Duke.

Who bids me spurn the foolish 'fads'
Put forward by the noisy 'Rads',
A set of very paltry 'cads'?
   My Duke.

Who is it kindly tells me what
I am to say and what I'm not
When in the House affairs get hot?
   My Duke.

Who is my scapegoat every day,
And bears my little sins away
When nasty things opponents say?
   My Duke.

Who, when he reads Sir Henry's chaff
About the member of his staff,
Will read it with a wearied laugh?
   My Duke.[5]

While we have discussed Gorst and his relations since 1895 with his two political masters, Devonshire and Balfour, we have said almost nothing about the important civil servants with whom he worked. We will mention several of them.

The Permanent Secretary at the Education Department, Sir George Kekewich, was educated at Eton and Oxford, had held his post for five years and was very conscious of his position. He wrote an interesting but at times somewhat bitter autobiography and is therefore not a completely reliable source. Indeed the historian Elie Halévy states the book is 'slanderous' (*sic*).[6] At first Sir George and Gorst got on well together, Kekewich welcoming Gorst's appointment on account of his commitment to reform. 'But for our personal friendship which I hope nothing will shake', Gorst wrote to him on New Year's day in 1898, 'our position at the Education department would be quite intolerable.' Yet two years later relations between the two men had deteriorated badly, Gorst reminding Kekewich that 'I am your official superior ... and I cannot allow you to intervene between me and the Lord President nor to hamper my initiative whenever I ... [suggest] matters of policy to him'.[7]

On the one hand Kekewich recognised Gorst's talents. He thought him for instance 'extremely clever and at times brilliant', describing him as a 'kind of Conservative and clerical Socialist'. In fact he was 'far abler than most Cabinet Ministers',[8] although his success in politics was marred by his erratic temperament. He also described him as having a 'keen sense of humour' and was a man who 'delighted in administering pin-pricks to the Cabinet for whom he entertained ... a whole-hearted and probably justifiable contempt'. Once he instanced how Gorst had read to him notes of a speech saying as he came to a particularly objectionable or cynical passage:

> 'This will tickle them up', 'them' being his own government!
> Or, 'Balfour won't like this bit; he'll squirm!'

Kekewich acknowledged Gorst's advanced views on education and his deep sympathy for children, especially for those who for no fault of their own were educated in the workhouse and commonly designated as 'pauper' children.[9]

On the other hand Kekewich could also be highly critical of Gorst. He related how unpopular he was at the office. When his Private Secretary left him to fight in the Boer War it proved difficult at first to fill the normally much coveted post,[10] the inference being that Gorst was a hard man to work for. Gorst could also, Kekewich found, be obnoxious and sulk. When he could not get his way he would go to the Duke. In this wise he was 'proficient in the art of stabbing in the back'. In course of time Gorst and Kekewich fell out over the role of school boards and by 1901 they were reputedly not on speaking terms. At the end of the following year Kekewich was forced to retire early. This, though, was not Gorst's doing.

Another man who disliked Gorst was Michael Sadler, the head of the section on special inquiries and reports. This included examining education systems in foreign countries. A high-principled man who would one day be Master of University College, Oxford, Sadler deplored how the Education department came to be divided into pro-Kekewich and pro-Gorst factions. Sadler got off to a bad start with the Vice President who demanded his urgent help in preparing the 1896 Education Bill. But Sadler was in Germany on duty and seemed slow in responding to Gorst's summons. By the time Sadler had reached the office in London, Gorst had completed and submitted his first draft of the legislation; he worked, of course, very fast, something

Sadler would not have known. According to Sadler's biographer son, the novelist Michael Sadleir, Gorst had once vilified his father in semi-public. This happened apparently in the dining-room of the House of Commons.[11] The precise circumstances are not known but there must be a suspicion that Gorst had fulminated about Sadler's apparently slow return from Germany.

It was one of Gorst's less endearing characteristics sometimes to strike out at those with whom he worked when he thought them at fault in their contributions. Michael Sadleir puts a generous construction on this unfortunate episode in the dining-room, attributing it to Gorst's resentment at his Bill's failure, and making allowances therefore for Gorst's behaviour towards his father.

Another figure was coming up fast on the outside rail. This was Robert Morant, seen by some as overly ambitious, an immensely tall and gaunt-looking Wykehamist who had read theology at Oxford and had then been tutor to the Crown Prince of Siam. He had become involved in trying to reform the education system of that country but after some intrigue he had been dismissed from his post.[12] He had joined the Education Department in 1895 in a junior capacity coming under Sadler. Gorst first met him at Toynbee Hall where he spotted his potential. Later Morant seized the opportunity presented in 1899 of becoming Gorst's Private Secretary, a position he used as a springboard to advance his career. He was soon to ingratiate himself with Balfour and was elevated to membership of the Cabinet committee preparing the Bill which became the 1902 Education Act. In that year, leapfrogging over every colleague and superior in sight, he was nominated successor to Kekewich as Permanent Secretary. The speed of his promotion took even Gorst's breath away.

Gorst's temperament sometimes let him down. Canon Barnett once described his temper as 'foul'.[13] Sir Richard Jebb, Gorst's brother MP for Cambridge University and a distinguished educationalist, was once button-holed in the Commons by Gorst in a 'vile temper' who addressed him in a bullying way on some departmental matter. This apparently gave Jebb a glimpse of what Gorst could be like when disagreeable.[14] On occasions in the Commons, when perhaps feeling despondent, Gorst would sit not on the front bench but in the darkest corners of the Chamber. He was certainly a curious mixture. An obituarist and fellow MP, who knew him well, wrote that Gorst was a 'somewhat genial man and was on the whole popular in the smoke rooms' and other places where members laid off politics.[15]

If offended by something in his Whitehall office Gorst would, according to Kekewich, keep away from the Education Department, and might go instead to the Science and Art Department in South Kensington which he found more congenial. Jack Gorst who, on leave, would frequently lunch or dine with his father in the House, confirms his father's moods when noting how he 'quarrelled with all his political colleagues and took up the position of a sulky discontented outcast'.[16] Jack had been wondering at the time whether his father might be able to give him a helping hand with his career (he did not in fact need one, for he was soon to become a protégé of Lord Cromer), but decided, on looking critically at his father and his situation, that there was no help to be obtained from that quarter.

Another who commented adversely on John Gorst's temperament was Hylda's husband George Hunter who regarded his father-in-law as 'an old pig'. According to Hunter, writing to his brother Duncan in the USA, there was speculation in the press (at the time of the Queen's Jubilee) that Gorst would be offered a peerage, an offer which – in Hunter's view – he would refuse because it would mean political extinction. Hunter, presciently enough, thought Gorst would get no further political promotion. In his letter he continued:

> He [Gorst] openly ridicules Lord Salisbury for a fool which is not quite the way to treat a chief with a view to personal advancement. He has the brains of most of them but not the sense not to let them see he knows it ... He's a rum card and can be most charming when he likes and equally damnably nasty when he doesn't like: I've only seen luckily the former side of him ...

Writing to Duncan four months later in December 1897, Archie, George's elder brother and a General in the army, said that Gorst had refused a peerage.[17]

Interestingly Harold Gorst never criticised his father's temperament when writing about working for him. For a time Harold acted as unpaid Assistant Private Secretary to John Gorst at the House of Commons. He had himself gone through a bad patch after his musical career had failed to blossom. Next he had incurred parental displeasure after marrying young without disclosing his marital plans to his father. But by the time his father employed him at the Commons, Harold was beginning to write quite successfully and was soon to become a parliamentary lobby correspondent. Harold enjoyed telling the story of how he had once found his father giving tea and buns to an actress in his room at the Commons. Suddenly the door burst open and Robert Morant entered to say that the Duke, expected much later, was going to arrive at any minute. Thinking quickly, Harold bundled the actress and tea-tray, and then himself, into the next-door room which happened to be empty. The actress was a lively person, and proceeded to give Harold a demonstration of 'high kicking'.[18] What John Gorst was doing with an actress in his room, history does not relate.

Gorst certainly had an unconventional streak. He took art lessons in one of the classes at the Science and Arts Department at South Kensington. At the Commons it was his practice to copy pictures in his room which was on the ground floor and overlooked the terrace. Inspecting Gorst's work through the windows would amuse the younger members and their visitors, especially when his efforts consisted, as was not unusual, of studies of the nude.[19] It would not have been untypical of Gorst to ignore gaping spectators and to continue with whatever he was doing.

Beatrice Webb, the social reformer and historian, gives us a glimpse of Gorst at about this time when he 'entertained a lively party of young people at dinner [in the House of Commons], retiring afterwards to his private room where we laughed and smoked whilst division bells were ringing ...' During these convivialities Gorst enjoyed, while sitting on a sofa with Beatrice and being egged on by her, gossiping about members of the Cabinet with a total lack of discretion.[20]

As had happened to him before in his political career, there were sometimes half-hearted ideas mooted about trying to have Gorst transferred from his departmental work to some quite different sphere. Once, for instance, the Duke was having a discussion with Kekewich, who was anxious to see the back of the Vice President. Kekewich asked the Duke whether he (Gorst) could not be induced to accept a colonial governorship 'a four thousand pounds one such as Trinidad or Jamaica'. The Duke slowly said, not moving a muscle of his face:

> I cannot imagine the government would offer Sir John Gorst the governorship of any colony they desired to retain.[21]

Sir Almeric Fitzroy, Clerk of the Privy Council and not an admirer of Gorst, was another with a suggestion as to how Gorst might be disposed of. He once proposed to Balfour that Gorst be made Chief Charity Commissioner, a job where he might regain, Fitzroy thought, some of 'the reputation so heedlessly lost in the last few years'. Balfour, however, foresaw difficulties in managing such a move.[22]

But not everyone saw matters as Fitzroy evidently did. People such as Stead and the Barnetts thought Gorst was doing a good job. Another such person was the strong-willed Liberal reformer and former schoolmaster Dr T. J. Macnamara, who would become Minister of Labour under Lloyd George in 1920. He wrote that Gorst again and again had 'insisted that the first great problem to tackle, if we are to get our system of national education on broad and lasting lines, is the problem of the Local Authority for Education'. It was clear that he accepted Gorst's idea of one comprehensive authority in each district.[23]

The passage of the Board of Education Bill in 1899 prompted Gorst to approach Salisbury about a move from education. Although his administrative plans for developing local education authorities were by no means complete, he decided at the beginning of August 1899 to write to the Prime Minister. He asked him now that his office was technically no more 'to take an early opportunity of transferring me to some other branch of the public service'. He told Salisbury that when he was appointed to his post four years before he understood he would be the virtual head of the department. Those expectations had not been fulfilled, although he went on to extol the virtues of the Duke as his chief. He referred, rather mysteriously, to his noticing a 'change of estimation' in which he was held. He then ended by saying that when the Prime Minister and Lord Randolph Churchill had 'obliged' him in 1886 to give up his profession he had become entirely dependent on the public service for employment.[24]

Not for the first time in his life the timing of an important letter to the Prime Minister was unfortunate. For in a speech on rural education at Dunmow in July that year, and reported in *The Times*, Gorst was said to have stated in typical vein that the 'greatest enemies [of education] in the country were the squire and the farmer', a quotation of his coming apparently from a speech he had made in the Commons. At once six Conservative MPs who counted themselves in these two categories wrote jointly an angry letter to Salisbury complaining about Gorst's remarks, which they considered offensive after all the support they had given to voluntary schools. This complaint reached Salisbury just a few days before Gorst's letter.

Salisbury in his reply to Gorst referred naturally enough to the complaint of the six MPs, and then also to other complaints by Conservatives about Gorst's 'attitude' in the last session. He reminded him too of their correspondence in 1891 when Gorst had sought the post of Postmaster General. Not surprisingly, he told Gorst that he had been 'at perfect liberty to pursue' his profession in 1886. No, there was no prospect of offering him another post 'without associating myself with your peculiar line of conduct'.[25]

This was a fairly crushing reply but it did not stop Gorst from defending himself in a letter written towards the end of September after his summer holiday. First he thought Salisbury's correspondents should have given him notice of their complaint. He did not dispute the content of his Dunmow speech but said the offending sentence had been taken out of context, and he had never said the squire and farmer were wrong to oppose education. If he were a labouring man, he argued, then he would probably take his children out of school in the summer to help in the hayfields instead of learning arithmetic and grammar. As to other complaints about his 'attitude' he was quite at a loss to understand what was meant. Once again he alluded to

> a certain class in the party [which] has seemed to dislike me personally ... But those in the party who approve and support me in Parliament and the constituencies are vastly more numerous ... they mostly belong to a class whose opinions are less likely to reach your ears ...

He finally begged Salisbury to see him and so 'suspend' his judgement until he could be heard in his own defence.[26]

In reply Salisbury declined to grant an interview. Further, he could not refrain from telling Gorst that when

> you are defending the policy of the government you give to both friends and foes the impression you are attacking it. Your manner of fencing seems to involve a not infrequent backhander aimed at those who are standing by your side or behind you. You are evidently yourself unconscious of the peculiarity of your manner ...

It was a chastened Gorst who replied to this candid letter. He told Salisbury that he could not help blaming *The Times* newspaper for blackening his character some 16 years before owing to some slight he had given the editor. Oddly enough, and a little sadly, he averred that 'few of the leading members of the party know much of me personally so that in my case there is little evidence of the false character being modified and corrected by the true one'. For this state of affairs Gorst may have had himself at least partly to blame. He nearly always dined, it was said, in the 'Irish Room' in the House of Commons restaurant. Moreover, he was 'often with an Irishman or an English Liberal – sometimes with a private Conservative, never with an official colleague'.[27]

In the general election in the summer of 1900, the 'khaki' election as it was known, Gorst was returned to the Commons by Cambridge University for the last time. He was to soldier on as Vice President, with the Duke still as his chief, but once again he was not in the Cabinet. Lucy, the parliamentary journalist, commiserated, and Gorst, in replying to his 'very kind letter', said it was

> mortifying to be passed over but I did not take any step to bring myself to Lord Salisbury's notice, partly because I knew it would be useless, and partly because I persuaded myself, like the fox in the fable, that a seat in the Cabinet was not an object to be desired. Some offence I gave Lord S in or before 1885. I know no more than you what it was, but he has never forgiven me and never will.[28]

When the new session of Parliament began in early December 1900 Gorst had been Vice President for more than five years. There was a rumour abroad that he was going to resign. He told Stead that there was not a 'shadow of truth' in this. Nobody had asked him to retire, and he would not dream of giving up as long as his health and strength lasted. He hoped too that something might be done 'for the good of the children of the land'.[29]

In looking back over those five years Gorst might have wondered what precisely had been achieved. The problem of reorganising education and bringing in new authorities had still not been resolved, although Gorst himself had done much to ensure that educational reform did not disappear from the political agenda. The search for a solution was, therefore, to continue, and Gorst spent a lot of time that winter preparing a new Bill. He was helped in his task by the publication of a Fabian tract produced by Sydney Webb entitled 'The Education Muddle and the Way Out', which proposed one public education authority controlling all kinds of education in its district. School boards should be abolished and the authority of the new education committees should extend to voluntary schools as well. Gorst liked these proposals which, after all, essentially reflected his own views. He had the tract distributed to his fellow ministers to show the time was ripe for carrying out a bold new measure.[30]

Gorst's new Bill was ready for the House by the spring and he introduced it on 7 May 1901. Devonshire was behind Gorst with his Bill, but this time Balfour had played no part in its preparation. Gorst described his measure as one which established in every part of England and Wales a local education authority to control and supervise all schools, whether elementary, secondary or technical. He specifically rejected the possibility of converting school boards into such authorities – the first time he had done this in parliament – and opted for using the counties and county boroughs as the basis for them. In this he broadly followed the pattern set in the failed 1896 Bill. So far so good.

But now, strangely enough, a flaw emerged in the Bill. He told the House that the education authority would be permitted to spend money generally for the promotion of education, but he did not want to 'draw a line between primary and secondary education'. He was picked up on this by Campbell-Bannerman and Bryce who were both not clear as to whether the newly conceived authorities were really comprehensive ones, and would thus be responsible as well for elementary education. Rather negatively, Gorst had to admit that grants were not to be spent on establishing and maintaining elementary schools.[31] And, indeed, the new authorities proved, on examination, not to be comprehensive ones. The Bill has been described as a timid measure, and one not doing justice to the Fabian tract.[32] The reception of the Bill was lukewarm on both sides of the House and the second reading was postponed.

The government was in a quandary. The Court of Appeal had upheld the lower court in the Cockerton judgement in April. Something urgently needed to be done about schools and classes, especially the evening classes, run by the school boards and held to be illegal. No one was more conscious of this than Gorst. Therefore the decision was made to drop Gorst's Bill and to introduce in its place a simple one-clause Education (No. 2) Bill, which in effect was to allow those schools and classes declared by the courts to be illegal to function without penalty for a period of one year. This, the 'Cockerton' Bill, was introduced by Gorst under the ten-minute rule on 2 July; this unusual procedure curtailed debate and consequently was criticised by the opposition, which, led by Bryce, divided the House.

During the second reading Gorst seemed to play down the actual number of pupils affected by the Cockerton judgement. He may, for instance, have been affected by the Chairman of the Cardiff School Board who had alleged to Devonshire and himself that 300 clever children of the working class were 'going to be turned into the streets' as a result of the judgement. Gorst told the House that, roughly, the number affected were: 4,000 pupils over the age of 15 in day schools (this was the age at which childhood was deemed to end); 1,000 pupils doing advanced work in schools of science run by the higher grade schools and some 228,000 pupils in 2,000 evening schools, half of them in London, run by school boards. Somewhat needled by Bryce about these boards, and no doubt frustrated to an extent by the course which recent events had taken, Gorst was suddenly side-tracked when he scathingly said:

> Are we to keep up in this House the farce that school boards are elected for educational purposes? Everybody knows that educational purposes are the very last ideas in the minds of the members of school boards. [Opposition cries of 'Oh'] I have heard they are elected, some on religious grounds, some on party grounds, but I have never heard of anyone being elected on educational grounds.[33]

The cartoonists were now enjoying some sport at the expense of Gorst, who was usually depicted as a jester. An article appeared in *Truth* entitled 'Chaos at the Education Department' suggesting that relations between Kekewich (as we have seen an upholder of school boards) and Gorst had reached rock bottom. The writer was unkind to Gorst, calling him an 'unpractical man and in matters of business an impossible colleague'. Then in a memorable and cutting turn of phrase he described Gorst as 'simply a pantaloon in a screaming harlequinade'. Yet the writer, not quite consistently, asserted he liked Gorst as a man, and admired his wit and philosophy.[34] Somehow Gorst managed to provoke either praise or obloquy. There seemed no half-way house.

Jack Gorst in his diary tells how in the middle of August his father arrived at Pitlochry in Scotland for a family bicycling holiday. There were plenty of other outdoor activities such as fishing, stalking or just plain walking. There is no evidence that John fished or shot for he was not keen on country pursuits. But he did enjoy his bicycle, once, though, falling badly from his machine. Happily he was not seriously hurt. Jack records how in the evening there was 'singing, bridge and romps'. It's a pity we don't learn whether John joined in with his children's 'romps' whatever these might have been (his youngest daughter Gwendolen was now 25). He was certainly not stuffy and earlier in the year was irritated to have been regarded as a spoil-sport. This had happened when he had been taken to task for criticising a school board for allowing young people at an evening class to engage in dancing under the guise apparently of 'physical exercise'. He had himself visited this class and been surprised at what he found. Gorst was to defend his stance in the House during a supply debate. Young people should organise dancing themselves, he asserted. All that was wanted was 'a piano and a young lady to play it and they can dance to their hearts' content'. But the money for this should not, he insisted, come out of the Consolidated Fund.[35]

The Prime Minister was ageing and his control over policy relaxed. Balfour was the heir-apparent and, taking more and more responsibility himself, now decided that once again he would give detailed attention to the preparation of a comprehensive Education Bill. He had been here before, and this time he could not afford to fail. For the last time, although he did not then know it, Gorst sat on the new Cabinet committee summoned to prepare this Bill. Morant too was on it, eager to shine. Balfour, demandingly, wanted from Devonshire first two and then three sets of alternative draft proposals. Gorst was still in Scotland while this was all being mooted but this did not stop him from writing to Devonshire giving his various thoughts on the way ahead. He ended: 'Having thus delivered my soul I can promise you the most loyal and hearty assistance in the preparation of Bills 1, 2 and 3.'[36] Back in London, Gorst was in the thick of considering the options. There was much drafting and re-drafting which must have thoroughly tested everyone's staying-power and patience. Despite all the efforts there seemed little progress, and in November a new Cabinet committee was appointed. This time Gorst was not a member. This was perhaps surprising considering the work he had done on the Bill and his undoubted deep knowledge of education. Devonshire had indicated Gorst was being 'most difficult', although we don't know why. Yoxall, an opposition MP and member of the National Union of Teachers, thought Gorst had too much influence with the Duke. Thus did Gorst's ministerial star begin its final descent. At the same time Morant's reputation rose. Later the Cabinet insisted that Balfour handled the new Bill when it came to the Commons – they would not have Gorst at any price.[37] This was a sad reflection on the man responsible for education in the Commons. Happily, it did not preclude Gorst from giving advice on the Bill to the Duke, and this he continued to do.

During his time as Vice President Gorst was not merely concerned with trying to get fundamental Bills reorganising the education system through the Commons. There were many other things to be done. For example he wanted to reform the education inspectorate, a vital piece of the machinery of education in his view, into a unified and independent body. While not achieving this aim in his time, he did bring female inspectors into the cadre as permanent staff and in 1901 arranged for all females in the inspectorate to be promoted to a new rank, junior inspector, to improve their career prospects. He was not unsympathetic to the problems encountered by the outspoken Kitty Bathhurst, one of the first female inspectors, who happened to be a cousin of his wife. He counselled her not to rock the boat with criticism. However she took no notice, and later on Gorst was obliged to tell Kekewich to dismiss her only as a last resort.[38] In a Commons debate some four years later Gorst gave his views of women in education when he said:

> he could not speak too highly of the work done in the education of the people by women. In the training and development of infants and very young children the experience and authority of women was absolutely invaluable.[39]

In a quite different field he disliked the concept of pupil-teachers. Also he was dissatisfied with pupil-teacher centres, which he considered exclusive. He set Morant the task of investigating this question with a view to seeing if the Welsh system of attaching pupil-teachers to secondary schools might be copied in England.[40]

Gorst always wanted to improve the professional standing of the teaching profession and to exclude incompetent teachers from it. In 1896 he had a Bill drafted for teacher registration but the measure, which gained support, fell with the main Education Bill. His proposals came forward again in 1899 and were only partly adopted, for the Board of Education legislation did not in the event provide for an independent registration council. This only came about when Gorst succeeded in having an Order-in-Council made in March 1902. In his last months as Vice President one of the questions he was considering was how teachers might best be protected from arbitrary dismissal by head teachers.[41]

There was one field close to Gorst's heart in which he made little progress while a minister. After a public-spirited woman, a Mrs Hoare, had revealed in 1897 that many children in London schools were employed in industrial occupations, the House of Commons called for a return from teachers about the problem. The return showed that at least 144,026 school children were in regular employment. For instance one boy had to deliver milk from 4 am until time to go to school. Another aged six peeled onions 20 hours a week for 8d. A little girl under six was employed as a nurse – she worked 29 hours a week for 2d and her food. Gorst wrote and spoke about this 'great social evil'. In due course an interdepartmental committee was set up and reported that at least 50,000 children (they were often called 'half-timers') were working for wages for more than 20 hours a week. Some worked as much as 40, and even 50, hours in addition to the 27½ hours spent at school.[42] A Bill to remedy the situation was introduced in 1901 but to Gorst's disappointment the measure was not proceeded with due to lack of parliamentary time. He had to wait until 1903 before the Bill was revived.

When Balfour finally presented his new Education Bill to the Commons in March 1902 it was seen to be a truly comprehensive measure. This did not stop its passage from being contested by vested interests and those frightened of reform. Its main provisions were:

1. School boards were to be abolished.
2. Counties and county boroughs were to become the local education authorities responsible for secondary and technical education, and also with some exceptions, for elementary education.
3. Voluntary schools and board schools were both to come under the new authorities.

The Act created 131 major local education authorities plus some 202 minor ones. These replaced the 2,568 school boards and 14,238 school attendance committees (where boards did not exist). It was a major reform.

Although Gorst did not contribute to the first reading (he was away ill: genuinely, it is believed), he made a long supportive speech during the Second Reading in May. On this occasion he followed Bryce who was pessimistic and thought the Bill inadequate. Gorst clearly took pains to demolish Bryce's arguments, and from this distance, with his wide grasp of his subject, what he said looks convincing. He reminded members that the policy contained in the Bill was the policy of the 1896 measure and that policy had not changed in the intervening time. He was also particularly strong on the need for local authorities to have control of finance.[43] Later on he took a vigorous part in the committee stage of the Bill, speaking in the last half of July 25 times. The House, and country, was now more ready for the reforms envisaged, and the Bill went through all its stages before the year was out.

Historians have given the credit for the Education Act of 1902 to Balfour and Morant. This is perhaps on the face of it understandable, but the events leading to the passing of this measure are quite complex as we may have succeeded in indicating. The conventional wisdom has now been reassessed by Daglish, who convincingly gives credit to the persistent Gorst for his part in reforming the education system while Vice President:

Without Gorst's activities during the preceding seven years, and especially in view of the educational goals and beliefs of Balfour, Salisbury and Chamberlain, it is debatable whether this much needed reform would have been achieved quite so soon.[44]

Not all historians have assessed Gorst's work so constructively. For instance Shannon, who tends to be dismissive of Gorst as a politician, states, in the context of the period before the introduction of the 1902 Bill: 'In the hands of Devonshire and Gorst the government's education policy was incoherent'.[45]

In July 1902, and before the Bill had completed its passage through the Commons, Salisbury resigned. Devonshire followed suit. Gorst did not want to go but, on realising that all members of the government technically had to tender their resignations, he too resigned. Jack Gorst puts it differently in his diary, noting that his father was 'politely told to go'. Balfour, there can be no doubt, was relieved that Gorst was departing as were *The Times* and the *Manchester Guardian*. However, the *Schoolmaster* and the *Journal of Education* regretted his going, while *The Speaker* compared the appointment of Akers Douglas as Home Secretary with Gorst's loss of office. The former had never distinguished himself intellectually in any way 'while Gorst had discharged his duties as Vice President when allowed by his superiors to do so with an intellectual distinction quite beyond dispute'.[46]

Rather idiotically, Balfour offered Gorst the Lieutenant-Governorship of the Isle of Man. He declined it.

The sympathetic Lucy was much more in tune with Gorst's feelings. A letter he had sent him was redirected to northern France where Gorst had gone to recover from 'the fatigues of politics'. Gorst's reply to his old friend had much charm:

> ... I think I have been delivered of a false position in which I have blundered about for seven years. The position of a free critic is preferable to that of a sham Minister. I have never reached the grapes, but I have sniffed them near enough to know how unripe they are ...[47]

However Gorst saw his term as minister, he had for many been revealed as a man committed to the education of the child in the widest sense. One contemporary had written that Gorst made education 'a living thing' even in the House of Commons. He did not confine himself to statistics, school places and grants but he talked of 'boys and girls'.[48]

NOTES

1. B. Simon, *Education and the Labour Movement 1870–1920,* London, Lawrence & Wishart, 1965, 192; Daglish, *Education Policy-making in England and Wales,* 72.
2. E. Halévy, *A History of the English People in the Nineteenth Century: Imperialism and the Rise of Labour 1895–1905,* 196–7; Eaglesham, *The Foundations of Twentieth-Century Education in England,* 34; Simon, *Education and the Labour Movement,* 193–4; A.I. Taylor, 'The Church Party and Popular Education, 1893–1902', unpublished DPhil. thesis, University of Cambridge, 1981, 257–99; Daglish, *Education Policy-making,* 110–111 .
3. Daglish, *Education Policy-making,* 114.
4. N. Daglish, 'Sir John Gorst as an Educational Innovator: A Reappraisal', *History of Education,* vol. 21, no. 3, 1992, 266; also see Eaglesham, *From School Board to Local Authority,* chapters XIII and XIV on the Higher Schools Minute and its effects.
5. Author and provenance unknown but verse dated 28 April 1899.
6. Halévy, *History of the English People,* 191.
7. Kekewich papers, G–Kekewich, 1 Jan. 1898 and 14 Jan. 1900.
8. G. Kekewich, *The Education Department and After,* London, Constable, 1926, 100–1.
9. Ibid., 100, 104.
10. Ibid., 101.
11. M. Sadleir, *Sir Michael Sadler 1861–1943,* London, Constable, 1949, 173, 175.
12. Daglish, *Education Policy-making,* 25; Eaglesham, *The Foundations of Twentieth-Century Education in England,* 38–9.
13. Barnett papers, A/FWA, S Barnett–F Barnett, 4 Feb. 1898 (probably an error for 1899).
14. Daglish, *Education Policy-making,* 96.
15. *Daily Telegraph,* 5 April 1916.
16. JG AN, vol. 2, 1896, 46.
17. D.H. Doolittle, *A Soldier's Hero: General Sir Archibald Hunter,* Narragansett, Anawan Publishing, 1991, 63, 121, 142.
18. MLL, 136.
19. Kekewich, *The Education Department and After,* 104.
20. N. and J. Mackenzie (eds), *The Diary of Beatrice Webb,* vol. 2, London, Virago, 1983, 107–8.
21. Ibid., 94–5.
22. Fitzroy, *Memoirs,* 28; Doolittle, *A Soldier's Hero,* 142.
23. T. J. Macnamara, 'Higher Education and the State', *The Nineteenth Century,* Apr. 1899, 665.
24. Salisbury papers. G–Salisbury, 2 Aug. 1899.
25. Ibid., Salisbury–G, 9 Aug 1899.
26. Ibid., G–Salisbury, 25 Sept. 1899.
27. Ibid., Salisbury–G, 27 Sept. 1899 and G–Salisbury, 30 Sept. 1899; *Daily Telegraph,* 5 Apr. 1916.
28. Lucy, *Nearing Jordan,* 248–9.
29. Stead papers, 1/29, G–Stead, 12 Nov. 1900.
30. Halévy, *History of the English People,* 200; Simon, *Education and the Labour Movement,* 206–8.
31. 4 PD 93, 7 May 1901, 971, 979, 987.
32. Halévy, *History of the English People,* 200; see also Simon, *Education and the Labour Movement,* 211–14.

33. 4 PD 96, 8 July 1901, 1170–1184.
34. Daglish, *Education Policy-making*, 138; *Truth,* 15 Aug. 1901.
35. 4 PD 98, 30 July 1901, 631.
36. PRO ED 24/79, G–Devonshire, 14 Sept. 1901.
37. Daglish, *Education Policy-making*, 151–2, 161.
38. Ibid., 233–4; Kekewich papers, G–Kekewich, 15 Oct. 1901.
39. 4 PD 144, 31 Mar. 1905, 68.
40. Daglish, *Education Policy-making*, 208–9.
41. PRO ED 24/22, citing a report in *The Times* of 27 May 1902.
42. John E. Gorst 'School Children as Wage-Earners', *The Nineteenth Century*, July 1899, 8–17; John E. Gorst, 'Social Reforms: The Obligations of the Tory Party', *The Nineteenth Century*, March 1903, 526–7; John E. Gorst, *The Children of the Nation*, 92–8.
43. 4 PD 107, 5 May 1902, 669.
44. Daglish, *Education Policy-making*, 196.
45. Shannon, *The Age of Salisbury,* 127, 128, 539, 546.
46. Daglish, *Education Policy-making*, 177–8 quoting journals cited.
47. Lucy, *Diary of a Journalist*, 157–8.
48. *History of Education*, 276, quoting H. Hodge in the *Saturday Review.*

20

The Children's Champion

When Gorst returned to the back-benches in the summer of 1902, a year and a half after Queen Victoria's death, he could look back on some 13½ years as a government minister. It was an unusually long, though interrupted, spell. Few people, if any, have been effectively Minister of Education for seven years. For his service he was awarded a pension of £1,200 p.a. (*c.* £66,600 now), paid out of a fund available for ex-ministers. MPs did not receive a salary until 1911, and this pension would enable Gorst to live in some comfort.

Freed from the 'chains of office' – Gorst's own expression – was he now at the age of 67 to sit back and take life more easily, resting on those laurels which a few progressive people thought he had earned? This would not have been his way, nor was it. In the words of his son Jack he was soon to revel 'in the for him very suitable occupation of the candid friend of the government'.[1] In other words he was, once again, an independent and radical Conservative. With more time at his disposal he threw himself for his final three years in parliament into the turmoil of politics with, if anything, redoubled vigour. Matters of unfinished business in the field of social reform commanded his attention, but he did not forget finance or colonial affairs.

For the moment, however, he did his best to ensure that the 1902 Education Bill reached the statute book (it did by the end of the year). For instance, in committee in a period of just over a month from mid October he intervened on no less than 35 occasions. At the same time, quite freed from any departmental responsibility, he punched home his valedictory message on education in a long article in *The Nineteenth Century*, reminding his readers that the Bill was to meet a national emergency. 'Unless reform is very promptly undertaken … English people would be less instructed than the people of the European States, of America and even of our own colonies.'[2] Although he might today be accused of a tendency to verbosity, he usually found something new to say. For instance, in urging that provision be made to ensure that religious instruction in schools was acceptable to parents, he even suggested that the tenets of the Muslim religion should be taught when there were Muslim children at school.

That summer Gorst had spent three weeks in August on holiday with his family in northern France visiting some of the places he had been to seven years before. This time Mary was with him. Jack, Edith, Eva and Gwendolen made up the party. To begin with, the focus of attention must have been on Jack who, as a result of his meteoric rise in the Egyptian government service to the post of financial adviser, had been made a KCB at the early age of 41. On the day of the Coronation of King Edward VII, 9 August, the Gorst family was staying at St Valery-en-Caux. In the morning a party walked along the cliffs. In the afternoon there was bathing. Places visited using train, motor car or bicycle included Fontaine-le-Dun, Veules, Quiberville and Fécamp.[3]

Not long after his return from France John Gorst moved his family from Cambridge to Cricket Hill House at Yateley in north Hampshire. We have no idea why he made this move for he was still MP for the University. It sometimes looks as if he judged a move was necessary to mark the end or the beginning of a phase in his life.

At the end of November Gorst was again travelling. He would be away from England for two months. This time he went to Egypt where he was to attend the opening of the Aswan dam. He reached Cairo on 4 December and was met by Jack. The next day he took the night train to Luxor with Jack, Hylda and Eva. Hylda lived in Alexandria with her husband, George Hunter, now Director-General of the Egyptian coastguard service, while Eva was staying as she often did with her brother. Sight-seeing at Luxor, naturally enough, included a visit to the tombs of the Kings and an excursion to view Karnak by moonlight. A huge throng of celebrities witnessed the opening of the dam on 10 December.

Back in Cairo Gorst found himself engaged in a social round of lunches, dinners, visits to the theatre and racecourse, and some further sight-seeing including a trip with Jack to see Coptic churches. John Gorst could be an entertaining man, and was said to be valued for his racy talk at dinner parties. Once he dined with Sir Ernest Cassels, King Edward VII's financial adviser. On another occasion he lunched with young Winston Churchill who had become Conservative MP for Oldham the previous year. Churchill while in Egypt apparently particularly relished the company of his father's old friends Hicks Beach and John Gorst.[4] Jack thought his father very much enjoyed his visit to Egypt and noted 'he [John Gorst] was especially pleased at the position of authority which I have attained here'.[5] As for Jack himself, his career went from strength to strength. After a spell at the Foreign Office in London, he would in 1907 succeed Lord Cromer as Consul and Agent-General in Cairo. Along the way he was to marry Evelyn Rudd, the heiress daughter of Charles Rudd, Cecil Rhodes's business partner in South Africa.

Jack had performed during his years in Egypt one enormous service to his five sisters. In cosmopolitan Cairo he provided them, just at the time they needed it, with an active and varied social life. This kind of life was something John and Mary had not obviously succeeded in arranging for their daughters. The fault surely lay with John. The unsettling and constant house-moving in and out of London could not have helped his daughters in their search for husbands. Perhaps immersed in his own affairs he had not given this important family question enough attention.

In reviewing the last decade, John Gorst had to admit to profound disenchantment with the ability of Parliament to bring in the social reforms he had campaigned for. He saw many problems unresolved: unemployment, poverty and hunger among the working class, and the neglect of children, the sick and the old. Disraeli, his mentor, had always insisted that his party should aim to promote social progress. Yet, Gorst asserted, although the Conservative Party had come to power in 1895 by pledging itself to an active and creative policy of social reform, nothing had been done despite the arousal of public compassion on many issues. For instance the government had resisted bringing in changes to the Factory Acts after the Berlin conference; little had come out of the Royal Commission on Labour; a select committee had been set up to look at the problem of unemployment but had achieved nothing, and the government had failed, to date, to reform the problem of the employment of school children.[6]

From the point of view of introducing legislation Gorst described the House of Commons as 'almost effete'. Nor did he see the necessary reforms as being likely to originate from central government departments. Some young civil servants had, he admitted, brilliant intellects but few could 'survive the blighting influence of routine, of having to act on precedent and of seniority promotion'. As for the most industrious minister, he had to spend long hours learning the routine of his office. Just as he felt competent to act he was, Gorst commented with much truth, 'whisked off ... and placed at the head of some other department, the work of which he is equally ignorant'.[7]

So how could things be improved? Gorst always had proposals to offer. He had come to the conclusion that the condition of the people could only be improved by giving more power to local government.

'Give up the dream', he said, 'of a benevolent central government ...
let every county and municipal authority become absolutely and
entirely ... responsible for the health and welfare of its own men,
women and children'. Local government had, he felt, significant
advantages over Westminster's. He had always considered too many
Conservative MPs came from privileged backgrounds. At a local level
people of a great variety, including representatives of the working
class, could come forward to address the problems. Also, amending
legislation would be easier locally. Far too much time at Westminster
was spent passing Acts to amend other Acts passed only recently. His
proposals for the devolution of power could not be borne, he realised,
just by the rates, but would need subventions from central
government. All these ideas and plans Gorst put forward in an article
published in March 1903.[8] It was to be his last great effort to put the
Tory party in the vanguard of social reform.

Whether or not Balfour and his ministers were really interested in
furthering a programme of social and welfare reform is a matter of
conjecture. In any case the government became involved in the spring
of 1903 in a serious internal dispute over tariff reform. By late summer
it was hopelessly split. Joseph Chamberlain, the champion of the
Empire, believed a policy of protection manifested through imperial
preference should be introduced contrary to the traditional free trade
policies pursued, now rather waveringly, by Balfour. By September
the Prime Minister, trying to preserve some unity in his government,
had dismissed Ritchie, the Chancellor of the Exchequer and a free
trader, while Chamberlain had resigned to fight for his views outside
the government. Lord George Hamilton and the Duke of Devonshire,
also free traders, resigned too.

Gorst had all his life been a free trader, and joined a group of 60
Unionist Free Traders in the Commons, led by Hicks Beach. In
particular he did not want to see the cost of food rise, which would
happen if a policy of protection were adopted. He also became active
in another grouping known as the Free Food League established in
July 1902 to impress its fiscal policy on the Conservatives. One of the
founders was Winston Churchill.[9] In October Gorst wrote to his old
chief Devonshire asking him to stand at the head of the Unionist Free
Traders, telling him that his researches showed that a majority of 'the
out-and-out party men' favoured Chamberlain's fiscal policy, but that
the great mass of the working class were solidly against that policy.[10]
The Duke did join the Unionist Free Traders but we cannot say what
weight he gave to Gorst's letter.

During the 1903 parliamentary session, Gorst was in characteristic mood in the range of subjects – fiscal matters apart – which caught his eye. In a long speech in February he declaimed in familiar style on the effects of the 'social disease' of unemployment and especially on the starvation prevalent among wives and families of those with no work. 'If we could put a million people on the land this country would be richer and stronger.'[11] Gorst also involved himself in debates on human rights in the Congo, affairs in Uganda, the state of the Services, and the effects of overworking shop assistants. He did not forget for one minute education and lent his strong support to the London Education Bill, which at long last turned the London County Council into a local education authority.

But at the top of his agenda came the children. He congratulated the government on reviving the Employment of Children Bill but saw no reason why travelling companies and circuses should be exempt from the protection to children offered by the Bill. He spoke too at length on pauper children, and praised Dr Barnardo for his methods of looking after children under his care. Boarding out children seemed the best course while the worst thing for the children was to be left in the workhouse.[12]

For some months Gorst had been in correspondence with Stead on a range of current issues including the Free Food League and the unemployed. At the end of the year he told Stead that he was ready to do anything to promote a proper discussion of the physical well-being of schoolchildren. He listed his remedies. They included:

1. Medical examinations: spot and annual ones.
2. Daily reports by teachers to the local education authority on every hungry, dirty and diseased child.
3. Periodical visits of trained nurses to schools.
4. A school breakfast of porridge and milk to be given to children on payment, and a dinner on similar terms. Parents to be held responsible for hungry children.
5. Arrangements on the Swedish pattern to deal with cleaning filthy children.[13]

Gorst, as can be seen, was in his enthusiasm over-optimistic with some of his proposals.

There had been a new and important development on the physical condition of the people which had prompted Gorst's last letter to Stead. An article had appeared in the January 1902 issue of the *Contemporary Review* written by an academically minded soldier, Major-General Sir Frederick Maurice, entitled 'Where to get Men'. In it Maurice had discussed the difficulty of recruiting soldiers during the Boer War. This was not due to low pay, lack of patriotism or the voluntary system of recruiting. It was simply the failure of the men coming forward to meet the physical standards required: only two men out of five could be passed as fit. This 60 per cent rejection rate, asserted Maurice, was caused by the poor living conditions of the working class. (The effect of these conditions on working-class children is illustrated by some official figures quoted in 1906. These compared the height and weight of 14-year-old boys coming from favoured and from artisan backgrounds. Boys from the former class were on average 5 feet 1 inch tall and weighed just over 7 stone, while boys from the latter class were 4 feet 9½ inches tall and weighed 6 stone. In other words a public schoolboy would expect to be 3½ inches taller and weigh one stone more than an elementary schoolboy from the East End of London.[14])

Maurice's article caused a great stir in the War Office and elsewhere, and the government was consequently moved to appoint in the middle of 1903 an interdepartmental committee on physical deterioration (ICPD) under the chairmanship of Sir Almeric Fitzroy, secretary of the Privy Council. The committee, to which both Gorst and Macnamara gave evidence, took until the summer of 1904 to deliver its report.

Gorst was now, and until the end of this parliament, to devote a great deal of his time both inside and outside Westminster to the welfare of children. In March 1904 he used the third reading of the Consolidated Fund Bill to demand when the Board of Education would take some practical steps to ameliorate the condition of children. He also asked when Fitzroy's report would be ready. The existence of malnutrition among children, Gorst told the Commons, was well known. The causes of the deterioration in their health were: 'want of fresh air, want of proper food, want of proper treatment and want of medical inspection'. He stressed that 'the mischief done by taking hungry children into schools and attempting to make them do intellectual or physical work was quite incalculable'.

A month later Gorst seconded a motion by a Conservative member which would compel the Board of Education to require suitable arrangements to be made whereby every elementary school child should have 'proper nourishment' before mental or physical instruction. Further, when proper food was not provided by the parents, food should be supplied by the local authority, which might then take suitable action to recover its costs.[15] This motion reflected the consistent line Gorst was henceforth to take on the issue of feeding. For a moment he may have thought he was making progress. But the response of Sir William Anson, the Parliamentary Secretary at the Board of Education and Gorst's successor there, was generally to stonewall. Anson had been a law professor at Oxford and only a short time in the Commons. He can be forgiven if he was a little bemused by the developing Gorstian bombardment.

The ICPD report was issued in July 1904. While concluding there was no sign of degeneration among the population as a whole, it recognised that in certain areas there was a problem about the condition of children and that there was a need for medical inspection. There were many recommendations. On the feeding of children it said that where the intervention of charitable organisations was inadequate, then it might be expedient to permit municipal aid. The evidence of Dr Eichholz, a schools inspector, was accepted that a third of the children at the Johanna Street board school in a poor part of Lambeth needed feeding. This was important as we shall soon see. The committee also acknowledged that the 'most uncompromising advocacy of public responsibility' for providing meals for school-children had been made by Gorst and Macnamara. The latter had indeed given graphic evidence of the hunger he had witnessed among his pupils when a board school teacher. For example, out of a school of 300, 25 or 30 children did not go home in the dinner hour because there was nothing to go home to. Thirty or 40 others would stay and have nothing to eat except a crust of bread or an onion. Two brothers he had seen in frosty weather making a meal of a turnip. Nonetheless the committee preferred that the problem of feeding should be left to school managers and to the voluntary agencies.[16] Perhaps it knew that Balfour had said on no account were children to be fed from the rates. On the other hand the committee did agree that neglectful parents would have to be prosecuted.

With the publication of the ICPD report Gorst, closely supported by the articulate Macnamara, began to step up his campaign. The climax was to come the next year. Gorst's first chance to speak in the Commons after the publication of the report came in a debate on the estimates on 10 August. He ranged at length on the issues close to his heart concerning children. He was not uncritical of the report, thinking that it sometimes did not go far enough, and regretted that no woman or member of the working class had been on the committee. Above all he appealed to the government to give power to the school authorities to feed hungry children when other means had failed. When he spoke about the inefficiency of the Board of Education's inspection system – inspectors wished too much to please teachers, their managers and officials in Whitehall – he was interrupted, being asked why he had not brought this to the attention of the House when minister. In answer, Gorst vigorously asserted he had done this many times.[17] Following Gorst, the up and coming Lloyd George thought Gorst's was an 'able' speech and that

> educationally they owed a great deal to the fact that the Right Honourable Gentleman was unmuzzled. The Board of Education ought to publish some of the memoranda written by [him] upon the educational condition of the country. They would be not only interesting and instructive but amusing, and would provide very good material for the controversies that arose from time to time regarding education.[18]

Before we leave the 1904 session of Parliament we should mention the support Gorst gave to Winston Churchill in March that year during a debate on the Easter adjournment. Churchill was not popular with his party nor with his constituents on account of his advocacy of free trade. When Churchill rose to speak on 29 March, Balfour and his front-bench ministers rose and left the Chamber, as did the Tory back-benchers, some of whom jeered Churchill at the door as they left. Churchill remained with only a few Unionist Free Traders at his side. One was Gorst. When Churchill had finished speaking Gorst at once rose and in no uncertain manner defended his old friend's son, who had suffered 'the most marked discourtesy' he had ever seen. He reminded the House he was an old colleague of Churchill's father, once the 'ornament' and leader of the party in the Commons. He continued '… if every other consideration of fair play failed, the hereditary right of the honourable member for Oldham to the respect and consideration of the House ought to have preserved him from such treatment as he received at the hands of his party this afternoon'.[19] Winston Churchill, who did not forget what Gorst had said, crossed the floor of the House two months later taking his seat next to Lloyd George, one his father had occupied when in opposition. Maybe surprisingly, Gorst was not happy about Churchill's action.[20] Perhaps he could not help seeing it in terms of Lord Randolph's ultimate failure in politics.

In the spring of 1904 Gorst went bicycling in the Harz mountains in Germany with Edith Deverell, a young and intelligent woman, who had been an inspector of schools in the Board of Education. Gorst and Edith were in correspondence over a period of 14 years. Gorst's letters, or some of them, have survived. It had all begun when in

October 1900 Edith wrote to Gorst, who was then Vice President, on a number of topics bothering her: the incidence of ophthalmia among schoolchildren, the lighting in classrooms and the methods of teaching drawing. Gorst replied to Edith at length and said he would like to show her letter to the Duke of Devonshire. Edith was friendly with another woman inspector, Kitty Bathurst (there were only six women inspectors working then) who was Mary Gorst's cousin. This may have explained why Edith felt able to write direct to the minister. The correspondence in its early days was mainly on professional or educational matters, but not entirely.

In a letter he wrote to Edith in January 1904 Gorst referred to 'your mysterious hint ... which led me to one interpretation only. It cannot lessen my friendship and esteem. But it reminds me of the fact that you are a woman which in our camaraderie we have both forgotten.'[21] Could Edith's hint perhaps have been a coy reference to an impending engagement? On 3 June that year he wrote to her that 'I must see you before you leave town ... could you come here [Queen Anne's Mansions where Gorst lived while in London] on Monday morning ... we could have a good talk and I would give you some lunch before saying good-bye.' Eleven days later Gorst wrote briefly again to her: 'I am sending you a copy of Faust as a memento of the pleasant cycling expedition we made in the Harz mountains'.[22] From this it rather looks as if this holiday took place in May. We know nothing more about the 'expedition', and have no idea who else was present.

By September that year Edith had married Francis Marvin, an academic, and gone with him to Leeds. But the correspondence between Gorst and her continued much as before. Some two years later when Edith's husband wrote to Gorst with the news of the birth of their son, Gorst replied with a rather charming little letter to Edith. 'I hope your son', he wrote, 'will grow up to be a good man and a comfort to his parents. You will find a new interest in life watching over his welfare.'[23]

We should perhaps avoid too much speculation about any possible Faustian symbolism concerning Gorst's gift (the older man pursuing the younger woman). But we may perhaps conclude that while Gorst must have admired Edith, the evidence points to an innocent relationship.

During the winter of 1904/5 Gorst's campaign on behalf of ill-fed and neglected children continued and if anything gained momentum. He was not put off by *The Times* newspaper, which in an editorial sternly criticised him and his proposals on the basis that he was undermining parental responsibility: 'It is easy, showy, comforting – everything that the sentimentalist loves – to put hungry children on the rates'.[24] In December he had been complaining to Edith about the number of engagements he had during the winter. He got a bit mixed up about them since his private secretary – his daughter Eva – was away in the Egyptian desert on an expedition with Hylda and George Hunter to buy camels for the Egyptian coastguard service.

On 20 January at the Guildhall in London, Gorst chaired the National Labour conference on the state maintenance of children. He told his audience that:

> The State, whose sacred duty is to protect the poor and helpless, has been robbing the children of the poor, and leaving them to perish for lack of that maintenance to which they are entitled. The injustice brings its own punishment for our national system of education is spoiled, and the children grow up feeble and diseased to fill our hospitals, workhouses and gaols, to weaken our empire and our nation, and taint our population with a crowd of incapables.[25]

But Gorst dissociated himself from the maintenance of *all* children. He wanted only *necessitous* children maintained. He told Edith that he had used the Guildhall meeting 'to frighten Mr Balfour and the rich. I say – see what you will come to, if you delay the moderate reform asked for by us moderate people'.[26] The meeting attracted comment in the press and one headline read 'Socialists capture the Guildhall conference'. At the end of the month he addressed two meetings at Barry and Cardiff on feeding hungry children. By now he was ready for the next session of parliament. At once, in February in a debate on the King's speech, he expressed astonishment that no action had been taken on the ICPD report. He promised to make life as difficult as possible for the government on the issue of feeding the children, warning the front bench he would bring up the subject at every opportunity and that included debates on the Irish, Scottish and English estimates. Nor would he neglect parliamentary questions and other parliamentary occasions.[27] He was true to his word.

We have already mentioned the sorry state of affairs at the Johanna Street school in Lambeth. Continual prodding by Gorst, Macnamara and now Keir Hardie, the founder of the Independent Labour Party, forced Anson to visit the school himself. But when asked by Gorst on 13 March a PQ seemingly designed to make the minister tell the House about his visit, Anson again stonewalled. In effect he implied that everything in the garden was lovely. Gorst was first dismayed and then decisive. On 15 March with three companions he paid an unheralded and rather dramatic visit to the Johanna Street school. This visit has been likened to the Jameson raid although in fact it turned out to be more successful than that dismal failure. Gorst was accompanied by Macnamara, who had taken the precaution of clearing the exercise with the chairman of the London County Council, and by Dr Hutchinson and Lady Warwick. Hutchinson, a late addition to the party, was physician to the Great Ormond Street Children's Hospital, while Lady Warwick, a great beauty of the day, was a society hostess who had taken up social work. Eventually she would become a member of the Labour Party.

At the school Hutchinson, helped by the headmaster, went from class to class identifying boys suffering from malnutrition and those who had had no breakfast that day. The results were horrifying and more than confirmed Dr Eichholz's findings. For instance, in the Standard III class 47 out of 57 children were in a state of malnutrition. Twenty boys were certified by Hutchinson as actually suffering from hunger. Armed with this information the four raiders at once went to see the Lambeth Board of Poor Law Guardians, who, conveniently found in session, courteously gave their consent to relief being given to the children, thereby establishing a precedent.[28] Back in the Commons the two MPs maintained their pressure on Anson, constantly bobbing up and down with speeches and questions. In a financial debate on 27 March Macnamara asked Anson to look into the matter of hungry schoolchildren with 'a little more warm-heartedness and full bloodedness'. Gorst spoke next – it must for him have been like the days of the Fourth Party – and strongly attacked the government for doing nothing for the children. He seemed tireless and relentless. One moment he would instance the rate of infant mortality in the country – in Preston he said 235 out of 1,000 children would die before reaching the age of one – and at another chide the government for still taking no action on the ICPD's recommendations. And why, he wanted to know, was he abused for proposing children should be fed before being taught? Children, he declared, were born with civil rights. What he wanted the President of the Local Government Board (Gerald Balfour, brother of the Prime Minister) to do was to instruct boards of guardians that 'every hungry child was entitled to immediate relief'. Nor did he forget – how could he? – to plug the need for proper medical inspections.[29]

If Gorst and his fellow campaigners were trying to shame the government into taking action, then they met at last with some success for their pains and tenacity. In April Gerald Balfour announced that, after discussions with the Board of Education, circulars were being prepared for issue to the Poor Law authorities to provide the sought-after relief. The necessary statutory Order followed. Under this Order guardians were to require the feeding of underfed children irrespective of the destitution of the father. If they thought fit, costs could be recovered. On 1 June Gorst told Gerald Balfour that he was deeply grateful for the action taken by the minister. Unhappily, the implementation of the Order was not a great success partly because of friction between the authorities involved. But at least the efforts of the campaigners, particularly Gorst and Macnamara, had breached, in the words of Daglish, the educational historian, 'the repressive nineteenth century attitudes to child welfare'.[30] Finally, W. T. Wilson, a new Labour MP in the next Parliament, introduced a private member's Bill for the feeding of schoolchildren. The measure was enacted in 1906.

Gorst had not been making a great fuss about nothing. On the contrary this was a campaign that needed to be fought. Gorst had made a signal and direct contribution to the process of alleviating social distress. To look ahead still further, the Education (Administrative Provisions) Act of 1907 included a section providing for the medical inspection of schoolchildren.

In the efforts made by Gorst over this period concerning children's welfare he had again shown himself to be a doughty fighter and an effective propagandist. In many ways he was at his best in publicizing the ills besetting the community and the failures of the government for not attending to them. The impression he sometimes gives is that this was the work he relished most. In his ardour he might speak in parliament at too great a length; thus he often side-tracked himself and tried to cover too much ground. Macnamara for instance was often punchier in his speeches. Notwithstanding these faults, there must have been many in the House and elsewhere who admired his remarkable knowledge, eloquence and persistence. Others, particularly those on the government front bench, no doubt found his constant interventions highly irritating, and were not persuaded by his harrying tactics.

One man always maintained his opinion of Gorst's capabilities. He was the veteran journalist Stead, who still carried high the banner of reform. Once, years before, Stead had suggested, tongue in cheek, that the Irish leader John Redmond should be made Prime Minister with John Gorst as his right-hand man. Gorst, he commented, was more in sympathy with the Irish Nationalists than with any other party.[31] Then in May 1905 Stead published another of Gorst's articles on social reform. In it Gorst would have the government learning from the Germans about insurance, and from the French and Belgians about how to feed schoolchildren. As for the Labour Party, Gorst urged them to go to the Irish Nationalists to learn about enthusiasm and discipline. Stead, agreeing with Gorst that parliament was a rich man's club and that it was vain to look in that direction for reform, made a startling proposal. 'The Labour Party is weak, disorganised, and without a leader. Here is Sir John Gorst's chance. I commend the idea to Mr J. R. Macdonald, Mr Keir Hardie and Mr John Burns'.[32] Finally, sensing that a general election could not be long delayed, Stead published a book towards the end of 1905 entitled *Coming Men on Coming Questions*, which carried a profile of Gorst at the age of 70. It was clear that Stead did not think Gorst was too old to achieve great things.

The reader might suppose that in the 1905 session of parliament Gorst was so absorbed by issues to do with children and especially their feeding that he had no time for other matters. This would not be quite correct. He spoke for instance on the threat from Russia on the North-West Frontier of India (a reduced one), on taxation in Ireland, what books should be in prison libraries and about his 'earnest desire' to see women made eligible for election to borough and county councils. The last recorded question which Gorst put in the House, which appears to have rung down the curtain on his 33-year career as an MP spanning a period of nearly 40 years, was a fairly typical one. He asked in early August whether the President of the Local Government Board knew about the inquest held at Shoreditch into the death of Annie Higgs, a middle-aged widow with three girls to support. The 'out relief' at first given her had stopped when her eldest daughter was 14. The Coroner's officer had

> found the room in which the woman and her children lived very clean but there was neither food nor money there and very little furniture ... death was due to heart failure, resulting from general bodily weakness from want of food and heart disease and that she had had no food recently, the stomach and bowels being empty ...

Would the minister, asked Gorst, inquire who was responsible for this widow being thus left to starve to death?[33]

The Prime Minister and his government had long been in trouble with bitter internal feuding over fiscal matters. Another issue had arisen the year before, causing the government embarrassment. This was its new policy of agreeing to the importation into the Transvaal of a great number of indentured Chinese labourers to work the mines, a subject on which Gorst had spoken in the House and shown his acute unease. He feared for how the Chinese were being treated both in transit and in the compounds at their places of work. Balfour was blind, however, as were many Conservatives, to the unpopularity of this policy with the electorate.[34]

Gorst had always maintained throughout his parliamentary career a keen interest in colonial affairs and particularly in events as they unfolded in southern Africa. He could not, of course, publicly air his opinions on those matters while a minister, but he confided to his friends the Barnetts just after the relief of Ladysmith in 1899 that he was still opposed to the Boer War. Years later he was to write that the British people had become 'intoxicated with the glory of conquering two little Dutch republics in South Africa'.[35]

At last, confronted with the increasingly powerful position being gained by Chamberlain with his tariff reform proposals and now by his capture of the National Union of Conservative Associations, Balfour resigned in December 1905. Campbell-Bannerman became Prime Minister and dissolved Parliament. In the ensuing general election in January the Conservatives were routed, the Liberals achieving a huge majority. Gorst, fighting as a free trader, lost his Cambridge University seat. This was the end of his career in the House of Commons. He would have received small consolation to know that Campbell-Bannerman had voted for him.

Friends wrote to Gorst commiserating with him over the loss of his seat. In thanking Bryce, now Chief Secretary for Ireland in the new government, for his 'kind' letter Gorst sounded a rather bitter note. He thought the Conservative Party, in rejecting most free traders from its ranks, had committed political suicide. The party would never again be trusted by the working class. All 'the genuine efforts of Disraeli and the pretended ones of Randolph Churchill ended in handing over the party to a gang of selfish and incompetent aristocrats ...' The word 'pretended' is revealing, although it is hard to know if this represents a fair assessment of what Gorst felt about Churchill's contribution. If he were now in the House, Gorst went on, he could do nothing but give 'friendly support' to the Liberals, who he hoped would achieve real progress in social reform.[36]

To Edith Marvin, Gorst confided that he had come to the conclusion that the House of Commons was 'a waste of time' – was this a touch of sour grapes? – and he doubted if he would ever go there again. Now that he had lost his 'regular employment [I] have to invent new methods of work. Like you I am writing a book'.[37] A few days later, writing from the Carlton Club, Gorst resigned as a trustee of the Primrose League since its 'present principles differed so entirely from those of the founders of the League'.[38] Although he was in one of his despondent moods, this did not mean that Gorst was quite breaking with the party he had inhabited for half a century and more. Nevertheless, disappointed that his vision of Tory democracy had not been fulfilled, he was beginning to approach the point of no return.

The year 1906 was to prove a literary one for the Gorsts. Quite apart from John's own efforts which we shall examine in a moment, his son Harold had published in that year his book *The Fourth Party*, which has since proved to be an historically valuable source to writers on that curious parliamentary episode in the 1880s. Earlier, Harold had published a study of Disraeli of which we have made use too, and a history of China.

John Gorst himself was already reaching for his pen, not that this was anything new. Once 42 years before, Gorst had decided after his searing experiences in New Zealand to write a book. Now again, and in the same vein, he had a burning desire to issue a message. The health of many working class children was, as he saw it, a social evil, and he wanted to bring this to the attention of as wide an audience as possible. The title of the book started out, rather unpromisingly, as *Public Health and Public Authority* but ended as *The Children of the Nation*. The work was published towards the end of the year while Gorst was out of the country. It was an indication of Gorst's still developing political outlook that he dedicated the book to the Labour members of the House of Commons in the belief that they were 'animated by a genuine desire to ameliorate the condition of the people'. The book, according to its publishers, Methuen, who included it in their 'New Library of Medicine', aimed at drawing attention to the national danger of neglecting children.

As a starting-point Gorst accepted that the prime duty of bringing up children rested with parents. Back in 1889 in a debate on the Prevention of Cruelty to Children Bill he had made the point that it was parents, and not the state, who had the first responsibility for the care and education of their children. Nevertheless the state too, he now wrote, had its duties: to see the child's rights were not violated by its parents; to give help and advice to parents to enable them to fulfil their obligations; and to perform the duties of parents when death or incapacity intervened.[39] Gorst was unashamedly an interventionist. He gave three reasons why the state needed, in the first place, to interfere with the individual in the field of public health. First there was public safety; no-one, he thought, would deny the government's right to protect the public against epidemics. Second there was the economic argument; it was expensive for the state to counter epidemics. The third reason was a broad one. Gorst believed that it was in the interests of the nation and community as a whole to ensure that those who contributed to the production of the nation's wealth should, when sick, be made fit and efficient again as soon as possible. By the same token every child should be brought up to be healthy and so a strength, not a burden, to the state.[40]

Gorst's book shows a depth of knowledge typical of how its author applied himself to a subject in which he was interested. Its range too was wide and covered: infant mortality; children under school age; nursery schools; medical inspection; medical aid, including insurance against sickness; school hygiene; physical training; child labour; parental responsibility; 'derelict' children (that is, orphans and those deserted by parents); the importance of good housing for the family; and proposals on the funding of reforms. There were also chapters on children's ailments and the 'ravages' caused by hereditary disease, for example by, in Gorst's view, alcoholism and syphilis. For these chapters Gorst must have had some help from doctors – he certainly quotes them frequently – although no doubt the medical views he sometimes expressed are outdated.

We learn from *The Children of the Nation* some things about Gorst and his opinions not known to us before. Thus, showing great concern for mothers, he advised they should not be employed in a period before and after childbirth. He accepted, though, that many needed to work or else their families would starve. He disliked the caning of children as a punishment and particularly the caning of girls by men. Once he visited *incognito* a school in Jersey where there was no corporal punishment – it was the most orderly and disciplined school he had ever gone to. As a result of visits made to poor neighbourhoods he made the point that it was often noticeable how well cared for Irish and Jewish children were by their parents. Then he regretted the absence of playgrounds in many towns and cities. In Salford it was said that the children, numbering 42,000, seemed to have forgotten how to play. Children, Gorst felt, should not be sent to school too young for this often harmed them. The Chinese civilisation he considered to be the most stable the world had seen, with its emphasis on home and family.

In France Gorst liked the example set by Parisians whose children in want received daily a wholesome hot meal fully subsidised by the municipality and community. He also cited with approval a public proclamation made in Paris on the evils of alcohol. Similar notices should be posted, he urged, in Britain at post-offices, libraries, churches, chapels, law courts and elsewhere. On the subject of alcohol Gorst may have had in mind the problem of 'overlaying'. This was when children, who slept in the same bed as their parents, were accidentally smothered. Over 1,600 children a year died in this way; many of these deaths occurred on Saturday nights and were attributed to drunkenness.[41]

Discounting King Edward VII's dictum that 'we are all Socialists nowadays', Gorst believed that some of the recommendations he made would bring upon him 'the vague accusation of Socialism, which to a public man is a calumny as terrible as it is unanswerable'.[42] He must particularly have had in mind his suggesting the possibility of having a system of free medical aid. But he was used to criticism after all these years and his principles were always more important to him than what people thought of him.

Throughout his book there are references, invariably flattering, to how Germany did things. It is fair to ask if Gorst played the German card too often. Yet Germany had much to offer, especially in the fields of education and municipal government. Indeed, better off people in Britain had for some time been sending their young to German schools and universities to complete their education. By the mid-1890s the author E. E. Williams had persuaded the general public that German manufacturers and traders posed a serious threat to British prosperity.[43] All this did not, however, stop Lord Salisbury from mocking Gorst's enthusiasm for Germany. But times were changing and things were going Gorst's way. Around the time he wrote his book, economists like William Beveridge (who was responsible in 1942 for the report given his name) were realising that Britain might profit from studying the methods used by Germany to deliver social welfare. Finally, Lloyd George went to Germany in 1908, a year after a visit there by Beveridge, on a working holiday to see what he could learn from German institutions. He came home impressed and soon began work on his national insurance scheme. Gilbert goes some way to suggesting that Lloyd George must have been influenced by Gorst.[44] This is not an unreasonable assumption to make. Gorst in and out of the Commons was an articulate and genuine messenger, as a speaker and writer, for social reform. Although Lloyd George and Gorst clashed on occasions in the Commons, the former often listened carefully to what the latter had to say.

In retrospect, and to move on to the years we have not yet reached in this story, Gorst must have been gratified by the programme of social reform unfurled and then implemented by the Liberal government. Infant-welfare centres and schools for mothers were established, while wide provision was made for the better treatment of children under the 1908 Children's Act. In the same year a non-contributory old age pension scheme was instituted. In 1909 labour exchanges were set up nation-wide. This was followed in 1911 by the National Insurance Act, whereby a sickness and unemployment scheme for the working population was inaugurated. Gorst may surely take some vicarious credit for what the Liberals achieved.

NOTES

1. JG AN, vol. 2, 85.
2. John E. Gorst, 'The Education Bill', *The Nineteenth Century*, Oct. 1902, 576.
3. JG d, 8–29 Aug. and Oct. 1902.
4. Randolph S. Churchill, *Winston S. Churchill*, vol. 2, 54.
5. JG d, 8–29.
6. John E. Gorst, 'Social Reform: The Obligation of the Tory Party', *The Nineteenth Century*, Mar. 1903, 519–32.
7. Ibid.
8. Ibid.
9. Randolph S. Churchill, *William S. Churchill*, vol. 2, 62–3.
10. Devonshire MS 2nd series, 340, 3007, Gorst(G)–Devonshire, 9 Oct. 1903.
11. 4 PD 118, 19 Feb. 1903, 323.
12. Ibid., 4 Mar. 1903, 1424; 11 June 1903, 682–4.
13. Stead papers 1/29, G–Stead, 31 Dec. 1903.
14. Lady Warwick, *A Nation's Youth*, London, Cassell, 1906, 24.
15. 4 PD 132, 27 Mar. 1904, 906–7; 133, 20 Apr. 1904, 789–92.
16. Daglish, *Education Policy-making*, 354–5; PD, 20 Apr. 1904, 792.
17. 4 PD 140, 10 Aug. 1904, 46–54.
18. Ibid., 54–5.
19. Randolph S. Churchill, *Winston S. Churchill*, vol. 2, 77–8.
20. Ibid., vol. 2, Companion pt 1, 323.
21. Marvin Papers MS, Eng. lett. C 257, G–Deverell, 23 Jan. 1904.
22. Ibid., G–Marvin, 14 June 1904.
23. Ibid., G–Marvin, 14 May 1906.
24. Quoted by Daglish, *Education Policy-making*, 360.
25. Quoted by Warwick, *A Nation's Youth*, 1; see also Simon, *Education and the Labour Movement*, 281.
26. Marvin Papers, G–Marvin, 27 Jan. 1905. There is some doubt about the date. This author prefers 1905 to 1903.
27. 4 PD 141, 23 Feb. 1905, 1143–5.
28. John E. Gorst, *The Children of the Nation*, 86–7, Daglish, *Education Policy-making*, 363–4.
29. 4 PD 143, 27 Mar. 1905, 1244–51.
30. Daglish, *Education Policy-making*, 365. See also John E. Gorst, *Children of the Nation*, 86–7; H. Bosanquet, *Social Work in London 1869–1912*, London, Murray,

1914, 252–3.
31. *Review of Reviews*, 31 May 1905, 499.
32. Ibid.
33. 4 PD 151, 7 Aug. 1905, 377.
34. 4 PD 130, 22 Feb. 1904, 636; R. Ensor, *England 1870–1914*, Oxford, Oxford University Press, 1936, 377.
35. Warwick, *A Nation's Youth*, xii.
36. Bryce papers MS, 71, G–Bryce, 7 Feb. 1906.
37. Marvin papers, G–Marvin, 3 Feb. 1906.
38. Middleton papers MS, Eng. c. 4833, G–Lane–Fox, 18 Feb. 1906.
39. John E. Gorst, *Children of the Nation*, 1–2.
40. Ibid., 2–7.
41. B.B. Gilbert, 'Sir John Eldon Gorst and the Children of the Nation', *Bulletin of the History of Medicine*, vol. XXVIII, 1954, 251.
42. John E. Gorst, *Children of the Nation*, 7.
43. Hennock, *British Social Reform*, 16.
44. Gilbert, 'Sir John Eldon Gorst', 251.

21

Return to New Zealand

At the end of the summer, after *The Children of the Nation* had been sent by Methuen to the printers, there was a new excitement in store for John Gorst. The New Zealand government had decided to stage an international Exhibition at Christchurch in November 1906. Lord Elgin, the British Colonial Secretary, determined in an inspired moment to send out John Gorst to attend the Exhibition as a special commissioner representing the British government. Elgin's junior minister in the Commons was Winston Churchill who approved the choice, telling his chief how he was 'delighted that you have sent old Gorst to N.Z. It will give him immense pleasure and I am sure he will do it well.'[1] Churchill was correct on both counts.

Taking his daughter Eva with him, John Gorst set out in late September for New York sailing in the White Star liner *Majestic* from Liverpool. He described the ship as 'a floating hotel in which every luxury in the way of entertainment is provided and in which the accommodation is as luxurious as the perpetual motion of the ocean will permit'. Once on dry land they continued to travel in style and comfort, crossing the American continent by railway in Pullman cars. They reached San Francisco only six months after the great earthquake of April that year which, together with the fire that followed it, had virtually destroyed the city, which was still desolated. On arrival there at midnight they drove 'through streets bordered by piles of rubbish with broken ruins of gigantic buildings looming through the darkness'. Next morning they made out the full horror of the ruined city, the Pacific breeze raising a pervasive fog of red dust from the ruins.

The mail steamer *Sonoma* made agreeable stops during its passage from San Francisco to Auckland – at Honolulu and at Paga Paga in American Samoa. But the ship had engine trouble and they docked at Auckland on 29 October, seven days late. Standing on the wharf as the ship was being made fast, Gorst noticed a very old and tattooed Maori with, in his words, 'the most benign face imaginable who had evidently recognized me . . .'[2] It was the 83-year-old Patara, his rival editor 43 years before, of the Maori newspaper *Te Hokioi*. The two men had in fact last met in England in the mid-1880s when Patara and other Maoris had made a visit to London to complain to the Privy Council about land problems (the visit was not fruitful). This happy reunion was for Gorst an augury for the success of his mission.

The Gorsts would now have to move fast to get to Christchurch in time for the opening ceremonies. So they were allowed only a brief two hours at Auckland before they were hustled onto another ship. This time it was a coastal steamer which took them to New Plymouth, then the most northerly point reached by the railway pushing up from Wellington. They had no time at the capital as the tourist department there hurried them onto yet another ship, one bound for the port of Christchurch. On board was George Fowlds, Minister of Education and Health, who took father and daughter under his wing. Between Gorst and Fowlds the theme of education provided common ground. Fowlds ensured that his visitor saw a number of schools during his stay in the country, and after Gorst's departure from New Zealand the two men corresponded for many years.

The Exhibition, which proved to be a well-organised and successful event, was opened by the Governor, Lord Plunket. The mother country had sent many exhibits. The most important one, in Gorst's view, was the Art gallery consisting of a collection of modern paintings, some on loan and some for sale, such as had never before been seen in the southern hemisphere.

In the grounds of the Exhibition was a model '*pa*' (Maori fortified village). Captain Atkin, the other British Commissioner to the Exhibition, at once carried Gorst off to see this special feature. Here Gorst met among the Maoris manning the *pa* an old chief who had been an ardent follower of Rewi. He shook hands with Gorst in the most hearty and friendly fashion.[3] Everywhere Gorst went in New Zealand the welcome he received from the Maoris was the same – he was remembered with respect and unusual warmth. At a dinner given in Christchurch by the government for the Maoris involved with the pah, Gorst, deputising for the Governor, made a short speech in Maori proposing the health of King Edward VII. More speeches and then songs of welcome followed. At the end every man was presented with a pipe and every woman with a workbox.

At length the Gorsts had to bid farewell to Christchurch and return to North Island. At Wellington Gorst and Atkin placed a wreath on the grave of Richard Seddon, the former Prime Minister, who had died suddenly some months before. Gorst considered that New Zealand owed a great deal to Seddon for his work over the years. From Wellington the visitors made a fairly leisurely journey north to the

Waikato by railway, steamer and coach, accompanied by James Cowan of the tourist department, who was to become a notable historian of New Zealand. But first they spent a few days in Masterton where Gorst's brother-in-law, Frederick Moore, lived.

Gorst was fond of travelling and, from the account he handed down in his book *New Zealand Revisited*, he relished seeing new sights including the geysers around Rotorua, besides meeting a vast number of people from all walks of life and Maoris connected with the old days. Eva, too, must have been entranced by the excitement of the journeying for, like her parents, she was made of the stuff of pioneers. Not many years later she would be off to the Balkan wars to nurse the wounded.

At Waharoa en route by train to Te Awamutu a hundred Maoris gathered to greet Gorst as he passed through. One of them was Taingakawa, the son of Gorst's old friend Chief Tamihara. The son was very like his father, and Gorst managed during his short visit to the Waikato to have several long talks with him.[4]

The climax to the whole visit to New Zealand must for Gorst have been his return on the evening of 3 December to Te Awamutu. The town board, the Europeans, and Maoris from far and wide did him proud. There were formal ceremonies, dinners, meetings and sightseeing. Bands played, hakas were danced and songs sung. Often the atmosphere was like a carnival with Gorst the central figure. Arrangements had been carefully planned. Five of his old scholars from the Technical School at Otawhao, all in their sixties, had met his train. They included William Hughes, once an apprentice carpenter and now an important chief with two young daughters.

The next day between 400 and 500 people came together at Victoria Park for a great meeting to welcome Gorst. Alas, the function was somewhat spoiled by heavy rain and people had to repair to the Town Hall. In a speech there George Fowlds, once again of the party, while acknowledging Sir John's 'brilliant' career in the old country, said he might have done better service to the Empire by remaining in New Zealand. As usual, Gorst was ready to speak in reply, this time in English. It was easier. Still full of energy, Gorst was taken on a tour of the surrounding countryside which held memories for him. He met, for instance, on this trip Roland Mainwaring (whose brother had travelled to New Zealand with him in 1860) and his wife, who had been little Jack's nurse in the Waikato. At Te Awamutu as elsewhere John Gorst and Eva were given presents, particularly Eva. Once she received a 'kit' made with kiwi feathers. On another, a green stone and gold pin, known as 'the pin of love' were presented to her by the

Hughes' daughters. These girls sang a charming Maori parting song as the Gorsts' train pulled out of Te Awamutu station on the journey north.[5]

At their next stop, Ngaruawahia, the capital of the former Maori King, a wonderful canoe journey had been arranged as a finale to the Gorsts' visit to the Waikato. A specially made white-pine canoe, 70 feet in length, with a crew of 15 Maori paddlers stripped to their waists, now took the Gorst party downstream to Waahi. The canoe was in the charge of Hori Te Ngongo, son of Gorst's old friend Chief Te Oriori. Along its journey the canoe was met by a state canoe specially sent by Mahuta, son of Matutaera, the former Maori king,[6] a signal honour for the former civil commissioner of the Waikato.

On this high note John Gorst's visit to the Waikato ended. There was a further round of receptions awaiting him in Auckland but could these have proved a bit of an anti-climax? In his book Gorst is the soul of tact and does not say. One gesture he clearly much appreciated. The mayor of Auckland presented him with a beautifully bound copy of the five numbers of the ill-fated newspaper he had edited, *Te Pihoihoi Mokemoke*.

During his travels Gorst could not fail to notice the enormous economic strides made by New Zealand in the previous 40 years. Auckland was unrecognisable with its well-laid-out streets, trams and neat houses. In the countryside he knew so well, and elsewhere too, bush had been cleared and everywhere there were prosperous farms. Beef, mutton, butter and wool production were rapidly on the increase. This progress had been matched by welcome political advances. Democratic government worked well. Women had been given the vote in 1893. In no other country in the world had they accomplished this so early. In the following year New Zealand would achieve dominion status. Gorst enjoyed hearing about the premium put on social welfare. For example, old age pensions had been introduced, and 12 years earlier a successful Arbitration and Conciliation Act had been passed which aimed to settle industrial disputes, and regulate wages and hours of work. In New Zealand, he was assured, there were no hungry children.

But what struck Gorst above all during his visit was the transformation visible in the relations between the people of European stock and the Maoris. At this he rejoiced and expressed his pleasure to everyone. Public opinion, he later wrote, regarded the Maoris as being entitled to equal rights and equal justice.[7] Maoris were admitted to both legislatures and a Maori had been a government minister. For their part, he observed, the Maoris had lost the former bitter feeling of hatred towards Europeans. There was one cloud on the horizon. This was the still vexed question of the land, about which the Maoris continued to have complaints against the government. Taingakawa, a spokesman, raised their grievances with Gorst, who advised very sensibly that they should take the matter to the government at Wellington and not to the mother country in London. In doing this he emphasised his visit was wholly without political significance.

On 10 December before the Gorsts embarked on their ship for Sydney, Atkin and Gorst, as the British Commissioners to the Exhibition, gave a farewell luncheon at the Grand Hotel in Auckland. Everyone was there including the mayor, Fowlds and Patara. Afterwards the former scholars, among them William Hughes, waved a last farewell from the quayside as the ship pulled away. The next day the ship passed the Three Kings islands at the top of North Island. Gorst would perhaps at this moment have found it hard not to feel a lump in his throat for he had a genuine affection for New Zealand and the Maoris. 'I watched the last bit of New Zealand territory', he was to write, 'till it faded away in the distance – Good-bye forever, Good-bye, Good-bye!'[8]

Shortly after Gorst returned home in February, a letter he had written many weeks before 'at sea off Australia' about what he believed Tory democracy stood for was published in *The Times*. This letter, from which we have already quoted, was prompted by Lord Rosebery's book on Lord Randolph Churchill which Gorst had read while in Australia. Gorst, loyal to the memory of Disraeli and Churchill, defended the principles for which Tory democracy stood, and away from which he believed the present Tory leaders had drifted.

Soon Gorst was to begin work on his book about his second journey to New Zealand, which would be published the following year. At the end of May he was needed for a visit being made to Germany by the Committee for the Study of Municipal Institutions Abroad, which went to a number of cities in the south of that country studying how local government worked there. As a whole-hearted admirer of German institutions, Gorst probably let his enthusiasm run away with him, for he was refusing to acknowledge that there was any military threat to Britain developing from the Kaiser and his government. He believed for instance that the skilled and expert workmen being turned out by the Technical School at Charlottenburg in Berlin were a 'far greater menace to British supremacy than a dozen Dreadnoughts'.[9]

Once more Gorst was affected by his propensity for having itchy feet. In early May 1907 we find him living in Letchworth, Hertfordshire. He had never had any great love of Yateley and its environs, once describing himself when there as being 'at rest in the stagnation of this country place'.[10] Why he went to Letchworth we cannot be certain, although there are pointers to his reasons. He had for some time been interested in the garden city movement which was being preached by Ebenezer Howard and others at the same time that pioneering work was taking place in Germany on town planning. Letchworth was the first of the English garden cities, being founded in 1903 and financed on the joint stock principle by wealthy shareholders. Later that summer when replying to a letter from his son-in-law, Mark Sykes, Gorst referred to the 'garden-city idea'. With the removal of the British workman from town to country in mind, Gorst was opining that 'the act of enjoying the country has to be taught like any new thing, and the British public is very slow to learn.' There is a nice postscript to Gorst's letter: 'The one great objection in the minds of many working men to country life is that the opportunity of getting drunk is more restricted'[11] Edith, John Gorst's fourth daughter, had some years before married Mark Sykes, heir to the Sledmere estate. Sykes, of whom it is said he could have made a reputation in at least half a dozen careers,[12] became an MP. He is especially remembered as the co-author of the Sykes–Picot agreement of 1916 which purported to partition Turkey in Asia, giving Syria to France and Mesopotamia (Iraq) to Britain. From the fragments of correspondence that survive it would seem that Gorst liked his son-in-law and encouraged him to pursue a political career. Sadly he died at an early age in 1919.

There was another aspect to Gorst's move to Letchworth. The Education Bill of 1907, enacted in August that year, had at last introduced a scheme for the medical inspection of children in elementary schools, an idea for which Gorst had long fought. The new scheme was due to begin in January 1908. Gorst decided that, although he was 72, there was a role for him to play in monitoring the performance of local educational authorities over implementing this new measure. No doubt he would be equally interested in seeing how these authorities were coping with the new responsibilities which had devolved on them under the Education Act of 1902. Showing, therefore, how quite often he was more enthusiast than cynic, Gorst took a post as manager of schools at Letchworth.[13] This was an amazing move for an ex-Minister of Education, but the job perfectly suited his purposes. We don't know for how long Gorst lived in Letchworth but he was there until at least August 1909.

Mary had no wish to live in Letchworth. She too was in her early seventies and had probably had enough careering around from house to house. In any case her daughter Hylda and her family now lived, when not in Egypt, near Bramshill, a few miles from Yateley. So John went to Letchworth on his own. Well, not quite. When he wrote to Edith Marvin declining an invitation to visit her in Leeds he suggested she came to visit him at Letchworth. He told her:

> I have one spare room comfortable and ready, and I have my very old friend Miss Johnson whom you have met at the House of Commons as housekeeper who will make you comfortable.[14]

This is the first time we hear in this story of Mathilda Jane Ethel Johnson, to give her full name. Unfortunately for a biographer, little is known about Ethel except that she was then 42 and the daughter of Edward Johnson, a solicitor, who had lived in the London suburb of Streatham. Jack Gorst, home on leave, visited his father that October and the succeeding August at his Letchworth 'cottage', but makes no mention of Ethel.[15]

So it was that John and Mary now mainly went their separate ways. Periodically they would come together. Not, though, at Yateley. Jack, after seeing his parents at Castle Combe, notes in a cryptic diary entry for 27 September 1909: 'Father's and mother's relations are very strained on the subject of Miss Johnson'. Harold, devoted to his mother but much less so to his father, makes no mention of Ethel in his autobiography. The Gorst daughters took the side of their mother, whom they all adored, and consequently disliked Ethel.

His post at Letchworth did not stop Gorst from travelling round the country. He continued to follow closely what was going on in parliament, and was still in demand as a speaker and writer on social issues. For instance, in 1908 we find him with speaking engagements in Lancashire, Yorkshire and Birmingham. At the last-named place he admitted in a speech that the cruel wrongs committed by drunken parents on their children had made him a temperance reformer. Yet he was not quite a teetotaller. He had spoken several times, mainly on technical points, during the passage of the Licensing Bill in 1904 which reduced the number of licences issued, on grounds of public policy, and compensated brewers for the closing of public houses. Gorst referred to the 'terrible sale of drink', and to the 'evils' which might result to schools when a public house was located near them. Nevertheless he voted for the Bill.

In contrast to the serious political issues Gorst normally espoused, we suddenly find him at the end of the year going off on a

Mediterranean cruise to Athens, Constantinople and the Holy Land where he visited Jerusalem.[16]

Always an advocate of Poor Law reform, Gorst wrote an article for *The Sociological Review* in which he analysed the majority and minority reports of the Royal Commission on the Poor Law set up by Balfour in 1905 and published in July 1909 (the rival reports filled a gigantic Blue Book with some 1,298 pages). Both reports agreed that the outdated Poor Law needed reforming by abolishing the local Board of Guardians system and its chief instrument the ghastly workhouse, which were based on the ideas and machinery of distant 1834. But the two reports differed on how this was to be achieved. Curiously Gorst, usually so forthright, did not offer his precise opinion on how the changes should be effected. His 16-page article was available, price 1d post free, from the National Committee to Promote the Break-up of the Poor Law. Gorst would not live to see reforms in this field. The minister, John Burns, was not enthusiastic, and then the war came. It was not until 1928 that Neville Chamberlain, Joseph's son, swept away the old discredited system.

As far as we know, John Gorst had a good relationship with his elder brother Edward who had lived the life of a country gentleman for some 35 years at Castle Combe. Edward had never been ambitious and was content in his rural retreat to be a JP, Deputy Lieutenant and High Sheriff of Wiltshire. In May 1909 he died. He was a bachelor and his estate of some 3,600 acres passed to John. For all his political life John had railed against the landowning class. Now he had joined it.

NOTES

1. Randolph S. Churchill, *Winston S. Churchill*, vol. 2, Companion pt 1, 583.
2. NZR, 3–4.
3. Ibid., 59.
4. *The Journal of the Te Awamutu Historical Society*, Dec. 1971, vol. 6, no. 2 and information from Te Awamutu Museum.
5. Ibid.
6. Cowan, *The Old Frontier*, 22; NZR, 294–6.
7. NZR, 67–8.
8. Ibid., 331.
9. J. E. Gorst wrote an article in 1907, 'Municipal Lessons from Southern Germany' for a journal which the author cannot identify .
10. Marvin papers, G–Marvin, 20 Sept. 1904.
11. Sykes Collection, DDSY (2)/1/4, G–Sykes, 17 July 1907.
12. R. Storrs, *Orientations*, 196.
13. Fowlds papers, MSS and Archives A–17, G–Fowlds, 20 Dec. 1907.
14. Marvin papers, G–Marvin, 6 May 1907.
15. JG d, 2 Oct. 1907 and 17 Aug. 1908.
16. *Alliance News*, 7 May 1908; Fowlds papers, G–Fowlds, 10 May 1909.

22

Fighting Preston

Towards the end of 1909 the country was plunged into a political crisis which was to last for not far short of two years. Even though he was rising 75, Gorst was to be involved in it.

The Chancellor of the Exchequer, Lloyd George, had to find for his budget an extra £15 million, then a large sum. To counter the growing strength of the German navy, new battleships were suddenly needed as in the music-hall refrain 'we want Eight, And we won't wait'. This was on top of money for roads (rapidly increasing motor traffic had turned these into dust and mud), the programme of social reform and other projects. Some of this money was to come from a proposed tax on the sale of land. Undeveloped land and mineral rights were also to be subject to new taxes. A complete valuation of land in Britain was therefore needed. The peers, who owned a great deal of the land, violently objected. Asquith, the new Prime Minister (Campbell-Bannerman had died in April 1908), stood firm. On 4 November 1909 the budget passed the Commons by 379 votes to 149; but in the Lords, where the Conservatives were ill-led, the measure was rejected two days later on its Second Reading by 350 to 75.

The financial powers of the House of Lords were at that time limited by the rights and privileges of the House of Commons, which were based on two resolutions of the Commons carried in 1671 and 1678. Briefly these laid down that 'the rate or tax ought not be altered by the Lords' and that 'all aids and supplies' were the 'sole gift of the Commons'. These principles were restated and amplified by resolution in the Commons in 1860. While, therefore, the Lords might in principle reject financial bills, to amend such bills would constitute a breach of privilege.[1]

In this sensitive field the Lords' move was seen by the Commons as an act of defiance, and consequently held by them to be against the constitution and a usurpation of their rights. There had been no such precedent, as Gorst was to remind his audiences, since 1674. A January election seemed inevitable. The issue for the Commons was plain enough. Were the Lords to have a veto? If so, the Commons would have lost its power so arduously gained in the seventeenth century to raise taxes. There was, however, an alternative lurking in the background. This was the precedent in 1832 when the Lords were coerced into passing the great Reform Bill by the Prime Minister's threat to have new peers created by the King.

Gorst entered into the fray with uninhibited enthusiasm. He was outraged at the Lords' behaviour. A House of Commons man through and through, he fervently believed that the Lords' challenge must be defeated. His old instincts aroused, there was only one thing he could do and that was to stand again for parliament. But not this time on the Conservative side. Never! Having surrendered his ministerial pension, Gorst was on 29 December adopted as a Liberal candidate on home territory at Preston, where he had already begun campaigning earlier in the month. There were five candidates fighting for two seats: two Unionists (as Conservatives were now frequently called), one Liberal (Gorst), one independent Liberal (Cox) and one Labour (Macpherson). The sitting members were Cox and Macpherson.

Gorst told his adoption meeting that most of the other questions facing the electors, important as they were – such as free trade, education, social legislation and even the budget – receded into the background against the main issue:

> Is the country to be governed by the House of Commons or by the House of Lords? ... It is a question whether the power of the people to regulate the affairs of this country is or is not to be preserved ... Don't deceive yourselves, you are going to fight a terrible battle against the House of Lords. You have to repel the invasion of the privileges of the people ...[2]

Meetings and speeches were followed by more meetings and more speeches. Gorst stumped round the constituency showing great energy. Sometimes he got carried away, as when on 5 January he told a mass meeting of Liberals at the crowded Public Hall that in his opinion 'the better plan would be to take the occasion of abolishing that House [the Lords] altogether.' He still could find a nice turn of phrase. The Lords, he conceded, had long been 'an ornament' of the state. So long as they remained one, all would be well. But now they had become 'an obstacle', and an attempt must be made to remove them.[3]

The Liberal candidate showed he had lost none of his passion for social reform, in regard to which the government was making great progress. Poverty, Gorst said, was the greatest discredit of the times and there was an urgent need for an improvement in housing. He admitted to a questioner that he had been in favour of women's suffrage since he was young. There is, however, evidence which shows him to have been a bit coy when a minister in speaking publicly on the subject. In 1898, for example, he declined an invitation from Lady Bective to speak on women's suffrage in Manchester, saying he did not wish to cause the government embarrassment. Going back a good deal further, Gorst had said in a debate in the Commons in 1878 on the Women's Disabilities Removal Bill that he was 'not one of the strong advocates of women's rights. I do not believe that women are much oppressed, or that their prospects, on the whole, are very bad'. Yet he nevertheless gave his 'cordial support' to the Bill – which was to give women the vote – on the grounds of personal liberty. His argument was that women should not be subject to legal restrictions which he disliked on principle.[4]

On foreign affairs Gorst told electors it was wicked of the Leader of the Opposition (still Balfour) to introduce a German war scare. Further, he, Gorst, believed that the Germans were 'our best friends'. From his own personal knowledge he knew the Germans had no more idea of invading England than the Englishman had of invading Germany.[5] As ever, Gorst put the best possible interpretation on German intentions and practice. He was not reported as referring to the question of the extra battleships needed.

The efforts he made on the hustings were, sadly for Gorst, to no avail. Major Stanley of the Derby family and A. A. Tobin, a KC, both Unionists, were elected with 9,526 and 9,160 votes. Macpherson was next with 7,539 and Gorst fourth with 6,281. At the declaration he made 'a brief and dignified little speech'. The results must have been a real disappointment to him. He attributed his failure at least partly to the success of the Unionists' tariff reform propaganda upon the 'poorer residents' who consequently, and against the trend in other Lancashire towns, voted for the Unionists. To Winston Churchill, who sent him a telegram of condolence on his defeat, he wrote that he felt 'a little ashamed of the want of shrewdness in my native place'.[6] In the country the Liberals returned 275 MPs, thus losing 102 seats, and now depended for power on Labour and Irish support. The Unionists won back 116 seats.

On 15 February Gorst wrote two separate letters to Churchill, one to congratulate him on becoming Home Secretary and the other to say that, as there was now likely to be a creation of peers (should a Parliament Bill reducing the power of the Lords be introduced),

I hope you will if you have the opportunity remind the Prime

Minister of me. My hope of getting back into the H of C is extinguished. But I think I could be a great help to the Govt in the H of Lords, both in the Constitutional struggle and in the discussion of social questions: and after the experience of the election I feel fit and anxious for political work.[7]

Gorst could not quite let go. He had told Edith Marvin some years before, as we have seen, that the Commons was a waste of time, and had now told the Preston electors that the Lords should be abolished. Yet he still wanted to be part of the political scene. But it was not to be.

The dispute between Commons and Lords continued well into King George V's reign. There was another election at the end of 1910 in which Gorst did not stand. The threat by the Lords to throw out the 1911 Parliament Bill did not in the event materialise, and so Asquith did not need to create a huge number of new peers. Nevertheless he did have a list of 250 Liberals whose names he was prepared, if need be and with the King's consent, to submit to George V for peerages. Gorst's name was on the list.[8]

Gorst had by now moved back to London and had a flat in Campden Hill Court not far from Hyde Park where he enjoyed walking. We do not know if Ethel was his housekeeper there, but it is likely she was. He periodically visited Castle Combe. Once we find him driving round the estate with Jack and the agent Robert Watkins in the big 35-horse-power Daimler given as a present to his parents by Jack.[9] Inheriting the estate from his brother had caused him, we know, some financial anxieties. There is no evidence that he loved the place like some of his descendants did, and he was quite content to leave its management in Watkins' not very capable hands. Jack was to inherit Castle Combe and consequently father and son made a careful resettlement of the estate. But Jack himself was not well. Overwork and stress in the unsettled aftermath of the assassination in February 1910 of the Egyptian Prime Minister, Boutros Ghali, may have been responsible for a stroke Jack had suffered in June of that year. His recovery was slow. Early the following year he was ill again and began to lose weight. Cancer was diagnosed in June and a month later he died aged 50 at the Manor in Castle Combe. Abbas Hilmi II, the Khedive of Egypt, made a special visit from the continent to Castle Combe to say good-bye to his much valued friend Jack Gorst, the man who had tried to liberalise British rule in Egypt.

John and Mary were much saddened by their elder son's death. There may have been a measure of consolation when the Khedive wrote comforting letters to John. Jack's services to Egypt would be long remembered, he said, and he would always look upon Jack as 'one of my best friends'. Moreover, the Khedive promised John to do whatever he could to help his daughters living in Egypt, now that their brother was no longer there to look after their interests.[10] He was referring to Hylda and Gwendolen. The Khedive was true to his word. And years later Hylda's elder son Archie became the Khedive's private secretary. Every year after Jack's death the Khedive visited his grave in Castle Combe to lay a wreath upon it. This was eloquent tribute to the esteem in which Jack had been held by Abbas Hilmi.

If there had been unrest in Egypt, civil strife of one kind or another was sweeping across Britain too. Labour troubles were acute, including constant strikes, the suffragettes were resorting to violence and the problem of a militant Ulster was looming. The Unionist Party, led since 1911 by Bonar Law in place of Balfour, was openly encouraging Ulster to arm in the face of the introduction of a third Home Rule Bill. Small wonder that Gorst, in writing to his friend Fowlds in New Zealand, said: 'The discontent of the masses is likely to find new and perhaps more reckless leaders who may guide us into a revolution'.[11] A month later, still in despondent mood, Gorst wrote to *The Times* about the state of education. He claimed that in most elementary schools the children were only drilled not educated, while secondary and university education was 'still fettered by medieval systems'. Furthermore, students were not educated but only prepared for examinations. Finally, he called for the 'tyranny' of the Board of Education over local authorities to be relaxed or removed. This may have been one of Gorst's last public pronouncements on education.[12]

These last four years could not have been easy ones for Mary, since her relations with John continued to be strained. She now lived at the Manor in Castle Combe where she was visited by her family. In the winter of 1909/10 she had spent some months in Egypt staying with Jack and with Hylda. While there she became ill with pneumonia, which pulled her down. On 29 January 1914, at the age of 78, Mary died at Castle Combe. Her children were devoted to her and must have grieved deeply. How John took her death we do not know, but the couple had been married for 53 years. Mary had been a loyal wife and a loving mother to John's children. There is no room for doubt that John Gorst had treated his wife badly. While there is plenty known about John's public persona, little light is shed on his family and private life. Gorst was compassionate about the nation's unemployed and needy, and about its children. But how far his compassion and love reached to his wife and daughters we cannot really be sure.

The same year as Mary died, and not quite eight months after her funeral, John Gorst married Ethel Johnson. This marriage alienated his family. It took place at the church of St Wilfrid's in Harrogate and was witnessed by Charles Johnson and John Rosier. The former was Ethel's brother and the latter Gorst's chauffeur. The same two men were witnesses to Gorst's will drawn up three days after his marriage. Under it Ethel received £800 a year for life and there was £30,000 (*c.* £1,650,000 now) to be divided equally among John's six living children (Jack's family having already been provided for). In a codicil John Rosier received £100 a year for life with £50 a year then being left to his widow for her life. There were no other legatees. Gorst had written to Edith Marvin a month before his marriage but, curiously perhaps, did not mention his approaching nuptials to her.

There are no surviving papers to show what John Gorst's reaction was to the declaration of war in August 1914. Edith Marvin visited him that winter in London, which obviously gave him pleasure. She sent him some books, and in thanking her for them just before Christmas he commented that 'the navy had more than fulfilled our expectation: but the waste of life and ships is most melancholy … everything good in German civilisation will be thrown back for years.'[13]

Mostly, John Gorst stayed in London. There were often long gaps between his visits to Castle Combe, and once he did not go there for eight months. One blessing Gorst had always been able to count upon was his health. It has been said that some time in 1914 he met with a slight accident – its nature is undisclosed but perhaps it was a fall – and that subsequently he did not enjoy such robust health. John's children had no fondness for Ethel and they probably did not see much of their father in his last years. At the end of March 1916 John caught influenza and a few days later, on 4 April, he died at home in London. He was nearly 81. Ethel survived him only a comparatively short time, dying of pneumonia, aged 53, at Trimingham, near Cromer in Norfolk, in September 1918.

NOTES

1. Thomas Erskine May, *Parliamentary Practice,* 14th edn, ed. Gilbert Campion, London, Butterworth, 1946, 763–79.
2. *Preston Guardian,* 1 Jan. 1910.
3. Ibid., 8 Jan. 1910.
4. 3 PD 240, 19 June 1878, 1844–8.
5. *Preston Guardian,* 8 and 15 Jan. 1910.
6. Randolph S. Churchill, *Winston S. Churchill,* vol. 2, Companion pt 2, 964.

7. Ibid., 1136.
8. J. A. Spender and Cyril Asquith, *Life of Henry Herbert Asquith, Lord Oxford and Asquith,* vol. 1, London, Hutchinson, 1932, 330.
9. JG d, 14 Aug. 1909.
10. Letters from Khedive Abbas Hilmi II to John Gorst of 30 June, 8 Jul 1911, quoted by P. Mellini in *Sir Eldon Gorst: The Overshadowed Proconsul,* Stanford, CA, Hoover Institution Press, 1979, 236.
11. Fowlds Papers, G–Fowlds, 25 Oct. 1911.
12. *The Times,* 27 Nov. 1911.
13. Marvin Papers, G–Marvin, 14 Dec. 1914.

23

Epilogue

Among many notices in the newspapers on John Gorst's death, a full and perceptive obituary came from the pen of T. P. O'Connor, a conspicuous Irish Nationalist MP and journalist who had known him over a long period. In his piece in the *Daily Telegraph* on 5 April 1916 of no less than 36 column inches, O'Connor began by asking why Gorst's career was

> of promise rather than achievement, of great possibilities and of small results. And it was somewhat difficult to say why it should have been so. It was not for want of intellectual powers for Sir John Gorst was beyond question one of the really ablest Parliamentarians of his time, nor was it want of industry … nor was it lack of conviction … cool, brave, sure of his facts, pointed, deliberate and careful in delivery, he had the power of making attacks which drew blood and … of never apparently losing for a moment his own self control.

O'Connor suggests that the key to Gorst's lack of success was Lord Salisbury. This dominating figure had the 'power to make or mar Parliamentary fortunes'. He had a 'stern and unbending' dislike of Gorst who was a 'very frequent offender against discipline and notoriously was dissatisfied with his lot'. There is certainly more than a ring of truth about this view.

Gorst was a complex man, and there were many factors contributing to what he must have perceived as his comparative failure as a politician. If the puzzle – and the *Daily Mail* said Gorst was always an 'enigma' – is to be solved, our net must be cast more widely.

There was one fundamental complication for an aspiring politician in Gorst's make-up. He was never a team player and never seen as a committed party man. The cat that preferred to walk alone, he was always the freelance. Even during his 13 years as a minister he was remarkably independent-minded, to the irritation of party leaders. First and foremost came his principles which he did not bend. He believed he was right and therefore wanted his way. This made him an uncomfortable and awkward colleague, sometimes being called disloyal and even treacherous. It is surprising, we might be tempted to conclude, that Gorst was ever a member of any government. The answer to this is that his vision and ideas, his knowledge of his subject, his courage, his resourcefulness, when allied to his great powers in debate – by some he was regarded as second only to Joseph Chamberlain – made it dangerous to leave him out. This was Salisbury's consistent view, although he drew the line at including Gorst in his inner counsels.

During his time in politics – his consuming interest, for he never gave enough time to the law to make his practice a real success – his career had something of the character of a switchback about it: a series of ups and downs. Of course political life by its nature tends to be so, but Gorst's ride was a more than usually bumpy one. For instance, after the Tory victory in 1874, and with no apparent reward in sight, he felt cold-shouldered by the party and was resentful. From 1880 he was centre stage in those heady days of the Fourth Party. Yet four years on, his hopes were badly dashed when Lord Randolph Churchill, ignoring him, came to an accommodation with Salisbury. A short time later he was exhilarated when appointed Solicitor-General, but in less than a year he found himself demoted to the India Office. And so it continued. His long tenure as Education Minister was a progression of summits and troughs.

His temperament did not always help him. A missionary in New Zealand had observed Gorst's tendency to be 'soon elated and soon depressed' (see p.60). In fact his character is not too easy to read. Some examples illustrate the point. While he was cool on the floor of the House, he was an impatient man and had a temper. He had undoubtedly a charm of manner and a genial streak but could be disagreeable, quarrelsome and contemptuous of colleagues. He was cynical, once being called the Diogenes of politics, but at the same time an enthusiast. While he might pretend not to be at all ambitious, he was *au fond* very ambitious. Too often his own worst enemy, this contrariness could have done him no favours as he struggled to climb the political ladder. Given his temperament, it is hardly surprising that Gorst made some serious errors of judgement in a career spanning over 40 years as an MP. For example he was surely foolish not to accept Disraeli's offer of a junior government post in 1875. This delayed his achieving ministerial office by ten years. He was unwise to fall out with Dyke and Smith, and should too have made more effort to come to terms with the grandees and landowners of the party. But then Gorst often fell down in his relations with those with whom he worked. The example of his friend Churchill, who could be notoriously careless of other people's feelings, would not have helped, but on the other hand his damaging prickliness was evident long before his Fourth Party days.

Above all, Gorst somehow failed to maintain the reasonably good relations he appeared to have with Salisbury in the 1870s. For all his political acumen Gorst was slow to spot that this leading figure would emerge as a powerful Prime Minister and, therefore, as a man not to offend. For tactical reasons at least Gorst should have attended Salisbury's dinner held in 1884 to mark the reconciliation between the leadership and the Fourth Party. As a result of his absence, Salisbury may have decided, if he did not think it already, that Gorst was a mere parvenu and unable to play the political game by its rules. Gorst's uninhibited pushiness often manifested itself through ill-judged letters he wrote to Salisbury canvassing appointments or promotion. The occasional gaffe he made, and his readiness to go his own way in apparent disregard of the niceties of party discipline, must have further exasperated Salisbury. The trouble was that the two men almost stood at different ends of the spectrum as far as politics went. Gorst wanted change while Salisbury stood for a cautious status quo. While the social base of Conservatism, obviously to Gorst's approbation, broadened by the end of the century, it was his misfortune that – as far as his career went – control of the party at the highest level was still in the hands of the land-owning élite.

O'Connor in his obituary notice appears to have ignored Gorst's relations with Balfour. They were almost as important as his with Salisbury. Again the two men seemed to get off to a good start as comrades-in-arms in the early Fourth Party days. But Balfour was two-faced with Gorst, who came to think that the nephew was the uncle's spy. Relations began to deteriorate as Balfour, always close to Salisbury, distanced himself from the Fourth Party. Mutual animosity between the two men was usually concealed, often cleverly, by Balfour. By the early 1890s Balfour considered the ever-independent Gorst was an 'impossible colleague' and wanted him sacked from the government for disloyalty. There is no room for doubt that Balfour went out of his way to block Gorst's political advancement.

If John Gorst's relations with his colleagues often left something to be desired – this was observed by his elder son – little is really known, as this history will have shown, about those he had with his immediate family. Nor is it clear how important to him, and so to his career, his family was. His wife Mary, and this much we do know, was a loving woman and protective of her children, who all adored her. That John treated Mary shabbily towards the end of their lives is not in dispute. As a father John was a bit of a martinet towards his two sons when they were young. Nevertheless, he took an interest, though often a stern one, in their schooling and careers, and could be helpful to them as they grew up. Jack was appreciative of the coaching for Cambridge his father gave him and of the European tour they made together afterwards. John was, of course, proud of Jack's achievements in Egypt, and the two men always remained on close terms. After the breakdown of Harold's musical career John held out a fatherly hand to him, employing him first in a firm of which he was chairman and then later as his private secretary. John's relationship with his daughters is almost a closed book. We do know that they were deeply alienated from their father by his second marriage. He had probably always been a bit of a tyrant in the bosom of the family, for Hylda's husband had said he was 'an old pig', surely reflecting something of Hylda's own opinion of her father. It is hard to imagine that John's awkward temper did not spill out sometimes at home.

The well-being of a family and the state of the breadwinner's finances are closely connected. In Gorst's case, what his precise means were, or for that matter his wife's, has never been clear. On the one hand he was regarded by Churchill as a poor man. It is true that his elder brother Edward helped pay his sons' school fees and also paid his election expenses at Chatham. Yet the indications are that he and his family lived in quite comfortable circumstances. While he did not make a fortune at the Bar there was a steady demand for his services as a QC with the occasional fat fee: witness his retainer for his jaunt to India. Until he inherited the Castle Combe estate late in life he never, as far as we know, owned a house, preferring to rent as he restlessly moved round the outer circumference of London. But he did not necessarily stint himself when it came to his choice of abode. For instance, the house he and his family occupied at Manningtree for five years was a small mansion set in spacious surroundings. He also had a number of directorships, which must have helped him considerably when he was not in receipt of a minister's salary. Then every so often he had holidays abroad, once taking his whole family to winter sports. He even paid his unmarried daughters (five of them all told) a reasonable quarterly dress allowance which shows some degree of affluence.

If Gorst did not have, for whatever reasons, the success he might have deserved in his career, then just what should he be remembered for by those interested in the history of his period?

We should not, as a start, forget his sympathetic championing of the Maori cause in his book *The Maori King*, still acknowledged in New Zealand as an important contribution to an understanding of the mid-nineteenth century history of that country.

Gorst first became politically prominent in the country when he made a name for himself after being appointed principal party agent in 1870. He was involved over the next four years in reorganising on a national basis the Conservative Party machine, then badly in need of an overhaul. During this time he founded Conservative Central Office. As a political administrator he met with conspicuous success. He brought to the job ideas, flair and attention to detail. As a result of his energy the party was in a high state of readiness for the election of 1874. Of course, there is scope for argument about the precise reasons for Disraeli's victory, but Gorst's work for the party undoubtedly played a significant part in it, and most historians give Gorst credit for what he achieved in these years. His further two spells at Central Office were, unhappily, not successful. On the other hand, his considerable skills as an organiser were again in evidence a decade later when he helped Churchill capture control of the National Union.

When Gorst was a member of the Fourth Party his name was almost a household word. Was he or was he not the *eminence grise* behind Churchill? And, concomitantly, to what extent was he responsible for promoting Tory democracy? These are questions which have exercised some fascination for historians. The term 'Tory democracy' had properly come into vogue after Disraeli's death and at the time the Fourth Party, led by Churchill, was challenging for the Conservative Party leadership. Significantly, it was Gorst who had taken an initiative in 1882 by suggesting to Churchill that the time was ripe for the rise of the 'Democratic Tory party'. This points to it being Gorst who was pushing for a redefinition of Conservatism. Gorst believed that the concept of Tory democracy owed its existence to Disraeli and to the democratic principles his former chief espoused. These included, as perceived by Gorst, the crucial need for a Tory programme of social reform.

Here we meet a difficulty. There is a school of thought, a persuasive one, among historians which considers that the Reform Act of 1867 was conceived by Disraeli essentially as a means of stealing a march on the Liberals, and that Disraeli was not so much a true reformer but rather a master party tactician. If this view is one which has to be accepted, then what of Gorst's beliefs? Either Gorst must have misread Disraeli or, alternatively and more likely, he interpreted the situation, using Disraeli's name and mystique to help develop the ideas coming from his own fertile mind in a fresh bid to democratise the Conservative Party.

If he were to carry forward his plans, Gorst saw that he needed a credible front man. Churchill, initially at least, fitted the bill. Unfortunately Churchill's and Gorst's aims were not the same, although Gorst did not perhaps see this until later. Churchill wanted power while Gorst wanted to change the nature of his party. In due course Churchill began to go his own way and eventually Gorst's plans ended in disarray when Churchill made his accord with Salisbury. In the earlier days of the Fourth Party, Gorst may have thought he was manipulating Churchill, but in the end it was Churchill who used, and then ditched, Gorst.

Gorst had not always been a reforming Conservative. He was unusual in one particular way. Politically his views moved from right to left. Most people tend to become more conservative with age. Not Gorst. He became more radical the older he grew. When he began his parliamentary career he was against the reform of the franchise and has been described by some as 'reactionary'. As a young man he did not think the working man, lacking education, was sufficiently responsible to vote. But, a realist, he saw with the passing of the Reform Act of 1867 that the Conservatives, if they wished to regain power, had to turn to their advantage the huge increase in the number of urban voters. These voters had to be encouraged and cajoled into supporting the Tories. Reservations Gorst had had about extending the franchise to the working class had, therefore, to be discarded.

After his four years at Central Office, and under the influence of Disraeli, Gorst emerged by the mid-1870s as a progressive and independent-minded Conservative, a stance he retained through the 1880s. When he became early in the next decade an ardent social reformer he was taking yet another step leftwards away from the image of the conventional Conservative of his time. The failure of the Salisbury and Balfour governments to introduce the reforming social legislation which Gorst believed was long overdue disenchanted him with his party and, to a considerable extent, explained why he eventually deserted the Conservative cause. The journalist W. T. Stead even saw Gorst in the early 1900s as a potential leader of the Labour

Party. This may have been fanciful but, significantly enough, Gorst dedicated his book *The Children of the Nation* to the Labour members of the House of Commons, who, he thought, genuinely wished 'to ameliorate the condition of the people'.

Gorst was through and through a House of Commons man, probably happiest as a back-bencher. His purple period, which has given him a niche in parliamentary history, was probably his four-year spell as a member of the Fourth Party helping to spearhead the attack on Gladstone's government. There was nothing Gorst liked more than goading the Liberals. As their fierce critic he displayed a masterly touch. The contentiousness or complexity of the matter in hand added spice to the occasion. If the Grand Old Man himself could be Gorst's target, so much the better. Always well-prepared, Gorst seemed tireless in his persistence while his agility as a debater was a by-word. There must have been many an occasion over the years when the minister responsible groaned as he saw Gorst, glasses glinting ominously, rising in his place to harass and torment the government in his evenly modulated voice.

Throughout his time on the back benches, Gorst loved above all to espouse the causes of the subject people in the Empire, never afraid to speak up on their behalf about their treatment. Foreign affairs, as opposed to colonial or imperial ones, were a field into which he rarely ventured. Thus while he spoke on Egypt, the Sudan and southern Africa, he never spoke on the Balkan crises or on relations, say, with France or Germany. Financial affairs, humdrum estimates and questions of supply and so on, also had a fascination for him throughout his career, especially if the navy were involved. He hated to see any profligacy on the government's part with taxpayers' money. Ireland and all procedural matters, parliamentary as well as legal ones, were also grist to his mill. There was a definite change of emphasis in the early 1890s when the labour question and social welfare began to command his attention, although he retained an interest in India and education until the end of his career.

As a minister Gorst cannot readily be rated as successful as he was when freelancing on the back-benches. His independence curtailed, it must have irked him at times to have to follow the government line and maintain at least a show of discipline. As Solicitor-General and later as Financial Secretary at the Treasury, posts he held only a short time, he was untested. It was a pity he was not given a second chance as a Law Officer for he should have been well suited to the work. In a long spell at the India Office his talents were under-used. In any case the position was regarded as something of a backwater, and Indian matters did not usually merit a good attendance in the chamber. The Manipur debate was an exception, and on that occasion Gorst let himself down, uncharacteristically failing to judge the mood of the House.

His last office, effectively Minister of Education, was an important one and he held it for seven years. Views differ as to whether or not he was successful. Because he and the party leadership were often in conflict, his performance was uneven. No one could doubt, however, his mastery of the complexities of the educational scene. While he saw clearly enough what needed to be done, he often stumbled over the execution of his plans. Thus, in the Commons, where he lacked effective support from Balfour, he failed twice with reforming Bills for which he was responsible. Nonetheless, he achieved notable and long-standing success, only recently recognised, as a result of his administrative measures, skilfully executed, which helped to devolve responsibility for education from central government to the local authorities. It is also obvious that his ideas were very much present in the famous Education Act of 1902, even if he gained no credit for it.

There is an area of Gorst's political activity which, as far as this author is aware, has mainly been overlooked by historians and which deserves to be remembered. This was Gorst's work as a propagandist both inside and outside the House of Commons when he busied himself alerting informed opinion about the great range of social issues needing attention: for instance, tackling the unemployment problem and the poverty that went with it; the improvements required in working conditions; the need for conciliation in the settlement of industrial disputes; the setting up of employment registries and the possibility of introducing compulsory social security schemes including free medical care for the sick. He was also, it has been justifiably claimed, the first politician to canvass publicly for old age pensions. This list of Gorst's interests in the employment and social welfare field is quite a full one, yet it still excludes the work he did on behalf of neglected children.

However, and this perhaps is the nub of the matter, did Gorst achieve anything as a propagandist? Certainly he must claim some credit for the establishment in 1892 of the Royal Commission on Labour (even if it had very limited success), for much preliminary work leading to Chamberlain's Workmen's Compensation Act of 1897 and also for the provision of government relief for the funding of hungry children in 1905. What is difficult to gauge is the extent of

Gorst's influence on the programme of social reform implemented by the Liberal government of 1906. Many of the reforms advocated by Gorst found their way onto the statute book. His proposals were invariably soundly based, cogently expressed by word and pen, and supported too by the veteran journalist Stead. Gorst had pointed out – some would say *ad nauseum* – the progress made in Germany over state intervention in social welfare. Lloyd George often listened carefully in the House to what Gorst had to say, and then in 1908 interestingly enough visited Germany, no doubt spurred on by William Beveridge's visit there, to see what he could learn from that state's institutions. He was impressed. We believe that Gorst should be given some vicarious credit, at least, for legislation such as the National Insurance Act of 1911, introduced by the Liberals before the First World War.

In reflecting on Gorst's political career, there is a great temptation to ask a residual and virtually hypothetical question. He saw himself, at least until towards the end of his career, as a stalwart though independent Conservative holding aloft the Disraelian torch. Yet was he in the wrong party? Dilke thought he was a Radical. Should he have been, as the Barnetts thought, a Liberal? Or should he have become one earlier than he did? After all, Gladstone and Winston Churchill – admittedly Titans both – crossed the floor of the House without damaging their careers. Certainly, in many fields, as for instance in colonial affairs, social reform, education and free trade, he was more Liberal in outlook than Conservative. In the Liberal Party Gorst would not, indeed, have had to contend with Lord Salisbury. Instead there would have been Gladstone.

There are always going to be some unresolved mysteries about Gorst and his life, including his relations with his family, and perhaps – although we hope we may have made a contribution during the course of our narrative to dissolving some of the mist – regarding his political persona and motivation. In many ways O'Connor's was an accurate assessment of Gorst, at least in so far as it went. To it we have had to add riders on his character and his relationship with Balfour. However able a man Gorst was, he did not do himself justice due to his wayward and awkward temperament which so often, sadly enough, alienated rather than attracted people. Nonetheless, in his ideas and pursuit of progress, he was often years ahead of his time, and no Conservative politician of his age matched him in promoting educational and social reform.

Our last word should perhaps be on behalf of the nation's

children. It was for them – both for their education and their welfare – that John Gorst, arguably, did his best work and for which he would wish to be remembered. He would have felt honoured by the memorial tablet to him placed on the chapel wall of St John's College, Cambridge, by Ralph Griffin of the Inner Temple, one-time registrar of designs and trademarks. Its Latin inscription reads in translation:

> … through life a strenuous advocate of the provision for all the children of the country of the means of acquiring sound learning, he did much while holding many high offices in the government to forward this object.

Bibliography

Note: Unless otherwise stated, books were published in London.

Allen, B. M., *Sir Robert Morant*, Macmillan, 1934.

Alverstone, Lord, *Recollections of Bar and Bench*, Edward Arnold, 1914.

Asquith, Earl of Oxford and, *Fifty Years of Parliament*, Cassell, 1926.

Balfour, Earl of, *Chapters of Autobiography*, Cassell, 1930.

Balfour, Sir Graham, *The Educational Systems of Great Britain and Northern Ireland*, Oxford University Press, Oxford, 1903.

Bassett-Lowke, W. J. and Holland, George, *Ships and Men*, George G. Harrap, 1946.

Blake, Robert, *Disraeli*, Eyre & Spottiswoode, 1966.

Blake, Robert, *The Conservative Party from Peel to Churchill*, Arrow, 1970.

Booth, Bramwell, *Work in Darkest England in 1894*, reprinted in *Opinions of Eminent Persons*, The Salvation Army, 1901.

Bosanquet, H., *Social Work in London 1869–1912*, John Murray, 1914.

Bradford, Sarah, *Disraeli*, Grafton Books, 1985.

Bridges, Yseult, *How Charles Bravo Died*, Reprint Society, 1956.

Bryce, J., *Studies in Contemporary Biography*, Macmillan, 1903.

Buckle, G. E. (ed.), *The Letters of Queen Victoria 1891–5*, vol. 2, John Murray, 1931.

Churchill, Randolph S., *Winston S. Churchill*, vol. 1. *Youth 1814–1900*, William Heinemann, 1966.

Churchill, Randolph S., *Winston S. Churchill*, vol. 2. *Young Statesman 1901–14* and companion part 2, William Heinemann, 1967.

Churchill, Winston S., *Lord Randolph Churchill*, Odhams Press, 1905.

Clark, G. Kitson, *The Making of Victorian England*, Methuen, 1960.

Clarke, Edward, *The Story of My Life*, John Murray, 1919.

Coleman, Bruce, *Conservatism and the Conservative Party in the Nineteenth Century*, Edward Arnold, 1988.

Cowan, James, *New Zealand Wars*, R. E. Owen, Government Printer, Wellington, 1922–23.

Cowan, James, *The Old Frontier*, Waipa Post, Te Awamutu, 1922.

Curtis, Edmund, *A History of Ireland*, Routledge, 1936.

Daglish, Neil, *Education Policy-making in England and Wales*, Woburn Press, 1996.

Dalton, B. J., *War and Politics in New Zealand 1855–1870*, Sydney University Press, Sydney, 1967.

Dixon, Conrad, *Ships of the Victorian Navy*, Ashford Press Publishing, Southampton, 1987.

Doolittle, D. H., *A Soldier's Hero: General Sir Archibald Hunter*, Anawan Publishing, Narragansett, USA, 1991.

Dunn, Michael, *John Kinder: Paintings and Photographs*, SeTo Publishing, Auckland, New Zealand, 1985.

Eaglesham, E. J. R., *From School Board to Local Authority*, Routledge, 1956.

Eaglesham, E. J. R., *The Foundations of Twentieth-Century Education in England*, Routledge & Kegan Paul, 1967.

Edwards, J. Ll. J., *The Law Officers of the Crown*, Sweet & Maxwell, 1964.

Ensor, Sir Robert, *England 1870–1914*, Oxford University Press, Oxford, 1936.

Feiling, Keith, *History of England*, Book Club Associates, 1950.

Feuchtwanger, E. J., *Disraeli, Democracy and the Tory Party*, Clarendon Press, Oxford, 1968.

Fitzroy, Sir Almeric, *Memoirs*, Hutchinson, 1926.

Foster, R. F., *Lord Randolph Churchill*, Oxford University Press, Oxford, 1982.

Fowler, W. S., *A Study of Radicalism and Dissent*, Epworth Press, 1961.

Gardiner, A. G., *Life of Sir William Harcourt*, Constable, 1923.

Gilmour, David, *Curzon*, Macmillan, Papermac edn, 1995.

Gorst, Harold E., *The Earl of Beaconsfield*, Blackie, 1899.

Gorst, Harold E., *The Fourth Party*, Smith, Elder, 1906.

Gorst, Harold E., *Much of Life is Laughter*, George Allen & Unwin, 1936.

Gorst, John E., *The Maori King*, Macmillan, 1864.

Gorst, Sir John E., *The Children of the Nation*, Methuen, 1906.

Gorst, Sir John E., *New Zealand Revisited*, Sir Isaac Pitman, 1908.

Griffith-Boscawen, A. S. T., *Fourteen Years in Parliament*, John Murray, 1907.

Gudgeon, Thomas, *The Defenders of New Zealand*, H. Brett, Auckland, New Zealand, 1887.

Halévy, Elie, *A History of the English People in the Nineteenth Century: Imperialism and the Rise of Labour, 1895–1905*, Benn, 1926.

Hanham, H. J., *Elections and Party Management*, Longman, 1959.

Harcourt Williams, R., (ed.) *Salisbury–Balfour Correspondence*, Hertfordshire Record Society, 1988.

Hardinge, Sir Arthur, *The Life of Henry Herbert, 4th Earl of Carnarvon*, Humphrey Milford, 1925.

Hennock, E. P., *British Social Reform and German Precedents*, Clarendon Press, Oxford, 1987.

Heuston, R. F. V., *Lives of the Lord Chancellors 1885–1940*, Clarendon Press, Oxford, 1964.

Hyndman, H., *The Record of an Adventurous Life*, Macmillan, 1911.

Jackson, Patrick, *The Last of the Whigs*, Fairleigh Dickinson University Press, USA, 1994.

Jackson, Patrick, *Education Act Forster*, Fairleigh Dickinson University Press, USA, 1997.

James, Lawrence, *Raj: The Making and Unmaking of British India*, Little, Brown, 1997.

Jameson, William, *The Fleet that Jack Built*, Rupert Hart-Davis, 1962.

Jenkins, Elizabeth, *Six Criminal Women*, Sampson Low, 1949.

Kebbel, T. E., *Lord Beaconsfield and other Tory Memories*, Cassell, 1907.

Kekewich, Sir George, *The Education Department and After*, Constable, 1926.

Kilbracken, Lord, *Reminiscences of Lord Kilbracken*, Macmillan, 1931.

Limbrick, Rev. Warren, *Bishop Selwyn in New Zealand 1841–68*, Dunmore Press, Palmerston North, New Zealand, 1987.

Lucy, Sir Henry, *Nearing Jordan*, E. P. Dutton, 1916.

Lucy, Sir Henry, *Diary of a Journalist*, John Murray, 1923.

Lyon, Jane, *Clipper Ships and Captains*, Mahwah, NJ (no date).

McKenzie, R. T., *British Political Parties*, Heinemann, 1963.

MacKenzie, Norman and Jeanne (ed.), *The Diary of Beatrice Webb*, vol. 2, Virago, 1983.

Matthew, H. C. G., *Gladstone 1809–1874*, Oxford University Press, Oxford, 1986.

May, Erskine, *Parliamentary Practice*, 14th edn, ed. Gilbert Campion, Butterworth, 1946.

Mellini, Peter, *Sir Eldon Gorst: The Overshadowed Proconsul*, Hoover Institution Press, Stanford, CA, 1979.

Moneypenny, W. F., and Buckle, G. E., *The Life of Benjamin Disraeli*, John Murray, 1910–20.

Moon, Sir Penderel, *The British Conquest and Dominion of India*, Duckworth, 1989.

Penn, Geoffrey, *Up Funnel, Down Screw*, Hollis & Carter, 1955.

Pimlott, J. A. R., *Toynbee Hall*, J. M. Dent, 1935.

Pugh, Martin, *The Making of Modern British Politics, 1867–1939*, Basil Blackwell, Oxford, 1982.

Raikes, H. St J., *The Life and Letters of Henry Cecil Raikes*, Macmillan, 1898.

Reader, W. J. (ed.), *Victorian England*, Batsford, 1974.

Rhodes James, R. V., *Lord Randolph Churchill*, Weidenfeld & Nicolson, 1959.

Roberts, Andrew, *Salisbury: Victorian Titan*, Weidenfeld & Nicolson, 1999.

Russell, Colin A., *Edward Frankland: Chemistry, Controversy and*

Conspiracy in Victorian England, Cambridge University Press, Cambridge, 1996.

Rutherford, J., *Sir George Grey*, Cassell, 1961.

Sadleir, M., *Michael Ernest Sadler 1861–1943*, Constable, 1949.

St Helier, Lady, *Memories of Fifty Years*, Edward Arnold, 1909.

Shannon, R., *The Age of Disraeli, 1868–1881*, Longman, 1992.

Shannon, R., *The Age of Salisbury, 1881–1902*, Longman, 1996.

Simon, Brian, *Education and the Labour Movement 1870–1920*, Lawrence & Wishart, 1965.

Sinclair, Keith, *The Origins of the Maori Wars*, New Zealand University Press, Auckland, New Zealand, 1957.

Sinclair, Keith, *A History of New Zealand*, Penguin Books, Pelican edn, 1980.

Sneyd-Kynnersley, E. M. *Some Passages in the Life of One of H.M. Inspectors of Schools*, Macmillan, 1913.

Spender, J. A. and Asquith, Cyril, *Life of Henry Herbert Asquith, Lord Oxford and Asquith*, Hutchinson, 1932.

Stead, W. T. (ed.), 'Coming Men and Coming Questions', *Review of Reviews*, 1905.

Steedman, C., *Childhood, Culture and Class in Britain*, Virago, 1990.

Storrs, R., *Orientations*, Nicolson & Watson, 1937.

Taylor, Bernard and Clarke, K., *Murder at the Priory: The Mysterious Poisoning of Charles Bravo*, Grafton Books, 1988.

Thomson, David, *England in the Nineteenth Century*, Penguin Books, Pelican edn, 1983.

Trevelyan, G. M., *History of England*, Longman, 1926.

Waldron, J., *Maamtrasna: The Murders and the Mystery*, Edmond Burke, Dublin, 1992.

Ward, Alan, *A Show of Justice: Racial Amalgamation in Nineteenth Century New Zealand*, Auckland University Press, Auckland, New Zealand, 1973.

Ward, R., *Life among the Maoris of New Zealand*, G. Lamb, 1872.

Warwick, Countess of, *A Nation's Youth*, Cassell, 1906.

Wells, Captain John, *Royal Navy: An Illustrated Social History 1870–1982*, Alan Sutton, Stroud, 1994.

Wolff, Sir H. Drummond, *Rambling Recollections*, Macmillan, 1908.

Woodward, Sir Llewellyn, *The Age of Reform 1815–70*, Oxford University Press, Oxford, 1979.

Sources

UNPUBLISHED

Barnett Papers, London Metropolitan Archives F/BAR
Bosanquet Papers, BOD MS, Autogr. d. 41
Bryce Papers, BOD MS Bryce, 71
Cambridge Union Society records, Cambridge
Charitable Organisation Society records, London Metropolitan
  Archives
Churchill, Lord Randolph, correspondence of, Cambridge University
  Library, Add. 9248
Devonshire MS, 2nd series 340, 3007, Chatsworth
Education Department PRO, ED 24/22, 24/79, 24/2099
Fowlds, George, Papers 1872–1934, University of Auckland Library,
  MSS and Archives A–17
Gorst, Sir Eldon, Autobiographical Notes and Diaries in private
  ownership (copies at St Antony's College, Oxford)
Hughenden (Disraeli) Papers, BOD 50/2, 125/3, 129/2, 137/4
Iddesleigh Papers, BL Add. 50041
Kekewich Papers, Duke University, North Carolina, USA, 3-3-71
Kimberley Papers, BOD, MS Eng. c. 4247
Marvin Papers, BOD, MS Eng. lett. c. 257
Middleton Papers, BOD, MS Eng. c. 4833
National Union of Conservative and Constitutional Association
  records, Conservative Party Archive, BOD
Paget Papers, BOD MS, Autogr. e. 12
Records of Rossall School
Ritchie Papers, BL Mss, Eur 342
St John's College, Cambridge, records
Salisbury Papers, Papers of the Third Marquess, Hatfield House,
  Hatfield
Stead Papers, Churchill College, Cambridge, 1/39
Sykes Collection, University of Hull, Brynmore Jones Library, DDSY
  (2)/1/4

PUBLISHED

Appendices to the Journals of the House of Representatives, Wellington,
  New Zealand

Bulletin of the History of Medicine
Bulletin of the Institute of Historical Research
Cambridge Chronicle
Chatham and Rochester News and North Kent Spectator
Durham and Newcastle Research Review
Fortnightly Review
Hastings and St Leonard's News
Historian
History of Education
Law Journal
Macmillans (magazine)
Nineteenth Century
North American Review
Parliamentary Debates, Hansard
Punch
Review of Reviews
Saturday Review
Solicitor's Journal and Weekly Reporter
Truth

Index

Note: In subheadings Gorst's name is abbreviated to JEG. When the names of his relatives appear as main headings, their relationship to him is put in parentheses.